Rough Rider in the White House

Sarah Watts

Rough

Rider

in the

White

House

Theodore Roosevelt and the

Politics of Desire

THE UNIVERSITY OF CHICAGO PRESS

CHICAGO AND LONDON

Sarah Watts is professor of history at Wake Forest University. She is the author of *Order against Chaos: Business Culture and Labor Ideology in America, 1880–1915.*

The University of Chicago Press, Chicago 60637

The University of Chicago Press, Ltd., London

© 2003 by The University of Chicago

All rights reserved. Published 2003

Printed in the United States of America

12 11 10 09 08 07 06 05 04 03   1 2 3 4 5

ISBN: 0-226-87607-1 (cloth)

Library of Congress Cataloging-in-Publication Data

Watts, Sarah Lyons, 1942–

   Rough rider in the White House : Theodore Roosevelt and the politics of desire / Sarah Watts.

    p. cm.

  Includes bibliographical references and index.

  ISBN 0-226-87607-1 (alk. paper)

    1. Roosevelt, Theodore, 1858–1919.   2. Roosevelt, Theodore, 1858–1919—Psychology.   3. Roosevelt, Theodore, 1858–1919—Language.   4. Presidents—United States—Biography.   5. United States—Politics and government—1901–1909.   6. United States—Foreign relations—1901–1909.   7. Political culture—United States—History—20th century.   8. Masculinity—Political aspects—United States—History—20th century.   9. Desire—Political aspects—United States—History—20th century.   10. Rhetoric—Political aspects—United States—History—20th century.   I. Title.

  E757 .W35 2003

  973.91′1′092—dc21

                         2003003576

Contents

Illustrations

Acknowledgments

Reflecting on Theodore Roosevelt's exploits in Cuba during the Spanish-American War, his close friend and political mentor John Hay said to him, "You obeyed your own demon." What demon, I wondered a hundred years later, and what obedience? And why did demonic necessity find such an easy and common currency among members of America's republican brotherhood, who, it seemed, feared social and moral degeneration on every front? How could such a youthful and virile man as Roosevelt summon, as he did, visions of desire and disgust that resonated with other men's fears and made them receptive to his strident calls for sacrifice and danger? And, for those men who entertained such urges, did the demon stand alone, uncontested and unexamined, perhaps because he lay at the root of how they constituted themselves as men? How would a historian go about investigating such psychological questions? The answer this book provides is a wild ride, but I hope it furthers our understanding of the ordinariness of what, for some observers anyway, is the dark side of the political moon.

Many people figured in the making of this book. First of all, I thank Frank Ninkovich for his comments at the American Historical Association panel session where these ideas were first aired, and for subsequently reading and criticizing an early version of the manuscript. Frank's sharp insights, his encouragement, and his selfless sharing of his time helped greatly in moving this toward a finished product. I am also fortunate to have as an editor Douglas Mitchell, whose early interest proved fruitful and whose close reading and deft suggestions improved the manuscript immeasurably. His broad knowledge, street savvy, and intellectual freshness provided me with an astonishingly deep resource.

I am indebted to other scholars who have provided

encouragement, discussions, criticism, and other sorts of help along the way. Kathleen Dalton, Theodore Roosevelt's most recent and, to my mind, most accomplished biographer shared generously her inestimable insights. I am grateful to Lisa Harteker, who shaped the manuscript at a crucial point, corralling the arguments into coherence and directing them at an anonymous reader. It would be impossible to adequately credit the importance of conversations, inspiration from their own work, and, in many cases, critical readings from Earl Smith, Paul Cobb, William K. Meyers, Michael Kimmel, Dick Schneider, Anna Rubino, Anthony Rotundo, John Fisher, Laure McKinnon, and the reviewers for the University of Chicago Press. Particularly, I thank the art historians David Lubin and Alex Nemerov for helping with photos and for providing interpretive insights, many of which I've borrowed. I also thank Wake Forest University's Department of History, the William C. Archie Fund for Faculty Excellence, and the Z. Smith Reynolds Foundation faculty leave program for generous support for research and preparation of this book. I am also deeply thankful to the librarians of the Z. Smith Reynolds Library, Wake Forest University.

Thanks also to Dominick La Capra and Stephen Nichols for inviting me to participate in the School of Criticism and Theory's 1996 summer institute, History and Psychoanalysis. There we analyzed how social and personal anxiety arises from the slippage between notions of perfect identity and the reality of a degenerate or unhygienic identity, an analysis which led to an understanding of how political elites make themselves into brokers of ideologies of purity and corruption and attach them to the modern nation. These understandings added to the complexity, and hopefully to the clarity, of the psychological arguments put forward in the book.

I thank the following people in no particular order since each in his or her own way provided stimulating criticism, encouragement, and friendship: Bruce Ritz, Gail Fisher, John Fisher, Ginny Rutter, Chuck Rutter, Mohammed Coovadia, Bryan Everly, Tom McNemar, Janice Walker, and Chris Bodenner. No two people had a greater influence on my conceptualization and interpretation of this material than Gale Sigal and Robert Beachy. They spent innumerable hours discussing history and theory with me and convincing me that I was taking a legitimate approach. Without their help this would be a lesser book. That it is not better is entirely my doing.

Finally, to members of my family, Sherry Watson and Ann Ketron, Amber Ketron, Barbara Crawford, Mario Pellicciaro, Carol Ryan, and Claire Lyons, I want to say how much your love and support has meant over the years. To you I dedicate this book.

1 *"The Hot Life of Feeling"*

Historians and biographers rightly portray Theodore Roosevelt as a progressive, a pragmatic rationalist, a modernizer, and a paragon of restraint. This respected statesman who believed in and practiced discipline and proper manners brought to politics a "mastery of affairs," the historian John Morton Blum writes, one that joined the "processes and purposes" of government and made Roosevelt "an exemplar for American statesmen" in the twentieth century.[1] Yet present-day writers, as well as Roosevelt's close friends and his peers among the gentry, in academe, and in government; and observers such as editors, cartoonists, and satirists all identify another side, a dark and irrational one that, to Woodrow Wilson, made him "the most dangerous man of the age." Mark Twain called Roosevelt "clearly insane . . . and insanest upon war and its supreme glories." Harvard philosopher William James found him pouring into the nation "a flood of abstract bellicose emotion." Biographer Edmund Morris writes that he had an "irrational love of battle" and "ceaselessly praised the joys of righteous killing." William Henry Harbaugh found in Roosevelt an "extraordinary severity of judgment and . . . a strain of ruthlessness and capacity for passing hatred."[2] He was "now and then possibly dangerous," Blum observes, because he was "not often surpassed in his excursions into hate and his paeans to conformity." In the hysteria accompanying the approach of World War I, "that part of him that had always seen the Jacobin in his opponents now ran amuck" and "fed the spirit that expressed itself in lynching, amateur witch hunts, intolerance of every kind." As he gave in to his "lust to rule," Blum concludes, Roosevelt's political mastery degenerated into demagoguery, chauvinism, and "a creed akin to fascism" (see figures 1 and 2).[3]

Yet despite the overwhelming evidence for "that part

Figure 1. Louis Dalrymple, "The Two Roosevelts," *Judge*

of him," present-day historians and biographers have not known what to do with it. They have reported it, but they have not probed its psychological depths, examined the way it contributed to Roosevelt's political vision, or explored how it resonated in the social psychology of Victorian society.[4] If, indeed, two popularly conceived Roosevelts lived in the president's body and in the nation's mind, it is not the rational, republican Roosevelt who needs further examination, but this Rough Rider who injected a rich vein of fantasy and emotionalism, an unabashed paean to violence, and a desperate fashioning of masculinity into political culture, and who, by doing so, offered ordinary men a sense that they actively participated in the era's aggressively insurgent manhood. Almost single-handedly among leaders of his era, Roosevelt drew men's sense of belonging into his own personal version of manliness and inscribed it in new and modern ways on the nation's collective mind.

Roosevelt was the first president to articulate the shared anxieties of his generation, and he provided its first seemingly coherent response to the cultural dislocations of modern society. One of the first political figures to interpret modernism as traumatic, he prescribed solutions in ways that drew white, middle-class men to him and inspired their confidence. Although Roosevelt was progressive and optimistic, his political vision encompassed his darker, emotional, antiliberal worldview of men and nations struggling against the forces of evil. Centering on what Mark Seltzer terms "relentless melodramas of degeneration and devolution," his vision

Figure 2. "Two Views of the President," *Eagle* (Brooklyn)

mobilized deep-seated anxieties about modern society and romantic, irrational longings for new sources of virility. It enlisted heroic men, and them
only, to establish manly boundaries between the nation and its modern enemies: effeminacy, eroticism, consumerism, and pacifism.[5] Indeed, the nation's longing for a warrior redeemer was so powerful, Jackson Lears
maintains, that one can locate the origins of twentieth-century Western
militarism in the reactionary responses to modernism in the late nineteenth century.[6]

Given apparently to both rational and "primitive" behavior, Roosevelt
embodied many of the contradictions in the new vision of manhood that
emerged in the late nineteenth century. Indeed, as Michael Kimmel observes, the era's thrust toward a more aggressive manhood coalesced
around Roosevelt precisely because he realized its contradictory elements,
both "the top rung of the ladder of social aspiration and the gladiatorial

animal arena sensed at the bottom."[7] He was the man who identified with the past yet embodied modernity, the patrician with an affinity for workers, the conservationist who proudly killed animals, the bodybuilder who loved poetry, and the civilized Easterner who made it in the barbaric West. As a preeminent historian, moralist, critic, naturalist, politician, and patriot, he narrated the rational march of racial civilization while advocating violence as an unfortunate but necessary, and even edifying, element in the grand themes that drove history.

For his part, Roosevelt would have immediately recognized the cartoonists' self modulated statesman and self-aggrandizing Rough Rider as the twin poles of his lifelong struggle to establish in the nation a "mighty manhood." If asked, he would have answered simply that manhood should feature both civilized society and savage freedom, and that, when the stakes were high, "men must trust to emotion for that safety which reason . . . can never give." Men must be judged "by the fire and vigor of their passions; by their deep sense of injury; by their memory of past glory; by their eagerness for fresh fame"; and by their achievement of goals which "give free space to . . . heroic feelings."[8]

While the popular view of two Roosevelts expresses the Victorian penchant for seeing the world in binary opposites, and although Roosevelt himself saw no contradiction in having it both ways, this view fails to account for yet another aspect of his persona, one that underlay both of the two Roosevelts. Within this masculine paragon his closest friends discerned a complex, darker, self-doubting, highly emotional, and sometimes erotic self, one that prompted Brander Matthews to describe his personality as "polygonal." Henry Cabot Lodge accused Roosevelt of having an underlying pessimism that made him "see things sometimes too darkly." William Allen White discovered "the shadow of some inner femininity deeply suppressed." This may have been a feminized version of what Owen Wister described as Roosevelt's simultaneous feelings of "perplexity and pain . . . the sign of frequent conflict between what he knew and his wish not to know it, his determination to grasp his optimism tight, lest it escape him."[9]

While less intimate observers overlooked this dark and feminine self, Roosevelt privately acknowledged it. He incorporated it into his vision of manhood, and he deployed his Rough Rider self in a lifelong assault against it. This book tells the story of how Roosevelt's manly self struggled with doubt, anxiety, and loathing, and with a fearful child within. His vision of manhood rested on the notion of a once strong but now fragile and ever weakening American male self, a notion that arose from his own emotional preoccupations, particularly his disgust for his own and other men's physical inferiority, his pervasive sexual priggishness, his anxiety about future sexual and racial degeneracy, and his fears of an interior cowardice that might be exposed to the outside world. While often coded "female" in the sense of poetic sensitivity, bodily weakness, or effete intellectuality, his inner self also appeared in the form of a simian ancestor, an "angel of peace," or a man who desired other men.

Throughout his life, Roosevelt met every appearance of this weakened self with aggressive disciplines and punishments. In his boyhood and youth, he subjected his frail and asthmatic body to a regimen of bodybuilding so extreme as to remake it, he said, into "a tough nut." No matter how he toughened himself, however, he could not escape living in a Victorian world in which normalcy was at stake and monstrosity was everywhere. One day, as a young man who had already absorbed society's loathing of the evolutionary likenesses of men and apes, he looked in his mirror and saw the image of an ape. Startled by the horror of species self-recognition, he immediately recalled a line from Robert Browning in which a purely civilized, aristocratic youth also sees a reflected image of the "pertest little ape," a spineless simian whose monstrosity "affronted" his human shape. Throughout his life, Roosevelt imagined apes and men contesting within a Darwinian montage, and evolutionary contests between races of men drove his theory of history. At every turn, in art galleries, in government houses, and in the hearts of men, he found examples of weakening racial selves.[10]

When Roosevelt's young teenage daughter Alice, who knew just how to tweak her father's fears, declared that she was going to give birth to a monkey, the outlandish claim left him livid with anger since it raised the twin specters of bestial miscegenation and biological atavism in his immediate family. Roosevelt would have been the first to admit that sex was hardly ever about sex, that it was more about the body, about politics, about the fate not just of individuals, but ultimately of civilization. Victorian anthropology envisioned human evolutionary progress fraught with the possibility of slipping backward, of producing a throwback child with mongoloid or anthropoid features, a child in whom one recognized primal ancestors. According to this vision, white parents had no control over such events. Apes that appeared in Roosevelt's mirror or in his child's fantasy signified his fear of regression to a savage self, of the loss of racial identity, of the failure of white reproduction, of the reappearance of simian monsters, and thus of the very precariousness of the civilizing process.

From early manhood, Roosevelt incorporated these fears into his theory of civilization. He assumed that modern life had bred in all white men, even his own civilized-statesman self, the same tendency toward decline.

He identified his fears as those of his social class and blamed them for what he saw as a national failure of nerve. Such concerns led him to equate "our mighty manhood" with "our nation," by which he meant the collective fraternal body of adult, white, heterosexual men whose immediate forebears had so recently conquered the frontier and created the republic. Yet by the end of the nineteenth century, as Roosevelt endlessly charged, the founding fathers' very success in nation building had transformed their descendants into the "hypercivilized man of the great industrial centers," a man whose lack of "contact with the rough world of actual life . . . saps the hardy virtues in a nation as it saps them in an individual."[11] Modern life created men "sunk . . . in a scrambling commercialism . . . busying ourselves with the wants of our bodies . . . content to rot by inches in ignoble ease." For Roosevelt, playing billiards, carrying umbrellas, and shopping signified men's capitulation to a "cloistered" life of "swollen, slothful ease," a life of erotic dissipation that made the "virile qualities atrophy" in the "class of better men."[12] Such a life humiliated men, Roosevelt thought, because it required them to submit to rather than resist their bodily desires.

Were bodily concerns not sufficient to produce pessimism as the new century approached, Roosevelt's own sense of weakness, like that of most men of his class, was mirrored in a seemingly brittle social order threatened by mobs of immigrants, raving "New Women," and the looming certainty that "race suicide" was pulling America back down the evolutionary ladder toward a "half-breed" culture. "We are all peering into the future," Roosevelt warned in 1895, trying to understand the "great dumb forces" of industrialism. By 1900, these had become "so complex," he told a Carnegie Hall audience, "their rate of movement so very rapid [that] the power of the forces of evil has been greatly increased."[13] Like Herbert Spencer, Roosevelt believed that modern society had generated its own social pathology and that American civilization had reached a crossroads from which it would either continue evolving upward or decline. He frequently used the words *cumber* and *retrogress* to warn that "poisons" had limited the nation's ability to maintain itself as a manly presence among nations.[14] "As a whole we are still in the flush of our mighty manhood," he cautioned British diplomat Cecil Arthur Spring Rice in 1901, but America had begun to show "signs of senility . . . of gross vice and moral weakness. Nobody can tell when or how soon disaster will come."[15]

By the 1880s, the mounting psychological and social crisis of modernity led to a growing acceptance of male violence. As many bourgeois men grew increasingly tainted with dandyism and an effete intellectualism, they began to value previously unaccepted forms of violent behavior such as sports activities that caused physical pain to themselves and to others. As they read social crisis as a sign of their own diminished manliness, they saw degeneration everywhere, among prostitutes, among the urban working class, in middle-class women seeking birth control, and even in the unsettling images in modern art. Even as violence declined in many areas of American life with the spread of factory management, urban policing, and bourgeois manners, Eastern men began to romanticize aggressive male endeavor and to appropriate its symbols, its rhetoric, and its psychological rewards.[16] They were increasingly drawn to all-male leisure activities such as sports and hunting, and they turned bodybuilding into a national obsession. The cult of the cowboy soldier arose in art, drama, and fiction, popularizing exaggerated and violent forms of masculinity.[17]

Roosevelt's attempts to jump-start masculinity in this charged cultural atmosphere were made easier by the instability of male identity in his era. The nation's expanding market economy created unsettled and constantly shifting grounds for establishing and maintaining male status and made its achievement both more difficult than before and more a matter of consciously crafting a socially visible self. New venues where bourgeois men could claim new statuses over women, minorities, working-class men, and especially men of their own class and race arose in the nation's media as well as in city parks and streets, in offices and stores, and in private meeting places from men's bars and gymnasiums to houses of prostitution. New society and sports organizations appeared, and an increasingly visible homosexual culture developed in the nation's largest cities.

Sensationalized entertainments, popular writers noted, had bred dullness among the citizenry, leading them to seek higher levels of artificial stimulation. At the Buffalo Pan-American Exposition of 1901, Mary Bronson Hartt observed fairgoers "dazzled" by panoramas of myriad world cultures and even the promise of a trip to the moon. After such a spectacle, she asked, "Where shall we go to get us a new sensation?" What can give us a "thrill of thorough-going surprise? Behold, the world is a sucked orange."[18] In an 1893 *Atlantic Monthly* essay, Agnes Repplier likewise turned to the subject of ennui, those "heavy moments stretching into hours" that brought the "dreadful weariness . . . of a dull existence, clogged at every pore." Beset with "amusements, which do not amuse," modern people "crave diversion . . . eagerly." Along with Roosevelt, William James, and many social critics of her day, Repplier identified fear as the "best antidote," fear that would spur the "zest of perpetual effort" that the Greek gods offered the ancients, those hardy souls who lived lives "filled with toil," "sweetened by peril," and "checked by manifold disasters."[19]

The problem, then, was that the same gender paradigm that under-wrote the civilized statesman also questioned his manliness. Roosevelt would have put it more simply: how to remain both manly and civilized? How to provide "emasculated" men with ancient adversities yet ones tailored to the demands of modern life? How to produce a civilized warrior who exercises "self-mastery over one's passions and follies." Only through their capacity for self-mastery, Roosevelt said, would "really high civilizations . . . supply the antidote to the self-indulgence and love of ease which they tend to produce."[20]

Toward this problem, Roosevelt directed a heady dose of outlandishly demonstrative manliness that positioned the Rough Rider against the statesman so as to address perceived weakness in psychologically protective ways. To negotiate the contradictory requirements of Victorian manliness, he imagined a "body politic," a national fraternity of white men, strong and pure, immune to sexual allure, attuned to manners and social hygiene, procreative in race-improving ways, eager for suffering, and capable of astonishing violence. As president, Roosevelt positioned his own body as a symbol of this imagined fraternity in the nation's political culture. He did not allow himself to be photographed or seen publicly using an umbrella or wearing tennis attire, and he especially would not be subjected to the "outrageous lie that I had been kissing babies." As a model of ideal manhood, his body became the analog for a nation that must not appear "vacillating and weak" to other nations.[21]

To strengthen the weakling in himself, his sons, other men, and the nation as a whole, Roosevelt made startling calls for ascetic self-denial, which he called "iron self-discipline." He filled his own days with desperate, self-punishing activities designed to enable his body to withstand ever higher levels of pain. This was a man who as president challenged officers of the regular army to extreme standards of horsemanship, who as a recently bereaved widower rode a horse almost to death, who as a loving father drove his ten-year-old son to a mental breakdown, who as a friend bullied other men into punishing physical contests in the name of sport.

Drawing no boundary between his own and his nation's body, he infused his political language with punitive solutions for the nation's problems, drawing exclusionary boundaries between pure insider and polluting outsider. He targeted men who had "certain dreadful qualities of the moral pervert."[22] He denounced the "soft, swollen eunuchs," those "men who were not men" who refused to father children, and the "sinister opposition," those congressmen who voted against naval appropriations. In debates with anti-imperialists and pacifists during and after 1898, he abhorred congressmen who voted against preparedness, men who preached "peace at any price," and men who refused to declare wars or fight in them. He called them "prattlers who sit at home in peace" exuding "silly, mock humanitarianism."[23] In Chicago in 1899, having just returned triumphantly from the war in Cuba, he gave his famous rallying speech "The Strenuous Life," in which he touted the value of the war against Spain, armed world leadership, and colonial responsibilities in Cuba, Puerto Rico, Hawaii, and the Philippines. In 1916, his frustrations with the lack of war preparedness led him to call Woodrow Wilson a "Miss Nancy."[24] And he made defeating these opponents of manhood into a matter of national survival. "In the long run," he proclaimed in 1917, "we have less to fear from foes without than from foes within; for the former will be formidable only as the latter breaks our strength."[25]

By using the word *we* in this passage, Roosevelt established boundaries between himself and an assumed virile male audience and nation on the one hand, and his enemies on the other, and set the stage for collective ritual attacks to contain or to excise those enemies. He interpreted their acts as effeminate, and their effeminacy as all the more damaging because he imagined the boundary between virility and effeminacy to be fragile and men's ideals to be easily and permanently corruptible from within or without. This facile slippage between notions of the perfect identity and the reality of the corrupted identity prompted him to claim in 1901 that "the *least touch* of flabbiness, of unhealthy softness, in either [Washington or Lincoln] would have meant ruin for this nation."[26] In Roosevelt's mind, a language of exclusion and the practice of bodily denial punished and exorcised the "foes within," and in so doing defined "we" against effeminacy.

Roosevelt's vision of manhood assumed cultural authority by appearing as a norm among those who imagined themselves real men against inferior categories of people. By adopting the language of gender polarity, Roosevelt joined the relentless forces policing the sexual boundaries between women and men and between robust heterosexuals and degenerate men. Thus Roosevelt's invectives against the "hermaphrodite" who compromised both male and female, the "circumcised" whose virility was corrupted, the "female brother" who embraced effeminacy, and the "skunk" who scavenged lowly victims all articulated the anxieties middle-class white men harbored about the blurring of absolutes and the collapse of difference. By articulating the rigid boundaries separating "real men" from corrupted ones, he helped to idealize the normative aspect of heterosexual male desire, to demonize its opposite, and to politicize both.

For the purposes of this study, the issue is less what Roosevelt's political language expresses or signifies than how it functioned to connect a man's emotional life and his preoccupation with his own body to the larger world and especially to the body politic. Without question, social anxieties are historical products mediated through language, but before that they are mediated through adult fantasies and longings, themselves products of childhood fears and hopes. It is this connection between the inner emotional self, which is deeply identified with the body and with childhood, and the "real" world that determines how a man refers to himself and how he sees the society in which he lives.[27] By understanding how strongly Roosevelt felt this connection and how effectively he communicated it to other men, we can begin to discover how ideals like maleness and whiteness take on the role of psychologically protective barriers against the feminine and the corrupt. Fears of divided identity or of a loss of self-control necessarily conjured demons in the form of half-men, hysterical men, or ape men. At the intersection of individual men's bodies and the nation's body, we can approach the question of why Roosevelt thought white men's bodies represented the fate of the nation and why he focused so obsessively on sexuality as the source of social breakdown. We can begin to understand how ideas of social corruption arose out of deep-seated needs to armor the male self against the feminine and how the demonization of women, nonwhites, and homosexuals became a way for men to manage their own fears and desires.

Unlike any other popular model of civilized manhood, however, Roosevelt's contained a startling and historically new prescription for cultivating those fears and desires and unleashing them in socially productive ways. Posed against the "weakling" that he feared in himself and in his nation, Roosevelt's Rough Rider self takes on new meaning because of its inherent violence. "There is not one among us," Roosevelt wrote to Edwin Arlington Robinson, "in whom a devil does not dwell," who at some point "masters each of us."[28] This beast within thrived on ancient forms of adversity and promised to resuscitate weak men because it punished softness and rottenness with brutality and pain. Roosevelt invited his devil into the nation's political culture in the form of a primal masculine sexuality.

Roosevelt's anxieties over the twin foes within, the civilized weakling and the manly beast, represented the contradictory requirements for repressive morality and primitive regeneration in Victorian manhood, contradictions that he interpreted as a challenge: how to master one's beast without overly stifling it—no small task, since too much self-mastery eventually halted the advance of a civilization based on virile male agency. If the beast were to revitalize the nation's men, it required discipline, but of a different sort than that required by the weakling. The latter invited punishment, but the beast demanded to be unleashed through carefully modulated bursts of primitive passion. Roosevelt's forays out West and his

Rough Rider experience in the Spanish-American War produced a political discourse that summoned a new type of men, those "seeking contact with the rough world," capable of "brutal heroism," and willing to develop the nation's "powers of endurance."[29] His politics called men to escape the confining bonds of civilization and indulge in the imagined vigor of the cowboys, hunters, and warriors who inhabited America's vanishing and increasingly mythic West. It encouraged men to imagine themselves bonded through the loyalty, bravery, and sacrifice that arose in rough play, the killing of animals, and war. It urged virile men to develop a tough exterior that would direct necessary violence toward the sinister opposition of other men: the corrupted and corrupting sensualists, pacifists, and sissies. Despite the admitted dangers inherent in such toughness, Roosevelt's politics of national manhood released men from conventional morality and invited them to indulge in sexualized martial fantasies that were strewn with recklessness, pleasureful pain, and easy death in an imaginary world seemingly no longer "a sucked orange."

Given this summons to extreme behavior, Roosevelt's masculinity was not just a reaction to the well-known sexually repressive Victorian mechanisms for cataloging and regulating male desire; nor was the civilization-savagery dichotomy a simple one. On the most straightforward level, among the late Victorians *savagery* denoted unrestrained desire, a transgression, or a fearsome excursion into the heart of darkness. On this level, as psychoanalytic theory would have it, an individual's unrestrained desire is displaced onto savages or wild animals and then mastered through disciplinary punishments or killing. In this figuration, such sublimations regulate male desire and point toward explaining why the power of self-discipline was, for the Victorians at least, an important manly quality.

To be sure, Roosevelt reclaimed this straightforwardly savage self with its accompanying punishments, but he assigned it a more prominent role in his psychological universe than merely grim displacement and punishment of individual desire. In Roosevelt's hands, the regulation of unrestrained desire rose into a giddy enjoyment of libidinal freedom strategically positioned across the political landscape. Approaching the boundary between restraint and desire became a pleasure-pain indulgence, a voluptuous experience that drew partisans of the cowboy-soldier cult to an emotional edge and had them peer into the depths of their own blood lust. Roosevelt actively sought this transgressive edge for the energizing power of standing face to face with the beast within. He knew the power of the beast, which he unleashed precisely in order to overcome it. He summoned unrestrained desire through calculated lapses of self-discipline, then reveled in it before he mastered it. In the heat of battle or while killing large animals, he simultaneously experienced what he termed a "hideous horror" and "the hot life of feeling," which alternately frightened and exhilarated him. Sometimes he drew back when the vehemence of these feelings frightened him. More often, however, the violence of hunting and soldiering was just fun, and he couldn't get enough. He said he was more alive during those times than at any other.

Men were drawn to the intensity of Roosevelt's passion. William Roscoe Thayer, Roosevelt's classmate at Harvard, said that he could stand near Roosevelt and "feel the powerful presence" of his "masterful will sheathed in self-control like a sword in its scabbard."[30] Such homoerotic feeling, however repressed, arose from the land of desire, but few of Roosevelt's or Thayer's fellows would have acknowledged anything but manliness in the one known since his Harvard days for iron self-discipline. Bourgeois men, negotiating a precarious masculinity that equally abhorred the sissy and the brute, recognized that Roosevelt's politics of hypermasculinity offered a way to loosen sexual energy within a framework of self-mastery. Roosevelt invited men to enlist this mastery in the interests of the nation. This statesman who loved his own suffering and who encouraged others to seek pain incorporated the masochistic and sadistic aspects of Victorian male repression into a revitalized manhood, one equal to the demands of both civilization and empire.

Understanding libidinal energy this way suggests that male sexuality serves as a vital force constructing social identity and authority in a way that, as Peter Stallybrass and Allon White find, "inevitably situate[s] the private self in relation to an imagined audience."[31] If Roosevelt was indeed, as John Hay said, "pure act," this act amounted to a vigorous investment of his libidinal energies into a heroic life and into the nation's future. This is why Roosevelt, perhaps influenced as an undergraduate by hearing William James speak on "Great Men and Their Environment" at the Harvard Natural History Society in 1880, abandoned Darwinian evolutionism, which to him seemed too random and directionless, in favor of a Lamarckian view wherein human acts constituted the raw factors of evolutionary progress. Roosevelt situated himself in history and created in himself not a mythical hero, but a man compulsively performing real acts to revitalize other white men for reasons of state.

Roosevelt summarized this libidinal energy as a national "unity" where "all the parts feel a subtle sympathy . . . and move . . . in response to some stir or throbbing, very powerful."[32] Fraternal sexuality in this form is not just sublimated through social relations in a one-way, individual-to-society trajectory where mental practices are projected onto a social scene. Instead, as Gilles Deleuze and Felix Guattari point out, individual psychology and social practices interpenetrate one another in a dynamic wherein social relations bring into play energies for which sex is a symbol. Not only expressive of individual longing and fear, desire throbs its way into history as socially productive action.[33] By this reasoning, through individual sublimation and direct social investment, and through his oft-repeated calls for "brutal heroism," Roosevelt transformed the primitive energy of the beast into the forward march of civilization.

BEYOND RHETORIC

Examining the languages of cultural politics is an exercise that necessarily begins on the rhetorical and discursive plane, where words are taken at face value. Traditional historians of U.S. foreign policy explain what leaders did and why, using analytical categories such as self-interest and idealism to understand rational security and economic decisions. Viewing politics as predominantly an expression of power and interest, many historians seem uneasy with emotional nationalism, treating it as mere hyperbole and underestimating its attraction and effect. Interpretations based on national interest place psychological evidence in a secondary role and thus leave unexamined the psychological roots of rhetorical violence expressed by individual leaders or in mass political movements. It is not very convincing, for example, that at the turn of the century Spanish colonial practices in Cuba threatened U.S. interests or that rational political or economic concerns drove the acquisition of Cuba and the Philippines. As Frank Ninkovich notes, the war and the subsequent campaign to suppress the Philippine insurrection required little in terms of national risk or sacrifice and the rationalization for them was couched in terms of identity rather than security.[34]

In the context of the late Victorian crisis of cultural authority, recent historians identify middle-class men's desires for "regeneration through violence," for "national salvation," for "redemption of the American spirit," for "regression to a more primitive state," and for "purging" the "false values of the metropolis."[35] Recent cultural studies of U.S. expansionism and the nineteenth-century cult of manhood, while remaining on the rhetorical level, show how Roosevelt represented a stratum of elite white leaders who, feeling the enervating effects of modernism, created ideologies of social and political power based on whiteness and manhood.[36] In the early republic, men considered whiteness, unity, and moral purity—those ideals of male equality that facilitated the capitalist market and guaranteed at the same time economic health and social inequality— necessary for political consensus, and they became the predominant modulating factors for national identity.[37] Several of the cultural studies examine the rhetorical fantasy integral to Roosevelt's aggressive and racialist masculinity and how he deployed it against decadence, but these studies fail to analyze his fantasy as integral to his politics.[38] They stress instead his liberal and progressive side and maintain that he won the fight for personal mastery of his primal emotions.

While many accounts of Roosevelt's politics remain powerfully effective on the discursive level, they allow terms such as *rape fantasy* and *primitive savagery* to serve as meanings in themselves and leave them unconnected to the emotional life that produced them. They offer little explanation for the special political appeal of Roosevelt's dark side or for the particular historical circumstances in which he chose to cultivate it. Failure to ground the rhetoric of aggressive masculinity in the emotional and libidinal fascination it held for bourgeois white men leaves the argument open to the charge that rhetoric is merely talk, unconnected to actual belief.[39] However hyperbolic, the politics of aggressive masculinity was not merely talk; it was talk grounded in meaningful fantasy. And that fantasy was not just fantasy; it was actual social engagement. But how do we get inside words like *regenerate* or *purge* or *redeem*? How do we discover why some men feel the need to cleanse society or to try other men by fire? How does symbolic violence urge men toward an actual use of force? How, exactly, does it identify its targets and prescribe their punishments?

Rather than accepting at face value that political rhetoric regenerates or purifies or otherwise satisfies certain psychological needs, this study seeks to understand identity at a deeper level than that of language and social discourse. Male behaviors based on irrational and largely unconscious needs and desires—fantasized on a collective level—provide the genesis of foreign policy as surely as do more acknowledged imperatives.[40] The nation's eagerness for war in 1898 evinced a response to internal, not external, enemies that must be examined in light of the emotional and often-unacknowledged threats they posed to normative white, male honor and middle-class identity. The evidence demands that we interpret rational politics in light of these perceived male weaknesses, underneath which lay fears of diminishing sexual and martial ability, of bodily deviance and deterioration, of the loss of class dominance in the face of social upheaval, and of violations of sexual taboos.

The very emotionality of the discourses of giving and receiving pain and of celebrating the blood-sport aspects of hunting and war begs a psychological analysis. While psychology alone cannot serve as a mode of historical analysis, it is the only discipline that targets the irrational as a formal subject of inquiry. The problem becomes how to study the emotional within the historical, a task this study undertakes by combining a psychological focus with an examination of male identity as a social logic or a strategy of self-presentation. Each of these spheres, the emotional and the historical, has a certain logic, and because men inject their fantasies into the historical dimension, the logic of one informs the other. Pure fantasy takes place partly in the unconscious, but, as Julia Hell and Klaus Theweleit observe of fascist politics, imagination also operates inside the historical process. Analyzing political ideologies through their fantasies "explains their power to seize unconscious drives," Hell writes, a power that accrues to them "because they bridge the social, and the individual, politics and desire . . . [on] different, variously articulated" cultural layers—the moral, the civic, and in the realm of the body.[41]

Thus it was that in England, France, Germany, and the United States, George Mosse finds, the bourgeois search for respectability—a search that distinguished normal from abnormal sexuality, rationality from passion, and the healthy from the diseased—became one of the building blocks of modern nationalism. It was the overarching vehicle of nationalism that turned private behavior like masturbation, homosexuality, or neurasthenia into a matter of public concern and assigned to the state the role of maintaining pure masculine and racial archetypes.[42]

PSYCHOLOGY

Kim Townsend, in *Manhood at Harvard,* holds that "most of Roosevelt's peers at Harvard limited, even damaged, their lives trying to be 'manly.' Imagining their bodies as so many forces to be controlled, they reined them in, fought and subdued them," and so doing, they lived lives that were "lonely struggles unto death."[43] Townsend finds entire generations of men from elite families locked in battle with the power of their sexual energy; longing for suffering; fraught with depression, psychosomatic illness, and neurasthenic breakdowns; and trying desperately to figure out how to live as men. If indeed men lived in such turmoil, this study seeks to unravel adult emotional needs in order to make it possible to write about them historically.

If psychologists are right, early childhood is key to that understanding. Psychologists' sense of how an independent self emerges begins with the intimate physical and psychological bonds that develop between mothers and infants. As the male child grows, he establishes a separateness from his mother and identifies with his father or some other male, and through this identification, he develops a sense of his own capacity for independent action. The principal psychological danger to an adult man's maintenance of an individuated self is a lingering and powerful urge to regress toward a comforting sense of oneness with the mother. The crafting of manhood,

David Gilmore concludes, "is a battle against these regressive wishes and fantasies, a hard-fought renunciation of the longings for the . . . idyll of childhood."[44]

For some men, psychic regression destroys the sense of independent selfhood and opens them to feelings of effeminacy, which must be resisted. The flight from the feminine emerges as a powerful force spurring the relentless maintenance of pure masculinity. Fear of women is not fear of *women* as such, but a metaphorical reduction of many other fears that signal the loss of singularity and independence. By this logic, resistance to longings for maternal connectedness prompts some men to erect psychological barriers, or ego boundaries, that take the form of a drivenness, a hard, unfeeling rationality. The more benign and harmonious a man's childhood, the less he displaces pent-up emotion onto adulthood. Depending on how much loss, insecurity, or anger some aggressively masculine men feel, resisting the pull toward maternal regression can take the form of violence against the feminine, distaste for sharing or communalism, or revenge against those perceived as weak.[45] Fear of letting someone get behind one's external barrier, of exposing weakness, of being somehow transgressed spurs some men to craft an exaggeratedly rugged and belligerent manhood, a "deeply conflicted, pressured, and forced" persona that strives for total control, competence, and isolating independence. Such men "experience a relentless anxiety," Gilmore explains, "that the external mask will suddenly fall away, revealing the trembling baby within."[46]

Displaced passions from private emotional life can, as a matter of course, inform public thought and action, drawing men to the enactment of rituals of purity and cleansing, to a fascination with authoritarian personalities, and to a preoccupation with maintaining social order and policing class, race, and gender boundaries.[47] The psychological explanation for how emotions translate into political life centers on men's attempts to maintain their own ego boundaries in the face of social upheaval and crises of sexual confidence. As Andreas Huyssen finds, "fear of the masses in [an] age of declining liberalism is always also a fear of woman, a fear of nature out of control, fear of the unconscious, of sexuality, of the loss of identity and stable ego boundaries."[48]

Recent research into the social constructions of masculinity in the United States underpins these psychological explanations for male autonomy and violence. Sociological studies of the appeal of violence, whether fictional or real, show that while most people seek to satisfy a curiosity about violence, watching it generally produces fear of injury or death rather than pleasurable reactions. The evidence is consistent cross-culturally.

Excluding the rare sadist who takes genuine pleasure in violence, most people's interest wanes as macabre acts, such as bodily dismemberment or necrophilia, appear. But whether the experience is pleasurable or distressing, we watch because of our curiosity, not because the images are appealing. The media exploit this curiosity.[49]

The audience and the setting in which the violence is presented also determine its meaning. Peer groups enforce aggressive and stoic masculinity and provide the moralistic justifications for violent acts. Violence appeals mostly to men, Dolf Zillman explains, usually to those exposed to high degrees of violence in their own lives, and especially to those who have high levels of aggression and a constant need for physical stimulation. Adolescent boys use cinematic horror to test courage and to demonstrate, ostensibly to their peers but essentially to themselves, their ability to control fear. For young men, playing war games or watching violent movies or sports constitute proof of the ability to manage fear, and thus mark male social identity. Male viewers distance themselves from their own uneasy responses to violence in order to render that violence tolerable. Even the strongest men wince, but manliness requires them to regard victims only in the abstract and to close off empathetic responses to their suffering.[50] In one study, young men who bravely watched fictional horror eagerly denounced others who reacted empathetically and emotionally. For men who positioned themselves as heroic or brave, superior manliness was equal to a proven callousness achieved at the expense of more squeamish peers. In the logic of this view, male violence is about other males. It is about overcoming one's own fear, identifying with a fraternal community of the fearless, and denouncing the fearful.[51]

When, if ever, is violence enjoyable? Rather than simply identify with violence, researchers find, men in U.S. society become emotionally involved in making moral judgments about it. They experience distress when good fictional characters suffer evil or bad guys obtain good outcomes. Viewers can overrule their empathy for someone's suffering if they deem it just—for example, if a villain is made to suffer. When viewers morally condemn the villain, they place themselves on a moral high ground that allows them to take great satisfaction from the violence that the villain has brought upon himself. The enjoyment of violent acts lies not in the violence itself, but in the meaning that viewers derive from it: a "moral right of rejoicing in response to exhibitions of righteous violence."[52] This suggests the reason that people who are fearful about becoming victims of violent crime condone severe punishments for criminals.

If indeed retribution elicits pleasure, it is possible that the more concerned the Victorian bourgeoisie grew with protecting its own moral interests against degenerate behavior, and the more desperate it became in its search for social order, the more it accepted social violence as morally justified. This explains, for Zillman, that "even the most gruesome, destructive violence fosters euphoric reactions, because moral sanction prescribes 'appropriate' retribution."[53]

It is also important to explore the appeal of Victorian-era warrior politics in light of how different cultures understand and construct manhood. In almost every culture David Gilmore examined in his ethnographic survey of male norms, men consider manhood to be an acquired attribute attainable only by some. Rather than a given that arrives automatically with physical maturity, manhood is a quality to be crafted or a prize to be earned in painful or dangerous rites such as circumcision and scarification or solitary stints in the wilderness. In most cultures, a youth demonstrates his transition to autonomous manhood by separating from his mother and performing successfully in coming-of-age rites. The fraternity of adult men welcomes these youths as equals. Boys who flinch or run away during such tests and adult men who have failed them or have remained dependent on their mothers or close to women in general are deemed cowards and weaklings and are never considered to be real men or suitable husbands. Manhood thus becomes exclusionary, and there are cultural sanctions for those who fail to achieve it. Adult manhood is almost universally "deeply conflicted, pressured, and forced, a mask of omni-competence and almost obsessive independence" that demands constant renewal and reestablishment.[54]

Cultural constructions of manliness vary from the extremely macho and aggressive to the less assertive and more egalitarian to the truly pacific. In general, cultures in which men and women work together and provide roughly equal amounts of food and child care tend to be the most egalitarian. Cultures with high proportions of male control of property and politics also tend toward high degrees of male violence against women. The roughness of male norms increases proportionally with the perceived amount of self-discipline and toughness needed for the daily work of providing for society's material needs. In this way, male codes of behavior direct energy toward a socially useful purpose. In aggressive warrior cultures, where women often undergo extreme forms of domination, men strive against one another to prove how hardened, cruel, and insensitive they are; male codes of behavior then serve as moral and social justification for aggression, warfare, and revenge. On the other hand, some peoples, such as the Tahitians and the Semai of central Malaysia, do not glorify toughness, for they have few enemies and little material want. In these cultures, men are freed from having to prove themselves, Gilmore explains, and are "allowed a basically androgynous script, which, significantly, they find congenial."[55]

Gilmore finds parallels in cross-cultural constructions of masculinity in the modern United States, where the common denominator in both Anglo-Saxon and ethnic subcultures is male worldly achievement constituted against laziness, effeminacy, or any other retreat from the work ethic. Furthermore, Americans follow the nearly universal belief in the constructedness of masculinity, that it is not the natural outcome of biological maturation but that it must be instilled through a period of tutelage, which if successful produces the hard-working, productive and reproductive man. The compulsion toward continual reenactment of this agency underlies modern manhood's vigorous self-fashioning and theatricality, making it, to James Eli Adams, "as much a spectacle as the feminine." Indeed, in Adams's figuration, the self-punishing aspects of modern manhood may not necessarily reflect men's tendency to repress longings for maternal comfort, but may also manifest the socially productive and demonstrative man. As such, repression understood as the energy of libidinal conflict emerges in outward displays of "masculinity as a virtuoso asceticism, a rigorous discipline staged before an imagined audience."[56]

Examining Roosevelt from these perspectives sheds new light on why many American men, in a period of profound social and sexual crisis, came to understand politics and political leaders not just objectively, but through their emotional lives. And it begins to explain why and how individual masculinity became a vehicle for establishing and maintaining the idea of the nation and its search for order. It suggests how, in Roosevelt's hands, politics, soldiering, and cowboying furnished grand national arenas for a pugilistic form of masculine self-fashioning. Roosevelt cultivated a political constituency among men who longed for a sense of agency and purpose or sacrifice or martyrdom in their lives, among men who saw enemies everywhere and wished the nation rid of them. He unlocked deep sources of interest, if not satisfaction, in vicariously experienced aggression that allowed partisans of his cult of national manhood to affirm the righteousness of excessive violence and their emotional reactions to it. He rendered men more responsive to calls for national purification by summoning their deep-seated need to reject the feminine. In his politics he encouraged men to stigmatize their emotional selves and project fears outward onto scapegoats, and in doing so he helped create his era's social rationale for persecuting outsiders. Insofar as men craved excitement in situations that reinforced male bonding, Roosevelt's fantasized violence provided radically excessive vignettes that held men's interest, no matter how troubling to them or how questionably moral. Men need not have enjoyed such fantasy in order to have thrived on it.

The chapters that follow demonstrate how Roosevelt's desire for toughening the nation's body against degeneration, his flight from effeminacy, his need to inflict pain on himself and others, and his rational use of men's capacity for "primitive" violence combined to cultivate an emotionally shared, exclusionary national community of white, heterosexual males. Few men of Roosevelt's time understood the deep emotional sources of these urges, for the president and for his era. Owen Wister did, though, when he remarked that Roosevelt's style of manhood "inevitably" led to the Great War, whose peculiar horror lay in "having our myths about blood and fire and mutilation and blindness come true."[57]

Inner Demons

It is just because
human blood-
thirstiness is such
a primitive part of
us that it is so
hard to eradicate,
especially where a
fight or a hunt is
promised as part
of the fun.
—William James,
The Principles of
Psychology

As it is with the
individual, so it is
with the nation.
—Theodore
Roosevelt, "The
Strenuous Life"

When William McKinley was assassinated in 1901, Theodore Roosevelt at age forty-two became the youngest man ever to hold the nation's highest office. To many Americans, the new president's ebullient optimism reflected the promise inherent in the era's astonishing material achievements. America would achieve great-power status, Roosevelt and most progressives predicted, expanding economically into the world's markets through private investment, advancing militarily by enlarging its deep-ocean fleet and acquiring colonies, and growing morally by providing tutelage for conquered peoples abroad. In the young nation's fate, progressives held, lay the entire future of civilization. Roosevelt's "panoramic vision of global evolution as a civilizing process" guided his foreign policy, Frank Ninkovich observes, and it served as the entering wedge for twentieth-century America's liberal internationalism, a political stance usually attributed to William Howard Taft, Roosevelt's successor in the presidency. Such "optimistic imperialist internationalism" provided Roosevelt and many of the era's politicians with the now familiar rationale for a controlled use of force to further civilization, bring international order, and preserve the white race.[1]

If destiny lay in many minds, the social Darwinism of Roosevelt's era made it easier to entwine racial, masculine, and national trajectories with that of civilization itself. Most Americans interpreted Darwinism to mean that persons, nations, and races evolved from primitive savagery to mature civilization, embodying along the way a succession of lower evolutionary physical and emotional characteristics. Ontology recapitulates phylogeny, they said. Within this evolutionary paradigm, Roosevelt mixed biological, social, and political ontologies to envision a world of racial nations, each positioned along a continuum from dark-skinned savagery to white civilization. Each nation experienced a "militant, savage stage of tribal morality," he wrote in 1913, when its "hot and lusty youth" bred the "hard men" and "masterful virtues" that ultimately produced civilization.[2] As the most highly evolved, the Germanic and Anglo-Saxon nations, with America at the forefront, represented civilization's vanguard.

Yet within the very optimism of this worldview lay the dark germ of defeat. True to republican and Puritan moralists before him, Roosevelt interpreted history as a recurring cycle of growth and stagnation. Rejecting Darwinist notions that random social or environmental factors governed human life, he envisioned history driven by a purposeful, Lamarckian evolution where individual men either created civilization through virtuous action or failed, like the Romans and the French, becoming engulfed in a morass of evil. "We climb through degrees of comparison," Roosevelt said; every step upward carried the dangerous possibility that the nation might fall backward. "We ascend or die."[3] In the anxious, ever-changing world of the late nineteenth century, when men and even nations had seemingly traded their youthful lustiness for the easy habits of civilized life, nations and men had to act, even if action brought only the opportunity, and not the guarantee, of upward ascent.

Thus, to Roosevelt, while the "frontier, barbaric virtues" drove civilization's advance, they did not alone produce more fit individuals, nations, and races. Only if and when men's moral character underwrote those barbaric virtues did they prove worthy of bearing civilization. Hardly armchair traits, barbaric virtues could not be learned apart from the forceful action that produced them. "You had to have the ideals," Roosevelt told veterans at Gettysburg in 1904. "That is why you won; . . . but if you had not been able to march and shoot you could not have put them into practice."[4] But even if men and nations practiced the ideals militantly, the evolutionary struggle provided no guarantees. No matter how strong any nation appeared, Roosevelt held, civilization tended toward a "certain decay" which "inevitably" befell every advanced nation. France's population had slipped into "gross sensuality and licentiousness" and had begun a long decline back down the evolutionary ladder for the same reason that the Romans, once "a thoroughly manly race," had ultimately "passed away."[5] Small wonder then that Roosevelt's closest lifelong friend, Henry Cabot Lodge, often found him brooding about civilization's future. Despite popular belief in Roosevelt's "buoyant and fearless" outlook, Lodge confided to the president in 1903, "I am one of the two or three people in the world who know better. I know you are, and always have been, a pessimist . . . and it does make you see things sometimes too darkly."[6]

Roosevelt's foreboding was greatly influenced by Brooks Adams's sweeping evolutionary theory of history, expounded in *The Law of Civilization and Decay* (1896). Martial virtues failed to reproduce themselves in men of the advanced nations, Adams argued with an eye toward the weak and nervous Easterners of his generation, and this failure brought not just individual humiliation but civilization's "last stage," the "end of history." Only national expansion could reverse national decline, Adams warned. Otherwise the nation would be "devoured by the gangrene which attacks every stagnant society and from which no patient recovers."[7] Accepting Adams's near-obsessive views, Roosevelt understood modern life as both civilizing and emasculating, entirely capable of limiting the nation's ability to maintain itself as a manly presence among nations.[8]

"The old iron days have gone," Roosevelt lamented in 1901 as he addressed the quarter-centennial celebration of statehood in Colorado Springs, "the days when the weakling died as the penalty of inability to hold his own in the rough warfare of his surroundings." The preservation of manly strength "will find a different expression now," he conceded, one more acceptable to civilized men, yet the "iron quality itself remains just as necessary as ever." For Roosevelt, the modern dilemma was how to discover this "different expression," how to preserve the "iron quality" of the nation's forefathers among men living in "softer times, . . . gentler and more humanizing."[9] He held out hope that the "masterful virtues" of virile heroism could be cultivated in a civilized context, that the sick nation could energize itself through "the warlike power of a civilized people."[10]

Preoccupied with visions of civilization and decay, Roosevelt developed a theory of nationhood that centered on the health of an imagined national body, one that he portrayed in vivid biological and sexual metaphors.[11] Nations live and die, he said. A nation's "community of interest," he told a 1901 veterans reunion in Burlington, Vermont, arises from the "great primal needs and primal passions that are common to all of us."[12] Here Roosevelt, like most men of his class, understood *us* to signify the select, fraternal, collective body of white male citizens, those men capable of expressing primal passions in a civilized manner. Though the nation was growing and becoming stronger, it had specifically modern diseases: effeminate behavior softened its fiber, and consumerism lured it into selfishness and ease. Roosevelt hoped almost against hope that "the healthy tissue will gradually eat out the unhealthy."[13]

As a young adult in the 1890s, Roosevelt saw unhealthy aspects of modernism looming everywhere. Urban life had liberated women, he and many middle-class men feared, just as the closing of the frontier had eliminated the world in which men engaged in hard physical work. Material greed diverted men from the republican vision of a disinterested, virtuous civic life. In Europe and America, a revolution in manners and morals attacked traditional sexual restraint and loosened the rigid prescriptions for male and female behavior. Companionate marriages eroded the patriarchal model of family life as philosophies of relativism and pragmatism beckoned the New Woman and the worldly men she associated with. New medical, scientific, and psychological definitions of normality and abnormality, together with the proliferation of instruction manuals for solving male sexual problems, the advertising industry's promises to help men "regain potency," the discovery of homosexuality, and a renewed focus on prostitution and the spread of sexually transmitted diseases, all heightened the focus on the male body and provided new grounds for male anxiety and for Roosevelt's vision of national manhood.[14]

After he became president, Roosevelt's concerns about male bodies grew. He began to encounter men in Washington and New York who had seemingly reverted to "a certain softness and luxury—a condition of mind and body in which long-continued hardship becomes intolerable." Such "stay-at-home" men drained the nation's hardihood because they "become fickle and hysterical under pressure of danger; they shrink from the grim necessities of war [and] will not show the necessary brutal heroism in attack and defense."[15] The masculine hardiness of warriors diminished, and along with it the nation's virility. "Did you ever look over the medical statistics of the half million men drafted during the Civil War?" Roosevelt asked the naturalist John Burroughs. "It would appear that the physical type in the Eastern States has undoubtedly degenerated . . . lighter built, . . . narrower across the chest. The decay of vitality, especially as shown in the decreasing fertility of New England and, indeed, the New York stock, is very alarming."[16]

Roosevelt's racial concerns cast whiteness as integral to his theory of national manhood. The possibility of evolutionary racial backsliding popularized by the era's social Darwinists led white men to fear that humans and apes shared common ancestors and that nonwhite populations posed a threat to white racial hegemony. Racial theorists fed these worries. Arthur de Gobineau, in *The Inequality of Human Races* (1849), argued that while the Aryan race had created Western civilization, it would inevitably degenerate through interbreeding with inferior peoples closer on the evolutionary scale to animals. "We do not descend from the ape," he announced, "but are headed in that direction."[17] Among many who attributed the decline in white birthrates—by nearly half between 1800 and 1900—to men's growing disinterest in procreation, Roosevelt feared that the Anglo-Saxon and Germanic races were committing suicide when men refused to father numerous children and when whites bred with members of "inferior" races.[18] After all, he said, Rome fell because "there sprang from its loins no children to defend it against the barbarians."[19] But he usually rejected ideas of inevitable decline, and instead urged American men to have more children, to "gird up our loins as a nation . . . to play our part manfully."[20]

POLITICAL MASTERY

Throughout nearly three decades in the public limelight, Roosevelt occupied a pivotal role as America's most important cultural broker of masculinity, embodying both an ideal type and the contemporary national mood. He drew many votes entirely on the basis of his manhood. William Allen White, a Kansas editor and Roosevelt's friend, estimated that of the four million votes Roosevelt received in his second and last campaign for president in 1912, approximately one million were cast by men for "no particular intelligent reason" other than that "you were a masculine sort of a person with extremely masculine virtues and palpably masculine faults."[21] Voters found his youthful political style personal, intense, and incomparably physical, and they considered him, according to his friend William Roscoe Thayer, "the most masterful politician of his time." "Known throughout the world as the incarnation of Americanism," Thayer wrote, Roosevelt had the ability to appear at once "most typically American and strikingly individual."[22] "He is not an American," Henry Cabot Lodge reported that an Englishman remarked after the 1905 Portsmouth conference, "he *is America.*"[23]

If Thayer's claim seems a bit enthusiastic, consider that in the late nineteenth century, the nation's press had suddenly reinvented presidential reportage. Although reporters had shown great interest in the presidency during the Civil War, after the scandals of the Grant administration and the impeachment of Andrew Johnson, they paid scant attention to presidents unless they married, gave key speeches, or traveled. But between 1870 and 1900, the number of daily newspapers quadrupled, bringing the number of readers to more than fifteen million a day, almost 20 percent of the nation's population. Similarly, the number of magazines rose from six hundred weeklies and monthlies in 1865 to 4,400 by 1890, dominated by a new generation of cheaply produced and sumptuously illustrated ten-cent magazines like *Muncy's* and *The Saturday Evening Post*. By 1905, these new popular magazines commanded a circulation of five million as they trained their readers' interest on sensationalized stories of police investigations, progressive reform, foreign relations, and events in the White House.[24]

The Spanish-American War and the explosion of the *Maine* in Havana
Harbor in 1898 intensified press interest in the president's actions, and
reporters' demands that McKinley respond to Spain's alleged outrages
heightened public attention. Wishing to avoid war and to restrain the public's war fever, McKinley had his chief of staff, George Cortelyou, shape
press coverage through carefully worded and timed press releases during
the entire crisis of the spring and summer of 1898. Reporters came to de-
pend on official White House statements as a source of news, a development that, in turn, magnified presidential leadership.

When Roosevelt succeeded McKinley, he retained Cortelyou as his
chief of staff until 1903. His wartime exploits had made him fully aware of
his ability to create news, and he cultivated well-known journalists, editors,
and writers, including Jacob Riis, Richard Harding Davis, and Lincoln
Steffens, and received, in turn, their approving attention. He invited reporters to accompany him on presidential travels and Western trips, and
even provided them with a train car.[25]

Reporters loved the exemplary physical and moral strenuousness that
Roosevelt called the "bully life," and they helped to integrate stories about
the president into the nation's sense of itself during his seven years in the
White House. Beginning with his days as a New York state assemblyman,
and throughout his political life, Roosevelt's raucous, explosive, moralistic
manner matched his imposing physical presence, and although he
offended some—Henry James termed him "the mere monstrous embodiment of unprecedented and resounding noise"—he always attracted a
large following.[26] "They were captivated by the flashing grin," biographer
Nathan Miller writes, "the determination in the blue eyes . . . and the
vigor in the staccato flood of words driven home by the . . . pounding of fist
on palm." "He was his own limelight," Owen Wister observed, "and could
not help it."[27] In the polarized and often corrupt world of party politics,
Roosevelt's "gift for political invective" made ordinary men think they had
found a champion.[28]

Many of the same Americans who identified with Roosevelt's theatricality also willingly consumed his version of the nation's history. Over his
lifetime, he produced a large quantity of articles and thirty-eight books,
many of which became classics: *The Naval War of 1812* (1882), *Gouverneur
Morris* (1888), and the wildly popular four-volume *Winning of the West*
(1889–96). As a historian and later president of the American Historical
Association, he understood the role of a national literature. More importantly, he assumed personal responsibility for creating a masculinized narrative of America's role in civilization's progress, and he enlisted himself as
one of its heroes. "It was as if the age-long fight between good and evil had

suddenly come to a head," said his good friend Jacob Riis; "we all leave our mark upon our day, and his is that of a clean, strong man who fights for the right *and wins.*"[29]

Such popular belief as Riis expressed, that the nation's strength arose from the bodies of virile white men like Roosevelt, helps explain middle-class Americans' relentless vigilance against the inner demons of moral, racial, and social decline and their incessant reinventing of ideal types. These reinventions made it easier for Roosevelt's more militant vision of manhood to focus men's anxieties on the physical body and to hold out dreams of national bodily wholeness against the risk of corrupted identity. Therein lay its appeal. To men who could never feel muscular or tough or brave enough, Roosevelt's promise of renewal through "endless feats of arms" helped change the standards by which they measured one another's masculinity.

Edward Alsworth Ross, the eminent University of Wisconsin sociologist, noted the growing social acceptance of ever higher levels of male aggression, particularly when exhibited by soldiers or chivalric gentlemen. He attributed this acceptance to the attractions of romanticized violence.

> It might at first blush seem strange that the aspiring millions of our democracy should embrace an ideal worked out among professional fighters. . . . But it is to be remembered that people will adopt as ideal only that type which charms and fascinates them. Our experience, as well as that of Japan, shows that an upper-class ideal, with its halo of luxury, romance, and feats of arms, is more apt to take by storm the hearts of plain people than one that springs from the soul of the prophet or reformer.[30]

Although the militant ideal that Ross alluded to had marked the European aristocracy since the Middle Ages and had infused American culture throughout the colonial and frontier periods, modern middle-class manners had come to exclude unruly male behavior in offices, parlors, and city life. Thus, few acceptable outlets remained for middle-class white men to do violence, making it all the more possible for their urges to be channeled into quasi-militant forms of aggressive physicality. A new social type appeared in the nation's cities, the "sporting male," to use Timothy Gilfoyle's term, a man who escaped civilization and joined other men in new realms of adult adventure: attending prize fights, frequenting prostitutes, drinking, and finding in working-class recreations an earthy vigor their own lives lacked. Drawing on boyhood groups like the Boy Scouts and college fraternities, fraternal clubs such as the New Improved Order of the Red Men encouraged grown men to rediscover primitive selves in bohemian and "Indian" rituals. Clubs and orders encouraged violence

through their initiation and membership requirements and provided ter-
ritorialized social space free from feminine influence. By 1900, clubs and
orders boasted a combined membership of 5.5 million out of a total of
nineteen million adult males.[31]

The era's fantastic literature, Peter Stearns observes, also provided
"moments of excitement that did not need to be internally censored."[32]
Fantasy fiction included hunting, Western, and medieval adventures; soft
porn; travel pictures of naked natives engaged in primitive rituals; and sen-
sationalist crime and disaster reporting. Lurid stories focused on heroes
who, in one way or another, set out on a quest and proved their manhood.
Davy Crockett, Gilfoyle points out, became a popular icon as he pursued
frontier adventures and engaged in "exhibitionist, non-reproductive" sex,
unfettered by home, family, or emotional intimacy.[33] For Anthony Rotundo, the powerful appeal of these stories rests on their having provided
"a resonant echo of those impulses and emotions that men had forsaken in
growing up."[34]

After the 1880s, the proliferation of amateur, college, civic, and professional baseball teams and boxing clubs, along with increases in the number
of organizations such as the Young Men's Christian Association (YMCA)
and the Boy Scouts, attested to the growth of an institutionalized sports
culture in which men could engage in ritualized displays of violence
among themselves. In the best Darwinian spirit, they came to envision
their own lives as a continual battle played out if not in the quickly closing
avenues to class mobility, then at least on the playing field.[35] Men began to
identify rough sports play and its correlates—struggle, strife, and domination—with a strong, masculine character. By the end of the century, it
became acceptable for middle-class men engaged in sports to cultivate
what they understood as the bestial and primitive, to encourage sexual aggression and even anger. At Harvard, as Kim Townsend points out, those
loyal to the scholarly ideal lamented the takeover of competitive athletics
and the marketing thereof to the detriment of the moral tone of the general
student population. "We have allowed the fighting impulse . . . to get the
better of the educational and developmental side," said Dudley A. Sargent, associate professor of physical training and director of the school's
Hemenway Gymnasium. "In other words we have lost control."[36] If this
sounds like the exact opposite of self-mastery, it had indeed become so, as
sports culture seemed to cultivate the open expression of the very passions
it was originally thought to suppress.

For many of the same reasons, men sought the new leisure excitements
and sexual freedoms of theaters, social dances, and brothels in the growing
tenderloin districts of large cities. In the 1860s, New York City's men sup-

ported over six hundred houses of prostitution, earning the city the nickname "Sodom and Gomorrah." By 1896, when Roosevelt became New York City's police commissioner, prostitution enjoyed so much Tammany police protection that payoffs from brothel owners and saloonkeepers amounted to de facto regulation. Beginning in the 1870s, the combined forces of Anthony Comstock and private groups like the New York Society for the Suppression of Vice began to work against pornography and prostitution in New York City, but they had made little headway by the turn of the century.[37] By providing pleasurable and often violent flights from ordinary life, sporting-male activities provided a sense of autonomy from women and equality with other men. Roosevelt's "strenuous life" and "bully" style enjoyed mass appeal for the same reasons that mass entertainments did, because his heroics were so out of the ordinary yet so close to the way ordinary men needed to feel. His fantasies of an eternal arrested boyhood and of male conquest and domination encouraged sporting males to consciously revitalize their own maleness, locate it in their bodies, and integrate it with an imagined national self.

BOYS TO MEN

Before the Civil War, white men considered manhood to be a quality opposed to boyhood and womanhood more than something they had to assert against other men. Parents took a somewhat negative view of boyhood, and they did not consider aggression or passion qualities of ideal manhood. Instead, middle-class notions of male agency rested on the self-made, civic- and family-minded, republican yeoman. By the 1840s, liberal political belief in the universal opportunities of democracy, together with classical economic notions of capitalist individualism, had made civic and commercial society the locus of most white male self-fashioning.

By the 1880s, however, the republican and capitalist sources of middle-class identity were rapidly eroding, putting masculine norms in great flux. Agribusiness and highly integrated corporations had overtaken the nation's Anglo-Saxon proprietary farms, shops, and small manufacturing establishments. The rise of new wealth and a large class of landless wage earners reduced the importance of place and family and elevated a distinctly modern anonymity and rapacity in business dealings. Such changes disrupted old social relationships and diminished the economic agency of the individual male even as he entered an urban work world where the cult of the self-made man encouraged ambitious, greedy behavior. The idea spread that men required passion and a certain absence of restraint to sharpen the competitive skills that allowed some men to achieve success by having bested others. "In a world where a man was supposed to prove his superiority, the urge for dominance was seen as a virtue," Rotundo argues, "and roles of domination and submission between men became respectable."[38] Although male success was defined primarily by achievement in the world of work, men went beyond market imperatives and infused competition into every aspect of manly life, even into previously less competitive areas like fathering children, converting nonbelievers, and physical exercise.

Thus, by the 1890s, the new markers of manliness were beginning to affect middle- and upper-class parents' expectations of boyhood behavior. People began to adopt more positive attitudes toward boyhood and to consider adult manhood to be its natural outgrowth. As they matured, young men were expected to strengthen the competitive skills of boyhood and to redirect their need for gratification and excitement into the adult world. Grown men came to endorse the pleasures of rough play and passionate exuberance—now thought to enhance the manly qualities of adult hunters, athletes, and soldiers. "Boys' vices suddenly became men's virtues," Rotundo observes.[39]

Conversely, the image of tamed, mannerly boys came to have a negative taint among middle-class men. Worried that there was something wrong with boys who were perfect gentlemen, who had only character to make them manly, parents began to support organizations like the YMCA, the Boy Scouts of America, and the Knights of King Arthur, which used strenuous outdoor activity to teach toughness and self-reliance. Ernest Thompson Seton, founder, with Robert Baden-Powell, of the Boy Scouts of America, seconded the new image of the competitive, savage child and enshrined it in the era's scouting tutelage. A popularizer of evolutionary growth metaphors, Seton argued that since the boy was "ontologically and essentially a savage," it was necessary for boys to play "Indian." Seton's book *Two Little Savages* told the story of a contemporary "young savage" in an otherwise civilized world, whose "bloodthirst" drove him to hunt in a nearby woods, where his "savage impulse to kill came quickly."[40]

Boyhood was expected to provide a "playful, libidinal, hedonistic" world, Rotundo finds, one that repressed tenderness and vulnerability and prompted boys to vent energy in aggressive fun "rarely free of cruelty or violence." Underneath the violence of snowball fights and schoolyard hazing "lay curious veins of casual hostility and sociable sadism." Boys routinely tortured animals to death "simply to inflict suffering," though they "held their deepest reserves of cruelty, . . . their fiercest fury for [human] enemies."[41] Upon the skinny, the weak, the bookish, or the ethnically alien, bullies imposed a cruel pecking order based on size, strength, bravery, and the ability to stand pain.

Stronger boys created peer groups in which they bonded through physical and emotional domination of the weak. Oftentimes "perversely affec-
tionate," boys demonstrated the fondness of these bonds through physical
contact that offered acceptable modes of release. "Where gestures of tenderness were forbidden" in the ordinary male world, Rotundo explains,
"physical combat allowed [boys] . . . bouts of intense embrace."[42]

Although boys could have close relationships with female relatives,
their cruelty and domination often extended to girls. Because the good behavior of sisters and other girls represented the domestic world boys had
only just escaped, they turned their disdain for that world into hostility
and contempt for girls, taking "vengeance on an earlier identity" for its de-
pendence on women.[43] As boys grew to men and developed love relationships with women, they found themselves attracted to a womanly ideal
laden with the old repulsions of boyhood. With conflicting feelings of sus-
picion and desire, males fantasized that feminine evil would lure them into
a female world of sexual excess or into the dangerous dependency of marriage. Spurred by these contradictions, the child's playful violence could
become real in the man, expressed in a desire to dominate, either through
protective gallantry or physical or emotional abuse.

Self-control loomed as an integral part of manhood, as middle-class
men were educated to think that they harbored dangerously strong sexual
passions, yet were constrained by a moral code that ostensibly restricted
sexual behavior to the marriage bed.[44] Men attempted to exercise self-
control at home, where their marriage partners supposedly helped them,
but middle-class women placed added demands on these efforts as they
limited family size, predominantly through abstinence and coitus inter-
ruptus. Through such restraints, "the new locus for 'true' male experience," Ed Cohen explained, became the "personal struggle between 'will'
and 'desire,' 'reason' and 'passion,' 'mind' and 'body' . . . , a contest
against oneself that must be 'won.' "[45] "Mastery over one's evil passions,"
as Roosevelt put it, required an active role for men in managing male desire. The struggle for this mastery heightened men's anxiety over sexual
excess, masturbation, and homoerotic feelings. It left them both attracted
and repulsed by their own passions and desperate to find acceptable outlets
for them.

Many men who courted and married ideal middle-class women separated the twin dangers of attraction and repulsion, finding recreational sex
not in spiritualized love relationships with women of their own class but
with women of a lower class. These men found themselves "slumming" in
working-class brothels and cabarets near the business district. Thus the
double sexual standard also represented a class bias, where men married

women from good families but indulged their baser impulses with working-class women and prostitutes. Engaging in "exploitative, impersonal" sex in casual relationships, Rotundo explains, led men to dissociate sexual passion from marriage and to equate it with something debased and vulgar, all the while retaining their own and their wives' respectability.[46]

DIVIDED SELVES

To understand the appeal of the new aggressive manhood and how it helped resolve men's contradictory feelings about their desires, it is important to remember that middle-class Victorians made sense out of the world through a complex system of categories that emerged during Europe's scientific revolution and the Enlightenment—habits of naming, numbering, classifying, and comparing just about everything. European philosophers and scientists arranged the great binary categories of human existence—civilization and savagery, purity and pollution, male and female, energy and fatigue—into hierarchies of progress and degeneration. Within these hierarchies, each act of differentiation became a judgment. To be sure, Victorian men and women inherited these distinctions and boundaries from the past, but they also created moral and social taxonomies out of the particular vicissitudes of their own era, such as prostitution, homosexuality, and race mixing. Blended with social Darwinist notions of continual flux and the political idea that America served as the vanguard of civilization, the polarity of the opposites seemed to dictate an all-or-nothing choice between two social extremes, with the fate of mankind at stake. In this way, as Sonja O. Rose observes, binary distinctions create order not simply because they arrange the cognitive maps that people follow, but also "because they are the outcome of struggles over the power to define."[47] Such polarities helped define, for example, the notion of a male psyche divided into human and bestial forms, and helped make men's minds and bodies a battleground. Thus Roosevelt's reach for a militant ideality at the end of the century involved more than an overt masculinizing process: as Arthur Brittan observes, "embodiment is not simply about the embedding of social practices in the body; it is also about the *exclusion* and rejection of other practices."[48]

The great fact of separating binary opposites into hostile camps meant that each pole required its opposite in order to produce meaning. This is how men of Roosevelt's era understood G. Stanley Hall's remark, "Real virtue requires enemies."[49] And binary habits of thinking explain why political discourse depicted struggles between enlightened progress and anarchy or between normalcy and deviance.[50] If real virtue required enemies, real heroes required villains. "Civilization is always in need of being saved from . . . internal enemies," William James observed, by people "knowing true men when they see them."[51] Thus binary opposites produced a dynamic that necessarily raised the question of outcomes. Albert Jeremiah Beveridge put it thusly in his *Meaning of the Times* (1908): "It is destiny that the world shall be rescued from its natural wilderness and from savage men."[52] As social concerns mounted at the turn of the century, the era's social critics produced a stream of books whose unsettling titles questioned Beveridge's optimistic outcome in binary language: Henry George's *Progress and Poverty* (1879), Brooks Adams's *Law of Civilization and Decay* (1895), and Matthew Arnold's *Culture and Anarchy* (1883). If these works seemed to foretell decline and final death, Max Nordau's *Degeneration* (1895) and James Balfour's *Decadence* (1908) confirmed it. Behind every hope for national perfectibility that these books held lay an Armageddon-like doom, one that Nordau called the "reddened light of the Dusk of Nations."[53]

Around any single binary pole, associated images elicited one another through common properties that were presumably transferable. Roosevelt used the associated categories of "race" and "nation" interchangeably and understood them within the interlocking metaphorical domain of white men's attributes—health, bravery, morality, and virility. Thus locked together, race, manhood, and nation stood in polar opposition to all elements of modern life that could threaten individual white men—moneyed Jews, dangerous women, wild Indians, or defiant Negroes. That any one danger might challenge "our mighty manhood," in Roosevelt's parlance, meant that it threatened all white men of "our" social class, as well as "our" nation and the trajectory of "our" civilization. This is why, for Roosevelt, "treason, like adultery, ranks as one of the worst of all possible crimes."[54] This is why in 1896 Roosevelt remarked about a Republican celebration of McKinley's presidential victory held by New York bankers that "at least half the guests were Jew bankers; I felt as if I was personally realizing all of Brooks Adams's gloomiest anticipations of our gold-ridden, capitalist-bestridden, usurer-mastered future."[55] Roosevelt's logic, which linked ethnic, economic, and nationalist fears, was held together not by deduction, George Lakoff points out, but by a rationale that was simply taken for granted.[56]

In nineteenth-century England, France, and the United States, that rationale enabled middle-class individuals to deeply identify with social and bodily processes deemed cleansing or polluting. "Abnormal" sexuality, venereal disease, and insanity prompted Victorians to develop a near-obsession with degeneracy as they acted out the social and psychological rituals that maintained boundaries between cleanliness and uncleanliness.[57] Boundaries created outsiders and transformed ordinary people and behaviors into dangerous enemies, allowing middle-class whites to embody in others what was disgusting in themselves. The nation's social critics identified the degenerate aspects of modernism. Edward Alsworth Ross noted in *Sin and Society* (1907), for example, "naturalism in fiction, 'decadence' in poetry, realism in art, tragedy in music, skepticism in religion, cynicism in politics, and pessimism in philosophy."[58] For William James, civilization's "internal enemies" included clerks and teachers, commercialism and corruption, "industrialism unlimited and feminism unabashed."[59] As the twentieth century unfolded, proper middle-class citizens began to imagine workers, prostitutes, the diseased, and the insane indulging in dangerous bodily excesses like masturbation and promiscuity. Disgust at such excesses helped define that hallmark of bourgeois identity, the autonomous, morally and sexually disciplined, white, heterosexual man who imagined himself at war with Roosevelt's "forces of evil."[60] Identity was formed at the point of exclusion.

In Roosevelt's mind, the civilization-savagery dichotomy metaphorically encompassed almost all the others, since every arena of life contained contending forces that advanced or retarded civilization. Using interlocking and overlapping metaphors of inclusion and exclusion and a near obsession with the maintenance of difference, he carried into politics powerful images of these great absolutes struggling over the nation's body. His speeches and writings resounded with images of "law, order and righteousness [that] succeeded to . . . barbarous and bloody violence" and of "orderly government . . . snatched from . . . the forces of darkness."[61] He offered his contemporaries psychological means to contain the fearful or disgusting aspects of modernity by projecting them onto scapegoats ranging from creators of avant-garde art to unruly unionists and by calling for disciplinary actions against those scapegoats.[62] Roosevelt's "fearless denunciation" of everything "wrong or low or weak . . . in our management of ourselves" and in the nation's affairs inspired praise, W. D. Trent wrote in 1896, for his "uncompromising, if not aggressive Americanism."[63]

Even Edward Bellamy, who harbored fewer class and racial anxieties than most writers, nevertheless deferred to those anxieties. In *Looking Backward, 2000-1887* (1888), one of the era's most popular novels, Bellamy refused to call his socialist utopia "socialist," because, he said, the term "smells to the average American of petroleum, [and] suggests the red flag, with all manner of sexual novelty and an abusive tone about God and religion."[64] Here Bellamy admits that given the Victorian sense of degeneration, Americans could not help but to conjoin revolution, sexual excess, sacrilege, and terrorism in the same threatening image. Roosevelt, too, linked associated evils in chains of historical causation, advising men to keep "mastery over their own evil passions," for "lawlessness in all its forms is the handmaiden of tyranny."[65] In this figuration, lawlessness was a woman whose body threatened dangerous excesses, sexual and otherwise. Still a maid, she nevertheless had become a political extremist serving the twin specters of anarchy and domination.

During the 1890s and throughout his presidency, Roosevelt would have disdained Bellamy's socialist utopia but agreed with his theory of decadence—that no single danger, not even lawlessness, could by itself destroy the nation. It was the combined pull of associated decadences that created the downward spiral. "What we have now to contend with," Roosevelt warned about the presence of freed slaves in society, "is not so much any one concrete evil as a general lowering of the standards."[66] This weakening could begin anywhere, proceed incrementally, inflict small losses, and culminate unexpectedly in racial decline, emasculation, or death. As a synergistic metaphor of decay, the "general lowering of the standards" necessarily unified its antidotes, making national survival dependent on the combined effects of "race hardening," territorial expansion, and assertive manliness. By linking national ideals, threats to those ideals, and antidotes to the threats, opinion leaders from both ends of the political spectrum reinforced and extended in the popular mind the domain of the closed, self-referenced theory of civilization contained in the binary opposites.

If associated virtues gained power through synergy, and if each binary pole required an opposite, the blurring of distinct categories disturbed this neat tautology. This was especially true when Roosevelt, as civilization's hero, showed weakness and provoked men's preoccupation with the alternately healthy and degraded aspects of the body and of its disciplinarian, the will. Known to many as an optimistic, moral, self-disciplined, and disciplining man, Roosevelt could nevertheless conjure doubts in himself and in other men and raise the possibility that a darker, more dangerous self, one less given to self-mastery, hovered underneath his poised surface. Media observers seized on Roosevelt's divided self, portraying him as capable of being seduced and exploiting his weakness for political power, as in this 1900 *Puck* cartoon "Not So Reluctant" (figure 3). At the end of the Cuban war, when his immense popularity propelled him to the governorship of New York, he provoked Republican Party leaders who wished to defuse his power by making him vice president. The cartoon's soldierly Roosevelt braces against the grasp of the matronly sirens of regional popularity but allows them to lure him, fully clothed and in control of his rational powers, into vice-presidential waters. Presumably, there he would not drown in sexual excess but would instead thrive politically.

Figure 3. Louis Dalrymple, "Not So Reluctant," *Puck,* 16 May 1900

At first glance, it appears that Roosevelt masters his sexuality by transforming the allure of temptresses into political service to the nation. Yet
the cartoonist uses sex as a metaphor for political desire, suggesting that
submission to either denotes a common weakness. Thus, Roosevelt smil-
ingly submits to the women's temptations, and descends not so reluctantly
into the water's flowing embrace. Victorian viewers most certainly read this
sexual subtext clearly because the cartoon invokes the eroticism of America's arguably most popular painting, Adolphe William Bouguereau's
Nymphs and Satyr (figure 4). The cartoonist places Roosevelt and the ma-
trons in the same positions as does Bouguereau his satyr and nymphs.
Thus, through his allegorical likeness with a satyr, Roosevelt could be pic-

Figure 4. William Adolphe Bouguereau, *Nymphs and Satyr,* 1873 (photo © Sterling and Francine Clark Art Institute, Williamstown, Mass., 1955.658)

tured as ostensibly chaste and rational yet actually inclined to cavort with maidens.

However prey to fleshly desires, Roosevelt represented to men of his era an astonishingly straightforward, virile, and sexualized body, leading some cartoonists to picture his sexuality less ambiguously and as even more

Figure 5. Llanuza, "On with the Dance," *San Francisco Chronicle* (Library of Congress Prints and Photographs Division, Washington, D.C., LC-USZ62-34271)

politically dangerous. "On with the Dance" pictures Roosevelt avidly embracing anarchism in the form of a woman with mannish muscles and hairy arms, a lighted bomb, and medusa hair, who snuggles close, posing a purely modern threat to the nation and its youthful soldier-statesman, much to the dismay of the gentleman watching from beside the pillar (figure 5). That anarchy can seduce even a uniformed and armed Roosevelt attests to her insidious power and reveals the vulnerability of the otherwise chaste, upright, and republican-minded leader, and by extension the corruptibility of the nation's male body and its politics. As the Roosevelt pulls her close and leads in the dance, his leering ardor suggests that his dark side seeks the red woman of a lower and more dangerous political order. Anarchy is dressed like a Gibson girl. Her clothes cling to her frame, and her high-heeled shoes lend her body a sinewy grace, forewarning of the dangers created by any woman, even one of the middle class, who enters the public dance of politics. This cartoon carries an indeterminate date sometime after 1910, and thus it is likely a reaction to Roosevelt's 1912 Progressive Party platform, which advocated such reforms as a graduated income tax, workmen's compensation, women's suffrage, federal conservation measures, and regulation of the labor of women and children. Whatever the precipitating event, the cartoon indicates that Roosevelt's dark persona offered his fellow men a disturbing metaphor for the blurred distinctions and alarming contradictions that appeared in men's psyches and on the streets of their cities. To understand the appeal of Roosevelt's dark persona, we must understand how the social demons common to men of this class could find expression in figures such as the dance partner, anarchism.

BOYS DON'T CRY

Many Victorian-era parents projected their own contradictions, anxieties, and self-disciplinary urges onto the lives of their male children through traditional child-rearing practices that required boys to repress emotion and desire under a stiff outward demeanor. Based on the Calvinist premise that children are innately sinful and must be painfully weaned from their depraved tendencies, these practices included strict instruction and the requirement of unending, laborious work. As parents administered corporal punishments to their sons "for their own good," they required them to keep a "stiff upper lip"; sparing the rod spoiled the child and produced "sissies."[67] In her study of nineteenth-century child rearing, the psychoanalyst Alice Miller maintains that parents who withheld affection and dispensed physical punishment traumatized their sons. Stern fathers could be kind and gentle and at the same time avoid intimate, emotional contact with their sons and never come to know or respect their feelings. In their quest to raise chaste and manly sons, many fathers inflicted a deep and lasting emotional trauma that constituted nineteenth-century civilization's great assault on the childhood of its middle-class males.[68] As Albert Beveridge observed in *The Young Man and the World* (1906), the modern father is a "pretty stern proposition. Raised by an earlier generation of even sterner fathers, he has 'been through the mill,' until the softness is pretty well ground out and little remains but the granite-like muscle of manhood."[69]

Toward the middle of the nineteenth century, a sentimental, romantic view of childhood challenged the sterner model. Progressive parents, educators, and reformers emphasized culture over nature and claimed that children adopted society's vices rather than being inherently sinful. These childhood experts emphasized children's innocence rather than their depravity and encouraged parents to nurture children's playful and emotional selves rather than to instill fear. This new model of child rearing did not cause the immediate rejection of the old, and many traditional families, like the Roosevelts, blended stern physical coercion with loving-kindness, a philosophy that reflected the culture's contradictory ideas about children's innocence and depravity.[70]

Parents who subscribed to stricter and more punitive models of child rearing caused boys not only to repress emotional needs but also to develop a fear and hatred of the father. Underneath what Beveridge identified as adult men's "granite-like" exteriors, repressed childhood longings for the emotional security fathers had withheld produced nagging but hardly identifiable feelings of inadequacy. Sons unwittingly internalized the authoritarian father and his sternness, toughening themselves in punitive ways and avoiding contact with their own emotions. Throughout their lives, these men continued to seek discipline from father substitutes and directed their own authoritarian and disciplinary urges toward those weaker than themselves. They viewed empathy as a sentimental capitulation to weakness. They projected their weak and emotional inner child onto other men, especially their own sons, whom they victimized as their own fathers had victimized them, thus passing on the legacy of their childhood.[71] Men projected anxious feelings into political contexts, as did that master of self-repression, Alfred Mahan, who, when applauding the role of U.S. troops in crushing the Boxer Rebellion in 1900, called the Chinese "children" who needed a "good shaking."[72]

Roosevelt's upbringing taught him, too, the importance of sublimating emotions. His father, also named Theodore, a prominent businessman, philanthropist, and public official, was loving and stern, Roosevelt related in own autobiography, and he was the "only man of whom I was ever really afraid." One of his earliest childhood memories was of his father's reaction when at the age of four he bit his sister's arm. His father chased him through the yard and into the kitchen, where the young Roosevelt hid under a table armed with a piece of dough the cook had given him. "My father immediately dropped on all fours and darted at me. I feebly heaved the dough at him, and . . . got a fair start for the stairs, but was caught halfway up them. The punishment that ensued fit the crime, and I hope—and believe—that it did me good."[73] Roosevelt did not describe the punishment, but he accepted it as necessary and salutary, so much so that his father never again punished him physically. Once disciplined, once "really afraid" of their father, Roosevelt said, he and his brothers avoided the consequences of further disobedience.

In a letter remarkable for its understanding of how his father instilled fear in him, and how he, in turn, did so in his son Ted, Roosevelt wrote to Edward Sanford Martin in 1900 explaining "the real underlying feeling which has made me fight myself and want Ted to fight." He approved of fighting only when it underwrote the practice of "virtue," Roosevelt wrote, only when a man was "decent and manly." He received this feeling from his father, who "refused to coddle me, and made me feel that I must force myself to hold my own with other boys and prepare myself to do the rough work of the world." He then retold the story of his earliest and only punishment. "In all my childhood he never laid a hand on me but once, but I always knew perfectly well that in case it became necessary he would not have the slightest hesitancy [to] do so again, and alike from my love and respect, from my fear of him, I would have hated and dreaded beyond measure to have him know that I had been guilty of a lie, or of cruelty, or of bullying, or of uncleanliness, or of cowardice." In the next paragraph he said of his son Ted, then thirteen, "Now I have striven to make him feel that if he only fights hard enough he is perfectly certain to secure the respect of all his associates for his virtues."[74] The most important respect for Ted to secure, of course, was that of his father. The question hung in the air between father and son, how hard was hard enough?

Roosevelt understood his father's regime of fear, and he used the same disciplinary technique on his own sons. "Be sure to make the children obey your first order," he instructed his wife, and both parents succeeded in doing so, according to biographer Edmund Morris, who described Roosevelt's fearsome paternal power: "There hung about his big, relaxed body an ever-present threat of violence, like that of a lion who, dozing, will suddenly flick out a lethal paw. His reaction to any form of wrong . . . was so quick, and so certain, that nobody, child or adult, crossed him more than once."[75]

Roosevelt had no lethal power as a youth. He was raised in a household of mostly women, who treated him tenderly: an indulgent aunt; a "distinctly overindulgent" grandmother, he said; and a mother who was a model of retiring Southern femininity. Known for being dainty, his mother never rode the carriage into town "without bundling up in veils and dust coat," recalled Roosevelt's sister Anna, "and putting on brown paper cuffs so that not a single speck of dust or smudge could touch her."[76]

Amid such fastidiousness and Southern gentility, Jacob Riis said in his popular 1903 biography of the president, Roosevelt grew up a "little lad . . . in stiff white petticoats, with a curl right on top of his head."[77]

Despite having had a wealthy and pampered childhood, Roosevelt considered himself a "sickly and awkward boy" and a clumsy youth, "nervous and distrustful of my own prowess," and he struggled with nearsightedness, asthma, and a speech impediment throughout his college years.[78] Young Roosevelt's consciousness of his "bodily inferiority," William Roscoe Thayer remembered, "made him seem shy and almost timid."[79] Roosevelt's father contributed to his feeling of bodily inadequacy, so much so that Roosevelt came to despise the weakling in himself. "I am as much inferior to Father morally and mentally as physically," he said, and he resolved to "lead such a life as Father would have wished me to."[80] In the childhood reminisces he recorded in his popular autobiography, serialized in *The Outlook* in 1913, six years before he died, Roosevelt admitted that when he was fourteen, bullies who sensed that he was a "foreordained and predestined victim" gave him the thrashing that prompted him to train physically so as to never again "be put in such a helpless position."[81] His father launched young Roosevelt into bodybuilding in order to make him tough, to help him combat his asthma, and to enable him to resist the moral temptations of his youthful body. He "made us understand" a "standard of clean living," Roosevelt later observed.[82] "I had to train myself painfully and laboriously not merely as regards my body but as regards my soul and spirit."[83] "I made myself into a tough nut."[84] Crafting his own manhood by mastering the weak, maternal-dominated body of his boyhood enabled him to imitate the physical muscularity and mental courage of his stern father and enlist them as psychological protection against the emotional longings for closeness with either parent. Making himself immune to emotional and sexual desire also taught him to consider women's attentions as an alluring but deadly manifestation of his own weakness, one that must be overcome before he could consider himself a real man.[85]

Few men completely repress emotions and Roosevelt was no exception. Throughout his life, he recounted striking examples of the emergence of repressed desires. Even as a youth, he procured "surreptitiously" the dime novels that he admitted his father had declared "*taboo*," and "I did read it, nevertheless, with greedy and fierce hope of coming on something unhealthy." But to no avail, for the "parts that might have seemed unhealthy to an older person made no impression on me whatever."[86] More modern observers may suspect that the "unhealthy" parts did indeed fulfill Roosevelt's "greedy and fierce" erotic desires. His admission that he sought forbidden erotica to begin with and his insistence that, once discovered, it held no allure attests to the power of these longings at the time and in his later life.

After Roosevelt entered public life in the 1890s, his self-acknowledged "priggish" manner and his exhortations to sexual chastity for men and women became well-known and highly popular. G. Stanley Hall, the era's prominent professor of pedagogy and adolescent psychology, attributed Roosevelt's popularity in part to his embodiment of the era's demands for sexual hygiene.[87] For Roosevelt, who often exhorted every man to have "thorough command over himself and over his own evil passions," such passions were forbidden behaviors that he thought to be morally and socially degrading: masturbation, homosexuality, and sex with prostitutes, though he never called these by name.[88] "The truth is," he warned, "that each one of us has in him certain passions and instincts which if they gained the upper hand in his soul would mean that the wild beast had come uppermost in him."[89] Roosevelt, who confessed his own repressed aggression by admitting that "wine makes me awfully fighting," and who acknowledged the "prig" in himself, elevated individual repression into national politics, emphasizing the need for men to control passion collectively.[90] "Woe to us as a nation if we ever follow the lead of men who seek . . . to inflame the wild-beast qualities of the human heart," he said in a 1900 address before the YMCA in Carnegie Hall. "What we need in our leaders and teachers is help in suppressing such feelings, help in arousing and directing . . . their extreme opposites."[91]

Politics furnished Roosevelt a venue for directing his considerable energies toward suppressing such feelings and arousing their opposites. He admired George Washington and Abraham Lincoln, partly because they exercised the "power of self-repression." In 1890, he became Civil Service Commissioner, his first federal appointment, and attempted to clean up civil service patronage and establish a merit system for officeholders. These efforts prompted political cartoonists to deem him the "Champion of Cleansing Reform." As New York City's police commissioner from 1895 to 1897, he responded to the efforts of the city's Committee of Fifteen to reduce white slavery by describing men who recruited women prostitutes as "far worse criminals than ordinary murderers." For such "brutes so low, so infamous, so degraded and bestial," he prescribed public whipping, though he held that strenuous calisthenics or sports could suppress such behaviors more effectively.[92] He also supported censorship of erotic materials in the schools. In an 1890 incident, an editorialist in the *New York Tribune* objected to Henry Wadsworth Longfellow as an "erotic poet" whose work contained sexual content that might corrupt young minds. Longfellow's poem "The Building of the Ship," which called the sea the "bridegroom" of the female ship, which was traveling on its "maiden" voyage, was said to suggest that a young engaged couple shared in the ship's sexuality by indulging themselves. When a great outcry arose over the poem, Roosevelt publicly sided with the censors on New York's board of education and approved the board's expurgated version that referred to the sea as the ship's grandfather, not its bridegroom, and made platonic siblings out of the romantic couple.[93]

Strenuous sports served an equally censorious role in Roosevelt's worldview. While in New York, he continued his college sport of boxing to improve his body, and following the nationwide trend in the 1890s, he established a young men's boxing club there. After becoming president, he continued boxing in the White House. As prizefighting expanded beyond working-class beer halls to become a respectable spectator sport, it satisfied middle-class men's growing desire to appropriate working-class men's aggressive virility.[94] Roosevelt admitted that boxing was "brutalizing." Gloves were not used and rules were few, and Roosevelt received a blow to the eye that contributed to later blindness. Nevertheless, he applauded when boxing became a popular middle-class sport because it rendered brutal passion acceptable and provided a palpable release for muscular energies.[95] "Powerful, vigorous men of strong animal development," Roosevelt wrote in an *Outlook* article, "must have some way in which their animal spirits can find vent."[96]

If these repressions and the management of energies indicated the power of the forces Roosevelt dealt with, he admitted that in some areas his own "atavistic puritanism" remained problematic. It made him recoil, he said, at the very mention of Oscar Wilde in a poem by George S. Viereck.[97] Though Roosevelt liked Chaucer, he found "The Friar's Tale" "nearly indefensible" on the score of "cleanliness," he declared "Sompnours" "needlessly filthy," and he suspected that of every ten men who read the tale of the wife of Bath, nine did so for "improper reasons."[98] Roosevelt's description of sexual "passions and instincts" and his plea for what he often called the "necessary discipline" of fathers, leaders, and teachers indicate his own need for suppressing sexual feelings in himself as an adult just as he had as a youth. In his adult life, he apparently convinced himself of his success in doing so and claimed not to tolerate men or women who were not "rigidly virtuous." "Thank heaven I am absolutely pure," he wrote in his diary in 1880 before his marriage at age twenty-two to Alice Lee, "I can tell Alice everything I have done."[99] After Roosevelt became president, cartoonists sensed the salutary effects of his Puritanism on political culture, picturing his efforts at trust regulation "The Soap-and-Water Cure," in which he vigorously scrubbed the nation clean (see figure 6).

Figure 6. Bernard Partridge, "The Soap-and-Water Cure," *Outlook,* September–December 1913

NECESSARY DISCIPLINE

Like his own father, Roosevelt was a loving and kind parent who read to and played with his children and became their friend, yet his stern application of "necessary discipline" conformed to the traditional pedagogy. In a 1900 article in *St. Nicholas,* "The American Boy," Roosevelt deplored the "effeminacy and luxury" of the boy born to rich parents, who "took to billiards as his chief innocent recreation, and felt small shame in his inability to take part in rough . . . sports." Roosevelt hoped that parental and peer pressure would shame such a young man into developing body and character "in the rough sports which call for pluck, endurance, and physical address." He considered the rearing of virile males a patriotic duty. As a nation, "we have a right to expect of the American boy that he shall turn out to be a good American man. . . . He must not be a coward or a weakling, a bully, a shirk, or a prig. He must work hard and play hard. He must be clean-minded and clean-lived, and must be able to hold his own under all circumstances and against all comers."[100]

Roosevelt's demands on the American boy fit neatly with sociologists' views of child education. G. Stanley Hall, author of *Youth: Its Education, Regimen, and Hygiene* (1904) and the massive, two-volume *Adolescence* (1904), deplored the sedentary school activities and "half hearted" play that had "emasculated" modern youth. Civilization's "delicate and tender nurture" and its neglect of the development of motor abilities had bred "sissies," "cowards, lady-boys, [and] milk-sops" with "puny and shameful bodies" whose "masculinity does not ring true."[101] By contrast, modern savages and man's primitive ancestors were true men, possessed of keener senses and more developed bodies that were capable of more endurance.

Luckily, Roosevelt wrote, those "primal, hereditary, . . . fundamental traits of savagery" survived in modern boys and had only to be reawakened in men. Rough, competitive "boy play" demanded the "heathen virtues of courage, endurance, bravery, and loyalty," which, in Hall's view, could "regenerate" a boy's savage self and direct its "rough instincts" toward modern needs, especially that of controlling adolescent sexuality. Rough play would enhance the "erectile value of strenuosity for every tissue" in the body, transferring immoral genital pleasure into bodily and "moral self-control." And like Roosevelt's valuing of moral action over mere morality, Hall specified a curious mind-body chronology that bypassed speech altogether, claiming that virile action, not armchair philosophizing, made a man moral. "Habits determine belief," Hall wrote; "deeds not words" produce the "willed action that is the proper language of complete manhood." And, like Roosevelt's use of nationalistic and racial language, Hall stressed that however redemptive the militant qualities of his regimen, however much the "rebirth" of manhood might bring "physical salvation" for civilization's "fallen beings," the future could just as easily entail "degeneration for our nation and our race."[102]

Roosevelt wrote to Hall agreeing that national survival rested upon "sound common sense, decency and manliness" in child education. "Oversentimentality, oversoftness, in fact, washiness and mushiness are the great dangers of this age and of this people," he added. "Unless we keep the barbarian virtues, gaining the civilized ones will be of little avail. . . . I feel we cannot too strongly insist upon the need of the rough, manly virtues. A nation that cannot fight is not worth its salt. . . . It is just so with a boy." Like Hall, Roosevelt emphasized the importance of pain for instilling hardihood and endurance in his sons. In this remarkable passage, he refers five times to discipline and punishment: "When it comes to discipline," Roosevelt assured Hall, "I cordially agree with you as to the need for physical punishment. With my own children (who I think I can say, are devoted to me, and who are close and intimate friends) I invariably have to punish them once physically so as to make them thoroughly understand that I will unhesitatingly resort to such punishment if they make it necessary. After that . . . I hardly ever have to proceed to extremities again."[103]

However extreme, Roosevelt applied this philosophy to rearing his eldest son, Ted, for whom life with father was an endless contest of rowing, hiking, canoeing, shooting, and hunting. Roosevelt taught Ted to swim by throwing him off a pier into water over his head. "Up to that time he had only paddled about in the shallows," Ted's older sister Alice recalled, remembering being reduced to tears herself when forced by her father to learn to dive, "terror of him finally overcoming my terror of the water."[104] Fatherly approval was contingent on manly performance, which his four boys, Ted, Kermit, Archie, and Quentin, strove mightily to achieve—perhaps too mightily in Ted's case, for at age ten he suffered what Roosevelt admitted was a nervous breakdown. Roosevelt instantly blamed himself. "I guess I have pushed him a little too hard . . . and his nerves have finally given away," he confided to William Cowles in 1898. "It has been a great temptation to push him. The fact is that the little fellow, who is peculiarly dear to me, has bidden fair to be all the things I would like to have been and wasn't. . . . Hereafter I shall never press Ted either in body or mind."[105]

By 1901, however, three years after Ted's breakdown, Roosevelt was again imposing high physical standards on the now thirteen-year-old boy, whom he described to Cecil Arthur Spring Rice as "small" compared to his peers. "I always believe in going hard at everything," Roosevelt wrote to Ted at Groton, and urged him to give his "last ounce of pluck and strength" in physical training. "To have you play football as well as you do and make a good name in boxing and wrestling and be cox of your second crew, and stand second or third in your class in the studies is all right." Worried about the consequences to Ted's health of maintaining such great effort at Groton, a school founded six years earlier as a preparatory school for Harvard, Roosevelt nevertheless admonished him not to drop near the middle of his class. Should this happen, "I would be rather sorry" father continued, because Ted would not enter college until age nineteen and would "therefore be a year later in entering life." Ted must do what he could to prevent any such "delay."[106] In September of 1901, he was injured, and he was unable to play for the rest of the season. "I was very sorry to learn that you had broken your collarbone," Roosevelt wrote to his son, "but I am glad you played right through the game, and that you seem to have minded so little."[107]

It was clear by January of 1902 that Ted had endured a football pummeling so vigorous that it had killed a front tooth. In letters written throughout October and November of that year, Roosevelt deliberated over whether Ted should continue to play. By the end of November, the president was counseling Ted to put an injured ankle in plaster for three weeks.[108] Mindful that teams used inadequate protection equipment, a Harvard football player watching one of Ted's games warned Roosevelt against allowing him to play against boys so much heavier. Roosevelt wrote to Endicott Peabody, the headmaster of Ted's school, and warned him that a Yale quarterback had concurred; Roosevelt added, "it was a pity a young boy should get so battered up, if it came from playing larger ones, as it might interfere with other playing later." Admitting that the boy would get "battered out before he can play in college," and probably agreeing also with the Yale player, Roosevelt expressed his concern to Peabody.[109] By October of 1902, however, Roosevelt had seemingly forgotten his concerns and was urging Ted, who had just turned fifteen, "So, killer of the buck and shooter of the prairie chicken, I hereby grant you unconditional permission to play on the third Eleven," the president wrote. "Now do not break your neck unless you esteem it really necessary. About arms and legs I am less particular, although . . . I prefer that even they should be kept reasonably whole."[110] A year later, the father's relentless pressure continued. "I do not in the least object to your getting smashed" for a worthwhile cause like making Groton's first string, Roosevelt wrote. But it was "a little silly" to risk one's body for lesser goals like the second or third string.[111] Surely Ted read these lines in the lightly humorous spirit his father intended, and just as surely he read the subtext that encouraged extreme effort and unnecessary risk.

Much was at stake for Roosevelt's sons since he made their physical abilities and resulting injuries a matter of honor among his own male friends.[112] He referred defensively to his sons' small stature, compensating for their size by asserting their determination and bravery. "Ted is a little fellow, under the usual size, and wears spectacles," he wrote to Edward Sanford Martin in 1900.[113] "My children are small, but they seem tough," Roosevelt wrote in 1904 to Bill Sewall, his Dakota ranch foreman and an accomplished hunter who served as Roosevelt's lifelong father figure. Ted "is of medium size but out on the football field or in boxing he will hold his own with other boys of his weight and inches, just as I have held my own in the political field."[114]

Roosevelt exhorted his sons to achieve his own level of strenuousness. In a revealing letter Roosevelt wrote to Ted in 1903, he recited his own prowess and bravery in the face of injuries sustained in singlestick jousts with his good friend Colonel Leonard Wood at the White House. Next, he compared his own and Ted's hunting and physical skills to those of Bill Sewall. "I told [Sewall] that I was still ahead of you with the rifle," Roosevelt wrote Ted, "but that you were ahead of me with the shotgun; that you could outwalk me, and were a very good rider." Roosevelt praised Sewall's two sons, who were a year older than Ted, for killing five deer apiece and for being good woodsmen and canoemen. "Sometime," the father continued, predicting future contests within Ted's generation of males, "you will have great sport up in the Maine woods with them."[115] Whether he sought or dreaded these contests, by age seventeen Ted proved manly enough to paddle a canoe at night to a remote island in a Canadian backwoods lake and kill a bull moose, Roosevelt boasted to Stewart White, with "horns that spread 56 inches."[116] Such quests on the part of the son fulfilled the father's emotional expectations. "I suppose life in the future will rarely hold such bright moments for him," Roosevelt had remarked when Ted killed his first buck at age thirteen.[117]

In 1905, Roosevelt wrote to praise his son after reading newspaper accounts that Ted had again "put up an exceedingly resolute and plucky fight" in football. Roosevelt conceded that his son had "evidently" proven himself. "In spite of being lighter than any other man in the line on either team," Roosevelt wrote, "you nevertheless held your own well until you got groggy under the battering plays directed at you."[118] But what did Roosevelt think Ted was supposed to prove? That he would willingly trade injury for approval? And what was Ted proving for himself? That if he brutalized himself sufficiently his father would finally love him unconditionally?

In 1905, Harvard considered abolishing football, partly because of the high number of injuries but mostly due to President Charles William Eliot's observation that sports led to campus riots, especially during the Yale game. Roosevelt summoned Eliot and Coach William Reid Jr. to the White House to urge them not to do "the baby thing."[119] In any case, the football craze made Roosevelt's admonishments unnecessary. Against Eliot's wishes it grew, in spite of unfair recruiting and rough play; it was made all the more popular by its exploitation of manly stereotypes. By 1906, even Roosevelt had become sufficiently alarmed by the excessive number of injuries and deaths sustained by college football players that he convinced a number of university presidents to join him in organizing the National Collegiate Athletic Association. New NCAA rules refined aggression in rough sports, specifying which punches or kicks were allowed. Though the new rules set limits, Peter Gay points out, they were designed not to "deny or end conflict but to recognize and tame it."[120] After all, Roosevelt wrote Henry Child's Merwin, the "main product we want to turn out of our colleges is men."[121] Not just any men, of course, but men in whose hands lay the nation's destiny. The time devoted to sports and the "injuries incurred," Henry Cabot Lodge explained, "are part of the price which the English-speaking race has paid for being world-conquerors."[122] Insofar as producing imperialists involved brutalizing them to the level of injury, that was entirely the point. The cruelest and most eager dispensers of suffering are those who have themselves suffered.

Although he acknowledged his role in Ted's breakdown, Roosevelt did not understand that he projected his own feelings of inadequacy and their resulting regime of pain upon his son. His own obsessive bodybuilding and constant proving of his bravery and stamina suggest that he never entirely overcame his fear of exposing the emotional child within. He did not understand that this fear came from his own father and that it drove him to identify that same child in his son, to call it weakness and to punish it to make it strong. By setting for himself extreme physical goals and incurring repeated injury in obtaining them, and by forcing his son into a perpetual state of striving toward nearly impossible standards, Roosevelt helped satisfy his own nearly insatiable need for physical punishment. He did understand that his own disciplinary needs outweighed his reluctance to punish. "I utterly disbelieve in brutality and cruelty" in childhood education, Roosevelt told G. Stanley Hall, "but I feel we cannot too strongly insist on . . . rough, manly virtues."[123] Roosevelt lacked enough self-reflection to turn his gaze from Ted to his own childhood, to his striving to please his father by compensating for the inadequacies his father helped establish in the first place.

One wonders if Roosevelt thought about young Ted's travails when reading Owen Wister's *The Virginian*, a book dedicated to him upon its publication in 1902, the second year of his presidency. The Virginian, a cowboy with a hard, unfeeling persona, uncharacteristically lapses into an emotional revelation when contemplating the upcoming hanging of his best friend. After the friend sends the Virginian a note saying that he could not speak of the hanging "without playing the baby," the Virginian muses: "I expect in many growed-up men you'd call sensible there's a little boy sleepin', the little kid they onced was—that still keeps his fear of the dark. . . . Well, this experience has woke up that kid in me, and blamed if I can coax the little cuss to go to sleep again! I keep a-telling him daylight will sure come, but he keeps a-crying and holding on to me."[124] As Kim Townsend observes, "it is an extraordinary confession," one that later cowboy heroes would never "allow themselves to make."[125] Wister's Virginian represses the inner child since he must soon meet the demands of mature manhood, in which he must overcome his fear of death, his longing for comfort, and his need for love. One wonders if the Virginian's father taught him how to be a man.

What was the message for America's men in Roosevelt's fatherly example? Roosevelt demonstrated how fathers made athletic sons into objects of masculine pride, and why they elevated athletics over academics. He instructed Ted that life was a painful physical contest in which a boy's performance at once guaranteed his father's love and provided watershed moments in both their lives. Failure came when sons hesitated or allowed the child inside to emerge, and it could result in parents withholding affection. Most importantly, Roosevelt's desperate striving for his own and his son's manliness signified the nationalist and racialist importance he placed on these efforts. The "duty of life," as he saw it, like the chief utility of sports, was "to encourage manliness and vigor, and to keep men hardy, so that at need they can show themselves fit to take part in work or strife for their native land."[126]

Other prominent men echoed Roosevelt's justification of rough sports. "I rejoice at every dangerous sport which I see pursued," Justice Oliver Wendell Holmes Jr. said in a speech, "The Soldier's Faith," delivered at Harvard in 1895.[127] "If once in a while a neck is broken," Holmes was later quoted as saying in a 1902 McClure's article, "I regard it, not as a waste, but as a price well paid for the breeding of a race fit for hardship and command."[128] In order not to be weak, men like Roosevelt and Holmes had to despise weakness in themselves, in their sons, in their friends and colleagues, and in the nation's body. Neither Roosevelt nor Holmes understood that the more they erected barriers of toughness, the more they yielded psychologically to the repressed emotions that could return in startling and unrecognizable ways.

UNPLEASANT SLIMY THINGS
Products of punitive and authoritarian child rearing, the century's white middle- and upper-class males matured into a world where they encountered the repressive bourgeois code of civilized morality. This code appeared in Europe and America in the 1880s and grew progressively more stringent toward the end of the century. Constituted against sensuous

gratification, it added new levels of prudery to traditional notions of virtue for both males and females. Social conventions as well as prominent physicians and psychologists held that men had limited sexual energy that they must learn from an early age to conserve and channel into socially accepted pursuits. As young boys matured, progressive self-help manuals warned them that masturbation and loose women would destroy their sexual energy and make them insane. Men were expected to confine sex to marriage and practice "continence," or control of their sexual impulses, through "pure" thoughts and arduous physical exercise.[129]

Few men understood the era's repressive moral code better than America's two most prominent psychologists, William James of Harvard and G. Stanley Hall of Clark University, who earned his doctorate in psychology from Harvard's philosophy department. In the early 1890s, these men laid the groundwork for the study of dreams and the discovery of the unconscious, and a decade later both played an important part in the American reception of Sigmund Freud's psychoanalysis. Against prevailing conventions that located emotional disorders in the body, James and Hall elevated psychological factors, especially primitive human "instincts," as keys to understanding human behavior and began to unlock the role of sexuality in early childhood. James understood the human mind as the site of warfare between instinctual habits and social standards, anticipating Freud's description of the id of the unconscious, the superego of social convention, and the ego that mediates between them. Dreams and emotions expressed internal conflicts, James held, and repressed emotions could reemerge as unconscious drives in adult life. Hall, too, recognized modern men's repressed nature and feared that "rudimentary organs of the soul, now suppressed, perverted, or delayed" could "crop out in menacing forms later."[130]

Other medical professionals and lay persons of the day came to recognize the existence of a frightening underworld of human emotion that men held tightly inside. Roosevelt's friend the Wisconsin sociologist Edward A. Ross claimed that men's indulgence in assault, dueling, vengeance, and sensual pastimes "show[s] that there is an unreclaimed jungle in man from which wild impulses break forth and lay waste the tilled fields. Despite the well-trimmed . . . lawns in front, there are unpleasant slimy things lurking in the rear ferns and undergrowth of the human soul. Consequently we must fight the devil with fire, quell one emotion with another, and . . . control through the feelings."[131] Hall's, Ross's, and Roosevelt's ascetic desire to conserve and direct men's sexual energy arose partly from their fears of wasting it. Men's sex organs could provide "force and energy" to their character, Hall and most health professionals thought, but men should conserve sexual energy and channel it into socially productive areas like business. Men who indulged their sexual desires, Hall warned, would find their powers flowing away toward women. "Delilah always robs Samson of his strength."[132]

Recognizing the danger posed by the return of repressed desires, Hall and many experts prescribed somatic solutions that called for even more repression. Boys must learn "drill, inculcation, and regimentation" in "mechanical training," Hall wrote. While these "special disciplines" may be "hard for the health of the body," it is possible nevertheless to quickly "break the child into them." Hall's fear of the child's "neo-atavistic past" prompted him to prescribe extreme punitive measures, which, he admitted, had little to do with education and constituted, instead, a way to force boys into the "higher qualities" of civilized life.[133]

If Hall and Ross, like Freud, emphasized a connection between repressed sexuality and civilization, William James thought that society was entirely too repressive and blamed it for late marriages and overly strict conventions of modesty that required people to say "retire" instead of "go to bed" and prevented them from calling "a female dog by name."[134] Though James's life was a tribute to those conventions, and though he remained reluctant to discuss what he called the "sexual instincts," he came to regret, for nationalistic reasons, the immense social and psychological costs of that suppression. "The critical atmosphere in which we have been reared [has] sealed up important energies," James said. "One part of our mind dams up—even DAMNS up!—the other parts. Conscience makes cowards of us all." For James, the code of civilized morality produced conscience, itself the repressive factor that led men to shrink from forthright action. This failure of nerve not only drained individual male "energies," it let loose cowards to roam the land, thus weakening white civilization, which could least afford it. "No scorn, no hardness, no valor any more! Fie upon such a cattleyard of a planet!"[135] James's former student Roosevelt also scorned idealists. Those who professed a "horror of war," he wrote to General Ian Standish Hamilton, commander of the Allied forces at Gallipoli in 1915, produced a "habit of mind" in which the "warlike virtues tend to atrophy."[136] This, then, was the dilemma of expert theorizing about male energies. Suppressing primitivism, as civilized men must do, created two problems: too much suppression created cowardly men; too little raised the specter of resurgent barbarism. Civilization had to tread a thin line between the two, and experts disagreed on where that line lay.

Enter Theodore Roosevelt, who understood the dangers in boys' sexual and emotional energies, but who nevertheless eagerly imported their natural wildness into his own adult political life. In Roosevelt's imagination, men should reinvigorate themselves but direct their "energies" away from women and self-indulgence and toward pursuits that enhance a chaste but aggressive manliness, one achieved by "cleansing and hardening" themselves. Given the seemingly contradictory psychic demands for both primitive regeneration, with its emotional and erotic undercurrents, and an austere, repressive morality, Roosevelt enlisted moral self-mastery as an agent for channeling dangerous forms of masculinity. In this manner, the Rough Rider helped reconcile his era's need for both repressing and unleashing the virile energy of bourgeois men.

Roosevelt's carefully modulated but contradictory demands for sexual continence and primitive energy elevated "iron self-discipline" to the role of controlling guardian of the "animal passions." His was the image of a hero who transformed a weakling self into a strong body and will and who used that will to govern the recklessness in his personal, military, and political life. His self-control under fire during the Cuban campaign, in which he rode a horse in clear sight of Spanish snipers, quickly became legendary. National campaigns of muckraking, a word Roosevelt coined, and "cleansing reforms" mirrored his own exhortations to individual men to strengthen themselves against bodily and emotional infirmity. Yet gradually after 1898, Roosevelt's political language elevated the need for primitive regeneration over the need for civilized self-mastery. The "iron self-discipline" of Roosevelt's warrior cult, as we shall see in chapter 4, called for men to unleash primitive instincts in new forms of aggressive manliness and direct them against civilization's perceived ills.

James and Roosevelt seized on war as the best way to revive men's repressed energies. Nothing channeled aggressiveness, they said, as well as military discipline. Like his fellow Harvard notaries Owen Wister and William Eliot, James was an anti-imperialist in the period of the Spanish-American War and the Philippine campaign, and, like them, he was not at all taken with aggressive sports or imperial masculinity. In 1910, however, James reluctantly concluded in an essay published in *McClure's Magazine* and in the *Popular Science Monthly* entitled "The Moral Equivalent of War" that only the "enduring cement" of martial virtues could save the nation. War's supposed "horrors," James wrote, "are a cheap price to pay for rescue from . . . a world of clerks and teachers, consumer's leagues, industrialism unlimited, and feminism unabashed." War was the "welder of men into cohesive states," the only site where "human nature can develop its capacity. The only alternative is 'degeneration.' "[137]

Why only war? For James, as for Roosevelt and Hall, pain figured importantly in the evolutionary trajectory of advancing civilization. To be sure, James's end product advocated imperial masculinity less nakedly than Roosevelt's did, but he did proclaim the same goals of saving civiliza-tion and advancing human progress. Historically, "Mankind was nursed in pain and fear," James explained. But released from the struggle for sur-vival by the comforts of industrial life—central heating, indoor plumbing, and railroads—men "reverted" to the pleasure economy. Stimulants and narcotics were readily available in medicines and drinks, allowing men and women to escape the sufferings of surgery or childbirth. In James's view, self-indulgence had produced in men a specifically modern weakness, the fear of losing life's amenities. This fear created a modern, feminized, "cowardly" male, given over to utopianism, socialism, and the individual desires that "repressed" men's "important energies."[138] To undo that re-pression and reconnect each man with his pain-hardy, primitive, and up-wardly evolving self, that soldier self, "always latent in human nature," he advocated war as "the only force that can discipline a whole community . . . against its weaker and more cowardly self." Even in peacetime, the na-tion should require military training so that its "gilded youth . . . paid their blood-tax, and [did] their own part in the immemorial human war-fare against nature."[139] Although James identified "nature" as the natural world, we might profitably, given his insecurities, take it to signify his own inner demons as well.

Indeed, though James ascribed men's "cowardly self" to their indul-gence in the "pleasure economy," he recognized to a remarkable degree that men's real struggles were directed "against [their own] nature." He understood, if imperfectly, that social pressures and harsh child rearing had repressed men's "important" emotional energies. A man who suffered from depression and sexual anxiety and who was uneasy with the homo-sexuality of his Harvard colleague George Santayana, James could see that men contained these emotions within unfeeling, disciplinary exteriors, that projected "impatience, grimness, earnestness, severity of character." He knew that to revive his energy a man must attack his "own interior self and its pet softnesses." He must make these inner feelings the "targets and the victims" of "sacrificial moods" that would bring pain, but a welcome and sacrificial pain. James understood, too, that men desired to impose regimes of suffering on others. "The pain may be pain to other people or pain to one's self—it makes little difference; for when the strenuous mood is on one, the aim is to break something, no matter whose or what." Emo-tions must burst forth violently in an "energetic character" that provoked men's "irascibility, susceptibility to wrath [and] the fighting temper."[140]

While James examined manhood critically and perceptively, Roosevelt understood his attempts to control his own emotions less well. Even though he identified aspects of his own psyche such as prurience and cow-

ardliness, he thought that other, equally discernable and consciously understood fears generated his anxieties. For these he sought conscious solutions. He claimed, for example, that when something frightened him, he
could acquire through "repeated exercises of will power . . . a certain fear-
lessness." "Many things I feared, but by acting as if I was not afraid, I was
not afraid."[141] In another display of this bravado, he remarked that "Black
care rarely sits behind a rider whose pace is fast enough." Curtis Guild,
who observed Roosevelt from his Harvard days into the presidency, identified the same bravado in Roosevelt's incessant pursuit of competitive
sports: "An attacker always," Roosevelt "sought to offset his fatally weak
point by leading swiftly and heavily himself without waiting for attack."[142]
We may doubt that even the Roosevelt of legendary self-mastery understood the difference between weak points or black cares that arose from the
outside world and those conjured within the realm of his own psyche.

And we may legitimately doubt that he—or most men of his generation—truly mastered their internally generated fears, since repressed anxieties rarely go away. Instead, they reemerge as phobias and longings,
neuroses and hysterias that produce a need to identify and to punish inner
demons. Most likely, men of Roosevelt's era directed such punitive feelings inward, toward and against their own desires. Just as likely, men also
projected their emergent fears outward, onto a self-fashioned, violent, and
wholly public masculinity. When ordinary men's repressions reemerged in
an upwelling of desire and burst through their resistance, "the wild beast
[had come] uppermost," as Roosevelt put it, producing a "savagery" he
once described as "hideous and revolting beyond belief and beyond description" and "all the more terrible because it could not be reckoned
with."[143] These fears led men to interpret certain national experiences
as traumatic and certain social groups as internal enemies—in Dominick
LaCapra's terms, as "destabilizing sources of phobic anxiety and quasi-
ritual contamination."[144]

DEMONS OF RACE AND CLASS

Roosevelt's urges for purification and punishment underlay his broadly
drawn social vision, which, as we have seen, encompassed biological, political, historical, and philosophical factors to explain the trajectory of
civilization across time. Addressed to the nationalist middle classes, his interpretations articulated anxieties about specific race and class enemies
and helped American men to come to terms with the deep social divisions
of the day. In this effort, he helped to popularize and politicize the ideas of
social theorists who after 1880 had provided new terms for understanding
social change and had introduced innovative, behavior-modifying tech-

niques of modern management and administration. Psychologists, managers, reformers, and educators like John B. Watson, Frederick Taylor, Jane Addams, and John Dewey prescribed various forms of tutelage designed to encourage groups of students, workers, or slum dwellers toward more responsible political behavior or more efficient work habits, and through such improvements, to foster social stability and individual moral worth.

Prominent among those social theorists, the Lamarckian Edward A. Ross held that the "social organism" was subject to the laws of biological evolution and influenced by environments for good or ill. In his most influential work, *Social Control: A Survey of the Foundations of Order* (1901), he argued that in modern America the increasing fragmentation of a formerly organic mass society bred moral weakness. He proposed a new collective ideal that drew upon the "surplus moral energy" of ministers, jurists, and educators, those "enlightened" citizens willing to forcefully impose the moral instruction required to overcome degenerate behavior.[145] Roosevelt promoted the ideas of social control theorists like Ross because they provided a means to reestablish control over an increasingly pluralist society. In Roosevelt's introduction for Ross's popular book *Sin and Society,* he expressed the hope that Ross's principle of social tutelage would rally public opinion against civilization's "really dangerous foes."[146]

Ross and Roosevelt infused political discourses with new racial terms— *race suicide, race consciousness, race war, race prejudice,* and *race question*—terms that heightened the self-awareness of white racial identity, contributed to whites' sense of racial exclusiveness, and raised the specter of inevitable racial conflict.[147] Roosevelt appropriated the terms *race suicide* and *criminaloid* from Ross, along with the terms *blood* and *breeding,* and used them to assign differential hereditary mental and physical traits to various peoples, with the "higher races" leading civilization to its destiny and the "lower" threatening to bring it down. Many race theorists of the times, not just Ross and Roosevelt, led readers to subsume categories like race and criminality under the rubric of national well-being and to summon their free-floating social anxieties to link seemingly unrelated groups like suffragists, socialists, and homosexuals into new and dangerous classifications like "degenerate."

Roosevelt's preoccupations with racial questions increased during the time of his presidency, as did his reading of racial theorists. He was broadly versed in the century's most important scientific and social scientific theory that, while split in the nature-nurture debate, nevertheless ordered the various human elements of history, society, and evolution around the all-controlling factor of race.[148] Many of his attitudes came from his reading of Arthur James Balfour's *Decadence* (1908), Houston Stewart Chamberlain's *Foundations of the Nineteenth Century* (1910), and Madison Grant's *The Passing of the Great Race* (1916). All these men conceived of a white race destined to rule the world. Chamberlain, for example, an Englishman of upper-class birth, was the most influential Teutonic racial theorist, Germanophile, and Wagnerite from the 1890s to the 1920s; Kaiser Wilhelm II acclaimed him as a "hymn to Germany." Hoping that Germany would come to dominate Europe, Chamberlain used scientific arguments to popularize Aryan racism and pan-German expansion. European racialist thought served Roosevelt's theory of civilization by providing continuity between Anglo-Saxon and Teutonic roots and American frontier characteristics. Thus the romantic nationalism and white supremacy that infused his works included the notion of "blood," according to which racial groups struggled against one another as they fulfilled their historical destiny.[149] Because so much of this historic racial struggle took place in Europe, racial-minded Americans understood "race" to be as much about preserving distinctions between groups of whites—Nordic Europeans, Slavs, Mediterranean peoples, Jews—as it was about distinguishing between whites and nonwhites.

As one of the nation's prime interpreters of the twin dangers of labor's radicalism and capital's materialism, Roosevelt positioned himself as a neutral broker of hostile interests and the guardian of the interests of all Americans. When he entered politics in the early 1880s, he positioned himself as friend of the working man. Even by 1895, Owen Wister recalled, "the threat of class war had not yet struck him as a peril against which to make ready."[150] He was the first president to openly court labor, to consult labor leaders, and to force business owners to arbitrate labor disputes. Samuel Gompers said that he was the first to use the phrase *organized labor* in a presidential address.[151] As almost all observers report, he maintained a remarkable egalitarianism in the context of the conservative Republican politics of his day. He eventually compromised his neutrality, however, by claiming that the large number of immigrants brought radical politics with their "blood" and kept the nation poised on the edge of anarchy.

Against genuine proof for Roosevelt's love of ordinary people, another picture emerges then, one of a man driven by foreboding and a deep fear of social disorder. As large numbers of the nation's workers organized, he came to interpret their demands as a "strike at the foundations of society." "The greater the total," as Alfred Mahan expressed it, "the more numerous the unworthy."[152] Admire labor though he did, Roosevelt also resisted what he thought were efforts of labor leaders to use class consciousness to alienate workers from mainstream America. In this he was one of the first modern politicians to decry labor as a special class interest aligned danger-ously against the classless whole.

Roosevelt's labor ideas evolved in an era of violent class conflict. In 1886, fifteen hundred strikes nationwide had affected over ten thousand businesses. During the Knights of Labor strikes in Chicago on May Day, a bomb disrupted a peaceful rally in Haymarket Square, killing one police-men and wounding seventy in the crowd. An uneasy public thereafter as-sociated the Knights with anarchist bomb throwers, concluding that the Haymarket incident signaled great national danger. In that tense atmo-sphere, Roosevelt compared his hardworking and patriotic Dakota ranch hands to Chicago's strikers. "My men . . . work longer hours for no greater wages than the strikers; but they are Americans through and through," he wrote. "I believe nothing would give them greater pleasure than a chance with their rifles at one of the mobs. . . . In relation to the dynamite busi-ness they become more furiously angry and excited than I do. I wish I had them with me. . . . My men shoot well and fear very little."[153] Four years after Haymarket, when Roosevelt held his first federal job as the U.S. civil service commissioner, he addressed Chicago's Marquette Club on "True Americanism." He congratulated Chicago's citizens for having executed the four "anarchistic dynamite throwers." In a passage later cut for the es-say's appearance in *The Forum* the next month, he told the audience that he hoped that they would treat future offenders with the same severity.[154]

Roosevelt's friend the prominent artist and writer Frederic Remington interpreted the great issues like labor unrest and immigration along simi-lar philosophical lines. As early as 1891, Remington had responded to the presence of immigrants by welcoming a "real blood letting." By 1893, when a nationwide depression led to layoffs, hunger, and growing unrest among Chicago's railroad workers, Remington wrote to his friend Poult-ney Bigelow, "I think in time we Americans will have to take down our Winchesters from over the fireplace and 'clean up' a lot of garbage that Europe has sent us." "When the massacring begins, . . . I can get my share of 'em and what's more I will. Jews—injuns—chinamen—Italians—Huns—the rubbish of the earth I hate."[155]

When *Harper's Weekly* sent him to cover Chicago's Pullman strike in the summer of 1894, Remington was primed for a confrontation. The American Railway Union's nationwide strike against the Pullman Palace Car Company focused attention on the Chicago terminus of twenty-three of the country's largest railroads. The strike ended when President Grover Cleveland summoned federal troops to move mail trains and "restore order." As twelve men died in the riots in and around Chicago, Remington developed a deep rage against Chicago's strikers and their supporters, which he aired in an article published in July at the height of the struggle, "Chicago under the Mob."[156]

The city is "in a state of anarchy," Remington reported. "Everyone goes about with his gun." Infantry companies of the Seventh, Third, and Sixth Cavalry under the command of General Nelson A. Miles had come from Indian fighting in the West to Chicago to defend both the trains and city residents against the "malodorous crowd of anarchistic foreign trash." One of Remington's dramatic drawings pictures soldiers with rifles "giving the butt" to strikers while a worker hits back with a club (figure 7). Another recreates the scene of the cavalry escorting the first meat train to leave Chicago's stockyards on 10 July (figure 8). In this drawing, charging cavalrymen lead a train bristling with riflemen through a "beery mob" that is throwing rocks at them and taunting them with "vile names."[157]

In Remington's account, the soldiers represented the moral and lawful side of the confrontation and the strikers the lawless and destructive. Whereas soldiers had previously defended the nation against outlaws and Indians on its frontier, in the modern battle of good and evil, they entered the heartland to fight its own people, whom Remington transposed into a "grim howling mob." For Remington, the soldiers represented the best specimens of American manhood. He referred to them as "his people," the "simple men" of the American West. The soldiers were "tall, bronzed young athletes," "clean" and "decent, pure and simple of speech." As defenders of the nation, the soldiers summoned their "sporting blood," which had been strengthened during the "enthusiasm" of target practice, where they learned to "hit a man at 500 yards with a Springfield." Confronted with a "seething mass of smells, stale beer, and bad language," they were "the perfect machine," trained to shoot and kill with "perfect mental calm." Despite all their marksmanship abilities, the soldiers did not receive commands to shoot, Remington told his readers, and were "bottling up a seething vat of wrath that will scorch something." In his fantasy, the soldiers wished "to create about eleven cords of compost" out of the "Hungarian or Polack, or whatever the stuff is." One soldier reportedly said: "Nay, do you know them things ain't human?" Forbearance was "too much to ask of such men," Remington concluded, and he eased some of his, and presumably the troops', frustrations by reporting that they were "refreshed morally" at least when someone shouted for the soldiers to fire upon the strikers and "kill 'em—kill every one of 'em."[158]

The events of 1894 made Roosevelt, too, think in terms of "sound chastisement" of dangerous mobs. "I like to see a mob handled by the regulars,

Figure 7. Frederic Remington, "'Giving the Butt' — The Way the 'Regular' Infantry Tackles a Mob," in his "Chicago under the Mob," *Harper's Weekly*, 21 July 1894 (Library of Congress Prints and Photographs Division, Washington, D.C., LC-Z62-096502)

Figure 8. G. W. Peters, "The Great Railway Strike—The First Meat Train Leaving the Chicago Stock-Yards under Escort of United States Cavalry, July 10, 1894," *Harper's Weekly*, 21 July 1894 (Library of Congress Prints and Photographs Division, Washington, D.C., LC-Z62-096508)

or by good State guards," he wrote to James Brander Matthews, "not over-scrupulous about bloodshed."[159] At the height of the Pullman Strike, in an essay in *The Forum* titled "True Americanism," Roosevelt again separated strikers who "seek to be other than Americans" from "real men" and "true" Americans.[160] Dividing workers' interests from those of society as a whole became a linchpin in Roosevelt's patriotism. At a Burlington, Vermont, veterans reunion in 1901, he compared the "true" American interests of Civil War veterans to the unpatriotic and selfish values of labor protesters. "In the breasts of men who saw Appomattox there was no room for the growth of the jealous, greedy, sullen envy which makes anarchy, which has bred the red Commune," he said at a Burlington, Vermont, veteran's reunion in 1901.[161]

Believing that rights and opportunities knew no class boundaries, Roosevelt attacked the growing socialist movement on the grounds that collective ownership of property violated the republican ideal of individual striving toward the social good. In response to the increase in socialist Eugene Debs's vote in the presidential election of 1904, Roosevelt came to

regard the growth of the Socialist Party as "far more ominous" than populism or any homegrown movement.[162] In 1908, he asked the postmaster
general to exclude from the federal mails the radical Italian language newspaper, *La Questione Sociale* of Paterson, New Jersey, on the grounds that it
advocated sedition and treason. In defending this request, Roosevelt wrote
to the Department of Justice that the paper sanctioned "murder by dynamite" and that to distribute it was "certainly as immoral as the circulation
of obscene and lascivious literature." If mailing the "anarchistic and murderous" newspaper published by the "enemies of mankind" were not already illegal, he would request Congress to make it so.[163]

Roosevelt often compared the failures of revolutionary France with
those of contemporary America; both were prey to the "folly of the reac-
tionaries" and the "folly of the demagogs [*sic*]." Irresponsible behavior by
first the propertied and then the poor brought the "Red Terror" and
Napoleonism, which were followed by the White Terror and finally the
July Monarchy.[164] For Roosevelt, the "extreme radicals" of eighteenth-
century France, with their "wicked folly" in advocating national work-
shops for the unemployed, corresponded to the followers of Debs, Bryan,
and populism, whom he denounced as "the Bolsheviki crowd" and "the
Jacobin Club." In the Chicago Coliseum, where Bryan had delivered his
"Cross of Gold" speech in the presidential campaign of 1896, Roosevelt
delivered a speech later that day in which he equated Bryan and the pop-
ulists with "the leaders of the Terror of France." "It is not merely school-
girls that have hysterics," he thundered. "Very vicious mob-leaders have
them at times, and so do well-meaning demagogues when their minds are
turned by the applause of men of little intelligence."[165] Roosevelt wrote to
Lodge in 1917 that Wisconsin's progressive governor Robert M. LaFol-
lette was "considerably inferior, in morality and capacity, to Robespierre,"
but showed the same dangerous tendencies as the man who "provoked the
Red Commune."[166] He warned that these forces could bring an "Armaged-
don of Labor and Capital, the merciless conflict of class with class."[167]

If Roosevelt valued the idea of democracy more than its reality, he tried
to have it both ways. "I am, in my own way, a radical democrat myself," he
wrote to Spring Rice in 1904, one who believes completely "in the democracy of the plain people." But his democratic loyalties had limits, since he
had "no patience with the tyranny of a mob."[168] Popular elections, while
"inevitable" and indeed "indispensable," were not "the only important
things in the life of a free people." At the heart of his political philosophy
lay the beliefs that "governing power should be concentrated in the hands
of a very few men" willing to actively take up its reins and that elections

"should not come too frequently."[169] "My whole career in politics is due to the simple fact that when I came out of Harvard I was firmly resolved to belong to the governing class, not to the governed."[170]

Democratic politics posed yet a further problem for Roosevelt in that it reduced the masculinity of elite leaders, making them into mere mouthpieces for democratic platitudes and panderers to public opinion. Those politicians, Roosevelt said, "who cant about 'liberty' and the 'consent of the governed,'" do so "in order to excuse themselves for their unwillingness to play the part of men." In 1899, enraged at politicians who had resisted declaring war on Spain, he told members of New York's Hamilton Club that such men did not have the strength to step in and take political control when necessary and that they would go so far as to let Apaches govern themselves.[171] Patrician politicians, who should furnish the front line of defense against socialism and economic democracy, instead wished to "coddle" the unruly classes through "wild and crude" social reforms whose "extreme" components ranged from wage-and-hour legislation to a graduated income tax. He even blamed the "mushy class" of wealthy philanthropists for stooping to "foolish and indiscriminate giving." Many reformers "became so appalled [with] the terrible suffering and stunting degradation in many parts of our great cities" that they were too sentimental to carry out the countermeasures needed if the country were to resist domestic and foreign radicalism.[172]

Representative government, Roosevelt's theory went, not only bred ineffectual leaders, it weakened the manhood of the entire male population. Liberal governments fostered a "certain softness and luxury—a condition of mind and body . . . in which the stay-at-home people become fickle and hysterical under pressure of a formidable foe." In 1898, this cowardly hysteria had caused the American people to "shrink from the grim necessities of war." During the Philippine campaign, Roosevelt complained to Spring Rice in 1904, American generals Nelson A. Miles and Thomas Forsyth had to "grapple with a public sentiment which screamed with anguish over the loss of a couple of thousand men, a sentiment of preposterous and unreasoning mawkishness." When fighting Indians in the West, Roosevelt pointed out, neither general had been distracted by public squeamishness over the loss of life. It was the selfish party leaders who made the generals' conduct in the Philippine war a target for easily manipulated voters. Even worse, antiwar hysteria also threatened the nation by rendering "large sections of the population . . . if drafted in war . . . utterly appalled by slaughter." Cowardly men who had become intolerant of slaughter, Roosevelt said in 1904, would need "long training before they became effective fighters" who were immune to the horrors of battlefield deaths.[173]

Roosevelt ended many of his discussions of democratic government with a call for strong men, and he always offered himself as the best example. Sustained and informed leadership in critical spheres like foreign relations should be left entirely to men with a higher understanding of the nation's needs. Otherwise internal dissension, as he sometimes termed the democratic process, could hamper the free exercise of a nation's will. Ideally, the U.S. government would combine the rule of the republican brotherhood at home with statesmen's free exercise of the "power to make head against foreign foes" unfettered either by popular or legal control exercised through "liberal institutions."[174]

Since the most dangerous aspect of the dangerous classes, Roosevelt felt, was their capacity for mob violence, only "strong-willed" men should initiate social change, and certainly not suffragists, unionists, or "mushy" reformers. Social hysteria had to be "reckoned with," he often said, by a man strong enough to resist special interests, to recognize the limitations of liberal government and to act with surgical certainty. "What we need more than anything else," he said in a letter to Francis Markoe Scott, "is to have a man at the head of affairs who will treat the tumors of the body politic with the roughest and most merciless surgery. We want a man who will put in the knife fearlessly."[175]

Roosevelt's use of the term *class* exposed his contradictory interpretations of the word. He did not dispute the existence of social class, and he sometimes used *capital* and *labor* to designate differences between income strata and between cultural groups. But he seldom used *class* in the modern social-science sense, to mean a group of people united by their relations to production. He considered class interest narrow and selfish, and he preferred interpretive categories like individuals, or races, or nations to understand historical change. He refused to believe that class interest was a legitimate source of political identity or that it could function as a lever for groups of people to effect social change. Foreigners could not be integrated into American society, he felt, until they renounced the class antagonisms they had imported from Europe and embraced law-abiding, community-spirited citizenship. Although he did not allow workers class consciousness, he prescribed it for the gentry. "The governing class ought to govern," he said.[176] At least some of his political clout among his class peers came from their perception of that resolve. Owen Wister, for one, felt that citizens should learn to identify men of good breeding in politics. In 1900, in an article he wrote about Roosevelt, Wister declared that "Americans like a gentleman when they see one," but that "in a republic such as ours, at present, the scum rises to the surface."[177]

Social class loyalty reared its ugly head, Roosevelt believed, only when ordinary men forgot their true, classless "community of interest." The "worst of crimes" against society were those in which demagogues inflamed "brother against brother" and encouraged the "unhealthy belief" that one class must dominate. Against the political disarray of mass society that diminished "national traits of hardihood and manliness," Roosevelt longed for an ideal brotherhood, a "community of interest" composed of an educated, cultured, Anglo-Saxon type who willingly used force to protect both propertied and working men's interests.[178] In an essay in *The Century* in 1890, he made individual men's "political will," not class interest, the basis of "proper political association." Many wills, acting together, would cohere into a brotherhood of "fellow-feeling" and a mutual "community of interest."[179] His early opposition to the political participation of women and Negroes arose from his view that they lacked the willful self-control of white men. The latter's ability to achieve "mastery" explained why "only the very highest races" obtained success at self-government and why the "utterly undeveloped races" could not be part of the republican brotherhood.[180] Political will, for Roosevelt, derived from true manhood. Only when men are genuinely interested in common manly aims do they come together in communities of interest. When a man "endeavors to throw in his lot with those about him, to make his interests theirs," then distinctions of birth or wealth disappear and the principle of "virile honesty and robust common sense triumph[s] in our civic life."[181]

Roosevelt's racialized homosocial republicanism reflected the social concerns of his mentor, Edward A. Ross, who defined society as an evolutionary organism that had finally developed, in the case of Teutons and Anglo-Saxons, the "more refined qualities" of honor, justice, and social order. The "aimless, arbitrary, and capricious" behavior of unruly crowds, the "swarm-life of aliens in tenement house and alley," Ross wrote, were abhorrent to the Teuton, whose intellectual and ethical superiority had prompted him to establish states with rational social order. Since the urge for social control evolved naturally out of the expansion of "property and economic organization," Ross taught, private property and a tendency to individualism were more highly evolved than socialism and communalism. Affixed to radical politics, the "passionate races" exercised their ability to "upset and wreck our personal schemes of life." Here *our* meant refined and educated white men, and *passionate races* referred to thirteen million immigrants. In modern societies, when social conflict "sapped social spirit and rent society in twain, the first effect is a weakening of social control and a drifting toward disorder." Democracy was no panacea, Ross maintained, since the "senseless mob" was "unfit to serve as Social Will." The mob reflected primitive instincts and was given over to hysteria, jingoism, and social intolerance. Roosevelt and Ross were both convinced that society needed political tutelage by what Ross called "the handful of thoughtful men" who could put "bits in the mouth of the mob and reins in the hands of the wise."[182]

Poets as well as academics affirmed many of Roosevelt's favorite racial, masculine, and national themes: the importance of acting in a "manly" fashion, defying fate, identifying dangers, and guiding the nation. Roosevelt greatly admired Eugene Fitch Ware's *Rhymes of Ironquill*, a group of poems containing remarkable bits of advice about popular forces and social classes. "They seem to embody an enormous amount of the philosophy of life," Roosevelt said when thanking Ware for a specially printed copy of the poems. "I have quoted them often in dealing with my own politics."[183]

Ware, like Roosevelt, thought that the expansion of white peoples into the Americas brought Europe's social disruptions. "The world is but an ocean of unrest," Ware wrote, "Whose tidal billows wander to the West." The ocean of demographic turmoil provoked fears of degeneration. "When communities turn loose Social forces that produce / The disorders of a gale," the poems advise, "Face the breeze, but close your jaw." Ware's dangerous immigrants swarmed across the Atlantic, filled East-coast cities, and flowed outward into the social backwaters of rural America. There, in degrading poverty, the poor whites of tobacco country worked "Stemming tobacco in a reeking basement." Left with few "hopes or joys," they formed "silent groups of many shaded faces," groups whose potential for social disruption was equaled by the dangers of "their blood the sewage of barbaric races." As members of failed races, such unfortunates filled their appropriate evolutionary station: "The races get what they deserve, / Some must fight and some must serve."[184]

Other groups in Ware's imagination, those of a hardier and more imperious strain, achieve more. Their "zeal and enterprise were tending west . . . / the restless movement of the race / Toward the western world is taking place." Quickly, Rome "builds and paves," and civilization expands in Europe, then crosses the straits of Dover and the Atlantic to find its best expression in America, a "bright new world . . . its hopes, its progress . . . / The sands of a fresh century start through." Driven by the expansionist fervor inherent in its racial and national heritage, this fresh country conquered "ancient nations and ancient creeds," which it "strung on empire like a row of beads."[185]

In Ware's poems Roosevelt also found confirmation of his notion of the political dangers caused by a voting populace that was sunk in luxurious living and subject to the evolutionary degeneration that produced effeminate men. People who "rest contented" with material accomplishments, Ware cautioned, eventually "retrograde and slowly sink away." Ware condemned timid men who dared not rise to destiny's call, and he summoned strong men to take their place in giving the nation "an ideal, / Some grand, noble, central project" so that it "refuses to decay."[186]

Ware's poems touched a nerve not just in Roosevelt, but in many racially minded Americans who predicted that civilization would disappear, overtaken by the dangerous sexuality of eastern and southern European immigrants, and even the Irish. Ware and Roosevelt integrated theories of race and sexuality with those of class difference. immigrant workers' seemingly excessive drinking, philandering, and spending was thought to indicate that moral failure and a lack of self-control lay at the root of their poverty.

Although Christian peoples had long understood sexual degeneracy as a consequence of Adam's fall in Eden, it gained new currency with social Darwinist ideas that strong nations expanded and weak ones died. In the minds of these thinkers, the presence of immigrants automatically signaled interbreeding between them and Anglo-Saxon, old-stock Americans, and the beginning of the nation's slide backward down the evolutionary ladder. Thus, Roosevelt was not alone in his fears that female sexuality, race suicide, class conflict, and evolutionary retrogression had special meaning when applied to the immigrant masses.

Writers of medical literature, too, linked the sexual deviance of women and children to that of so-called primitive peoples. Women and children in otherwise civilized countries, the prominent medical theorist Richard von Krafft-Ebing wrote in 1903, were capable of perversions that were similar to the random and uninhibited sexual behavior found among cretins and the insane. Savage and primitive sexuality were the natural state not just of mental defectives, women, and children, but of Indians, Africans, American Negroes, and Cubans. Indeed, the capacity for sexual deviance increased as one "descended" to the lower classes. But human sexual evolution had progressed "upward" from sexual "shamelessness" in the "swamp" to a male-dominated, monogamous society that was of necessity ordered by law, religion, and morality. Out of chaotic and primitive promiscuity, civilized order had produced monogamy, he held, giving European Christian men "mental and material superiority over the polygamic races, and especially over Islam."[187]

The problem of modernism, to Krafft-Ebing, was that even "superior" cultures produced pathological, "primitive" sexuality, as when middle-class men visited prostitutes or engaged in recreational sex. Thus the nation harbored seeds of decline not only within its traditionally dangerous social classes and nonwhite groups but also among its whites and middle-class people. Given the potential for sexual retrogression to pollute "natural drives," the state had to assume the burden of responsibility for suppressing both individual pathologies such as masturbation and homosexuality and social ones arising from prostitution and cross-class sexual relations.[188]

Roosevelt, too, entwined theories of class, sex, and race and made them matters of national concern. He equally castigated the lower-class women who had "fallen" into prostitution and those disposed to radical political tendencies. In this transference, Roosevelt's sexual enemies became class enemies, adding the specter of mob violence to the sexual struggle that engrossed him throughout his life. Drawing on the nineteenth-century commonplace that revolutionary change would inevitably be accompanied by unimaginable sexual crimes, Roosevelt helped to spread more widely fears that different sorts of mixing, from class "hybridization" to racial miscegenation, would contribute to the gradual degeneration of the social body. For example, he wrote to Arthur Hamilton Lee in 1908 that Japanese immigrants, who were "still coming here at the rate of about five hundred a month," might, through the "wickedness" of "sexual misconduct," provoke "horror" among ordinary Americans.[189]

While most of Roosevelt's Anglo-Saxon racial exclusivity targeted Mediterranean peoples, he felt that the degenerate rural whites of his own stock posed their own unique threat. It is clear that Roosevelt formed some of his impressions of poor rural whites while conducting his research for *The Winning of the West*. In this study, the West was the trans-Appalachian backcountry of eighteenth-century Kentucky, Tennessee, and North Carolina. Here Roosevelt found men and women of the "true, hardy backwoods stock, fitted to grapple with the wilderness," steadily pushing back Indians and improving their means by "thrift and industry." Those pioneers who failed at this attempt were the "crackers," or poor whites— "lank, sallow, ragged creatures." He thought these unfortunates chose to live in "poverty, ignorance and dirt," even though they had "every chance to rise." Remaining "weak, irresolute, or shiftless, often warped and twisted, mentally and morally," these people had "unfortunately survived" down to Roosevelt's own day. They constituted "a rank, up-country growth, containing within itself the seeds of vicious, idle pauperism, and semi-criminality."[190] From the Alleghenies to the Rocky Mountains, he wrote, these "mean whites . . . still half-till their patches of poor soil, and still cumber the earth."[191]

Roosevelt's characterizations of poor backwoods whites resonated with late-nineteenth-century sociological theory. Armies of investigators representing the newly professionalized social sciences collected demographic statistics that grouped people according to new definitions of mental, moral, and physical degeneracy. Sociologists created a range of professionally demarcated degenerates, such as criminals, lunatics, and misfits, and assigned them a social role so dangerous that by 1913 nine states had passed laws permitting sterilization of criminals and defectives, with Indiana leading the way in the number of such operations performed.[192]

An article entitled "Backwaters of Humanity" that appeared in 1913 in *The World's Work* shows the obsessive scrutiny with which observers uncovered and categorized degenerate characteristics in suspect groups of people. The article's anonymous author bemoaned the "depressing influence spread throughout [the] community" from the "backwaters of dead mentality," evidenced by sociological investigations the New Jersey State Department of Charities undertook in the pine belt.[193] Testing 199 members of several generations of one family, investigators found among them persons of the following descriptions:

Normal	13
Partly normal	4
Normal and criminal	1
Degenerate	124
Degenerate and criminal	20
Degenerate and almshouse	6
Degenerate, almshouse, and criminal	2
Degenerate and illegitimate	15
Degenerate, illegitimate, and almshouse	2
Degenerate, illegitimate, almshouse, and criminal	2
Illegitimate, partly normal	1
Miscellaneous, died, or unknown	9

Although the investigators did not explain what criteria they used to determine categories, they made clear the degree of pathology they uncovered. In this one family, the combined deviant sexuality, criminality, poverty, and insanity of 93 percent of the members harbored ominous warnings. Mental incapacity and sexual deviancy were genetic and familial—that is, transmitted by sexual union—and combined to present a dangerous class threat coming from the poor people in the rural pine barrens.

The swarming millions were attacked for contradictory reasons: they had too many children; they did not produce enough soldiers; they were a directionless mass without a center; they were a tightly organized conspiracy bent on social revolution; they surged across borders in mighty floods;

they seeped backward into stagnant slime. The contradictory feelings that arose in Roosevelt when he wrote about these issues help explain why he felt the need for a national "cleansing and hardening" as a means to guard against what he called the "mighty tide of immigration."[194] Were this protection not effective, his sometimes pessimistic notion of the historical march of "civilization and culture" led him to predict, the "cultured folk" would "sooner or later . . . be engulfed, and the leveling waves of barbarism wash over them."[195]

Cartoonists and writers reinforced the sense of inundation Roosevelt felt by picturing immigration as something that was as persistent, unstoppable, and inevitable as a flood or an ocean. Owen Wister's protagonist in his novel *Lady Baltimore* anguished over "old stock" Americans "who are neither going down nor bobbing up, but who have kept their heads above the American tidal wave." From the morass of this tidal wave, race mixing in the form of "tempting dances" beckoned men from good families, taking them "deep among our lower classes that have boiled up from the bottom."[196] In a 1903 cartoon in *Judge*, the "riff-raff" swimming ashore wear hats that read Pauper, Mafia, Degenerate, Anarchist, Illiterate, and Outlaw (figure 9). These names connect the politics of anarchists and outlaws, the biology of illiterates and degenerates, and the conspiracy of mafiosi into one common "danger to American ideas and institutions" that sends Uncle Sam scrambling to avoid drowning.

Figure 9. Louis Dalrymple, "The High Tide of Immigration—A National Menace," *Judge*, 22 August 1903

Roosevelt's use of water metaphors indicated that his psychological defense against any social threat took place against the feeling of drowning or of being engulfed by the ocean or sucked down by mire. He commonly called upon Americans to protect the nation against the "influx" of a "mass of Orientals . . . that would mean the submergence of our own people."[197] For men who viewed women negatively, fears of their own effeminacy could emerge in images of drowning floods or dissolving tides, stagnant swamps, devouring pits, or red caverns. Using images of swimmers, waves, floods, and "oceans of unrest," Roosevelt and other critics of immigration fantasized the drowning of "our own" in a tide of aliens, thus expressing deep anxieties about the racial and sexual integrity of the nation's body.

As immigrants poured across the nation's borders, swelling and surging in tidal billows and oceans of unrest, the possibility of slipping backward down the social ladder into a watery morass and the moist sexuality of race suicide all expressed the middle class's vulnerability to invasion, to foreign footholds, and to penetration. Socialism threatened a redistribution of wealth to be sure. But by emphasizing the social against the individual ownership of property, socialism also conjured darker images of equality, of sharing with the undifferentiated masses, of a lowering of class barriers and a leveling of class distinctions, of allowing oneself to be engulfed in a watery oneness. To upright, property-respecting republican brothers, socialism's deadly leveling and stripping away of boundaries washed away the individual self.

Such feelings exposed and weakened the boundaries many men simultaneously kept around the emotional self and the nation and help explain why Roosevelt warned that the nation's fraternal brotherhood could not long survive the inundation of "alien matter." In his 1894 essay "True Americanism," published in *The Forum*, he called for Americans to check immigration "by much more drastic laws than now exist." Such laws would keep out workers who depressed wages, "races" that did not readily assimilate, and "unworthy individuals . . . not only criminals, idiots, and paupers, but anarchists." For groups that were, in his mind, more racially compatible, like Germans and the Irish, Roosevelt would solve the problem of assimilation by instilling in them an "intense and fervid Americanism." "More than a third of the people of the Northern States are of foreign birth," Roosevelt noted, and "we have no use" for the German or Irishman who "remains such." When foreigners became "Americans like the rest of us," they posed no threat, since America is a land of "mixed blood." But when they "cling to the speech and customs . . . of the Old World, . . . we ourselves also suffer from their perversity."[198] If immigrants failed to assimilate, Americans would become "dwellers in a polyglot boarding house," "a contemptible knot of struggling nationalities," or worse, like Latin America, a "squabbling multitude of revolution-ridden States."[199] With such language, Roosevelt invoked retaliatory feelings and pointed fantasized violence at targeted groups. Barbara Ehrenreich explains this need for containment expressed by Roosevelt and Mahan: "All that is rich and various must be smoothed over. All that is wet and luscious must be dammed up and contained; all that is 'exotic' (dark, Jewish) must be eliminated."[200] Alfred Mahan warned that Americans should avoid "tolerance towards the unfit," for it made them reluctant to "strike the individual in the interests of the community." To him, those Americans "reluctant to punish" must develop a desire for social efficiency and the "hardness of heart" needed to deal with large numbers of the "unfit."[201]

THE ARMORED, EXPLODING SELF

On the social-psychological level, then, important personalities like Roosevelt, Ross, Mahan, Wister, and James exhorted middle-class men to project their own self-purifications onto the nation's body and to undertake a national self-hardening as a radical antidote to modern ills. These men imagined a tough collective national exterior that took the form of a modern steel navy, the domination of militarily weaker or less civilized nations, or repeated disciplinary actions at home against race and class enemies. In this sense, the search for social order that produced the era's purity crusades, court injunctions against strikers, penal codes, and modern strategies of factory management emerged from the deepest levels of men's psyches. In Roosevelt's hands, the strength of these disciplinary needs encouraged dreams of national transformation that mandated a thrilling transgression of ordinary moral restraints.

By the end of the century, popular writers had noted the nation's growing tendency to appreciate the extremities of war James and Roosevelt called for. "There is a remarkable and very significant tendency to praise all war songs, war stories and war literature generally," Agnes Repplier wrote as early as 1891, "in proportion to the discomfort and horror they excite, in proportion to their inartistic and unjustifiable realism."[202] In the years surrounding the Spanish-American War, the nation's martial appetite sharpened as the yellow press encouraged the basest of motives. In this period before the two world wars and the rise of fascism questioned organic nationalism, the *Washington Post* could even speak of the peculiar preferences of the nation's palate: "The taste of empire is in the mouth of the people, even as the taste of blood in the jungle."[203] As such feelings mounted, Roosevelt's political language suddenly set about summoning the agents of radical transformation, exploiting the excitements of horror, and unleashing what James called an "evolutionary savagery" whose "remote origin in the evolution of the race" placed it above rational justification.

Part of the great appeal of disciplinary and exclusionary language lay in the thrill of exposing the "wild beast qualities" of the human heart, for, as James pointed out, many men sought rather than avoided the beast within. For this reason he thought that "showing war's irrationality and horror . . . had no effect on modern man" because the horrors themselves "make the fascination. War is the *strong* life; it is *in extremis*. . . . History is a bath of blood, . . . horrible reading because of the irrationality of it all." "Especially for non-combatants" like city-bred onlookers, war provided "the supremely thrilling excitement, . . . an explosion of imaginative energy. The dams of routine burst, and boundless prospects open," and "the remotest spectators share the fascination of that awful struggle."[204] Only in battle, James thought, could the primitive beast within legitimately rise to the surface, break the dams of ego maintenance, and explode. And, as James emphasized, the city-bred reader could imaginatively ride this tide of exploding emotion.

Cultural notions of latent beasts within that erupted "in extremis" drew from nineteenth-century psychological, social, and evolutionary theories that held that humans could "revert" to behaviors of their biological ancestors. In an age that had conjured apocalyptic visions of a destiny out of control and had emphasized modernism's hidden and dangerous aspects, fear of losing control produced its own ecstatic power. Fear that civilization was only a veneer, that it might revert to savagery unless civilized men waged ceaseless war against the beast within, was an acknowledgment of the thrilling resurgent power of the repressed. As with men's fascination with horror, which James knew, disgust and desire "seem necessary to each other," writes William Miller; disgust does not simply dissuade a person from pleasure but heightens that pleasure. "The damlike barrier . . . works both to obstruct access to the desired object and to provide the means for storing quantities of desire sufficient to overcome the barrier."[205] The warmongering fiction and outlandish political fare of late Victorian society provoked lurid interest in the thrills of forbidden sights and tastes and in the fascinations of extreme danger and terrible savagery.

For Roosevelt and his contemporaries to acknowledge the compelling allure of unleashed emotions, of excitations to horror indicates that they at least partly understood the psychological function of the great rush of feeling accompanying transgressive behavior. In the social psychology of political culture, such behavior endorses the collective indulgence of repressed desire on a national level. This is why Roosevelt could cultivate individual men's heightened appreciation for ever-widening thresholds of violence and appropriate it into political culture.

The psychological appeal of those attractions Roosevelt called the "hideous and revolting" threatened and even sometimes promised to dissolve the internal boundaries, James's dams, established to contain them. In this manner, the return of repressed desires provoked contradictory feelings some men held about their inner emotional lives. Ego maintenance, or "self-mastery," demanded that otherwise unacceptable prurience, rape fantasies, or acts of violence be reconciled with moral precepts. Notions of altruistic duty provided psychological armor for men that raised their actions above the level of fleshly or deathly urges. The mental habit of interpreting the killing of enemies as responsible and dutiful abstracted the brutality of the act, shielding it behind a self-protective ego armor that allowed men to distance themselves from what would otherwise be war's outright horrors.

For many men attracted to the soldiering or hunting life, ego maintenance manifested itself in the new language of aggressive manhood, which described killing as civilization cleansing, race hardening, and nation strengthening. Highly evolved whites were so civilized, many men thought, that even performing acts of slaughter could not make them into savages. With such habits of mind, men would maintain what Mark Twain called "the white man's notion that he is less savage than the other savages."[206] In 1898, as Roosevelt set off for Cuba, John Hay called him a *wilder werwegener*, an adventurous savage, an endearing term that converted Roosevelt's blatant war eagerness into romantic, imperialist adventurism.[207] The true savages, as everyone knew, were the Spanish colonial authorities, aptly demonized in the nation's press. Civilized adventurers reluctantly but necessarily defined violence as what the *New York Tribune* blithely termed "intelligent barbarism" and Roosevelt called "brutal heroism."[208]

Social theorists provided the logic for the intelligent barbarism that obtained among the fraternity of warriors and would-be warriors. Ross, in his analysis of aggressiveness in combat and sport, found that white men fought one another fairly and obeyed rules that arose naturally from their "sheer love of fighting on equal terms." Out of white men's racial penchant for fair play, he maintained, progressive society "manufactures conscience," which, in turn, forces men to subsume their "panther traits" under the rules of warfare and sport. Under these circumstances, "the great conquering, civilizing races" benefited from men's aggressiveness because it was thought-out, fair-minded, and filled with a "healthy sense of justice." In Ross's figuration, violence, per se, was neither civilized nor uncivilized. It depended on whose it was. Aggressiveness was not a problem among civilized men of the "winning race" for they united their "pushing, combative disposition with self-control." "From the standpoint of world peace and order," he wrote, "the race most hopeless is not the hard and aggressive race, but the race afflicted with seething, explosive passions."[209] Ross may have had in mind Roosevelt, who was widely known as master of his own passions and yet appreciated for his aggressiveness. Owen Wister, recounting Roosevelt's many battles, observed, "Mr. Roosevelt was busy fighting the first time that I ever laid eyes on him." "He takes no mean advantage of an adversary; he stops when 'time' is called, he fights 'on the square'; he is what the West calls a 'white man.' "[210]

In more modern parlance, we might say that men repressed their emotional selves under an armored exterior to create a self-contained, self-controlled, rule-bound exteriorized man. Strong ego armor turned the solitary individual into a forward striving, restlessly toiling, sexually disciplined, racially pure machine, one that could unleash emotions only in carefully controlled situations to protect the national body against its enemies. As with modern institutions such as schools or prisons, where organizational discipline penetrates the social body, the military enveloped the individual physical body with its emotions and fleshly desire, enclosing it within the collective body of the organization, which appeared to observer and participant alike all discipline and hardness.

According to this logic, Anson Rabinbach and Jessica Benjamin observe, war became a "symbolic system of desire" that furnished real and armchair soldiers the "most profound mirror" of their external armor identity.[211] In war, men could denounce their own bodily interiors and retreat into collective ego-boundary maintenance through "hardness, destruction, and self-denial." They could, in the perfectly rational cause of civilization, link with like-minded males to undertake group rituals of formalized bloodletting that released repressed emotions. The pleasures of breaking boundaries and the eruption of desire endorsed the aesthetic attractions of violence, as the most violent and outlandish acts of hunting and war took place within the mental boundaries of cleanliness, order, precision, and certainty. On this level, war and its accompanying parades of armaments, mounted warriors, marching formations, and gun salutes provided the visible elements of armor identity in the system of desire. Toward the century's end, America's splendid little war served as a magnet for the social-psychological strands of belligerent masculinity, Western amorality, the need for trial by fire, and the urge to hurt someone.

Writing in 1901, Ross identified that "daring and disobedient breed . . . the restless, striving, doing Aryan, with his personal ambition, his lust for power, his longing to wreak himself, his willingness to turn the world up-side down to get fame or fortune," who "is under no easy discipline."[212] Here Ross identifies the disciplinary affect of the soldier male who uses pain to repress and contain his desires. Ross also indicates the difficulty of maintaining repression, given the tendency of desire to resurface in vari-ous levels of violence or unruliness. Self-disciplinary pain is not a private psychological mechanism, for in disciplining themselves, men like Roose-velt came to discipline others and to popularize the punitive qualities of the armored and disciplined warrior-male. In this manner they invoked the sadistic and masochistic impulses of national manhood, its striving turned outward in irrepressible violence and inward to wreak havoc on the self.

SCAPEGOATS

When suppressed fears and emotions reemerged, many men projected them outward onto objects of transferential identification, or scapegoats. For middle-class men, the national scapegoats collectively embodied the inner demons that men repressed, making the presence of individuals such as prostitutes, pacifists, and Jews, and behaviors like effeminacy a palpable and immediate danger.[213] As corrupters of ideal masculinity, degenerate groups carried Roosevelt's "illness of modernism" in that they threatened the nation's civilizing role and white men's place in it. As representatives of rottenness, corruption, and passion, degenerate groups embodied urges that, were they to "come uppermost" as Roosevelt warned, would undermine the ego boundaries men had established to con-tain them. As we shall see in the next chapter, the vehemence with which men converted seemingly unhygienic and degenerate social forces into a separate and distinct Other attested to the degree to which they were threatening and, therefore, a source of repressed anxiety.

On a visit to Aden in 1867, Captain Alfred Thayer Mahan, the nation's preeminent naval expansionist, expressed this transference of inner dis-gust onto scapegoats. Of the "divers peoples" that came together in the port, he said, "the Jews most attracted my attention, . . . an attraction of repulsion . . . though I am without anti-Semitic feeling. The physiognomy commonly associated with the name Jew was very evident. . . . Cringing and subservient in manner, . . . behind the . . . exterior a fierce cruelty of expression which would make a mob hideous, if once let loose. A mob, in-deed, is ever terrible; but these men reconstituted for me, with added vividness, the scene and the cry of 'Crucify Him!' "[214] For Mahan, fear of his own weakness or "cringing," disgust at his own capacity for "cruelty," and the dread of his own punishment by "a mob hideous" clearly named

what he repressed as well as identified those same qualities in the scape-
goat. Most tellingly, Mahan's revulsion provoked in him a violent urge.

In the hands of political leaders, scapegoating, to the extent that it produced a paranoid, narcissistic, radically exclusionary phobic anxiety, functioned as a displaced form of ritual purification, a displaced but very real
collective purging of the nation's internal "unclean."[215] Roosevelt loathed
the contaminating blood of hypersexualized women and the social deviance of "reds." Beveridge abhorred wild Filipinos, and Jews disgusted
Mahan. James feared being mired in a mass of clerks and teachers, and
Ross in "slimy unpleasant things." Like Ahab's struggle with his own "in-
tangible malignity," Mahan's "attraction of repulsion" for Jews, James's
"fascination" for war's "horror," and Roosevelt's "greedy and fierce hope"
for something sexually "unhealthy" revealed the power of the repressed
desire, the steely allure of masochistic violence, and the obsessive and uncontrolled dimensions of the scapegoating. Melville, true to his own genius, saw deeply into this aspect of Ahab's psyche:

> The white whale swam before him as the monomaniac incarnation of all
> those malicious agencies which some deep men feel eating in them, till they
> are left living on with half a heart and half a lung. . . . All that most maddens
> and torments . . . ; all that cracks the sinews and cakes the brain; all the
> subtle demonisms of life and thought; all evil . . . visibly personified. He
> piled upon the whale . . . the sum of all the general rage and hate felt by his
> whole race from Adam down; and then, as if his chest had been a mortar, he
> burst his hot heart's shell upon it.[216]

Women, Apes, and "Baneful Things"

Since the [white man] has become a house race, the sufferer boldly takes to the life in tents. Half our diseases are in our minds and half in our houses.
—Boy Scouts of America handbook for 1910

On becoming president in 1901, Roosevelt became the self-appointed watchdog for guarding against effeminacy in national life. No man more convincingly inscribed politics with fears about his own body or offered that body as an example of what a regenerated male could do for the nation. In the previous decade, as husband and father, New York assemblyman, Rough Rider, and governor of New York, he had distanced himself from the feminizing effects of domestic space by mastering politics, hunting and outdoor life, and, finally, military service. In the nation's political spotlight, he used his bodily strength to contest any image that sullied the ideal white, male body—homosexuals, shirkers, sissies, pacifists, and even ape-men. On the September 1904 cover of *Physical Culture,* the president exhibited this strength, asking, "What Shall We Stand For in Politics?" (figure 10). "We," the nation of forthright white men, shall "stand" just as he stood: not in a suit, but in riding clothes, with boots firmly planted, hand on hip, resolute, confident, and challenging, ready for a life of hardy strenuousness. Staring challengingly at his viewers, the nation's most popular specimen of male physicality exudes the authority of mastery over horses and men. He is one who countenanced no resistance from women, workers, blacks, second-generation ethnic Americans, or anyone who threatened to share public space with ideal men. Readers of *Physical Culture* would have only to try to imagine him holding an umbrella, wearing tennis attire, carrying a child, or standing naked to sense the craftedness of the image.

Roosevelt brought a new bodily presence to international politics too, and he was determined to reflect American power through his own style of masculinity. A British cartoonist caught his stern, moralistic demeanor and physically bombastic political technique, picturing

79

Figure 10. "What Shall We Stand For in Politics?" *Physical Culture*, September 1904

him during his grand tour of Europe at the conclusion of his presidency as a large and imposing bulk delivering "straight talks" to "effete civilisations" (figure 11). European viewers understood that the cartoonist was satirizing Roosevelt's puritanical moralizing, just as he exaggerated his body size in relation to that of the attentive imperial officers and decadent monarchists at his feet. At the height of British empire in the years before

the First World War, few British would have accepted directives of any
kind from an American, especially moral ones. The cartoon's mocking
tone was probably lost on Roosevelt's countrymen, who were more likely
to appreciate the frowning, preacher-like authority with which he bestowed the "wisdom of the West." Taken together, these two images (in figures 10 and 11) suggest that Roosevelt established a considerable moral

Figure 11. Leonard Raven-Hill, "Roosevelt's Straight Talks to Effete Civilisations," *Punch*

and physical presence, in the United States at least, partly on the basis of racial and class images of male authority and power. How did he establish his authority among American men? How did his inner demons help him choose the scapegoats, the objects of scorn against which that authority was deployed? How did his articulation of that scorn help construct a historically new version of masculinity?

KNICKERBOCKER SEX

Devoted to Victorian images of the ideal woman, most men of Roosevelt's class preferred their wives and unmarried daughters to remain inside the home in order to provide a moral haven for men who were forced to venture into the cutthroat professional or business world. Men viewed women as subordinates, and even after the advent of companionate marriages in the 1890s, when wives became partners in domestic relationships, men seldom considered them independent or competitive enough for the "real" world. Upper- and middle-class women served to protect the family and civilization from the very society created by men, who, in turn, expected the women to be gentle, graceful, dainty, and nurturing, and above all, uninterested in and even ignorant of their sexual possibilities. Sex was reserved for marriage, and medical experts idealized the woman who relegated it to an act of procreation. Middle-class women's passion lay not in their enjoyment of sex, it was thought, but in their moral and spiritual power, which was a source of strength for husbands and children.

In the era's religious and scientific literature, women appeared less rational than men, and by virtue of being in touch with more primitive selves, they were both innocently superior and capable of dangerous moral lapses and of switching between good and evil at a moment's notice.[1] Roosevelt, too, linked moral capacity to male rationality and agreed with experts that most women suffered from a vacillating personality and so had a diminished capacity for rational, and therefore moral, thinking. He expressed his own vision of the ideal upper-class wife and mother in his descriptions of his two wives. "She is so pure and holy that it seems almost profanation to touch her," he said of Alice Lee shortly before their wedding in 1880. Perhaps he saw her in the Victorian tradition of the child bride who never grew up—she was fourteen in his favorite picture. Though his second wife, Edith Carow, was a strong equestrian, hiker, confidant, and mother of six, he often pictured her, as he had Alice, as passive, childlike, and pure. When he became president and rode horses with Edith in Washington, he was pleased that she looked "so young and pretty" that someone remarked, "she must be his daughter, for she is only a girl."[2] He often described both Alice and Edith as having contradictory if not irrational natures, though not flagging morality. Alice Lee was "pure and sweet" one day, he wrote in 1880, and the next a "little witch [who] led me a dance before she surrendered" to his marriage proposal.[3] Well into his second marriage, he could write of Edith alternating between her submissive "goddess" side and her dominating, "Commodore Hull" side.[4]

Forever nervous about the boundaries between virtue and degradation, Roosevelt insisted that standards of female purity be strictly upheld in every aspect of life, even the imaginative. In a 1904 letter to novelist Martha Selmes, he chastised her for allowing her fictional heroine to indulge in morally ambiguous behavior. "Personally I prefer virtue," he wrote, "but if one deviates from virtue then for Heaven's sake take the opposite course thoroughly." His was an extreme position, he admitted, this willingness to assign evil to an insufficiently virtuous woman. "I am writing as if I were a prig," he conceded. Roosevelt's habit of thinking in moral absolutes left him uneasy with any blurring of his strict boundaries that separated good and evil.[5]

Though Roosevelt's ideal remained that represented by his wives and those of his friends, he admired the hardy pioneer women he met out West. These women rode horses, maintained frontier homes, or managed cattle ranches, and produced children along the way.[6] He compared tough, outdoor women to those effete, childless, Eastern middle-class women most responsible, he thought, for the nation's declining birthrate. He was distressed over their "willful" reproductive "irresponsibility." Exhausted by the "selfishness" of too much reading, shopping, and theater-going, educated women of the Eastern elite, Roosevelt and most medical professionals thought, suffered from weakened bodies and diminished capacity for childbearing. He extended to women his prescription for ideal men's bodies, which must suffer "risk and pain." Eastern women should undertake "bodily hardening" because childbearing remained women's primary duty, even in the industrialized world. Bodily strengthening would allow a woman to be the "wise and fearless mother of many healthy children," he said; it was her "duty to the nation." Indeed, by having children painfully and unhesitatingly, women signified their willingness to partake in a nationalistic ritual of bodily purification.

He admired women's suffering and considered it not merely mandatory, but deserved, presumably because of Biblical prescriptions for painful birth. He compared women who confronted "the fear of maternity, the haunting terror of the young wife," to soldiers in war who also risked their lives to serve the nation. "Of course" one could risk too much, he observed. "I do not wish to see a woman worn down and perhaps killed by too much maternity; but my parallel of the soldier holds good."[7] This was a

close subject for Roosevelt, torn as he must have been between his wish
that women have many children and the fact that Alice Lee, his first wife,
died after bearing their first child. He had built his large, twenty-three-
room home, Sagamore Hill, on Oyster Bay, Long Island, for her and in anticipation of her childbearing potential. Twelve of its rooms are bedrooms.

If Roosevelt's presidential exhortation was insufficient to spur women
to patriotic, if painful, childbirth, he accused those who refused of en-
dangering the race-nation. If women "flinch from breeding the deserved
death of the race takes place even quicker."[8] When a nation's women
"shrink from pain, . . . that nation is rotten to the heart's core," he said.
"When men fear work or fear righteous war, when women fear motherhood, they tremble at the brink of doom; and well it is that they should
vanish from the earth, where they are fit subjects for the scorn of all who
are themselves strong and brave and high-minded."[9] The woman who
"flinches from childbirth stands on a par with the soldier who drops his
rifle and runs in battle." For those "contemptible creatures" he prescribed
"extinction."[10] From such high moral and martial ground, the nation exercised a greater claim to women's bodies than women themselves, at least
for breeding purposes, just as it laid claim to men's.[11] Over the nineteenth
century, the middle-class birthrate had declined by half, and Roosevelt's
solution was to "standardize" the Anglo-Saxon birthrate at four to six
children.[12]

Roosevelt's desire to maintain white racial purity led him to designate
as ideal fathers those men who were of "thoroughly" American stock. In
1900, Roosevelt was "delighted" to congratulate Leonard Wood and his
wife on the birth of their first child. "I am a believer in seeing good stock
perpetuated, and I always feel angry when I see those whom I respect, . . .
who do not leave behind them their seed to inherit the earth."[13] When he
began his campaigns for a higher white birthrate, his daughter Alice
mocked him by forming the Race Suicide Club, in which she and her
friends exchanged birth control information. If his own daughter found
cause for mirth in his strident prescriptions for upper-class breeding, so
did the president's critics. When Roosevelt congratulated ex-President
Grover Cleveland on the birth of a boy, an *Ohio State Journal* cartoonist
emphasized the Anglo-Saxon "common ground" of "no race suicide" in
Roosevelt's praise (figure 12). Another cartoon shows President Roosevelt
seated at his desk and warning that "Race Suicide Is a Crime" while beam-
ing over the words "126,000 new New Yorkers." Mr. Knickerbocker, the
upper-class progenitor, enters the room with his arms full of babies and
asks the president, "Will This Do?"[14]

For Roosevelt, a sufficient birthrate alone did not guarantee racial sur-

Figure 12. Harry James Westerman, "On Common Ground," *Ohio State Journal* (Columbus)

vival. Martial virility was of equal importance. "The race should never cease to breed," William James concurred, "for every one is sensitive to its superiority." One duty of "mankind," James maintained, was "keeping military characters in stock" if not for wartime use, then as "ends in themselves" and as "pure pieces of perfection—so that Roosevelt's weaklings and mollycoddles may not [make] everything else disappear from the face of nature."[15] In this context of selective breeding, Roosevelt's ideal national manhood was threatened by miscegenation, birth control, abortion, male effeminacy, and homosexuality because they deflected white, upper-class progenitors from the task of reproducing the homogeneous nation. Breeding was one of Roosevelt's "three prime requisites for any race, the three essential qualities for any nation." "Work—fight—breed": unless a race does these things, "it certainly must be worthless."[16] Working, fighting, and breeding created action boundaries between the normative men of "our race" and an assumed "impotent," dark-skinned, or otherwise weakened man. Translated into politics, this hierarchy valorized not just a flight from the feminine, but also the phallic conquest of small, weak, brown-skinned, allegorically effeminate peoples. In a social Darwinist morality, the logic of this politics held that strong and civilized races must dominate weaker ones for their own good, and that weaklings invited outside force by being unable to control their passions, govern themselves, or advance toward civilization. To Roosevelt and James, civilization and the main vehicle for its advancement, the race-nation, remained the umbrella ethos for spurring on soldiers, workers, and procreators.

If women, and especially mothers, figured importantly in civilization's advance, they did so as distinctly second-class citizens. Even as he advocated equal rights for both sexes, as early as his senior year at Harvard in 1880 he used a pathological analogy between women and infirmity to dispel any notions of inherent equality. "A cripple or a consumptive in the eye of the law is equal to the strongest athlete, and the same justice should be shown to a woman whether she is or is not the equal of man."[17] Though he considered women unequal to men, Roosevelt clearly favored their participation in economic life and seemed not to believe that having a job, even for middle-class white-collar women, interfered with having children. During his six years on the Civil Service Commission from 1889 to 1894, he advanced progressive causes by converting 26,000 jobs from patronage to merit selection and by allowing women to compete with men for them. This policy greatly increased the presence of women in government. By 1898, he conceded to Susan B. Anthony that "woman . . . is in many cases oppressed," but he nevertheless believed at that point that a woman did not need the vote, since she "can get all the rights she can take" under current law.[18]

After he became president, however, Roosevelt began to understand that voting women would have more social leverage. Prompted by considerations of racial superiority, not the civil rights arguments of suffragists, he began to advocate women's suffrage. By gaining the vote, he hoped, women would more effectively promote marriage and the family. It was his desire to enlist "strong" women to uphold their maternal duty to produce children themselves and to alleviate fears of childbearing among their sisters. He remained nervous about entrusting the vote to a sex that could not, like men, "fight in defense of their rights," a weakness that "makes a powerful argument against putting the ballot into hands unable to defend it."[19] But he anticipated that political activity would spur American women to submit their reproductive capacity to racial and national imperatives. Like other socially conservative advocates of progressive reform, Roosevelt's plea for white women to "uphold" the race reinforced Victorian notions of female inferiority, extending into political culture popular themes of sacrifice that he knew only too well from classical and Victorian art and literature, wherein women madly stabbed or drowned themselves for love or virtue or for religious martyrdom. Indeed, Bram Dijkstra finds that even before medical men did, nineteenth-century politicians raided images of sacrificial women from art and literature quite profitably for their own careers.[20]

After Darwin had seemingly seconded notions of female inferiority and medical experts had pronounced motherhood the only proper social role for women, traditional-minded males of Roosevelt's era interpreted politicized or hypersexualized women as dangerous. Middle-class men found the entry of any women, but especially their own wives and daughters, into public life disturbing, in part because previously women's inaccessibility within domestic life had ensured their purity. Women who entered the public sphere at best adopted male roles or asserted their sexual presence. At worst these women unleashed the forces of degeneration. The increasing popularity of Charles Dana Gibson's liberated Gibson girl, who appeared in the 1890s in *Life* and after 1900 in *Collier's Weekly*, attested to the way in which images of women had been transformed from the straitlaced Victorian ideal of the nineteenth century to the New Woman of the twentieth. Slim, sophisticated, and sexually liberated, the Gibson girl set standards of dress, behavior, and attitude for an entire generation of women.

Given medical arguments that a woman's whole persona was constructed around her womb and that procreation was her biological fate, many men worried about women who refused to have children. Such women practiced or advocated birth control, many men thought, so they could indulgence in sexual pleasure with no other object than pleasure itself. This idea was so horrifying to some medical experts that they expanded the womb-centric model of women's nature to include lust as an important but dangerous ingredient. Medical literature abounded with denunciations of aggressive sexuality and even raised the specter of female masturbation. Since women lacked self-discipline, according to this literature, any pleasurable or "selfish" sex weakened their minds and bodies. In his aptly titled *Satan in Society* (1870), eminent professor of medicine Nicholas Francis Cooke identified women's willingness to have sex for any other purpose than procreation as a "monstrous heresy against religion, society, and common sense." He castigated women's various birth control methods and suggested instead that they have "at least six or eight children; a healthy woman can give birth to sixteen; examples are not wanting in which [women have had] as many as 24 children."[21] Selfish sexuality among women defied conventional notions of femaleness and conjured a threatening form of the New Woman—a sex starved, predatory, hedonistic type, dangerously approaching the Victorian category of fallen women.

The growing public presence of white, middle-class women who demanded the vote, attended art exhibitions, shopped unchaperoned, and used birth control aroused dread in men of Roosevelt's generation. Cooke predicted that the woman who gained "rights" would quickly degenerate, or evolve backward, "cease to be the gentle mother, and become the Amazonian brawler."[22] One of Roosevelt's favorite poets, Eugene Fitch Ware, expressed "Our terror of that day" when "The atmospheric spirit of the age, / Have made these women / So we cannot trust 'em. / Who knows what ills the present may presage?" In this poem, ironically titled "A Romance," Ware's narrator deplores how a "man can go distracted on a female, as her lover" and, reciprocally, "why a woman likes a man / With such horrible devotion." No friend of love, Ware recounts his fictional couple's "frantic," "furious," "rabid," "reckless" lovemaking that "sickened all the boarders of a second-class hotel" and set off a chain reaction of business collapse, tax delinquencies, foreclosures, and bank failures that ultimately ruined an entire town. Men should avoid loving women intensely, the poet advises, since women have "made the world a circus ever since the days of Eve."[23]

Roosevelt's domestic life richly abounded in play with and tenderness toward his children and wife, while at the same time it contained disciplinary barriers against indulgence, sexual or otherwise. More affluent than almost all other Americans, Roosevelt avoided what he deemed overt "richness and luxury" in his home or dress and restricted himself to a few strenuous pleasures. One friend remarked that eating was his only indulgence. Sex, obviously, was another, though as a youth he sublimated his passion to physical exertions and remained "pure" until marriage. After marrying, he was the faithful husband of two wives who together bore him six children. Roosevelt loved, entertained, read to, and corresponded with women throughout his life, though usually about literature or domestic life and hardly ever about politics. He also judged, exhorted, interpreted, defined, and disapproved of them in ways that bespoke the extreme importance he placed on controlling emotions and thoughts about women. Sometimes this self-control reached an extreme. After his first wife, Alice, died, he forbade anyone in his extended family to mention her name or that of her daughter and namesake, who was now growing up in his second family. Throughout her life, he referred to this child as Sister.

As many New Women abandoned corsets for bicycles, Roosevelt and many other fathers tried to enforce traditional morality and behavior. In his own household, his oldest child, Alice, scandalized her puritanical father. At age nine, she knew how to launch threats that aroused his sexual prejudices and fears with amazing accuracy. She announced that she no longer wished to be a girl and that she had decided to wear pants, bob her hair, and give birth to a monkey. By threatening to cut her hair short, she was making a declaration against the Victorian ideal and in favor of a boyish style that blurred male-female distinctions. Her announcement that she would give birth to a monkey evoked in Roosevelt three of his era's most fundamental fears: the blurring of distinctions between humans and animals; Negroes, who were likened to apes; and child sexuality. Wittingly or unwittingly, Alice lent racial and bestial overtones to her father's fears of uncontrolled female sexuality, for, in order to bear a monkey child, Alice must presumably find a simian father.

Alice, who admitted to her "proclivity toward malice," scandalized and disappointed her father on other fronts.[24] In 1897, when Alice was fourteen, her father complained that she was "running riot with the boys and girls."[25] During Roosevelt's presidency, as Alice entered her twenties, she shocked polite society as well as the president by smoking in public and gambling at the racetrack. She drove her red "electric" from Newport to Boston accompanied only by a female friend, a feat that caused a scandal in the newspapers. "A letter came from Father," she wrote in her autobiography, "that . . . enumerated the iniquities that I had committed . . . [and] scorched the paper on which it was written."[26] When Owen Wister remarked on Roosevelt's lack of parental control, he retorted: "I can be President, or—I can attend to Alice."[27]

Newport, Rhode Island, was the resort town where New York's "Four Hundred" richest families kept summer mansions. It was home to the New York Yacht Club, where the "Harvards" and the "Oxfords" held regattas. In the summer, men who worked in Manhattan took the overnight ferry from New York to Newport, where their families resided. Under the watchful eye of Caroline Astor, Newport's elite displayed their fashionable lives to one another in elaborate entertainments. "In those days Newport was supposed to be the Mammon of unrighteousness," Alice wrote rather proudly as she described the goings-on at one of the Vanderbilts' fancy-dress parties.[28] It was in the Newport Casino in 1893 that Ava Willing Astor had played a tennis match dressed in bloomers, to the shock of traditionalists, including her mother-in-law, Caroline. *Vogue* magazine featured Newport's fashionable, athletic women as "the moderns," trendsetters who served as the basis for the Gibson girl.[29]

Roosevelt deplored Alice's socializing with the decadent Newport crowd. "Sister continues to lead the life of social excitement," the president wrote to his son Ted, "which I think is all right for a girl . . . for a year or two; but . . . I do not regard it as healthy from the standpoint of permanence."[30] In 1901, he confided in a letter to Cecil Arthur Spring Rice that he felt "contempt and anger" at the lives the Four Hundred led, "which vary from rotten frivolity to rotten vice." They "contribute nothing useful to intellectual, civic or social life [and their] unwholesome influence . . . has rather grown worse."[31] In the mind of her father, Alice's defiance of convention placed her sexual purity and therefore marriageability in jeopardy—and what would she be if not married?

APES AND BRUTES

Evolutionist notions left middle-class, white men preoccupied with imagining that Jews, Negroes, and Asians, who they thought were closer on the evolutionary scale to the primitive, had hairy bodies and sloping foreheads. Capitalizing on white men's desire to distance themselves from apes, promoters of world's fairs and other exhibitions at the turn of the century placed indigenous people on display in supposedly authentic settings that pandered to voyeurism and titillating revulsion. In 1906, the monkey house of New York's Bronx Zoo exhibited a Congolese pygmy man, Ota Benga, in a cage he shared with an orangutan. Newspapers, prompted by the bones zookeepers had placed around him, suggested that Benga's filed teeth were meant for eating human flesh.[32]

Like many fairgoers familiar with Darwinian theory and with what must have seemed evidence of its veracity, Roosevelt dreaded the idea that humans and apes shared an evolutionary likeness. His childhood recognition of his own apelikeness in the mirror prompted him to refashion himself against the ape. He admitted to Herman Hagedorn that his compulsive bodybuilding efforts in his early teens were not just attempts to please his father, but were prompted by the horror of self-recognition in Robert Browning's *The Flight of the Duchess*. Here, an effete aristocratic son is the "pertest little ape / That ever affronted human shape. . . . All legs and length, / With blood for bone, all speed, no strength."[33] Conflating humanness and apelikeness remained equally horrifying to Roosevelt throughout his life. Shortly before his death, when pundits alluded to Lincoln's "rude and uncouth" background, they sullied Roosevelt's notion of ideal males. "I do not understand," Roosevelt said, "why some persons like

to portray Lincoln . . . as a lineal descendant of the Pithecanthropus. . . .
He was by no means first cousin to the cave man in appearance."[34] During
his political career, Roosevelt turned disgust with anthropoid origins into
racialized political invective. Distancing "civilized" politics from the
Latin variety, he wrote John Hay that Venezuelan president Cipriano Cas-
tro was "an unspeakably villainous little monkey," and he labeled President J. M. Marroquin of Colombia a "Pithecanthropoid."[35]

   In an age when Darwinism insisted on the hominid origins of the
human species, popular images abounded of heroic figures defeating anthropoid ancestors. The scenario was most vividly presented by one of
Roosevelt's most admired poets, and the most popular writer in the
English-speaking world, Rudyard Kipling. In the prose and poetry of his
twenty-volume works, published in 1900, the Nobel Prize–winning author placed the destiny of white civilization and the burden of empire on
the shoulders of heroic soldier males, assigning them the necessity of using
racialized strength against evolutionary dangers. In "The Seven Nights of
Creation" (1899), Kipling's devil undertakes to emulate God and create
an Adam, but produces instead "baneful things—fogs, poisonous plants,
venomous creatures," and, worst of all, an ape. In the poem's illustration,
the devil's ape cannot stand erect, but instead crouches primitively on the
ground, uprooting grass with his "hairy, spider arms" (figure 13). The
ape's "wrinkled palms . . . stretch forth helplessly and beat the dark," says
the narrator; his "strange, black lips . . . cry and protest"; he wretchedly
implores his creator, "why . . . hast thou breathed Spirit in this foul body?"
Yet piteous or not, the ape appears dangerously primordial to the poem's
civilized narrator. "I saw all wild things crouch beneath that eye . . . [that]
glow[s] with the sense of power," the narrator says as he turns his gaze
from the dirt-bound ape to the muscular true inheritor of the earth, the
majestic winged Adam, who triumphantly and in flames rises heavenward,
where "God gave him great dominion over all." The devil admits that he
failed to create an Adam and concedes that "evil is less powerful than
good."[36]

   Yet in the illustration, Adam's feet remain rooted in the ape, whose
"sense of power" ties Adam to his earthy past and calls into question the
ability of contemporary men to escape their primitive origins. This fear of
being rooted in murky and primitive animality, in "baneful things,"
haunted Victorian men's sense of themselves, certain as they were that the
"superior" races were locked in struggle against the "lower" ones. Turn-
of-the-century racial theorists speculated freely on the final outcome of
this struggle. The French count Arthur de Gobineau, who published his
influential *The Inequality of Human Races* after the revolutions of 1848–

Figure 13. Frontispiece in Rudyard Kipling, *The Writings in Prose and Verse of Rudyard Kipling*, vol. 17, *Early Verse*

1849, predicted that the Aryan race that had created Western civilization would ultimately degenerate through interbreeding with inferiors. "We do not descend from the ape, but are headed in that direction," he prophesied.[37] Somewhat more optimistic than Gobineau, Roosevelt remained disgusted with visual confirmation of the evolutionary likeness of apes, primitive men, and modern men. Though his dark views sometimes surfaced, he clung to the hope that in the ceaseless struggle of civilization against degeneration, each historical stage would produce a stronger race.

If scientific theorists contemplated with distaste the continuum from prehuman to human existence, artists like Frederic Remington marketed the morbid attractions of hominoid primitivism to the nation's magazine-reading audiences. In *Pony Tracks*, a collection of articles appearing in *Harper's Weekly* and *Harper's Monthly* between 1890 and 1895, Remington describes a Dakota Sioux man as "a perfect animal" whose face was "replete with human depravity . . . ferocious, arrogant [with] ghost shirt, war-paint, feathers, and arms." "As a picture," the Sioux was "perfect; as a reality, horrible."[38] In "Massai's Crooked Trail," Remington tells the story of a Chiracahua bronco buster who gets away with murder and rape. "In Massai you have struck a note of grim power as good as anything you have done," Roosevelt wrote to Remington. He praised Remington's "whole account of that bronco Indian, atavistic down to his fire stick; a revival, in his stealthy, inconceivably lonely and bloodthirsty life, of a past so remote that the human being as we know him, was but partially differentiated from the brute."[39] Both Roosevelt and Remington understood that in the brute's horror lay his appeal, even as Easterners would have to reconcile their disgust at his brutishness with the allure of his violence.

In 1906, Remington provided American culture with an apelike figure as powerful in bronze as Kipling's in poetry. *Paleolithic Man* crouches with dangling arms and clawed toes, ears alert. He grasps a clamshell that signals his rootedness in a primal ocean (figure 14). He uses the clamshell as a human tool and challenges the viewer with knowledgeable and clearly human eye contact. Remington described *Paleolithic Man* as a "human figure bordering on an ape," and he sent President Roosevelt a copy, which he identified as the "original inhabitant of Oyster Bay," Roosevelt's family homesite. By noting this lineage, Remington humorously provoked what he knew to be the president's uneasy feelings about having descended from such an ancestor. In his reply thanking Remington for the sculpture, Roosevelt avoided Remington's point about his own forebears and coolly remarked that the clamshell in the man's hand was "appropriate" since Paleolithic man ate oysters.[40]

Remington's crouching *Paleolithic Man* was a relatively harmless mem-

Figure 14. Frederic Remington, *Paleolithic Man,* 1906 (photo by James O. Milmoe; courtesy Rockwell Museum of Western Art, Corning, New York)

ber of the larger cultural genre of more threatening primordial men. Amid widespread fears of miscegenation, turn-of-the-century art and fiction depicted lurid images of Negroes, Indians, and gorillas abducting helpless young white women for sexual purposes, creating the opportunity for their rescue by white men. Irving Couse's 1891 painting *The Captive,* for example, portrays the actual captivity in 1847 of Lorinda Bewly, who the

Figure 15. Eanger Irving Couse, *The Captive*, 1891 (photograph by Craig Smith, collection of Phoenix Art Museum, Phoenix, Ariz., gift of Mr. and Mrs. Read Mullan and others, by exchange)

Cayuse chief Five Crows reportedly wanted for his wife (figure 15). Bewly lies on the tent floor unconscious or sleeping, with a peaceful expression. Although her dress is demurely tucked about her crossed legs, which perhaps signal initial resistance, she otherwise rests completely at the whim of the Indian sitting beside her. Her hair is pulled back, suggesting a handhold already used to bring her to this position and to be used again when she awakens. Some of the indignation captive fantasies provoked among urban readers, Alexander Nemerov finds, resulted from writers' and artists' suggestion that captives were at least partly willing participants in their sexual domination.[41]

Similarly, Charles Schreyvogel painted *The Rescue at Summit Springs* in 1908 to commemorate the Battle of Summit Springs in which the U.S. Fifth Cavalry attempted to rescue two white women from a group of Indians (figure 16). One captive kneels and covers her face, perhaps horrified by the imminent scalping, but in any case entirely inert in the fray, as William Frederick "Buffalo Bill" Cody, the Fifth Cavalry scout, arrives just in time to destroy the brute. The artist's portrayal of the captive's helplessness implies that had she not been rescued, she would still be kneeling before her abductors.

Figure 16. Charles Schreyvogel, *The Rescue at Summit Springs,* c. 1908 (Buffalo Bill Historical Center, Cody, Wyo., bequest in memory of the Houx and Newell families, 11.64)

Emmanuel Fremiet's sculpture *Gorilla Carrying Off a Woman* (1887) depicts a naked woman struggling fruitlessly against the grip of a virile and entirely savage animal (figure 17). Three strong elements of the sculpture, the woman's buttocks and the gorilla's snarling face and heavy weapon, emphasize the woman's nakedness, her panic, the futility of her struggle, and the gorilla's determination. Fremiet turned the captive toward the gorilla and arranged her arms so they are pushing against her captor's neck and chest. The two figures are locked in what to male viewers must have suggested a sexual embrace, emphasized by the bodily contact and by the arms that, while resisting, could have looked suspiciously as if she were acquiescing. These images become all the more satisfying and entertaining because they direct the male viewer's imagination toward the gorilla's reason for carrying off a woman in the first place.

Not surprisingly, few of the era's fictional females struggled successfully against their captors since the nineteenth-century male artists' imagination allowed few roles for women beyond submission. Most artists would have thought it impossible for a woman to outwit her captors and escape, even if she wished to, which most doubted. Many popular captivity narratives relate stories of white women who initially resist capture, but in time became a willing wives to their Indian captors. Artists, and pre-

Figure 17. Emmanuel Fremiet, *Gorilla Carrying Off a Woman*, 1887 (photo copyright
Giraudon /Art Resource, New York)

sumably their patrons, preferred to imagine sexual complicity, for this provoked and entertained viewers' fantasies of abduction, struggle, and rape:
immersed in the fantasies of bondage and rape served up in Victorian culture, men could imagine women who struggled at the moment of capture
but secretly desired and thus ultimately submitted to sex. By laying Bewly
out prone and unconscious before her captor and before male viewers,

Couse delays and thus heightens the excitement of the anticipated moment of sexual conquest, the moment of rape transference realized in
Gorilla Carrying Off a Woman.

Viewing such images fueled Roosevelt's fears of, if not his sexual curiosity about, evolutionary ape-men, in his language "half-breeds" and
nonwhites who were capable not only of polluting wives and daughters,
but also, through race mixing, of causing the civilization that produced
them to slide into prehistoric savagery. As Henry Fairfield Osborn, a racial
theorist and correspondent of Roosevelt's, put it in 1916, "If the valuable
elements in the Nordic race mix with inferior strains or die out through
race suicide, then the citadel of civilization will fall for mere lack of defenders."[42] In their sexual complicity with animals and brutish men, captives did not defend civilization, much less conform to racial and womanly
ideals, and men viewed them as dangerous. Many men who might refer to
themselves, as Roosevelt did, as prigs or prudes in sexual matters, allowed
women they viewed as dangerous to both trigger sexual fears and provoke
aggressive feelings. As a number of middle-class women asserted themselves politically, men portrayed them as conflated social-sexual threats:
aggressive race polluters or anarchists who were dangerously sexual and
whose alluring mouths and disheveled hair concealed a threat of dismemberment and death. Recall brutish anarchism, Roosevelt's cartoon dance
partner. He might court her, popular fears ran, but she would destroy him.

ROOSEVELT THE CRITIC

By the end of the century, Christian, classical, and Victorian literature and
art abounded with graphic expressions of wanton and lascivious women
beheading, drowning, and otherwise engulfing men. Accentuating widely
held notions that women of every social class were capable of sexual aggression, artists provided elaborate fantasies of men victimized by feminine evil, visions that indicated both the artists' and presumably the
viewers' attraction to and repulsion by forbidden sexual liaison. In 1902,
the Reverend E. Cobham Brewer's monumental four-volume *Character
Sketches of Romance, Fiction, and the Drama* collected the pre-Raphaelite
illustrations to the works of Homer, Walter Scott, Tennyson, and Kipling,
and to various medieval epics. In these images, women and devils erotically
and savagely tempt saints, who endure the proper punishment for sexual
excess. Heroes, presumably less abstemious than saints, sometimes resist
and more often succumb to the fleshly wiles of sea nymphs, vampires,
Amazons, Valkyries, and other temptresses, who in scene after scene drag
helpless men into dangerous waters or dark caves. In the epic *Nibelungen-
lied,* appearing in Brewer as an accompaniment to Richard Wagner's *The*

Figure 18. Hans Makart, *Alberich's Pursuit of the Nibelungen Ring*

Ring of the Nibelung, one of Roosevelt's all-time literary favorites, the warrior Alberich, in pursuit of the Nibelungen ring, is beckoned by naked and sporting nymphs of the Rhine to "riot and revel with us" (figure 18). As two nymphs pull him farther into the surf, a third holds the ring and her naked body just beyond his reach, drawing him closer to drowning. As a counterpoint to the robust nymphs, the popular nineteenth-century cult of female invalidism, with its fainting, tubercular, wasted, broken-backed waifs, portrayed women as sexually alluring and, because of their helplessness, equally menacing. Shakespeare's ever-popular Ophelia, driven mad after Hamlet victimized and abandoned her, dressed herself in "fantastic garlands" and fell to a "watery death" in a stream. Although Ophelia should appear as a sympathetic character, an illustrator reconfigures her as a demonic, if fractured, seductress whose bare breasts and enticing expression lure men into the same watery death as her own (figure 19).

Roosevelt's wide and eclectic reading of the popular literature, classics, criticism, science, and history exposed him to these images, and his running public commentary in the books and journals of his day made him one of the most important observers and popularizers of the era's notions of female decadence. He found female corpulence dangerously erotic. "I am not at all fond of Rubens" Roosevelt wrote to his sister Corrine during a European trip in 1881, reacting to the painter's large canvases dominated by "fleshly, sensuous" nudes, beefy women with muscular arms, legs, and necks. Curiously, Roosevelt tolerated Rubens's women when they were

Figure 19. Madeleine Lemaire, *Ophelia*

posed as rich Flemish housewives. Calling them "handsome animals," he approved of the artist's connecting them to the animal world. But he was disgusted when the painter corrupted his notion of ideal womanhood with the same animality. He found Rubens's virgins "either ludicrous or revolting," and they were "not much better as heathen goddesses." "I do'n't [*sic*] like a chubby Minerva, a corpulent Venus and a Diana who is so fat . . . she could never overtake a cow." He "fails in his female figures," Roosevelt concluded when too much animal-like fleshly excess in the body of virgins or goddesses brought them down to the level of "heathens" and sullied their chaste ideal.[43] Corpulence, with its overheated sexuality and taint of femininity, could render men's bodies disgustingly alluring too. Roosevelt described Hubert O. Thompson, the New York commissioner of public works, as "a gross, enormously fleshly man, with a full face and thick, sensual lips."[44]

For Roosevelt, avant-garde art presented equally unsettling images. In 1913, the New York City Sixty-Ninth Regiment armory exhibition of European and American art presented a highly publicized, sensational, and well-attended show of modernists, including Picasso, Matisse, Kandinsky, Gauguin, Van Gogh, and Duchamp. Traveling to Chicago and Boston, the exhibition's paintings and sculptures gave the nation its first airing of modern art. The show's many representations of women included nudes and portrayed prostitutes and working-class women realistically and without moral comment. It was estimated that a half-million people viewed the exhibit, especially after vehement attacks by the public added to its huge success. Art critics reacted with indignation, and public officials threatened to close the show, charging that the "lunatics, charlatans, and political subversives" who produced it had breached public morality.[45]

Deeply disturbed on viewing the armory show, Roosevelt immediately published a stinging review in *The Outlook* that castigated modern artists for producing degenerate female images.[46] At the turn of the century, Western art had begun to incorporate human visages from Africa that many white Americans considered primitive and barbaric. In his review, Roosevelt attacked the "fantastic developments" among modern art's "lunatic fringe," the cubists and futurists like Chagall, Picasso, and Giacometti, who willfully ridiculed, eroticized, and disfigured what he considered the bodily ideal.[47] Cubist pictures of "misshapen nude women" were "repellent from every standpoint," he fumed in his review, and referring to the animality and exposed breasts of Wilhelm Lehmbruck's *Kneeling Woman*, he commented that she appeared "obviously mammalian" (figure 20). To *Kneeling Woman*'s "smirking pose of retrogression," "praying mantis" position, "deformed pelvis," and "tibia of giraffe-like length"

Figure 20. Wilhelm Lehmbruck, *Kneeling Woman*, 1911

he ascribed "pathological rather than artistic significance," reminding himself, perhaps, that the female praying mantis preys upon the male after copulating.

The armory show included Edvard Munch's *Nude with Red Hair* (1901), which was also titled *Sin*. Although Roosevelt provided no comment about this painting in his review, his priggish reserve and sense of racial purity must have been discomfited by her fractured face and staring, vacant eyes framed by unkempt and seemingly menacing hair (figure 21).

Instead of offering the easy pleasure of comfortably enticing if animal-like female bodies like those Rubens painted, this nude has a gaze that is challenging, repulsive, and frightening. Her eyes bring a disconcerting asymmetry to the face: one is rounder and bulging, with a fixed black pupil; the other is almond shaped and looks askance, giving the face a strange, distracted demeanor. The appearance of the nude's breasts and navel, which, eye-and-nose-like, displace the viewer's attention downward, suggest the vagina in the position of the mouth. It is likely that Roosevelt had never before encountered such an image of disfigurement and entrapment. It must have reminded him of the sexual "recklessness" of Ware's fictional women, who sought to make the world a circus or worse.

Roosevelt's strong criticisms of female images in the armory show reflect his belief that the represented female was not just consumer entertainment, but a culturally strategic means for upholding ideals. Lehmbruck's kneeling woman distilled into one vision all that he hated about the New Woman and her corrupting effects. She mirrored his fear of female sexuality in her distorted, "pathological," mockingly submissive, "smirking" pose, evoking the dangers of disfigured and possibly diseased women. Art that violated the boundaries of the ideal surely hastened social degeneration. Such art, Roosevelt told readers of his armory show review, "may mean death and not life, retrogression and not development."[48] With this warning, Roosevelt connected the seemingly harmless world of art to the nation's fate, and most of his readers probably took his words seriously. Men had little way of knowing that the sexual interpretations they drew from artworks like those of Rubens, Munch, and Lehmbruck reflected their own fears that the era's changing sexual norms would lead to chaos. Even less would men have understood that their free-floating anxieties found women convenient targets.

These are the underlying psychological reasons that led Roosevelt to cultivate the manly icons of national identity so tirelessly, especially those produced by artists. Sculptors, he said, should never portray George Washington or Abraham Lincoln clad in a classical toga.[49] For Roosevelt, the toga's soft and dresslike folds that closely followed the contours of a statue's body detracted from the statue's ability to signify the nation's manhood. In 1908, when Roosevelt heard that the sculptor Augustus Saint-Gaudens intended to sculpt General William Tecumseh Sherman led by a winged Victory, he feared that Sherman's image would become a "folly which . . . portrays Graces, Muses, or Angels, obviously unreal and irrelevant, disporting themselves around an obviously fleshly hero." Roosevelt imagined the incongruity of sexually playful females tempting a semiclothed and sexually corruptible Sherman, an image as disgusting as

Figure 21. Edvard Munch, *Nude with Red Hair,* or *The Sin,* 1901

if Saint-Gaudens had placed cavorting nymphs around his "mighty statue of mighty Lincoln." Roosevelt simply could not bear to have national heroes, as he imagined them, seductively dressed and snared in erotic play with minions of feminine evil. In an address to the audience at a Saint-Gaudens exhibition at the Corcoran Art Gallery, a much-relieved Roosevelt praised the "extraordinary" finished equestrian statue of Sherman. The sculptor, Roosevelt said, captured the essential man; his grizzled, homely, democratic demeanor; and his "courage of tempered steel."[50]

Roosevelt extended his self-described protest against the degenerate effects of female sexuality to Rudyard Kipling's poem "The Vampire." Vampire stories became popular fare in England and the United States in the late nineteenth century, especially after Bram Stoker's *Dracula* (1897) translated medieval lore into a literary classic that expressed British racial phobias of Eastern Europeans. In this novel, Count Dracula journeys from Transylvania to England, bringing the incubus of vampirism to prey on pure English girls and transform them into seductive vampires.[51] Kipling said that he wrote his poem upon viewing Philip Burne-Jones's painting *The Vampire*, exhibited at a London gallery in 1897. An etching of the painting often accompanied the widely popular poem and appeared as the frontispiece for volume 10 of the *Sahib Edition of Rudyard Kipling* (figure 22).

In Burne-Jones's illustration and in Kipling's poem, the wild-haired, powerfully seductive vampire of the nineteenth-century male imagination straddles a prostrate man and raises her head, having just sunk her bared teeth into his neck. The dying man is in love, the poem explains, but with some alien and consuming thing he does not understand. Readers discover that this alien is actually the man's wife of many years. "A fool there was," Kipling writes, who with "honor and faith . . . wasted years, tears, and work of . . . head and hand" on "the woman who did not care." Considering the woman his "lady fair," the fool is blind to her true nature—merely "a rag, a bone, and a hank of hair." "Some of him lived, but most of him died," Kipling laments, as the man succumbs to the archetypal predatory female despoiler, who, sated from having sucked his blood, rises to wreak death on other unsuspecting and well-intentioned men.[52]

The sucking of blood was a common Victorian metaphor for moral and material draining; thus, the vampire wants not only sex, but to consume the man entirely. Her slow, sexual draining of the man's life juices produces a death in life and renders the man blind to his plight and helpless to prevent his fate ("a fool must follow his natural bent"). The man approaches his vampire-lover with "honor and faith," yet "his goods he spent" in trying unsuccessfully to satisfy her. The man's final shame is not

Figure 22. Philip Burne-Jones, *The Vampire*, c. 1897

the degradation of moral and material bankruptcy, or even that the vampire drains him and renders him useless. His shame lies in the waste of his efforts on a woman who obliviously "threw him aside," never knowing or caring what she did. Both Kipling and Roosevelt interpreted the drained and helpless man in terms of empire, for his final degradation renders him useless to the nation.[53]

When, in 1894, Roosevelt wrote to thank his friend Kipling for sending a book of poems that included "The Vampire," he did not express the reservations that he later confided privately to Elbert Hubbard: "The Vampire," he wrote, has "always struck me as being in a decadent tone."[54] Perhaps Roosevelt did not convey this to Kipling because of the mutual admiration each man had for the other. After all, Roosevelt considered himself and Owen Wister the American Kiplings. Perhaps he hesitated to criticize the poem to its author because he found himself without the proper vocabulary to protest a horribly degrading and death-dealing act of penetration by a sexually dominant female. He did, however, ask Kipling not to "think me altogether a prig" in wishing that the story ended with an uplifting "moral," one that presumably would have left the man as master of his own energies.[55]

Through the same lens, Roosevelt read an equally dangerous social and moral degeneracy in the pacifism and sexual preoccupations of Leo Tolstoy, whom he called a "hysterical and morbid type of reformer" who "has in him certain dreadful qualities of the moral pervert."[56] In Tolstoy's novel *Anna Karenina*, Roosevelt found one character, Kitty, "perfectly healthy," but the title character "prey to the most violent passion, . . . and her reasoning power so unbalanced" that she could be described as "in a certain sense insane."[57] Singling out Tolstoy's "The Kreutzer Sonata" as a shocking tale of modern debauchery, Roosevelt charged that the "filthy and repulsive book" presented "gross and criminal aberrations of the sexual passion."[58] Tolstoy's preoccupation with what Roosevelt called the "worst excesses" of sexual passion indicated, as the president wrote to Robert Grant, that "the man has a diseased mind. He is not wholesome. He is not sane, and therefore . . . prone to the hysterical excess of a wicked kind."[59]

What "excesses" could have provoked such an outburst? "All men have upon our souls hundreds of the most varied and terrible crimes in regards to women," The protagonist of "The Kreutzer Sonata" claims. Men are guilty not just for imposing their sexual excesses on women but for "killing" those who die in childbirth. Because all women fall under men's desires, he equates upper-class marriage to prostitution, both "swinish union" held together by men's "animal excesses." Yet while the protagonist condemns men's treatment of women, he blames women for purposefully seducing men, who have no control over their sexual will. "Ladies of high society" and prostitutes alike, Tolstoy wrote, make themselves into the same "weapon of sexual excitement, intoxicating men with their poison." They entice men through the "same costumes, the same perfumes, the same baring of arms, shoulders, and breasts . . . the same entertainments, dances, music and singing." "When I see a woman all dressed up," the protagonist exclaims, "I cannot help seeing something dangerous for men and illicit, and I feel like calling a policeman and asking protection against a peril, and demanding that the dangerous object be removed."[60]

"The Kreutzer Sonata" provoked the intense anxiety of the prig in Roosevelt, who denounced Tolstoy's frank discussions of "hideous evils attendant upon unregulated or twisted passion."[61] Both Roosevelt and Tolstoy deplored the sexual adventurousness of upper-class women and both understood the degrading consequences of men's passion for women. For Roosevelt, this passion suggested debauchery so degrading that once it was committed no one could atone for it. "Boys or men of foul life," he wrote in 1900, "cannot become good citizens, good Americans, until they change; and even after the change scars will be left on their souls."[62] For Roosevelt, the fundamental evil of sexual license was that it sullied men not just morally or socially, but politically, removing them forever from his ideal brotherhood. Although Rubens's corpulent nudes or an "obviously fleshly" General Sherman disgusted him, and although he and Tolstoy shared a revulsion for sexual pleasure, Roosevelt rarely spoke directly of sexual passion. When he did, it often was in vehement outbursts such as his strident condemnations of decadent art and literature.

Roosevelt's reaction to aggressive female sexuality likewise emerged in a 1904 letter to Amelia Glover, who had recently passed along to the president a letter from an unnamed Colorado woman who had written the editor of a local newspaper criticizing the president. Though its exact content is not clear, the critical letter was enclosed with Glover's letter to Roosevelt. In his vehement reply to Glover, Roosevelt equated the letter writer's "lies" with the despicable "ideal of womanhood" that the character Selma embodied in Robert Grant's *Unleavened Bread*. Roosevelt advised both women to read Grant's novel in order to learn of the abhorrent values Selma portrays—"especially in her sexual relations," which clearly repulsed him. "In all the ages," he fumed, "there has been no more contemptible ideal."[63] Writing to Grant the next year, Roosevelt revealed that the reason for his contempt was the prospect of female independence and easy divorce, which he believed showed an "atavistic return to the system of promiscuity" and lay behind the declining birthrate among whites. Grant had condemned easy divorce in a *Public Opinion* article, and Roosevelt responded by sending him a copy of a speech he had delivered before the National Congress of Mothers, deploring the declining birthrate and calling for nationally standardized and more restrictive divorce laws. Roosevelt told Grant, "I know that the effect on 'the Four Hundred' of easy divorce has been very bad. It has been shocking to me to hear young girls about to get married calmly speculating on about how long it will be before they get divorces."[64]

Few women provoked as strident an outburst from Roosevelt as Grant's Selma. The day after he finished reading *Unleavened Bread* in 1900, he wrote Grant that "I became so absorbed in it that I could not put it down until I finished it. It is melancholy, indeed a painful book, but it is the strongest study of American life that has been written for many years. I am delighted with it."[65] Selma, the *Unleavened Bread* of the title, is a modern, culturally refined, emancipated woman who, frustrated with domestic life, wants to participate in the nation's politics. Yet her unleavened, raw qualities—she is a vain, selfish, materialistic social climber—render her nothing short of evil. As "proud as Lucifer and sometimes as beautiful," Grant writes, Selma teaches men a "new lesson," that they must defer to her devilish allure and fulfill her sexual and material needs. After her first marriage to an uneducated but prosperous varnish manufacturer somewhat beneath her station, she finds the notion of having children "vaguely disgusting" and indulges in sex only for pleasure. She finds her own unexpected pregnancy "irksome" and later neglects the child, who dies of an illness, after which she begins to practice birth control. In succession, each of her three husbands "inevitably" falls prey to the "witchery of her intense moods" and to the "germs of intimacy." The first husband she uses as an economic stepping stone, the second dies from overwork trying to fulfill her insatiable demands both for sex and for the material trappings of high society, and the third becomes the unwitting dupe of her political aspirations.[66]

At the novel's beginning, Selma does not aspire to be a destroyer of men. Initially content with the best small-town, republican tradition, she appreciates a liberal, socially fluid society where men of talent and diligence rise, elevating their women along with them. Though raised to live within modest means, she moves to New York, where the city's "finery" dazzles her. She soon replaces her "stern democratic faith" with a disdain for her lower-middle-class origins, which she transforms into an engulfing, homogenizing morass, "despair[ing] to see the long lines of houses, street after street, and to think she was [once] merely a unit, unknown by name, in this great sea of humanity." Thwarted by class and gender barriers and frustrated by her own social ambitions, she finally realizes that equality is a "sham," that social distinctions are everything, and that "the better sorts *are* better." Having paid the price of admittance to high society by abandoning republican virtue, she agrees with a wealthy matron who remarks that there is "something in the Declaration of Independence about being free and equal that was put in as a bluff to console salesladies." Though men of all stations can vote, the society matron concedes, "equality ends there," and sophisticated women like Selma should not be deceived "by the Sunday-School, Fourth of July . . . [sentiments] of the American people. . . . [They] are at heart a nation of gamblers," each striving for the economic and political power that belongs exclusively to the rich.[67]

Selma becomes a striver too, but toward the end of the novel, high society closes its doors in her face, and she, in turn, repudiates her rich acquaintances. Now the lives of the "the ultra conservative, solid, stupid aristocratic set" who live in "crude . . . barbaric splendor" in their Fifth Avenue mansions remind her "instinctively of Sodom and Gomorrah." She imagines that an "angel with a flaming sword" comes to destroy the houses and their owners "as symbols of mammon and contraband to God." Because she cannot join the envied rich herself, she fails to understand why such people should be allowed to exist.[68]

Grant intended his character Selma to expose those lower-middle- and working-class women whose sexual demands degraded men, whose materialism subverted republicanism, and whose social pretension bred class envy. Roosevelt, who never tired of valorizing democratic leveling and hard-working husbands, was horrified with Selma's emphasis on class differences. In his broadly homogeneous national ideal, any emphasis on class seemed undemocratic because it could quickly lead to dangerous class antagonisms. Selma's denunciation of the lavish Fifth Avenue mansions may have made any man of wealth uneasy, not just Roosevelt, whose father's home at 28 East Twentieth Street prominently displayed the family's wealth, and who himself purchased his first home at 6 West Fifty-Seventh Street. From his early twenties onward, Roosevelt was an important figure in the social life of New York's Knickerbocker set, and along with members of the city's other elite families, he enjoyed the invitations of Mrs. William Astor. While he never hid the inherited wealth and family prominence that automatically conferred membership in upper-class hunt and polo clubs, he cultivated in political rhetoric his oneness with working-class men.

Making Selma an erotically charged, sexually promiscuous, willful, and domineering woman, Grant deployed sexual metaphors to clarify class distinctions, holding up against Selma's model of class-conscious womanhood an image of the ideal bourgeois wife, sexually demure, politically innocent, properly mannered, economically frugal, and knowing her place. Against Selma's weak-willed husbands, Roosevelt premised male middle-class identity on a husband's ability to be master in his own house, on his self-discipline and his effectiveness in disciplining, especially the moral excesses of a wife who has become sexually demanding or obsessed with material things. In an era when bourgeois men delayed marriage until they could provide a decent family income, the dual regime of sexual and economic restraint required them to show great self-discipline, which the women of the household must mirror. Like the victims of Kipling's vampire, Selma's husbands unwittingly seek the corrupting charms of a woman who ruins them with the twin weapons of her own sexuality and an obsessive consumer culture that has adopted feminine allure as its most powerful icon. Thus, in a manner characteristic of Roosevelt's age, the psychological disturbances men found in erotic feminine display came to equal the allure and threat of modernity.[69]

Roosevelt employed these very distinctions of class identity and sexual and economic austerity when he contrasted Grant's Selma with Owen Wister's *Lady Baltimore* (1906). Wister's title character, Roosevelt wrote to the author in 1906, constitutes a "sturdy protest against what is sordid, against . . . spangle-covered baseness, against brutal greed and sensuality and vacuity." For Wister and for Roosevelt, who admitted his own "possibly priggish way of looking at novels," *Lady Baltimore*'s two female characters epitomized the extremes of "decent" and "sordid" womanhood. Roosevelt told Wister that his novel "teaches admiration of manliness and womanliness . . . as understood by those capable of holding a high ideal." Praising the novel's "good, straight, decent people," Roosevelt admitted to Wister that he "earnestly" wished to see "the most effective kind of warfare waged against exactly what you denounce. Smash vacuous, divorce-ridden Newport."[70] Wister, similarly angered about sullied womanhood, might like to smash Philadelphia, at least the Board of Education meetings his otherwise genteel wife attended as a member. "I have at times a rush of blind feudal hatred," he wrote his mother, "at seeing my girl on her feet in public, talking to men—and such men."[71]

Wister's novel of polite life takes place not in the Newport playground, but among the genteel folk in turn-of-the-century Charleston, South Carolina, the last bastion of "good" American society. In a Southern social hothouse, amid a great deal of bowing, blushing, and honorable propriety, upper-class white men and women hold out against declining standards of manners, decency, and chastity. The novel's chaste Miss Eliza La Heu represents one of the "last of [her] kind, the end of the chain [of] the bold original stock, the great race that made our glory grow." For Wister, the racial element underpinned what had been, for the likes of Miss La Heu anyway, a "well-knit country" with that "exquisite personal unitedness" among people of the "good old native blood." Modern disruptions brought on by upper-class greed, the "invasion of the proletariat," and the resulting race mixture could be quickly ended, according to the novel's moral protagonist, "if we could only deport the negroes and Newport together."[72]

In Wister's novel and in his own imagination, the nation's "original" Anglo-Saxon racial stock was fast disappearing "in the breathless, competing North," where white men were being "ground into oblivion between the clashing trades of the competing men and the clashing jewels and chandeliers of their competing wives." The novel centers on a high-stakes mating game in which the drunken dukes of a declining European royal line come to America to court and marry the daughters of rich American republicans. The chaste Eliza vies for the attentions of one eligible bachelor with the novel's anti-heroine, Hortense Rieppe, a red-haired "specimen devotee" of the Newport cult, itself the "rottenness of smart society." Her "beauty flash[ing] with devilment," Hortense lives the life of the New Woman, who smokes, orders highballs, and revels with young rich men in autos and steam yachts. "Insolent," "experienced," "sophisticated," and "constructed for pleasure," this "bacchanalian" woman seduces wealthy men for sport. In a frenzied and sexually charged atmosphere, the Newport crowd, driven by "the cold fear of ennui [which] gnaws at their vitals," seeks higher but ever-diminishing plateaus of lavish and outlandish entertainment, a bored quest that provides the entering wedge for women like Hortense.[73]

For Roosevelt, as for many middle-class men of his era, the implications of the sexually free New Woman trading sex for material goods formed a common basis for his strong reaction to the stories of Kipling, Tolstoy, Grant, and Wister. Her effect on men, marriage, and the family concerned every patriotic man, and prompted one man to ask in *Lady Baltimore*, "Is the whole country sick?" and another to confirm, "Sick to the marrow, my friend."[74] Roosevelt believed that marriage and the family were the very foundations of the state and that a woman's highest duty was fulfilled in her separate sphere, that of homemaking and childbearing. Men should seek the ideal mates, those for whom "the home in its widest and fullest sense should be the prime end of life," Roosevelt wrote to Harvard psychologist Hugo Munsterberg. "Able, intellectual, cultivated women . . . make the best wives and mothers," he continued; they were "infinitely better than the vain, frivolous, shallow, tricky type."[75] When women like Selma or Hortense broke those bonds, he was horrified.

Although at the turn of the century most people would have said that the new companionate marriages were made for love, upper-class marriages still revolved around considerations of good breeding and property, and marrying "beneath one's station" was looked upon with horror.

Figure 23. "An Awful Possibility under Our Blue Laws as Roosevelt Enforces Them," *World* (New York)

Roosevelt was outraged when his free-living cousin Cornelius Roosevelt, semi-exiled in Paris, "distinguished himself by marrying a French actress! He is a disgrace to the family—the vulgar brute. P.S. She turns out to be a *mere courtesan! A harlot!*"[76] By bringing a near-prostitute into the family, his cousin had, in Roosevelt's estimation, betrayed not merely his class, but his entire cohort of American men. Cartoonists, as usual, picked up on Roosevelt's discomfort, as in a New York *World* cartoon depicting him as a Puritan burning the New Woman as a witch (figure 23).

Vampirish, sexually predatory, and tricky types like Robert Grant's Selma or alluringly lascivious types like Owen Wister's Hortense, Tolstoy's women in "The Kreutzer Sonata," and even Cornelius's wife figured in Roosevelt's fears of race suicide. For Roosevelt this matter loomed "fundamentally [and] infinitely more important that any other question in this country." A woman who "desire[s] to be independent," who "dislikes having children," and who engages in "mere vapid pleasure . . . is in effect a criminal against the race and should be an object of contemptuous abhorrence by all healthy people."[77] In Roosevelt's interpretation, a woman such as Selma, by masquerading as an ideal woman, intentionally sought to corrupt white men and subvert the race-nation.

In Roosevelt's estimation, Tolstoy and Kipling were the greatest fiction writers of his day, each furnishing an ideal type of his race and nation. Though both men wrote of female subversion, Roosevelt was willing to forgive Kipling the lurid scene in "The Vampire" because he thought that almost all Kipling's works contained moral lessons. Tolstoy, however, could not be let off so easily, for in creating a character similar to Grant's Selma, he, like Dracula, sowed in the West the seeds of Eastern racial degeneration. "After all," Roosevelt wrote while discussing the two writers with the aristocratic British diplomat Spring Rice, "it is the Slav, and not the Englishman, who shows decadence."[78]

For Tolstoy to liken marriage to prostitution and to equate a married noblewoman with a courtesan blurred the boundaries Roosevelt maintained between high- and low-class women and between the commercialized, criminalized sex of the streets and the sanctified sex of the marriage bed. Above all, this blurring intimated that just as prostitutes' degeneracy tainted upper-class male clients, so did the sexual predations of respectable women of those men's own class. It seemed to many men, not just Roosevelt, that aggressive female pleasure was on the rise among women of all classes and threatened to dissolve male ego-boundaries. It was as if lust were some contagion that female bodies carried—a social disease that might burst its bounds, overwhelming unsuspecting men and casting them into debauchery and race suicide.

"Fruitless pleasure," to Roosevelt, appeared equally unwholesome in men. Roosevelt described it in florid language that revealed his anxieties about the spread of contagion and the muddying of absolutes. Sexual deviance had already appeared in France, he wrote in 1899, where "the race has begun to decrease and the nation is decaying mainly because of the way men and women look upon the relations between the sexes."[79] In a 1901 address in Minnesota at the outset of his presidency, he warned Americans against "that vainest of all vain pursuits—the pursuit of mere pleasure as a sufficient end in itself. The willfully idle man, like the willfully barren woman, has no place in a sane, healthy, and vigorous community. . . . The gross and hideous selfishness for which each stands defeats even its own miserable aims. . . . The happiest woman is she who has borne and brought up many healthy children [and] the happiest man is he who has toiled hard."[80] Men's pursuit of pleasure was connected, in Roosevelt's mind, not just with frivolous sex, but also with prostitution and syphilis. Having sex with presumably racially inferior, lower-class prostitutes, he thought, displaced "race-strengthening" with sex that not only was degrading and criminal but also could produce insanity. Criminality, insanity, sexual perversity, and poverty often came together in the Victorian mind, most notably where the person of the prostitute was concerned.

The allure of independent, sexually available women, however repugnant they were in polite society, underwrote the great appeal of the new subculture of prostitution that allowed the sporting male, married or unmarried, middle or working class, to seek sex outside the legal, economic, and emotional entanglements of marriage. *Sporting* here refers not hunting or playing games but to seeking sexual favors from certain women. As Timothy Gilfoyle explains in *City of Eros*, married upper-class men frequented prostitutes in New York City between 1820 and 1920, knowing that they could keep the vice-ridden tenderloin district separate from idealized home and family even as prostitution became an integral, if ostentatious, part of commercial entertainment in bars, theaters, and restaurants and at formal balls.[81] As urban public and commercial life increasingly determined norms of courting and sexual behavior, popular sporting male culture held out individual choice and personal pleasure as goals. Moral reformers, of course, saw the same freedoms as sin. For scientifically minded Victorians, the danger of syphilis and the hereditary nature of social deviance made intercourse between men and "degenerate" prostitutes extremely risky. Many men, not just moralizing reformers, began to harbor uneasiness about the fate of the nation's white male population. As prostitution became more visible and reform efforts increased in the decades before the turn of the century, the public was less inclined to be understanding toward prostitutes as victims of the city's evils than they had been early in the century. Now, true to prevailing fantasies of feminine evil, prostitutes, like vampires, were thought to spread evil by ruining unsuspecting males morally and financially. Against these fantasies, and much to the dismay of reformers like Roosevelt, a countercurrent of naturalism in literature and art arose toward the end of the century, one that portrayed prostitutes sympathetically as the products of social conditions, somewhat harmless and not so different from anyone else.

THE BODY BESET

If these cultural assaults pressed some men to fantasize a manhood beset by evil and degeneracy, scientific discoveries about the basis of bodily fatigue compounded their anxieties. Beginning in the 1870s, scientists began to describe the physical laws governing heat and energy. The first law of thermodynamics, the law of conservation of energy, posited a stable universe full of indestructible energy, while the second, the law of entropy, paradoxically predicted a downward spiral and ultimate exhaustion of that same energy. Thus theories of physics, like biological, political, and racial theories, held out the possibility for either progress or decline. Practitioners in the newly professionalized sciences of physiology, psychology, and sociology assumed that the same physical laws that governed the material world also governed human bodies, and investigators and society at large set about applying those laws. By 1900, a *Popular Science Monthly* article, "The Human Body as an Engine," explained how scientists had developed instruments for determining the body's metabolism by measuring its electrical and thermal energies, and held out the promise that men, though not women, could possess the unlimited energy of a machine or the universe.[82]

Prominent among the scientists who invented mechanical instruments to assess male energy was Dudley A. Sargent, director of Harvard's Hemenway Gymnasium after 1879, who included a chapter titled "The Physical Proportions of the Typical Man" in his book *Athletic Sports* (1897). Sargent developed a "uniform system of measurements" for selected bodily properties, with which he formulated "standards" by which to judge men's "symmetry and strength." Ignoring the law of entropy, Sargent maintained that the nation's "better class of men" could realize a near-perfect body through strenuous exercise and that they were obligated by patriotic duty to do so. Sargent's idealized "eugenic body" for individuals had its political complement in his vision of an "imperialist physique" for the nation, an " 'innately' superior moral, mental, and physical nature that can express all forms of power."[83]

By the end of the century, however, scientists had abandoned some of this optimism and reluctantly concluded that bodies did not follow the physical laws governing the efficient conversion and expenditure of energy, but were instead more subject to thermodynamics' second law—that of fatigue and entropy. Scientific and medical literature pessimistically pictured health as depending on the temporary conservation but ultimate loss of the body's energy, including its mental or nervous energy. Interpreting the body's mechanical energy and its will as the twin sources of its muscular force, scientists neatly extended the physical laws of the body to the mind, making it, Cynthia Russett remarks, "liable to all the evils that flesh was heir to."[84] By the early twentieth century, French physiologist Théodule-Armand Ribot and others had turned energy conservation into a psychological issue, having discovered, they thought, the sources of male neuroses. In the workplace, technological and managerial imperatives disciplined men externally, but more importantly, men were disciplined internally by a "psychophysiology" of the will, a force that drove men to compete, and that, for some, resulted in a condition of mental and moral exhaustion known as male neurasthenia.[85]

First described in the 1860s by a New York physician, George Miller Beard, in *A Practical Treatise on Nervous Exhaustion* (1880), and expounded more fully in his *American Nervousness: Its Causes and Consequences* (1881) and *Sexual Neurasthenia* (1898), male neurasthenia became the medical way to blame "modern civilization" for white men's loss of virility. By 1900, nervous disease among white, middle-class, urban men, even—or especially—in prominent men like William James and Owen Wister, had pushed male neurasthenia to "near epidemic proportions."[86] For Beard, the pressures of industrial life and sedentary living and the corresponding increase in intellectual life depleted the finite supply of nerve force. The chief cause of male neurasthenia was overwork—especially "mental labor," "ambition," and stress. In the body's zero-sum thermodynamic economy, the brain's work competed with the body's work for energy, exhausting citified men who thought too much or bought stocks on margin. In the worst cases, the disease led to a complete breakdown.[87]

According to Beard, "industrialism" had brought the white-collar jobs that produced male neurasthenia. In the late nineteenth century, work outside the home was the chief factor in determining a man's social identity—how others saw him and how he understood himself. It was widely held that through his own efforts, the middle-class self-made man created his own and his family's status. His wife, in keeping with her domestic station, furnished their home and entertained in a style that reflected and bolstered the couple's social position. A middle-class man's ability to maintain this status depended on his job, and white-collar employment had greatly expanded along with the economies of scale in the new industrial economy. On the eve of the Civil War, 88 percent of American men were farmers or self-employed businessmen; by 1870, that proportion had dropped to 66 percent, and by 1910 it was less than half. Through these same years the demands of large corporations for engineers, managers, accountants, executives, salesmen, and clerks steadily increased the percentage of white-collar workers to one-fifth of the male workforce by 1910. As the size of the industrial bureaucracy grew, the chances for upward mobility into executive levels in the company diminished, as did the opportunities for men to find independence and self-actualization in the workplace. Workplace frustrations increased the likelihood that men would gravitate toward affirmations of manhood outside their jobs. If they found no such outlet, Beard held, workplace stresses and the pressures for material consumption from socially competitive wives caused men to develop male neurasthenia.[88]

Although women developed neurasthenia as often as men, Beard diagnosed it differently for each sex. For women of the "comfortable classes," "mental activity" produced "bright eyes" and "sprightliness of countenance," both of which only superficially indicated intellectual capacity since women's minds were kaleidoscopes of surface impressions that rendered them "exquisitely susceptible" to suggestion. "All of female character is in the clothes," Beard wrote, "for him who can read their language."[89] Superficiality and susceptibility, together with childbearing, made high-strung upper-class women prime candidates for nervous diseases. In contrast with women's neurasthenia, which derived from pathological sources, Beard thought, men's came from overwork—in other words, from fulfilling their social responsibilities. Doctors who treated neurasthenic males, the historian E. Anthony Rotundo found, respected their patients, for they came from the ranks of society's most harried professionals. Doctors prescribed rest, fresh air, and exercise, or a trip to Europe for male neurasthenics. For female neurasthenics, doctors often prescribed isolation in a dim room with reduced sensory input, as Charlotte Perkins Gilman so vividly relates in *The Yellow Wallpaper* (1899). Doctors never imposed such a "cure" on men.[90]

If professional brainwork depleted the energy of middle-class men, the physical demands of industrial wage work did so for the industrial army of semiskilled and unskilled blue-collar workers. Together with the subdivided and deskilled labor processes introduced by modern management, mechanization and routinization had begun to separate individual workers from control or ownership of the labor process and to reduce them to extensions of the machine. In his influential *Social Problems* (1883), Henry George charged that labor-saving devices resulted in "positive evils" for workers by "degrading men into the position of mere feeders of machines"—a condition not thought degrading to women and children who toiled at the same unskilled jobs. Machines themselves became "absolutely injurious . . . rendering the workman more dependent; depriving him of skill and of opportunities to acquire it and his hope of improving it; cramping his mind, and in many cases distorting and enervating his body."[91] Though working-class men and women rarely had the luxury of being diagnosed with a nervous disease, some middle-class reformers and policymakers did at least worry over the ultimate effects of reducing republican yeomen to a nation of machine tenders. Roosevelt's worries about the working class, however, like his worries about women, apes, and danger, provoked his inner demons rather than eliciting any desire to reform the conditions of labor. Bypassing the criticisms of observers like George, Roosevelt centered his concerns for men's bodies around psychological urges to self-protection and self-hardening against failures of nerve and against sexual, moral, and economic loss.

HETEROSEXUAL ANXIETIES

As if all these psychological pressures were not enough, the invention of homosexuality in the late nineteenth century took place in the context of the emergence of aggressive masculinity, a heightened interest in the male body, and its correlate, and an obsession with male effeminacy. These uncertainties produced a need among men to separate and individuate their bodies from those of other men. Throughout the earlier half of the century, few restrictions governed men's touching or even caressing one another in ordinary social interactions. It had been common practice for men to sleep with other men in boarding houses and hotels, and pictures of athletic teams that adorned the pages of *Physical Culture* routinely showed men casually draping their limbs about one another. Gendered political language existed in the early national period, but it was usually employed as an abstraction rather than in ad hominem attacks, and it seldom directed attention to the male body. Thus, a man's virtue or his pastimes could be charged as effeminate, but seldom his person. Toward the end of the century, however, sexual epithets like *eunuch, sissy,* and *hermaphrodite* came into common usage to signify weak, timid, or submissive men who preferred the company of women and who, supposedly, could be recognized by their bodily traits.[92]

Preoccupations with the growing visibility of homosexual communities in large cities, Anthony Rotundo observes, "produced a powerful new weapon for maintaining the boundaries of manhood."[93] Medical and social scientists, armed with nineteenth-century theories of mental and social pathology, began to develop theories that defined homosexuality and redefined men's social relations to one another. Urban homosexuals whose behavior violated notions of normality drew the attention of police, who had rarely prosecuted homosexuality before 1860. By 1880, experts defined homosexuality as a pathology and imposed legal prescriptions against it in America and in England, where Oscar Wilde was an early victim. While visiting the United States in 1882, Wilde had dressed stylishly, penciled his eyebrows, and lived and traveled with great artistic flair, creating confusion about his effeminate behavior and seemingly indeterminate sexuality. If most Americans remained dimly aware of homosexuality, journalists helped reduce the confusion and make homosexuality an issue, avidly speculating on Wilde's visit with Walt Whitman and describing his youthful following in the cities he visited. An article in the *Brooklyn Daily Eagle* described "the school of gilded youth eager to embrace his peculiar tenets," and a *Washington Post* journalist wrote of those young men who painted their faces "to resemble those of girls." Journalists also portrayed Wilde's affinity for street boys, newsboys, messenger boys, stock boys, and especially bad boys, and closely recounted the national craze of Wilde impersonating and cross-dressing, and the brief appearance of an entire art genre of aesthetic and feminized style among men. A few men around the country, including a senator from New Jersey, courted and lived openly with younger men. Americans educated themselves on the seeming style of homosexual culture, and, contends Mary Blanchard, they initially viewed the homosexual "with tolerant good humor," but eventually found themselves uncomfortable with gender ambiguity. Wilde returned to England, where, in 1895, he was prosecuted as a homosexual, convicted of "gross indecency," and jailed.[94]

To appear ordinary, men now had to respond to a new category of difference, that of the homosexual, an imperative that immediately quashed the Victorian tradition of intense male friendships. Now men would not be fully masculine until they had excised from their person any beliefs or practices associated with dalliance, sodomy, masturbation, or anything else that suggested that they had succumbed to bodily desires.[95] Some homosexual men had attracted public attention by behaving effeminately or dressing as women, and bourgeois male heterosexuals assumed that this was typical of all homosexuals. Labeling an entire community with the outward attributes of some of its members focused the definition of homosexuality on external bodily appearance and behavior. As new norms of masculinity emphasized physical muscularity, homosexuality became coded with skinny bodies, weak spines, thin muscles, and deficient genitalia.

For heterosexual men with homoerotic urges, and for men who needed to repress emotionality, the homosexual emerged as a clearly defined binary category to which men could assign these unacceptable urges and feelings. As heterosexual men began to fear that any man could give over to such "tendencies," they needed to distance themselves from homosexuals and prove themselves "real" men. The more a man feared he might be or become a homosexual, Rotundo writes, "the more he needed to prove himself a man or—what was more difficult—come to terms with what was not manly about himself."[96] This repulsion signals less the "normal" man's chance of becoming a homosexual than that of him finding himself weak, emotional, or unable to perform sexually.

Normative or hegemonic masculinity, Ed Cohen explains, defined "normal" or "healthy" white, middle-class male sexuality, morality, and physicality over against anything considered degenerate. Manhood, which had been defined in the early nineteenth century in relation to boyhood and womanhood, now had to be defined in relation to the masculinity of other adult, white, middle- and upper-class men. Increasingly, men adopted strident negative referents for describing one another. Some emphasized the differences between men's masculine and feminine sides, the adventurous versus the timid, the assertive versus the bookish, or the militant over the peaceful.[97] Others began to contrast toughness with tenderness and to fix a gendered hierarchy with each of these qualities arranged within the male world of work and politics. Though the United States had no notoriously gay man equivalent to Wilde to heighten public awareness and to serve as a locus of public denunciation, men cultivating a manly demeanor found plenty of pacifists, aesthetes, reformers, and socialists to decry. Accusations of homosexuality became a powerful tool for stigmatizing the unmanly man, and ultimately any man.

Rafford Pyke explained "What Men Like in Men" in a 1902 article in *Cosmopolitan* that was almost entirely a tirade against sissies' bodily attributes. A sissy was smooth-faced and vacuous, and usually had light brown hair and pale blue eyes. His mouth was "wavery," his lips "imperfectly closed," his shoulders sloped. He was ungainly, his neck too long, his Adam's apple too protruding, and his hands and feet too large. A sissy's asexuality made him "absolutely harmless" around women and "essentially a tame cat." Altogether "incomplete," a sissy made "normal men," feel "a most intense repulsion."[98]

Against such "men who were not men," Roosevelt was a master of the political invective. He hurled the most humiliating criticisms at other leaders, criticisms that created images of the undesired body in contrast to that of the ideal represented by him and other "better men."[99] McKinley, he said, had the backbone of a chocolate éclair. Some men's "shoulders slope like a champagne bottle." Mugwumps were "political hermaphrodites." Henry George typified the "emasculated professional humanitarian." Opponents of naval appropriations, a group for which Roosevelt reserved special ire, constituted a "small bunch of eunuchs," and one was a "circumcised skunk." Anti-imperialists were "beings whose cult is nonvirility." He thought that the "lunatic reformer" in Eugene Fitch Ware's poem "Retrospective" was aptly described as "our short-haired female brother."[100] He decried the "utter physical worthlessness" that rendered army officers poor horsemen and made them "objects of ridicule." To strengthen the officers, Roosevelt issued an executive order requiring each to "prove his ability to walk fifty miles, or ride one hundred, in three days." To quell a congressional outcry at the extremity of this demand, Roosevelt himself rode ninety-eight miles in a January storm on frozen roads in a little over seventeen hours, shaming the officers and congressmen who had protested.[101] He wrote to a friend that the country harbored an "immense multitude of philanthropists, Congressmen, newspaper editors, publicists, [and] softheaded mothers . . . who think that life ought to consist of perpetual shrinking from effort, danger and pain."[102] Sometimes Roosevelt was more direct. In one case he charged a sitting president with being effeminate: in 1916, enraged over Woodrow Wilson's reluctance to declare war on Germany, Roosevelt called the president a "physically cowardly demagogue" and a "white-handy Miss Nancy," a term men used to refer to womanish men they thought to be prudish, overly cultivated, or cowardly.[103]

With such words, Roosevelt helped create an entire cultural category of men whose lack of virility arose from what he supposed were female qualities. Hermaphrodites, eunuchs, sissies, Miss Nancys, and female brothers lacked proper, or properly used, male genitalia, a deficiency that left them little more than women and incapable of the masculine rationality and hardness required for practical politics. For Roosevelt to refer to circumcision in an insult suggested that to him, and presumably to many men of his era, the practice tampered with a man's virility. Saying that a man had a soft and creamy white mass for a backbone implied at best that he could not stand unassisted and at worst that he had a limp penis. Such insults transformed ordinary somatic differences into markers of behavior and made manliness into a political contest. By insisting that out-of-shape officers "felt shame" and that the nation's small navy was an object of international ridicule, and by calling a Democratic president a coward, Roosevelt linked the emotional and bodily vulnerabilities of his targets to their political viability, and in doing so, constructed a national politics of exaggerated hypermasculinity.

By the early twentieth century, middle-class men had defined the realms in which American manhood lay in doubt. Amid scientific warnings and images of national decline, the challenges to male physical and economic viability from the New Woman and male neurasthenia created threats equal to those of the exhaustion of races, the death of nations, and the entropy of the universe. Roosevelt figured prominently among the writers and social theorists who linked the thermodynamic economy of male bodies and the nervous condition of male minds to the health and fate of the nation. He did not invent the stigma of energy loss, emasculation, homosexuality, or race suicide; nor did he invent the threat of female aggressiveness, but he staked individual male honor and the nation's survival on the nation's ability to fortify its males against those dangers. Most importantly, through social Darwinism, race theory, and progressive social thought, he linked men's inner demons to the larger political culture, helping them to identify the social factors that seemingly produced such trepidation.

Cowboy Soldiers

Is America a
weakling to shrink
from the world-
work?
—Theodore
Roosevelt, to the
1900 Republican
National
Convention

I owe more than I
can ever express to
the West.
—Theodore
Roosevelt, "In
Cowboy Land"

For those men at the turn of the century who were psychologically ripe for models of essential masculinity,
Roosevelt almost single-handedly caused a "sudden,
radical shift," Theodore Greene argues, in the American
hero model. "It was one of those utterly unthinkable co-
incidences," William Allen White, the Kansas editor, remarked, "that a man of Roosevelt's enormous energy
should come to the Presidency of exactly that country
which at exactly that time was going through a transi-
tional period—critical, dangerous, and but for him terrible."[1] Roosevelt emerged as a central purveyor of the
cowboy-soldier hero model because he more than any
man of his age harnessed the tantalizing freedom of cowboys to address the social and psychological needs that
arose from deep personal sources of frustration, anxiety,
and fear. More than any other he sensed that ordinary
men needed a clearly recognizable and easily appropriated hero who enacted themes about the body; the need
for extremity, pain, and sacrifice; and the desire to exclude some men and bond with others. In one seamless
cowboy-soldier-statesman-hero life, Roosevelt crafted
the cowboy ethos consciously and lived it zealously, providing men an image and a fantasy enlisted in service to
the race-nation.[2]

Rather than creating the new archetype, Roosevelt
accelerated and focused several cultural themes that
converged in it. As we have noted, men were changing
their ideas of how to be men, appropriating more aggressive models in response to a growing sense of male
diminishment. The republican heroes of antebellum
America, Greene found by studying elite magazines,
consisted largely of those gentlemen, scholars, and pa-
triots whose reputations rested less on their wealth than
on evidence of their character—honesty, sobriety, hard
work, and civic service. By century's end these heroes

had been joined by Daniel Boone, Leatherstocking, and Civil War generals, but while all remained enormously popular, they somehow fell short in providing what was needed in a specifically modern hero.[3] In keeping with changing models of masculinity, Greene says, mass-circulation magazines began to feature a Napoleonic "idol of power," a man of action who used iron will and "animal magnetism" to crush his rivals and dominate nature. Biographers of plutocrats and robber barons encouraged readers to envision themselves in a social Darwinist world of ruthless competition where character alone appeared effeminate and sentimentalism dangerous. Earlier notions of manliness had counseled reason over passion; now the hero must unleash his "forcefulness."[4]

Enter a new type of charismatic male personality after 1870, a cowboy soldier operating in the new venue of the American West on sheer strength of will and physicality. Eastern readers instantly recognized him as more masculine precisely because he met the psychological desires in their imagination, making them into masters of their own fate, propelling them into violent adventure and comradeship, believing them at home in nature, not in the hothouse interiors of office buildings or middle-class homes.[5] Writers pitched the cowboy ethos against Christian values of mercy, empathy, love, and forgiveness, against domestic responsibility and the job demands that complicated men's lives and dissolved their masculine will. The cowboy was not interested in saving souls or finding spiritual purity or assigning meaning to death. His code of conduct arose as he struggled against the overwhelming wildness of men and beasts and carved out a prairie existence with guns, ropes, and barbed wire. Readers suspended ordinary morality as they fantasized about life at the margins of civilization and sampled forbidden pleasures of taming, busting, subduing, shooting, hanging, and killing.[6]

The cowboy cult drew on other important cultural themes as well. Its racial component arose in part from developing notions of national unity that began to overcome Civil War sectionalism. As industrial society's racial and class tensions grew and war wounds healed, Nina Silber finds, Northerners adopted a more sympathetic view of Southern white manhood, one in which Southern elites came to be admired for their racial acumen. Northerners abandoned critical views of slavery for nostalgic reminiscences of plantation life in which white Southern men had effectively managed a racial society, keeping blacks where they belonged and protecting white women's virtue. In the theaters, novels, and traveling shows of the 1890s, popular themes of happy plantation slaves reflected Northern acceptance of the Southern white view of race and the Jim Crow limitations on suffrage, mobility, education, and economic life. Even if many, though not all, Northerners drew the line at excusing lynching, Silber observes, they nevertheless accepted the idea that Southern white men lynched black "rapists" in the attempt to prove themselves men. Concerns about protecting Southern womanhood reflected Northern men's anxieties about promiscuous sexual behavior and the preservation of women's proper sphere. Finding a common ground of white manliness among former enemies, Silber explains, helped Northern whites to "cast African-Americans outside the boundaries of their Anglo-Saxon nation," to romanticize Southern notions of chivalry, and to justify turning Southern race relations over to Southern whites entirely.[7]

Northerners drew racialized bonds of white brotherhood around men so recently considered traitors by conjuring an abstracted, essentialized white manhood untainted by sectional or class divisions. In the 1890s, the appearance of Flag Day and veterans commemorations and organizations like the Daughters of the American Revolution emphasized sectional harmony and elevated a new form of nationalism based not on identifiable values, but on an empty and exceedingly blind loyalty. In an 1895 Memorial Day speech, "The Soldier's Faith," given at Harvard's Soldier's Field, a football arena named in honor of six of the school's Civil War dead, Oliver Wendell Holmes Jr. best expressed this new patriotism: "The faith is true and adorable which leads a soldier to throw away his life in obedience to a blindly accepted duty, a cause in which he little understands."[8] Such logic, which placed unthinking dutifulness over understanding, left little room for moral discretion and made blind response a virtue. Such martial abstractions rallied many men, patriotic speakers knew. In the installation ceremony for the General William Tecumseh Sherman monument in Washington, D.C., Roosevelt honored the "valor and devotion to duty" of former Confederate as well as Union veterans, for the Confederate soldiers had merely responded to a "loyalty toward what they regarded as right."[9]

These abstractions suited well both the demands of national unity and the myth of the cowboy as a loner true to his own code of honor. The cowboy style of manliness drew on the antebellum notion that white men possessed the core, essential quality that Melville's Ishmael detected in Starbuck, the *Pequod*'s first mate, who radiated "that immaculate manliness we feel within ourselves, so far within us, that it remains intact though all the outer character seems gone."[10] Toward century's end, Mark Twain, one of Roosevelt's favorite interpreters of the American West, identified this essence in the "magnificent, glorious giants" who tamed the American frontier:

It was a driving, vigorous, restless population in those days. . . . It was the *only* population of the kind that the world has even seen gathered together. . . . For, observe, it was an assemblage of two hundred thousand young men—not simpering, dainty, kid-gloved weaklings, but stalwart, muscular, dauntless young braves, brimful of push and energy, and royally endowed with every attribute that goes to make up a peerless and magnificent manhood—the very pick and choice of the world's glorious ones. No women, no children, no gray and stooping veterans—none but erect, bright-eyed, quick-moving, strong-handed young giants—the strangest population, the finest population, the most gallant host that ever rode down the startled solitudes of an unpeopled land.[11]

In Twain's heroes, it was not virtuous character or principled action but a forceful physicality, totally male and forever young, that primed his idealized giants to ride over smaller beings and virgin landscapes, doing what Roosevelt later called the "world-work" of soldier statesmen. Jacob Riis, only one among many who avowed that Roosevelt embodied in real life the masculine essence Melville and Twain expressed in literature, predicted that America "shall make of [Roosevelt] a king in his own right, by his undimmed manhood,"[12] In depicting a "royally endowed," "immaculate," and "peerless and magnificent" manhood, Melville, Twain, and Riis uncovered an essentialism born of a desire for an aristocratic, exclusionary yet unifying, purified strongman. "If this sounds like a prescription for Theodore Roosevelt," Greene points out, "it was."[13]

THE CRAFTED COWBOY

For an Easterner to cross the divide into essential manhood, he must somehow appropriate the amoral energy of the American West that Mark Twain had described. Roosevelt's own cowboy-soldier life testified to that, but first he had to create a persona that he most surely was not born with. He entered the New York state assembly in 1881 at age twenty-three, having overcome poor health just like his idol Abraham Lincoln. He still appeared unmanly, and newspapers and his fellow assemblymen ridiculed his "squeaky" voice and dandified clothing, referring to him as "Jane-Dandy," "Punkin-Lily," and "our own Oscar Wilde."[14] The New York *World* proclaimed him "chief of the dudes."[15] Duly insulted, he began to construct a new physical image around appropriately virile Western decorations and settings, foregrounding the bodily attributes of a robust outdoorsman that were becoming new features in the nation's political iconography.

At age twenty-five, on his first trip to the Dakota badlands in 1883, Roosevelt purchased a ranch, bought a herd of cattle, hired ranch hands, and, spending considerable time there, began to develop his Western image. He took "obvious delight," his younger cousin Nicholas observed, in the "apparently pathological extremes" of his exploits in the Dakotas— "rides of seventy miles or more in a day, hunting hikes of fourteen to sixteen hours, stretches in the saddle in roundups of as long as forty hours."[16] During his early years as a ranchman, Roosevelt's appearance, in studio photos at least, suggested a Leatherstocking frontiersman of the eighteenth-century Appalachian wilderness. In 1883 or 1884, he posed in a fringed buckskin outfit, complete with hunting cap, moccasins, cartridge belt, silver dagger, and rifle (figure 24). Yet without Western attire, a horse, or an open prairie, he still looked like an Eastern would-be.

In 1885, returning East after a bighorn hunting trip to Montana, Roosevelt had another studio photo made. This time he appeared as a self-consciously overdressed yet recognizable Western cowboy posed as bold and determined, armed and ready for action (figure 25). "You would be amused to see me," he wrote to Henry Cabot Lodge in 1884, in my "broad sombrero hat, fringed and beaded buckskin shirt, horse hide chaparajos or riding trousers, and cowhide boots, with braided bridle and silver spurs."[17] To his sister Bamie, he boasted, "I now look like a regular cowboy dandy, with all my equipments finished in the most expensive style."[18] Only the fringed buckskin shirt remained from his Leatherstocking outfit. Buckskin, he said, represented America's "most picturesque and distinctively national dress," attire worn by Daniel Boone and Davy Crockett and by the "reckless, dauntless Indian fighters" who led the "white advance throughout all our Western lands."[19] Buckskin and whiteness notwithstanding, this 1885 image still seems forced, and his attention focused on the costs, accoutrements, and style of cowboy life. He does not even wear his glasses, without which he could see only poorly.

During his time in the Dakotas, Roosevelt hardened his body, a task, Nicholas remembered, that was not completed "to his satisfaction" until his late twenties.[20] Roosevelt's struggles against cattle thieves and lawless gangs and his skill in breaking and riding wild cow ponies provided the physical courage "which his soul had aspired to in boyhood," William Roscoe Thayer observed. His asthma abated, and finally he developed a body "which could back up any resolution he might take."[21] "I am well hardened now," Roosevelt wrote to his sister Anna in 1884; "I have just come in from spending *thirteen* hours in the saddle."[22]

Strengthened by the rough life of a cattle rancher, Roosevelt continued

Figure 24. Roosevelt in Leatherstocking costume, c. 1883–84 (Library of Congress Prints and Photographs Division, Washington, D.C., 215922. LCUSZ6 24172 3)

to develop his Western image. Beside his horse in another photo, undated but probably from the late 1880s, he wears essentially the same outfit as he did as a studio cowboy, minus the chaps (figure 26). This image reveals a more resolute, saddle-worn, authentic cowboy standing beside a working cow pony against a bona fide Western backdrop. Still posed, though not so

Figure 25. Roosevelt, c. 1885 (Theodore Roosevelt Collection, Harvard College Library)

Figure 26. Roosevelt as a cowboy in the Dakota Territory, c. 1885 (Theodore Roosevelt Collection, Harvard College Library)

stiffly as in the studio shot, he rests his hand on his gun and is more believably ready for action because he now wears glasses.

As Roosevelt's cowboy image evolved, his popular image changed along with it. When he bought his first ranch, both Westerners and the Eastern press ridiculed him for looking like an overdressed, overeducated tenderfoot. By 1886, his Western exploits had visibly hardened him. "What a change!" the Pittsburgh *Dispatch* exclaimed; "he is now brown as a berry and has increased 30 pounds in weight." His high and squeaky voice was now "hearty and strong enough to drive oxen." Reviewers of *Hunting Trips of a Ranchman: Ranch Life and the Hunting Trail* (1888) and *The Wilderness Hunter* (1893) allowed Roosevelt the full legitimacy of Western cowboy life. The *New York Times* certified that "Mr. Roosevelt has had full practical experience of what he writes about" and noted that "to be a cowboy . . . is by no means an easy task." Ranching life held "a special charm for the gilded youth of the Eastern states," *The Dial*'s reviewer reported, "and Mr. Roosevelt seems to have followed it."[23]

It was not just how a cowboy looked that separated him from Easterners, but how he lived. In their struggle against nature, the *New York Tribune* noted, cowboys had to live lives of "intelligent barbarism" that involved "barbarous and crude forms of dissipation."[24] "I heartily enjoy this life, with its perfect freedom," Roosevelt wrote, "for I am very fond of hunting, and there are few sensations I prefer to that of galloping over these rolling, limitless prairies, rifle in hand."[25] "He craved once more to be alone with nature," reported the naturalist John Burroughs; "he was evidently hungry for the wild and aboriginal,—a hunger that seems to come upon him regularly at least once a year, and drives him forth on his hunting trips for big game in the West."[26] In this intense contact with a heightened reality, Roosevelt claimed to have discovered the raw and primitive man in himself—what Easterners must have been like before being drained of their life juices. "This is what I was like when I had the bark on," he later wrote.[27]

Though himself a New Yorker, Roosevelt enjoyed demeaning the tame outdoor pastimes of Easterners. He preferred his Western life of wild horses, wild terrain, and wild game to Eastern foxhunting, he wrote in 1884 to Lodge, an Eastern patrician and foxhunter. Western hunting required natural buckskin shirts, rifles, and rugged cow ponies, Roosevelt said, rather than tailored red coats worn during scripted jumps over fences chasing a ground-dragged scent. "A buffalo is nobler game than an anise seed bag," and one could kill buffalo only in the West.[28] In 1883, when he had killed his first buffalo, Roosevelt spontaneously danced a "war dance" that he repeated thereafter in a lifetime of famous hunting. In the aristocratic gentility of the hunt club, no member would ever have allowed himself such freedom.

Thomas Nast was one of the nation's first image makers to transport Roosevelt's cowboy body into the nation's political culture. In a cartoon of 1889, the first year Roosevelt served as the U.S. civil service commissioner in Benjamin Harrison's administration, Nast blended Roosevelt's Wild West bronco busting with current notions of progressive reform (figure 27). In this remarkably predictive portrayal, a youthful and determined cowboy at "Uncle Sam's Ranch" disciplines the out-of-control "Spoilsman" with "Civil Service Reform." During the following six years, Roosevelt gained national attention by removing thousands of jobs from political patronage, thus making civil service reform a popular cause. This move surprised the Republican party machine and provoked the unenthusiastic

Figure 27. Thomas Nast, "A Popular View of the Commissioner's Victory over the Spoils System," 1889 (courtesy Theodore Roosevelt Association)

Harrison to remark that Roosevelt "wanted to put an end to all the evil in the world between sunrise and sunset."[29]

By the time of the Cuban campaign, Roosevelt's Rough Rider performance completed his evolution from Leatherstocking to a hardened, purposeful cowboy–cavalry hero. In an 1898 photo, Colonel Theodore Roosevelt of the Rough Riders prepares to embark for Cuba (figure 28). Roosevelt as Rough Rider presents himself as a solid and muscular, mature, battle-ready horseman, ready to charge roughly over Spaniards and ride confidently into the nation's political consciousness. With authentic cowboy and warrior accoutrements, Roosevelt had remade the youthful, slim, decorated, and slightly feminized body of the studio photos into a battle-hardened man of action worthy of national acclaim.

Figure 28. "Col. Theodore Roosevelt, of the Rough Riders," 1898

After serving as governor of New York and McKinley's vice president, Roosevelt became president in 1901. *Punch* commemorated the ascent of the nation's favorite cowboy to the highest office. Sending its "best wishes," the magazine pictured the Rough Rider, complete with an American flag saddle blanket, reporting for duty as president of the United States (figure 29). By this time, the entire nation knew of Roosevelt's youthful bodybuilding to overcome frailty, his cowboy and hunt-

Figure 29. Bernard Partridge, "The Rough Rider," *Punch*, 25 September 1901

ing exploits in the Dakotas, his pugnacious style in New York politics, and his bravery under fire in the war against Spain. Seconding Roosevelt's own tireless self-promotion, national magazines and newspapers faithfully recorded his every move. A million Teddy bears were for sale in New York City alone. Young boys began strengthening regimens, and grown men reveled in what the *New York Tribune* in 1907 called Roosevelt's "opulent efficiency of mind and body."[30] By then well into his second term, the five-foot-eight Roosevelt weighed over two hundred pounds. He was a "strong, tough man; hard to hurt and harder to stop," remarked his heavyweight sparring partner, a professional boxer who came regularly to the White House for workouts. "His large frame and thick neck gave the impression of a big man," his cousin Nicholas Roosevelt observed, and "his chest was powerful and well developed."[31] General Arthur MacArthur remarked to Roosevelt how pleased he was that at last the nation had a president who could review troops on horseback.[32]

Given its bulk, Roosevelt's cowboy-soldier body contrasted with and eventually won out over an equally powerful ideal. Frederic Remington's drawing "An East-Side Politician" depicts a man dressed in a pinstriped suit, top hat, and patent leather shoes, with a gold watch chain stretched across an ample stomach that attests to his eating habits (figure 30). Health professionals like the prominent neurologist George M. Beard praised the corpulence of members of the "well-to-do classes" as a matter of national pride and equated plumpness in men with health and vigor, and in women, with beauty. Many of the nation's prominent men weighed around three hundred pounds, among them Remington himself; twice-president Grover Cleveland; speaker of the House and presidential aspirant Thomas Reed; William Howard Taft, who, it was said, ran for the presidency on a platform of reinforced concrete; and Brigadier General William Rufus Shafter, commander of the Fifth Army Corps in Cuba, to which the Rough Riders were assigned.

Though Roosevelt never approached the size of Remington's East Side politician, he too was given to overeating, and he steadily gained weight during his presidency. He complained about his stiffness and bulk even though he continued to ride, hike, and row strenuously, something few other men of his size did. Fat, an especially insidious problem to a man who equated bodily flabbiness with moral failure, drove Roosevelt to Jack Cooper's health farm in Connecticut to lose weight, in keeping with a trend that, in the new century, found a significant number of Americans favoring a slimmer physique.[33]

But the president's crafted cowboy image had entered the American consciousness, and it compared favorably not just with bulky upper-class waistlines but with the bodies of working-class men who were, as Beard observed, often rendered by long workdays and substandard wages "thin, angular, stooping, anxious, and, in not a few cases, emaciated." Advertisements directed at fattening undernourished men dotted the pages of working-class periodicals like the *International Socialist Review*. "Let Us Make You Fat" read an ad for a "concentrated flesh builder." "It is no longer necessary to be thin, scrawny, and underdeveloped" (figure 31). Now workers

Figure 30. Frederic Remington, "An East-Side Politician," 1894

could beef up and avoid the "humiliation and embarrassment which only skinny people have." Physicians focused almost entirely on flabby middle- and upper-class bodies. Beard cautioned doctors who treated neurasthen- ics to prescribe therapeutically "small doses" of horseback riding and gymnastics. He made no mention of what to do about frail working-class

Figure 31. "Let Us Make You Fat," *International Socialist Review*, June 1913

men, who in any case did not frequent elite physicians like Beard.[34] For Roosevelt, concerned as he was with the military importance of the average man's physique, the answer was not better-paying jobs or improved diets, but athleticism and "toughness."

The nation's growing preoccupation with physical strength led biographers and fiction writers to promote a new hero in the 1890s, Greene notes, who had the "firm face of a fighter" and the "squared shoulders of an athlete"; he was "in every way a large man." Nearly six feet tall and weighing almost 250 pounds, the hero had a prominent chin that showed his "aggressive spirit." When he was in the "full flush of strength," his "intense animal vitality" gave him "tremendous even gigantic physical endurance." Villains, of course, had flabby bodies. By the end of the nineteenth century, American readers considered physical size and strength an essential part of good character; in fact, they came to understand them as the same thing.[35]

Drawing on English and German enthusiasm for bodybuilding, Americans flocked to competitive sporting events, exercise clubs, hunt clubs, YMCAs, and the Boy Scouts in the 1890s. Amid a growing sense that the nation's future depended on the health of white young men, mass demonstrations of schoolyard calisthenics, such as that of "The School Boy Army" that performed in 1913 in New York City's Central Park, addressed the issue of undermuscled youth. "10,000 Boys at Play Take All by Storm," reported the *New York Times,* with a picture of an enormous grid of perfectly aligned white boys in white shirts and dark pants, arms outstretched and fingertips almost touching.[36] Organized by New York's public schools and city officials, the mass rally, "largest of its kind in the world," advertised the "civic results of physical and hygienic training" that was undertaken by 700,000 boys thrice weekly in the city's public schools. Cordoned off on a 240,000-square-foot green, two hundred "armies" arranged themselves in ninety rows precisely six feet apart. From the square's center, where three large American flags flew, an open corridor ran to the flag-draped reviewing stand. There stood an array of judges, aldermen, borough presidents, police and park commissioners, representatives from the Russell Sage Foundation and the Playground Association of America, and prominent businessmen, among them Vincent Astor and S. R. Guggenheim. The rally's highlight came when the guest of honor, former president Theodore Roosevelt, ascended the podium amid cheers to give a rousing speech that praised the benefits of muscular nationalism and affirmed his role as its personification.

For the demonstration's organizers and adult participants, the boys' tight, military-style formations and collective response to commands showcased a solid and unified group exterior. Girls, whom event organizers termed "non-combatants," were only allowed to observe the "heroes" from the sidelines. By presenting group calisthenics as a white-only, male-only patriotic act, organizers made the exercise a metaphor for the nation's body. But why was it so machinelike and exclusionary? Bodybuilding activities, directed on one level at purposeful physical training, affirmed on another level the collective, emotionless exteriors that men formed around their interior selves. These exteriors, like the ten thousand equidistant and untouching boys, reinforced an aseptic, formalized exclusion of femininity and eroticism. Everywhere from schoolyards to navy yards, men could link to other men safely and emotionlessly in formal groupings around activities whose unwritten rules foreclosed individual intimacy in favor of group loyalty. As Klaus Theweleit observes, ritualized group reinforcement of these exteriors promises men the "reintegration of hostile [interior] components under tolerable conditions" and "the dominance of the hostile 'female' element within themselves."[37] In the minds of advocates of muscular nationalism, strengthening young men was the analog of Roosevelt's having made his own body a "tough nut."

Roosevelt's capacity for machinelike action, so psychologically protective in his own life, made him the perfect advocate of the same protections for any militant group, and especially for the nation. U.S. cartoonists, remarkably alert to the various manifestations of Roosevelt's persona, often pictured him as a fully armored warrior defending the nation's body. In "An Impregnable Shield," the centurion-president holds the phallic sword of utter certainty in one hand and the shield of public welfare in the other, guarding against the arrows of his critics (figure 32). The Spaniards, losers in the imperial struggle of 1898, depicted Roosevelt as the "rising sun of Yankee imperialism," holding sword and olive branch and backed by the votes of his democratic but equally imperialistic constituency (figure 33). His feet are planted on Cuba and the Philippines, and in the latter country seminaked ape-men fight each other with fists and sticks. Presumably the warrior's armor held Spain at bay while protecting the squabbling colonial subjects below, whose diminutive size suggests a femaleness in their primitive bellicosity.

Roosevelt created boundaries against an effeminate self by living the "strenuous life" that gave rein to self-willed virile action. For him, self-congratulatory toughness and near-maniacal physical strenuousness became an act of armoring, an antidote that allowed him to seem more virile than any other Easterner. William Roscoe Thayer observed that physical extremes were a lifelong daily regimen for the president, whose "inexhaustible energy hungered for action."[38] It was well known that Roosevelt filled each presidential hour with exhausting work and play and made leisure activities like picnicking or reading into laborious toil. His own father had not allowed idleness in his children, and Roosevelt passed on this insistence on constant action, refusing to tolerate unstructured, purposeless leisure for himself or anyone around him.[39] "The only thing I am afraid of," he wrote to his sister Anna in 1896, toward the end of his second term as New York's police commissioner, "is that by and by I will have nothing to do."[40] Roosevelt's remarkable capacity to substantiate himself, to believe in and then to make real his own bodily force impressed many men. "The president himself is a good deal of a storm," observed the naturalist John Burroughs during a trip to Yellowstone in 1903, "a man of such abounding energy and ceaseless activity that he sets everything in motion around him. He is doubtless the most vital man on the continent,

Figure 32. "An Impregnable Shield"

Figure 33. Opisso, "Roosevelt as the Rising Sun of Yankee Imperialism," *Hojas Selectas* (Barcelona)

if not the planet, to-day."[41] "A wonderful little machine," Henry James wrote of the president's body, "it functions astonishingly and is quite exciting to see."[42]

THE COWBOY CULT

The growing cowboy cult, with Roosevelt as one of its favorites, drew on and quickly absorbed themes of essentialized manliness, amoral violence, ascetic nationalism, and homosocial bonding. In the golden years of open-plains cattle ranching between 1865 and 1885, cowboys drove large herds from Texas to railroad towns like Abilene, Kansas. Just as the open range and the frontier closed and the Indian wars ended, editors of American books, magazines, and newspapers discovered that Easterners had begun to marvel at the lives of cowboys, Indians, and cavalrymen and at the topography of the American West. Theater and show producers, writers, artists, historians, and chroniclers set new standards of action and realism and provided a value system for the cowboy easily appropriated by the purveyors of American imperialism. William F. Cody was the most notable of the real-life Westerners whose experiences and autobiographies elevated the cowboy to national prominence. Readers avidly consumed Cody's story of his experiences—first as a Civil War scout for General William T. Sherman, later as a scout for the Fifth Cavalry in the wars against the plains Indians, and even later as a Pony Express rider and commercial buffalo hunter—which appeared in over five hundred variations, including Ned Buntline's story *Buffalo Bill, King of the Border Men*, serialized in the *New York Weekly* in 1869 and published as *Buffalo Bill* in 1886. In the 1870s, capitalizing on this popularity among readers, Buntline lured Cody to Chicago, where he played himself onstage in *The Scouts of the Prairie*, a melodrama that turned the cowboy hero into an instant theater success and romanticized what were becoming central features of his life: heroism in the face of overwhelming danger, celebration of the edifying effects of violence, and fascination with Western animals, weapons, and landscapes.

During the winters of the 1870s, Cody toured with *The Scouts of the Prairie* and in the summers returned to the prairie as a real scout and Indian fighter for the Fifth Cavalry. In 1876, a few weeks after the battle of the Little Big Horn, Cody avenged General George Armstrong Custer's death by killing and taking the scalp of the Cheyenne chief Yellow Hand. The next year, he staged his version of events for theater audiences in *The Right Red Hand; or Buffalo Bill's First Scalp for Custer*.[43] By 1882, the success of Western themes led Cody to produce an outdoor Fourth of July show, *Old Glory Blowout*, near his Nevada ranch. The play's wild reception by local audiences prompted him to launch Buffalo Bill's Wild West Show and Congress of Rough Riders of the World. By the mid-1880s, this spectacular touring production had performed before multiple large audiences and had further whetted the public's appetite for violent adventure and Cody's appetite for fame and profit.

Using Anglo-Saxon cowboys, Indians, and soldiers and live horses, buffalo, deer, elk, and cattle against a painted Dakota panorama, the show staged hunting scenes, cavalry charges, and stagecoach rescues. Real Indians, including the Sioux chief Sitting Bull, appeared in melodramatic reenactments that took place even as actual wars between Indians and the U.S. Cavalry continued in the West. In 1890, General Nelson A. Miles summoned Cody to negotiate with Sitting Bull, whom he considered part of the Ghost Dance movement, but President Benjamin Harrison called off the conference at the last minute. A month later, when Sitting Bull refused to surrender, troops from General Miles's Seventh Cavalry killed him along with many others. During the battle, Sitting Bull's horse, having been trained to do tricks in Cody's Wild West show, mistook the gunfire for a cue and began performing tricks as if he were on stage. Eleven days later, at Wounded Knee, the Sioux resistance ended with a massacre of men, women, and children, and thereafter Cody quickly added Sitting Bull's death and the "Battle of Wounded Knee" to his Wild West show. But the career of Sitting Bull's horse was not over. The horse was given to Cody, and it appeared in the staging of his Wild West show at the Chicago Columbian Exposition in 1893.

If Sitting Bull's horse was confused, the contradiction between Indians' fighting for survival against the U.S. Cavalry and playing themselves in shows must have alternately teased and boggled the public's imagination. The presence of actual participants from the real events helped make the staged events believable. Such "fictions of the real," to use Alan Trachtenberg's term, helped dissociate war against the Indians from its brutality and misery and reestablished it as vaudeville entertainment that appealed to the nation's romantic sense of itself.[44] These fictions lent an aura of theatricality, of display and posing, of crafted heroism to the dreams of armchair cowboys who vicariously rode with the men. Not the real thing, Cody and his audiences knew, the show was as close as many men would ever come. Close enough for Mark Twain, who noted in a letter to Cody that the show "captured the spirit of America . . . down to its smallest detail. . . . It is wholly free from sham and insincerity." Yet however real the show was, Twain also understood that its spectacles were mythical, though they recreated in him, he said, effects "identical" to those of the real frontier of his youth.[45]

Cody's advertising extended the claim of authenticity even as it identified his show's viewers as more masculine. One poster read: "More than Historic: It is History itself in Living Lessons—Not the Imitations of Fancy, but the Stupendous Realism of Facts—Not an Empty Cheating Echo, But Daring Deeds Incarnate, Telling its Thrilling Tales with Rifle, Sword and Spear, using in Place of Halting Words Inspiring, Splendid Action."[46] With the title's repeated "Not," Cody positioned real cowboys and true action against fictional accounts that were imitative, fanciful, hesitant, and devious—in short, effeminate figments of literary and historical imagination.

In 1888 the now famous "Buffalo Bill" Cody published *The Story of the Wild West,* and the book and his show became popular in Europe. In 1892, Frederic Remington saw Cody's show in London, and to signify his approval, he drew ten illustrations of it, which *Harper's Weekly* published under the title "Buffalo Bill's Wild West Show in London."[47] By 1893, when the Wild West show played at the World's Columbian Exhibition in Chicago, the Congress of the Rough Riders included Arabian Bedouins, Russian Cossacks, Mexican *vaqueros,* Argentine Gauchos, German cavalrymen, French lancers, and English guardsmen. In 1898, Cody appropriated Roosevelt's wartime experiences in his theater production Roosevelt's *Charge up San Juan Hill* and played Colonel Roosevelt of the Rough Riders himself. (Roosevelt had asked Cody to join the Rough Riders when he first organized the regiment. Unable to go himself, Cody had sent several of his best "shootists.")[48] Soon thereafter, he added a dramatization of U.S. Marines fighting in the Boxer Rebellion, demonstrating that he, like his friend Roosevelt, saw the cowboy soldier as fulfilling America's imperial destiny on the world stage.[49]

By the 1890s, driven by the public's intense interest in the representations in the Wild West shows, the cowboy cult was firmly entrenched in the nation's culture. Copycat touring shows proliferated, and stories of Western horsemen told in dime novels and comic books sold as hot items in theaters, museums, and art galleries. Reenactments of the charge up San Juan Hill and the Battle of Santiago appeared at numerous public fairs, including the St. Louis Louisiana Purchase Exposition in 1904. Talented writers such as Jack London, Rudyard Kipling, Owen Wister, Frank Norris, and Mark Twain, and artists such as Frederic Remington, N. C. Wyeth, Charles Russell, and Charles Dana Gibson poured out cowboy stories in the nation's magazines, widening the scope and variety of the reading public's experience.

After the turn of the century, the infant movie industry, inspired by Cody' historical recreations, distributed Westerns worldwide. America's first film, Edwin S. Porter's *The Great Train Robbery* (1903), was a Western, and it was followed by others such as *Bronco Billy and the Baby* (1907) and *The Virginian* (1929). When Cody ventured into film in 1913 with *The Indian Wars Refought,* featuring the scene "The Battle at Wounded Knee," he brought on the retired Nelson Miles as a consultant, used actual Indians and cavalry, and starred in the movie himself.[50] The first movie of the famous cowboy actor Tom Mix, *Ranch Life in the Great Southwest* (1909) echoed Roosevelt's book *Ranch Life and the Hunting Trail.* Mix's director elaborated on current ideas about cowboy fashion taken from fiction and literature, dressing the actor in ornately tooled leather holsters, belt, and boots, and a white satin shirt and white hat, and he raised audience expectations for violence by adding a second six-shooter and an extra cartridge belt that displayed larger bullets.

Taking advantage of Cody's pioneering entertainments, Frederic Remington and Owen Wister made a living almost entirely out of romanticizing cowboy life, energizing the new archetype with new forms of dramatic realism. Remington, a New York artist who claimed he painted "men with the bark on," was sent to the Western plains by *Harper's Weekly* in 1885 and 1886 to cover the Indian wars that were drawing great public attention.[51] In 1885 and again in 1886, Geronimo escaped from Arizona's San Carlos reservation and fled to Mexico, pursued by the Third U.S. Cavalry. "Here was the real thing," exclaimed Poultney Bigelow, the first editor to see Remington's work. "No stage heroes these; no carefully pomaded hair and neatly tied cravats," he said in a sly slap at melodrama. "These were men of the real rodeo, parched in alkali dust . . . under the furious rays of the Arizona sun. Genius was in those rough drawings, and I loved them for their very roughness."[52]

By 1890, the appeal of Remington's Indians, soldiers, horses, buffalo, and cowboys had made him the nation's most well-known chronicler of the West. Nearly every widely read magazine carried his illustrations, and commissions poured in. Over his career, Remington produced 2,700 drawings and paintings, and in 1888 alone, when his Western themes began to appear in exhibits and win prizes, Remington published no fewer than 177 pictures in *Harper's Weekly, Outing, Youth's Companion,* and the *Century.* He won a silver medal at the Paris Exposition in 1889. By 1900, *Harper's* billed him as the nation's preeminent Western reporter and said that he had barely escaped harm at the "battle" of Wounded Knee. In that same year, he won the American National Academy Prize, and in 1903, *Collier's* chose him to illustrate western themes in a series of centerfolds.[53]

Roosevelt went West the first time after his graduation from Harvard, then again in 1883 to treat his asthma and look for financial opportunity, and a third time in 1885 after the deaths of his mother and his wife. Wister first journeyed West in 1885 on the advice of his physician, S. Weir Mitchell, to treat a neurasthenic breakdown brought on by parental pressures and family and career concerns. He had struck up a friendship with Roosevelt at Harvard, and he, Roosevelt, and later Remington enjoyed a friendship and active correspondence over the next quarter-century, in which they traded stories about politics, trips out West, writings, art, and wartime adventure. All three men belonged to the Boone and Crockett

Club, for which Wister and Roosevelt helped create an exhibit, a log cabin on an island, for the 1893 Chicago Columbian Exposition. All three, but Remington and Roosevelt more than Wister, removed themselves periodically from the company of women and civilization to travel West and enjoy exclusively male adventures. All three claimed that the great drama of the West had added immeasurably to their lives, and all three lamented its end.

The three friends closely followed and frequently participated in one another's careers. Remington took many of his early Western scenes from photographs Roosevelt had taken in the 1880s, and he included images of Roosevelt in several of his pictures.[54] Roosevelt chose Remington to draw ninety-nine illustrations for *Ranch Life and the Hunting Trail,* which was serialized in six issues of *The Century Illustrated Monthly Magazine* and released as a book in 1888. The national attention Roosevelt's Western tales received boosted his friends' careers. Wister wrote his first Western tale, "Hank's Woman" after a trip to Wyoming in 1891, and that story was followed quickly by "How Lin McLean Went East," *Red Men and White* (1895), *Lin McLean* (1897), and *The Jimmyjohn Boss and Other Stories* (1900). Wister's *The Virginian* (1902), the nation's favorite Western novel, which enjoyed fifteen printings in its first eight months, was illustrated by Remington and dedicated to Roosevelt. In October of 1907, when Remington was at the height of his fame and Roosevelt was president, *Pearson's Monthly* featured the artist in "Frederic Remington: Most Typical of American Artists." Remington's sculpture *Bronco Buster* appeared on the cover, and President Roosevelt contributed a letter in tribute to the artist's status as a chronicler of the West.

Roosevelt, Remington, and Wister lavished praise upon one another's work. Each understood that the other two men's vision had influenced his own interpretation of the West. "Half of the men" whom Roosevelt described in his own Western and Rough Rider adventures, he said, "might have walked out of Wister's stories or Remington's pictures."[55] Roosevelt praised the "grim stalwart men" who provided the "note of manliness which is dominant throughout the writings of Mr. Wister."[56] Remington read Roosevelt's four-volume *Winning of the West* in 1897, then wrote to Roosevelt praising the books. Roosevelt wrote back that he was enthusiastically reading Remington's articles and felt that they "come closer to the real thing . . . than any other man in the western business."[57] "You in your line," Roosevelt wrote to Remington, "and Wister in his, are doing the best work in America today."[58] Roosevelt told *Outlook* readers in 1913 that "fortunately" for the nation, Wister and Remington had made Westerners live "as long as our literature lives."[59] He likened Remington's skill in portraying the plainsman and soldier to Kipling's expertise with his chosen subjects, and he predicted that Remington's works "will make the cantos in the last Epic of the Western Wilderness."[60]

Wister and Remington first met at Yellowstone in 1893, and immediately they began an artistic and literary collaboration that ended only with Remington's untimely death in 1909 at age forty-seven. There they resolved to write and illustrate articles that would transform the cowboy into an American archetype, agreeing to enshrine the authentic West in the American imagination before the arrival of what Remington termed "the derby hat, the smoking chimneys, . . . and the thirty-day note."[61] Wister, Remington, and Roosevelt resolved to capture Western energy for Eastern men who were being drained of their manhood by what Remington called the "enfeebling present."[62]

Their collaboration produced a seminal series of articles for *Harper's Monthly* written by Wister and illustrated by Remington: "The Promised Land" (April 1894), "Kinsman of Red Cloud" (May 1894), "Little Big Horn Medicine" (June 1894), "Specimen Jones" (July 1894), "The General's Bluff" (September 1894), "The Second Missouri Compromise" (March 1895), and "La Tinaja Bonita" (May 1895). The capstone article in the series, "The Evolution of the Cow-Puncher," appeared in September 1895 and gave the country its most complete look at the nature of the "grim lean man" who was to become a mythic hero of twentieth-century stage, film, and novel.[63]

Wister and Remington decided to produce "The Evolution of the Cow-Puncher" upon reading Roosevelt's 1894 essay "What 'Americanism' Means," in which he argued that to evolve a distinctive national identity, Americans must separate from European culture and unite around some original American ideal. In the West lay the genesis of an authentic America, Roosevelt told an *Evening Post* reporter: "It is in the West that as a nation we shall ultimately work out our highest destiny."[64] This destiny would rescue the nation's men, Roosevelt predicted, simply because the West had produced the cowboy. Pleased with Wister's and Remington's contribution to national destiny, Roosevelt wrote Wister that he "heartily" approved of "The Evolution of the Cow-Puncher" and *Red Men and White,* for they constituted "a new page in . . . contemporary historical writing" by vividly portraying manly "types that should be commemorated."[65]

Throughout the 1890s, Wister, Remington, and Roosevelt constructed their cowboy of the imagination purposefully as an energizing tonic for jaded Easterners. For their readers and viewers, the world came alive with the explosive physical energy of men mounted on half-wild horses perpetually in need of taming. "Be very profane and have plenty of shooting,"

Remington advised Wister on how to write a Western; "Put every person on horseback and let the blood be half a foot deep."[66] Each of the three men portrayed fictionalized cowboys with the same "rude virtues of perfect courage" he had seen among cowboys in the Dakotas and Arizona. To be a rancher, a man had to be " 'all man,' " Remington wrote, "because it is 'a man's job.' " The cowboy's lawlessness and his capacity for amoral acts figured importantly too. "The cow-men are good friends and virulent haters," Remington explained, and "if justified in their own minds, would shoot a man instantly and regret the necessity, but not the shooting."[67] It was this revival of the cowboy's frontier virtues that mattered most to Roosevelt, for the cowboy's raw power and his eagerness to kill, so necessary for survival in the West, had also become necessary for successful American nationhood.

For its themes, the Western drew from the captivity narratives of the Indian wars of the seventeenth and eighteenth centuries and from the stories of heroes of the American frontier like Miles Standish and Daniel Boone. James Fenimore Cooper's *Leatherstocking Tales* appeared in the mid-nineteenth century in popular dime novels. These early fictional treatments of the cowboy established themes followed by Cody's Wild West Show and by later writers of fiction and of popular biographies of Cody, George A. Custer, and Kit Carson. As John Cawelti shows in *The Six-Gun Mystique*, formulized Westerns required certain key ingredients: vast and forbidding landscapes; violent conflict on the border between civilization and savagery; and a moral and masculine hero who operates as a liminal figure, saving the town and its damsel but refusing to settle down. Directors generally made the movie cowboy develop close personal relationships, not with women, but with his cow pony and his Indian pal, each of whom appeared as a character with a name and a personality.[68]

To the early Westerns' racial and civilizing themes, Wister, Remington, and Roosevelt added elements that more directly addressed late-nineteenth-century men's social and psychological concerns. As they replaced the scouts of the colonial and Appalachian frontiers with the horsemen of the great plains, they disagreed on how to fashion this new figure. In the 1870s and early 1880s, Easterners' image of the cowboy had been conditioned by news reports that pictured cowboys as poor, half-breed, half-civilized laborers who easily turned horse thief or vigilante. In 1881, President Chester A. Arthur asked Congress to authorize the U.S. Army to control bands of violent and "armed desperados known as 'Cowboys,' " who terrorized the Great Plains.[69] Remington preferred to remain true to this more realistic, raw type represented by the Mexican *vaquero*, the true "Texas type of cowboy," a "brave fellow, a fatalist, with less wants than the

Figure 34. Frederic Remington, "The Texas Type of Cowboy," *The Century*, June 1888 (courtesy Frederic Remington Art Museum, Ogdensburg, New York)

pony he rides," who had "invented the whole business of running steers to Abilene" (figure 34).[70]

Wister, ever the proper Philadelphian, preferred to place a more re-fined, Anglo-Saxon hero in the context of civilization's advance, and ultimately he had his way in what had become a lucrative commercial undertaking. By 1895, although Remington upbraided his friend for im-posing Anglo-Saxon racial qualities onto authentic Mexican and Texan cowboys, both men had forsaken the distinctly unheroic, scruffy, Western range rider in favor of the clean-cut Anglo-Saxon more accommodating to Eastern class and racial tastes.[71] Their foregrounding of violence and racializing of the cowboy suggested that the two artists purposefully constituted him over against both Eastern effeminacy and the immigrant threat felt by many Anglo-Saxon, middle- and upper-class whites. Locating the action on the border between civilization and savagery helped resolve some of the tension that arose between an Anglo-Saxon social order and its seeming enemies—Indians, immigrants, and blacks—guaranteeing that the former advanced against the latter. Thus, as Cawelti finds, the frontier setting allowed Easterners to exult in lawless violence "without feeling that it threatened the values or the fabric of society."[72]

In "The Evolution of the Cow-Puncher," the *vaquero* serves as a foil against which to portray the Anglo-Saxon cowboy as a product of an evolutionary "testing of the fittest." Unified in a fraternal brotherhood by "the bottom bond of race," the new cowboy "improved" the figure of the "small, deceitful, alien" Mexican *vaquero,* Wister wrote, and transformed him into an Anglo-Saxon with the "grittier qualities" needed for fighting the mounted Indians of the Great Plains. Mexicans, by this logic, were unworthy heroes because they were too close racially to Indians. In the antimodern essentialism of the cowboy cult, it took a white man to do the job. "Destiny" plucked the Anglo-Saxon Easterner from impending decline in "the library, the haystack, and the gutter [and] set him upon his horse" out West. "Face to face with the eternal simplicity of death, his modern guise fell away," Wister wrote. "It was no new type, . . . just the original kernel of the nut with the shell broken."[73]

The cowboy's destined appearance at civilization's evolutionary forefront signaled his superiority in the racial trajectory of Teutons and Saxons across world landscapes. Unlike either Mexican *vaqueros* or Natty Bumppo of the *Leatherstocking Tales,* whose appeal lay in his anarchism, this new American cowboy was a harbinger of white civilization. The "spirit of adventure and courage" required to "survive in the clean cattle country" necessitated Anglo-Saxon self-sufficiency, Wister wrote. "You will not find many Poles or Huns or Russian Jews in the West." The cowboy emerged as a horseman, unlike the Swede, who farmed; the Frenchman, who stayed inside; the Italian, who sold fruit; and the Teuton (at least the non-Prussian Teuton), who had become a "tame slippered animal . . . swaddled in a dressing-gown." Bypassing these inferior types, the cowboy was heir in a direct line of European heroes and heroics, Wister wrote, from the "slumbering untamed Saxon" of Walter Scott's novels, through Viking rovings, to Camelot, William the Conqueror, the Spanish Armada, Waterloo, and "yesterday in Samoa and today's round-up at Abilene." The Norseman, the medieval knight, Daniel Boone, and the cowboy "are nothing but the same Saxon in different environments." Marching into the Western edge of civilization, "the race was once again subject to battles and darkness," which brought out the "Viking portion" of each man. "None but the plucky ones could survive." The white man's "fittest instinct" made him "through the centuries, conqueror, invader, navigator, buccaneer, explorer, colonist, tiger-shooter."[74] Thus Wister's and Remington's cowboy came to embody a militarized version of national manhood, honed to elemental perfection in Western civilization's racial, evolutionary, and territorial expansion against "darkness."

The cowboy's masculine and racial qualities came from his having abandoned urban life and civilized morality and become a law unto himself. One of Wister's "evolved" Anglo-Saxon cowboys, he said, had "the bluest eye, the longest nose and the coldest face I ever saw." He "took wild pleasure in existence" but "laughed seldom." He lived rootlessly, "as wild and lean and dangerous as any buck or bull." He comprehended "no middle ground between the poles of brutality and tenderness" and was always "indifferent to death, uneasy about corpses and the dark." Living as far from civilization as possible, Wister's and Remington's cowboys avoided women above all. While the cowboy might "draw the eye of a woman," he "never settled down," and he remained immune to charms that threatened his life of adventure. "War they made plenty, but not love," and they "begot no sons."[75] Remington, like Wister and Roosevelt, counted excessive sexuality as one of the "enfeebling influences of luxury and modern life," so he made his fictionalized and painted cowboys "simple and chaste."[76]

Though the cowboy's racial qualities and martial skills had gone dormant in the modern world, the West's "gymnasium for mind and body" fostered his readiness for theft, sport, or killing. "No angel," Wister wrote, this "Angle" stole riches and territory alike. On the open, flat prairie, whose "extreme barrenness . . . held tamer people at a distance," Wister wrote, the cowboy made his "nightly bed in a thousand miles of snow and loneliness." He reveled in "glorious days" on this "playground" where "battle and murder and sudden death [were] every-day matters." In this land, "his spirit was in the permanent attitude of war. No fiercer blood ever stained a border."[77] In a similar celebration of amoral bloodthirstiness, Remington said that the cowboys in his paintings lived in jeopardy of the "enormous, the formidable, the terrible." As they were captured and tortured or fought in last stands or fled for their lives, they were "wrenched out from the quiet uneventful round of everyday life, and flung into the throes of a vast and terrible drama that worked itself out in unleashed passions, in blood, and in sudden death."[78]

As the cowboy cult evolved, Easterners ascribed higher and ever more mythical levels of amoral violence to the archetypal cowboy-heroes and villains of the frontier. From colonial times to the late nineteenth century, the West was never as violent as either the South or Eastern cities; the demands of Eastern readers for violence in Westerns may have been more a result than a cause of high levels of social violence in American society. Given the cowboy's capacity to "bring a sense of moral significance and order," Michael Bellesiles writes, he reconciled readers' anxiety over actual violence in their cities and the desire for violence in their hearts.[79] Cowboy narratives distinguished between good and bad men and between moral and immoral acts. The hero's violence cleansed and purified; the villain's violence was undisciplined and savage. Cowboys used violence reluctantly and according to their own strict code of honor, which brought order to the lawless range. But, like one of Roosevelt's heroes in *The Winning of the West*, "once provoked," the cowboy was capable of astounding feats of mayhem. As readers grew more eager for the hero's clean-cut violence, stamped with the moral imprimatur of advancing civilization, Cawelti finds, they found it "graceful, aesthetic, and, even, fun."[80]

Wister's and Remington's cowboys lived lives that did not serve civilized morality. In *What an Unbranded Cow Has Cost*, one of Remington's five paintings for a scene in "Evolution of the Cow-Puncher," everyday violence renders morality irrelevant (figure 35). On the unfenced range, where large herds of nearly wild cattle belonging to different ranches grazed together, roundups and calf branding took place each spring, when calves could be identified by their mother's brand. In the painting, cowboys from three different ranches claim an unbranded animal, and without warning, begin shooting one another and the horses. "In a few minutes fourteen riders lay dead on the plain," Wister wrote. Amid the dead and dying men and horses, a lone cowboy lowers his gun but remains alert, his left hand steadying a fallen comrade while "the tied animal . . . bawled and bleated in the silence."[81]

Although in his article Wister romanticized this carnage as "skirmishing enough for a ballad," he was shocked upon first seeing Remington's painting. "It is not only vast, it states itself utterly. It struck me dumb," he wrote to Remington. "So much has never before been put on any page of Harper."[82] Wister's reaction, coming as it did from a writer who preferred happy endings, reflected the difference between his portrayal of the West and Remington's less glorious one. *What an Unbranded Cow Has Cost* is neither romantic nor heroic, but imparts a tone of finality and exhaustion after the cowboys have wreaked a vengeance dearer, it seems, than life itself. On one level, the pathos with which Wister and Remington portray the casual mutual executions indicates the acceptable "cost" in human and animal lives. On another, the emotional cost of a cowboy's life is its demand

Figure 35. Frederic Remington, *What an Unbranded Cow Has Cost*, in Owen Wister's article "The Evolution of the Cow-Puncher," *Harper's Monthly*, September 1895

that men renounce morality and compromise, its demand that given the slightest provocation they do violence to themselves. But even if Wister had understood these self-punishments, he could not have assigned them meaning. The painting left him speechless. Remington's cowboys show "neither redemption nor atonement," the historian Ben Vorpahl writes. "When death came, it saved no one, culminated nothing."[83] Such a dire existence, Wister admitted, "soon makes a strange man of any one," and it ultimately places the cowpunchers entirely outside civilization's manners and morality, "unlike all people but each other and the wild superstitious ancestors whose blood was in their veins."[84]

Unwilling to explore the slaughter's numbing emotional costs, and ignoring its sadistic and masochistic psychological rewards, Wister attempted to end "Evolution of the Cow-Puncher" on a redemptive note. "True unto their own frontier justice, [the cowboys] have settled their differences according to its dictates," dictates in which the instantaneous avenging of admittedly "evil deeds" had the "saving grace of courage."[85] However thin and self-justifying Wister's logic of frontier justice, and however amoral the cowboys who administered it, evil deeds were redeemed by having produced the manly quality of courage. Wister had no option but to justify the carnage in terms of courage, and his readers, seeking meaning in their own lives, bought the justification. Roosevelt did his

Figure 36. Frederic Remington, *The Last Cavalier*, in Owen Wister's article "The Evolution of the Cow-Puncher," *Harper's Monthly*, September 1895 (courtesy Frederic Remington Art Museum, Ogdensburg, New York)

part to validate the emotional landscape of the cowboy world too, using the same logic as Wister to make sacrifice worthy by dint of manly glory. "We knew toil and hardship and hunger and thirst," he wrote in *The Wilderness Hunter.* "We saw men die violent deaths as they worked among the horses and cattle, or fought in evil feuds with one another; but we felt the beat of hardy life in our veins; and ours was the glory of work and the joy of living."[86]

"Evolution of the Cow-Puncher" carried another Remington painting that figured importantly in constructing the cowboy cult. In *The Last Cavalier,* a knight-cum-cowboy rides across a panorama of his mounted evolutionary forebears—armored Teutons, Spanish conquistadors, plumed gentry, and buckskinned mountain men (figure 36). To Wister, the painting represented the cowboy's fierce spirit even as it foretold his doom because modern life—at least until the appearance of the Rough Riders three years later—offered little hope of producing any more heroes. "*The Last Cavalier* comes home hardest," he wrote to Remington, "I love it and look at it—It's so very sad and so very near my private heart, . . . a poem much better and more national than Hiawatha or Evangeline. *The Last Cavalier* will haunt me forever. He inhabits a past into which I withdraw and mourn."[87] Remington was so touched by Wister's appreciation of the painting's tragic sense that he withdrew the canvas from sale and gave it to his friend.

The Last Cavalier mourns the American cowboy as the last in an evolutionary line of heroic horsemen. The strenuous environment that produced him had been overtaken by the "exhaustion of virgin pastures, the . . . wire fence, and Mr. Armour of Chicago," Remington said. Like the cowboy Wister immortalized seven years later as the Virginian, who gave up cowboy life to settle down, the cowpuncher of "Evolution" moved to town in order to marry and get a job or "fence in a little farm."[88] Although Roosevelt, too, thought the cowboy soldier vital for subduing the frontier, his theory of history as the unfolding of white civilization allowed him a more optimistic view of the cowboy's fate. "It was right and necessary that this life should pass," Roosevelt wrote for *Outlook* readers, for it was a "temporary stage" that must give way to the establishment of family farms, which were a more advantageous use of the West "from a National standpoint."[89]

Henry James appeared more eager than Wister to romanticize the American experience, and he objected to *The Virginian*'s unfittingly domestic ending. James expressed what Easterners were beginning to demand of their fictionalized and commercialized cowboy, not that he reconcile wildness and society by settling down, but that he choose to remain apart. Eastern readers wanted a cowboy onto whom they could project their emotional needs, one who flaunted his amoral, anarchistic wildness, who lived spontaneously and thrillingly and then died fulfilling a tragic destiny. "I thirst for his blood," James wrote Wister; "I should have made him perish in his flower and in some splendid and somber way."[90]

In Roosevelt's writing, the West delivered this splendid and somber death, a similar amoral ethos, and more. He transformed war and the West into the prime cultural sites for integrating the "mighty thrill" of "mighty manhood" into the nation's identity. Roosevelt took to the West with "inchoate enthusiasm and intuitive identification," Richard Slotkin observes, living out the national myth of frontier regeneration as fully as any man of his class and generation, and retelling it as compellingly as any other writer.[91] His trilogy, *Hunting Trips of a Ranchman, Ranch Life and the Hunting Trail,* and *The Wilderness Hunter,* as well as the ever popular *The Winning of the West,* figured importantly in constructions of Western imagery in the nation's mind. In 1888, *The Century* serialized Roosevelt's stories of ranch life in five articles that contained sixty-three illustrations by Remington: "Ranch Life and the Far West" (February), "The Home Ranch" (March), "The Round-Up" (April), "The Ranchman's Rifle on Crag and Prairie" (June), and "Frontier Types" (October). These writings established Roosevelt as the nation's most important historian of the trans-Appalachian migrations and connected the frontiersman to the Western cowboy.

Editors appreciated Roosevelt's contribution to the cowboy cult, noting the racialized and nationalistic manliness of his characters. In 1895, the *Atlantic Monthly* praised Roosevelt's "sketches from real life" for "rescuing from forgetfulness" the West's "extremes of human condition" and "representative figures." Roosevelt's cowboys represented the "original wilderness hunters," the *Atlantic* opined, and would, like their forebears, soon "ride away into oblivion." In 1897, the *Nation* remarked that Roosevelt's story of cowboys and roundups "marks a stage in the development of the country that cannot be ignored." The *New York Times* said that Roosevelt's *The Wilderness Hunter* performed a service for American men. "No other qualities [possessed] by a nation can atone for the lack of that vigorous manliness which the chase cultivates," the paper reported, and it praised Roosevelt for "stimulating a love of country in the rising generation." Similarly, in 1896, an unnamed writer in *The Forum* praised Roosevelt for writing "history that enlarges . . . comprehension of the character of the nation" by unfolding the "heroic and noble deeds" of earlier generations and connecting these with the historical trajectory of the Aryan race, "especially the English portion of it." "He is a man and an American," the writer concluded.[92] W. D. Trent, in an 1896 review of Roosevelt's historical work for *The Forum,* thanked him for "giving the nation a history" of the wars of "civilization against barbarism and savagery." But most of all, Trent wrote, "I thank him still more as a man . . . [whose] large and manly heart . . . enables him to live with and be one with his characters."[93]

In tandem with those of Wister, Remington, and Cody, Roosevelt's Westerns drew on earlier accounts of frontier nationalism that had accumulated since colonial and revolutionary times, stories through which conquest entered the nation's sense of itself. He drew heavily upon Francis Parkman's seven-volume *France and England in North America,* in which romantic heroes developed character and virtue by conquering savages. Taking up where Parkman left off, and dedicating *The Winning of the West* to him, Roosevelt continued many of Parkman's tropes, but tailored them to modern male concerns about civilization's fate. In his account, the colonial and early-national frontiersmen emerged as forgers of national manhood and as evolutionary precursors to the more violent, nineteenth-century heroes produced in the prairie West. He made national well-being contingent on the cultivation of "vigorous manliness" and located its origins in the racial and territorial struggles of whites against savages and outlaws on the frontier. In the contest between race-nations that constituted history, Teutonic warriors triumphed over Rome, spread through Western Europe, and conquered the Americas, where a new strain of Anglo-Saxon-

Dutch settlers peopled the frontier. This struggle to establish civilization against savagery necessarily employed force since competition drove human evolution. Domination of inferior races was the natural vindication of superior ones like the Americans, who, a product of the long evolution of the Teutonic and Anglo-Saxon "blood line," represented the highest stage of human development.[94]

In *The Winning of the West*, Roosevelt revealed how the raw Appalachian frontier brought out primitive behavior in civilized white men, forcing them to forgo empathy for themselves or any other human. He admiringly described the "savage" heart of William Campbell, an eighteenth-century settler of "giant strength," a "true type" of the "earnest, eager men who pushed the border ever farther westward." While a "firm friend, staunch patriot, and tender and loving husband," once angered he was "subject to fits of raging wrath that impelled him to any deed of violence." Campbell could write an amorous letter to his wife in which he remembered her "lovely face" and promised to bring her a three-week-old scalp he had taken from a killed Indian. He hunted down Indians, Tories, and horse thieves with "furious zest" and a "relentless and undying hatred," dispatching them with "a certain ruthlessness" and a "merciless thoroughness." If such men failed to learn mercy or develop moral character in the backwoods, Roosevelt wrote, "at least they knew that it is still better to be just and strong and brave."[95]

Mercy and morality again took second place to strength and bravery in Roosevelt's account of the 1780 Revolutionary War battle of King's Mountain. North Carolina militia commander Colonel Benjamin Cleavland was a "good friend and neighbor, devoted to his country, and also a stanch Presbyterian." Yet he was famous for the "brutality in his character" and for "persecut[ing] his . . . foes with ruthless ferocity, hanging and mutilating any Tories."[96] While Roosevelt admitted that "many of the acts of brutality were past excuse," even considering the "wrongs" these backwoodsmen and militia suffered at the hands of Indians and Tories, his rousing language betrays an admiration born of identification with the violence. In their campaign against the Cherokee in 1776, the Southern backwoodsmen had "wasted and destroyed to [their] heart's content," he wrote, until "all the Cherokee settlements west of the Appalachians had been destroyed from the face of the earth."[97] Even Cleavland's wife emerges as a "worthy helpmeet" for having decided the fate of a Tory horse thief captured by her sons. "Taking from her mouth the corn-cob pipe, . . . she coolly sentenced him to be hung, and hung he was without further delay or scruple."[98]

Sometimes Roosevelt's histories resounded with Old Testament zealotry, bidding a terrible and purifying wrath on the enemies of frontier expansion. In the third volume of *The Winning of the West,* he describes the massacre of "harmless Moravians" by more virile backwoodsmen who "laid slight stress on pity, truth, or mercy." These men expected to be "censured lightly" by their God "for merely killing members of a loathed and hated race." Roosevelt depicted the American frontier as another Canaan inherited by "another chosen people," who destroyed the land's current inhabitants, the "red savages," for their "abominations." The backwoodsmen "strove mightily to bring about the day when the heathen should have perished out of the land; for they had read in The Book that he was accursed who . . . kept his sword back from blood. There was many a stern frontier zealot who deemed all the red men . . . corn for the reaping. Such a one rejoiced to see his followers do to the harmless Moravians as the Danites once did to the people of Laish, who lived quiet and secure, . . . and who yet were smitten with the edge of the sword, and the city burnt with fire."[99] In Roosevelt's portrayal, backwoodsmen like Campbell and Cleavland invoked the essence of a virile and untamed national manhood: strength above scruple, the satisfactions of ferocity, and the capacity for "any deed of violence" against even harmless whites. As radically excessive as these characters' qualities of "vigorous manliness" seemed, Roosevelt stressed that they represented "all that is best in our national life."

For Roosevelt, as for Wister and Remington, the prairie's "grim and forbidding" landscape created a specific type of man. Although Abraham Lincoln and Andrew Jackson had honed their manliness "grappling with wild surroundings," Roosevelt maintained, landscapes figured less in their world than they did in the world of the later part of the nineteenth century.[100] In the cowboy cult, harsh Western landscapes became players in their own right, whose role was to inflict psychological pain on the hero. In his own Western life, Roosevelt said, landscapes produced exquisite feelings of "hopeless, never ending grief" and bred a love of nature's terrors and an admiration for the stoic and determined men who refused to flinch in their grip. Harsh winters required a special heroism. In them, Roosevelt wrote, "all the land is like granite; the great rivers stand still in their beds, as if turned to frosted steel. In the long nights there is no sound to break the lifeless silence." Winter brought "great hardship and exposure," and its loneliness could produce "iron desolation." Weaker men went mad, Roosevelt wrote, but in others the "stern and unending struggles with their iron-bound surroundings" generated "abounding vitality" and "bronzed and rugged strength."[101] The landscapes' trial by fire hardened men into "reckless riders" who lived a "free and hardy life" and "unmoved looked in the eyes of life or death."[102]

Roosevelt's fictional Western cowboy lived in an imagined landscape of epic magnificence and elemental savagery where never-ending struggle against outlaws, Indians, brutal weather, and impossible terrain summoned equally elemental responses. The bleak and merciless qualities of the sky and the landscape made the cowboy the way he was: silent, unfeeling, unquestioning, and uncomplaining.[103] His existence depended on using brute force without a moment's hesitation. Roosevelt's cowboys appeared "sinewy, hardy, self-reliant" in their adventures as "grim pioneer[s] of our race." Grim, perhaps, since they were "rather silent, self-contained men," given "to drink, and when drunk, to shoot," but for Roosevelt they exhibited the essential American qualities. "A cowboy will not submit tamely to an insult and is ever ready to avenge his own wrongs; nor has he an overwrought fear of shedding blood." He possessed, in fact, "few of the emasculated, milk-and-water moralities admired by the pseudo-philanthropists"; instead he possessed, "to a very high degree, the stern, manly qualities that are invaluable to a nation."[104] In the fantasizing imagination, Jane Tompkins observes, he was superman: without God, armed to the teeth, and invincible.[105]

Promoting, in his popular writings, his own bodily prowess gained out West and in the Cuban campaign, Roosevelt made the cowboy's requirements the same as the nation's: masculine authority, mastery of self, productive and reproductive work, and especially the capacity to suffer and to unleash violence on others. "Daring and hardihood and iron endurance," he said, "in endless feats of arms are not merely indispensable traits for pioneers" in the "ceaseless strife waged against wild man and wild nature"; they were traits needed by "every mighty and successful people."[106] Roosevelt located American superiority in the self-actualization of its pure males and promised to make the nation mighty through "daring" acts that hurled "iron endurance" against new, modern forms of wildness. Yet for him, the final realization of pure manliness was not the end goal of history, for triumph would bring an annihilating stasis. In Roosevelt's worldview, the quest for civilization constituted a "ceaseless" struggle with "endless feats of arms," an insistence that drove him toward a theory of perpetual war.[107]

William James, the nation's most influential philosopher, attributed to human instinct men's growing taste for the sense of social isolation coupled with fantastic moral invincibility that was packaged so neatly in the cowboy cult. Although men also have amiable instincts, he observed, the "hunting and pugnacious instincts," once aroused, overwhelm sociability because men give in to the emotional excitement. In war or the hunt, these excitements drive out peaceful instincts, and the "pleasure of disinterested cruelty . . . inhibit[s] our sympathy absolutely. This accounts for the cruelty of [groups] of men hounding each other on to bait or torture a victim. The blood mounts to the eyes," James said, "and sympathy's chance is gone."[108]

Giving philosophical if not biological license to notions of instinctual male primitivism, James encouraged Eastern men to reclaim their manhood from the moralists. Only when men risked pain and death in the face of insurmountable odds could they imagine themselves as true men, men who in the throes of immediacy could not stop to evaluate a moral code that appeared meaningless by comparison. The amorality popularized by fictionalized cowboys and legitimized by a moralist of James's stature was reflected in the seemingly unconcerned reaction of Americans to acts of brutality committed by the U.S. occupation army in the Philippines between 1899 and 1902. Official codes of amoral behavior employed by American troops and officers on the Pacific frontier became public after the Senate investigated a series of atrocities. Widespread airing of the atrocities provoked a noisy outcry among anti-imperialists like Mark Twain, William Jennings Bryan, and James. Yet few leaders feared that ordinary Americans might be offended, and no general cry of alarm arose. As Americans followed daily news about the wars, the value system embedded in the cult of the cowboy soldier provided a means of psychologically absorbing accounts of the otherwise disturbing and seemingly barbarous actions of the U.S. Army. Alfred Mahan summed up the general feeling: " 'Our country, right or wrong,' may be very bad morality," he wrote, "but it is a tremendous force to reckon with. Disinterested emotion, even unreasoning, may be just the one factor which diplomacy cannot master."[109] As Roosevelt explained it more simply in his popular autobiography: "Out on the frontier, life is reduced to its elemental conditions."[110]

"Stubborn tenacity" and "stubborn fixity of purpose" were two of Roosevelt's favorite phrases for describing the unemotional exterior that marked a true man and enabled him to ignore the outcry of armchair moralists. Tenacity represented "the only quality the lack of which is as unpardonable in the nation as in the man. It is the antithesis of levity, fickleness, volatility, of undue exaltation, of undue depression, of hysteria and neuroticism in all their myriad forms." In Roosevelt's mind, tenacity always necessitated suffering and martyrdom. It could only be acquired through pain, from which the fickle and hysteric shrank or at which they flinched. "Grinding need," experienced in times of national crisis, trains "either nation or individual" to "greatness." "The lesson of unyielding, unflinching, unfaltering perseverance in the course in which the nation has entered is one very necessary."[111]

COWBOYS TO SOLDIERS

Just as Americans neared the end of 250 years of war against Native Americans, the West ceased to provide a proving ground for Roosevelt's "stern, manly qualities," and it seemed logical that war with Spain and suppression of the Philippine insurrection would provide the next frontier. Three years after the publication of "Evolution of the Cow-Puncher," Remington suddenly found himself reporting what he called "the Cowboy's War." From their vantage points in Cuba, no fewer than five prominent writers and artists—Roosevelt included—interpreted the six-week war in the American imagination. Stephen Crane and Jacob Riis were there, both reporting on the Rough Riders. William Randolph Hearst of the *New York Journal* sent Remington and Richard Harding Davis, who also wrote for *Scribners' Magazine* and *Harper's Weekly*, to see the war "up close." These writers interpreted the war for their readers, encouraging them to side with their government, to look favorably on war's tragedy, and to open themselves to its seductive violence.

In 1898, Roosevelt was thirty-nine and in his prime. He desperately wanted to go to war, and his cowboy credentials gave him an authentic voice to call men to arms. Friends like Winthrop Chanler knew "Roosevelt is going mad wild to fight and hack and hew."[112] If unable to participate, Roosevelt said, "I shall be eating my heart out; I like action."[113] Twenty years later, he would feel "deep sympathy" for the men of 1918 who were also "eating their hearts out because they cannot get into the fighting line."[114] He would have left his wife's deathbed to go to Cuba, he said, and he quit his job as undersecretary of the navy and left her home sick with the six children. A determined Roosevelt convinced Secretary of War Russell Alger and General of the Army Nelson A. Miles to give him a lieutenant colonel's commission in the army and to allow the formation of a volunteer regiment. Swamped with over twenty thousand applications, he chose a regiment of one thousand cowboys, hunters, ranchers, miners, former football players, polo players, oarsmen, and other men whom William Roscoe Thayer called "lovers of adventure from the great Eastern cities," many of whom Roosevelt knew personally.[115] Roosevelt carefully fashioned the regiment, manning it with a preponderance of unruly Southwestern cowboys leavened with Ivy League athletes, Jews, Irishmen, Italians, Scandinavians, and part-Indian scouts, the latter segregated in a separate company. His drew his officer corps from wealthy recruits from the Ivy League whom he called "the very inspiration of young manhood," a clear representation of white national manhood at the core of the Rough Riders. No blacks needed apply and none were sought, since mixing in the "most inferior" races would sully the melting pot.[116]

"It was a remarkable spectacle, this flocking to a man not yet forty," William Roscoe Thayer wrote. "But Roosevelt's name was already known; it excited great admiration in many, grave doubts in many, and curiosity in all."[117] From Western novels and Cody's extravaganzas, the press appropriated the term Rough Riders and applied it to the nation's favorite cowboy-cum-soldier. "The fact that [he] had become so prominent a figure in the West," his sister Corinne observed, "proved the essential factor in the flocking to his standard of that mass of virile manhood."[118]

Roosevelt chose Leonard Wood as the regiment's colonel. A thirty-seven-year-old Harvard-educated career army surgeon, Wood had won the Medal of Honor fighting Apaches. Roosevelt found that Wood "combined, in a very high degree, the qualities of entire manliness with entire uprightness and cleanliness of character." Yet Roosevelt equally emphasized his primitive qualities. "By nature a soldier," he said, Wood was a man of "extraordinary physical strength and endurance" who could withstand "intolerable fatigue, intolerable thirst, never satisfied hunger . . . against the most cruel and dangerous foes." He was "one of the two or three white men who could stand fatigue and hardship as well as an Apache."[119]

Part of a generation privileged with a propertied upbringing, an elite education, and a sense of obligation for public service, Roosevelt and Wood shared a common perception about history and a similar vision of the country's needs. "We had the same ideals, the same way of looking at life; we had kindred tastes; we were fond of the same sports; [we were] men with families."[120] Many of Roosevelt's friends recognized that both men lived and loved the strenuous life to an extraordinary degree. Jacob Riis liked to see them together in Washington the year they became friends "because they are men of the same strong type."[121] Wood had acted as what Roosevelt called his "playmate" after they first met in Washington in 1897, and throughout the war and into the White House years the two men wrestled, hiked, rode, and played the game of singlestick: "We put on heavily padded helmets, breastplates and gauntlets and wrap bath towels around our necks, and then we turn and beat one another like carpets."[122] Their obvious delight in physical jousting attests to the powerful psychological unity found in regular, strenuous bodily contact between men who deemed themselves worthy specimens of masculinity mirrored in one another.

At the San Antonio camp where the Rough Riders trained, Roosevelt fairly exulted in his and Wood's exploits. The regiment battle cry was "rough, tough, we're the stuff. We want to fight and we can't get enough." When in May of 1898 the regiment's colonel finished reading the men their orders for Cuba, the troops cheered, Roosevelt danced his war dance that he had theretofore used upon killing game, and he and Wood "embraced like schoolboys."[123] Part of a national elite from which emerged many statesmen and military commanders, Roosevelt and Wood shared a common ambition to prove themselves as warriors and to bring to the nation the things they valued in themselves.

In 1898, Remington was thirty-nine and, like Roosevelt and Wood, desperately wanted a part in the Cuban campaign, albeit a safer one. "There's bound to be a lovely scrap around Havana," Remington wrote to Wister in June of that year, "a real bloodletting" and "a big murdering" that would "make men glad and death easy."[124] "With the Fifth Corps," published in *Harper's Monthly* in November 1898, was one of ten articles Remington wrote and illustrated on the war action. His reporting impressed many who took part in the fighting. U.S. Navy captain Robley D. Evans, commander of the *Iowa* in Sampson's fleet off Cuba, congratulated Remington on his "wholly satisfying and satisfactory," realistic descriptions of the fighting. "With the Fifth Corps" is "bubbling over with vitality and . . . raciness," Evans wrote; "you have greatly moved me."[125]

Remington admiringly described Major Generals Henry W. Lawton, Civil War Medal of Honor recipient and captor of Geronimo, and Adna R. Chaffee, Indian fighter. Both men had been Roosevelt's commanders in Cuba, and Roosevelt had described each of them as "anxious to get first blood."[126] "What satisfying soldiers Lawton and Chaffee are!" Remington wrote, "both seasoned, professional military types. Lawton, big and long, forceful, and with iron determination. Chaffee, who never dismounts but for a little sleep . . . and whose head might have been presented to him by one of William's Norman barons." Warming to his subject, Remington linked Chaffee's head to Europe's racial heritage and chivalric past. "Such a head! We used to sit around and study that head [that] belonged to . . . the period . . . when the race was young and strong; and it has 'warrior' sculptured in every line." In his paintings and drawings of the war, Remington made certain, he said, that such racial archetypes as Chaffee "look their part" since "war is a primitive art." And he reminded his readers that "life never runs so high in a man as it does when he is charging on the field of battle."[127]

Life ran high for Roosevelt. Disembarking with his regiment in June, he was assigned to support regular army troops assaulting Spanish positions in the hills east of Santiago. The fighting lasted only three weeks, and the Rough Riders saw action in three of the war's four major battles, Las Guasimas, Kettle Hill, and San Juan Hill. On 1 July 1898, Roosevelt's dramatic charge up Kettle Hill routed the Spanish defenders. He then gathered remnants of several regiments into a reserve force that supported regular army forces assaulting San Juan Hill. He praised his men's bravery as they lay on their stomachs and returned Spanish fire. He rode his horse back and forth in full view of the Spanish, never taking cover while bullets flew all about. Given that Roosevelt was the only mounted soldier in the battle, any witness would have laid odds that the Spanish would kill him. By the time the battle ended, ninety of the 450 Rough Riders had been killed or wounded, including Roosevelt, who received three minor wounds.[128] But this is exactly what he had come for. Surveying the battlefield that evening, Roosevelt's close companion and Rough Rider Bob Ferguson observed that "T. was just reveling in victory and gore."[129]

In 1898, at the end of the war, Roosevelt commissioned Remington to paint the war's most famous event. In *The Charge of the Rough Riders at San Juan Hill*, Remington captured its essence (figure 37). Jacob Riis provided commentary in the *New York Sun*. As a mounted Roosevelt with drawn revolver led a group of charging and dying Rough Riders and army regulars in an assault on Spanish fortifications,

> bullets were raining down at them, and shot and shells from the batteries were sweeping everything. . . . "Forward! Charge!" Lieutenant-Colonel Roosevelt led, waving his sword. Out into the open the men went, and up the hill. Death to every man seemed certain. Up, up they went, . . . in the face of death, men dropping from the ranks at every step . . . [yet] not a man flinching. . . . Roosevelt was a hundred feet in the lead. Finally his horse was shot from under him, but he landed on his feet and . . . charged up the hill afoot.[130]

Americans avid for war reportage enthusiastically received Remington's paintings and articles. To consumers used to fictions of the real, it mattered little that Roosevelt actually led the charge on nearby Kettle Hill, not San Juan Hill; that Kettle Hill was smaller and much less well defended; that the Rough Riders arrived at San Juan only after it had been taken by regular army troops; or that Roosevelt had discarded his sword earlier that week and had left his horse at the base of the hill. And it did not matter to them that the actual charge up Kettle Hill was a slow crawl on the soldiers stomachs, that several regular army platoons reached the hill's summit simultaneously with Roosevelt, or that most of the losses on Kettle Hill were actually borne by the Tenth Regular Cavalry, a contingent

Figure 37. Frederic Remington, *The Charge of the Rough Riders at San Juan Hill*, 1898 (courtesy Frederic Remington Art Museum, Ogdensburg, New York)

of black soldiers.[131] Only one black soldier appears in Remington's painting. What mattered was that the nation came to believe that the charge actually took place on San Juan Hill. What mattered, the *Santa Fe New Mexican* reported, was that the Rough Riders taught the civilized world "that America possesses a class of men who, when . . . brought face to face with the enemy, never quit fighting until victory or death comes."[132] What mattered was that Remington's and Riis's account established Roosevelt's masculinity as a spectacle where men visualized a mounted hero charging at the head of his troops toward the enemy, prepared to sacrifice his life for the nation and displaying a courage that bordered on suicidal recklessness. What mattered was that these and similar accounts affirmed the Rough Riders as true inheritors of the cowboy tradition of white, aggressive, nationalist manhood. What mattered was, as Riis wondered, "In how many American homes was that splendid story read that morning with a thrill never quite to be got over?"[133]

Roosevelt, for one, never got over it. Throughout his life he considered the day of the charge "the great day of my life."[134] When Charles G. Washburn, an old friend from his Harvard days, asked Roosevelt which life experience had given him "the most pleasure," Roosevelt replied, "The charge up San Juan Hill." Important politicians did their part in making Roosevelt's acts into moments of national glory. In July of 1898, John Hay congratulated Roosevelt on his "brilliant campaign." "You obeyed your own daemon," Hay exuded and then quoted Sir Walter Scott: "One crowded hour of glorious life / is worth an age without a name." Hay continued: "You have written your name on several pages of your country's history."[135] In outlandish displays of self-congratulation, Roosevelt culti-vated Remington's and the media's popular image of him and never at-tempted to correct the account historically, helping instead to inscribe it in national memory as the public had come to understand it. In early 1899, he published a number of articles on the Cuban campaign, and *Scribner's Magazine* serialized his dramatic account of the fighting, *The Rough Rid-ers*, published later that year as a book.

The "Cowboy's War" soon placed the man Mark Hanna called "that damned cowboy" in the White House and furnished the means by which Roosevelt imported Western icons first into the Cuban battlefield and thence into political culture.[136] Together with literary versions of the ro-mantic cowboy life, Roosevelt's histories, Buffalo Bill's Wild West Show with performing U.S. Army regulars, Remington's paintings and draw-ings, and Wister's "Evolution of the Cow-Puncher," Roosevelt's and Wood's wartime exploits merged into an archetype of the nation's new semifictional warrior-hero. Remington painted many scenes of this hero, but never more tellingly than in *Portrait of Major General Leonard Wood* (1909), now located at the United States Military Academy at West Point (figure 38). Remington had pressured his longtime friend to come to his Connecticut home and sit for the portrait, which he finally did a decade af-ter the war. As he and Wood reminisced about Arizona and the "old times" and talked about the new American "Island Empires" of the Caribbean and Pacific, Remington thought that "without in the least sensing it, Wood has been a king."[137] True to Remington's image of him, in the painting Wood is self-possessed and majestic as he sits astride a finer horse than he would have ridden in Cuba. The general's mouth is open as if he is giving a command to off-picture soldiers while behind him others advance with rifles ready. Ramrod-straight and dignified, his physical body, like that of his fine horse, conveys mastery, intactness, cleanliness, precision, and dominance.

Remington's artistic skills figured in another commemoration of the Cowboy's War. In September of 1898, as they mustered out at Montauk Point, Long Island, the men of the Rough Rider regiment presented Rem-ington's *Bronco Buster* to Roosevelt (figure 39). "There could have been no more appropriate gift" as this bronze by Frederic Remington, Roosevelt appreciatively told his assembled men. "The foundation of the regiment was the cow-puncher, and we have him here in bronze." He would value the bronze, he said, "more that I do the weapons I carried through the campaign."[138] *Bronco Buster* was the nineteenth century's most popular, and probably most profitable, bronze sculpture. Remington made over two

Figure 38.   Frederic Remington, *Portrait of Major General Leonard Wood,* 1909 (courtesy West Point Museum Art Collection, U.S. Military Academy)

hundred casts of it in his lifetime. Among many who praised it, *Harper's Monthly* editor William Dean Howells said the sculpture "took me tremendously." However, the greatest compliment Remington ever had, the artist wrote Roosevelt, "was when the Rough Riders put their brand on my bronze." Roosevelt wrote back, "I have long looked hungrily at that bronze, but to have it come to me [from the Rough Riders] seemed almost too good."[139] Popular notions of the cowboy's ability to dominate the untamed spirit and raw energy of the West were condensed into Remington's image of him busting a thousand pounds of lunging horseflesh. In 1913, the editors of *Outlook* illustrated "In Cowboy Land," part of Roosevelt's serialized biography, with a full-page photo of the *Bronco Buster,* combining in the public mind Roosevelt's actual cowboy life with Remington's artful rendition.[140]

In *The Rough Riders,* Roosevelt constructed his soldiers in the style of his own, Wister's, and Remington's archetypal cowboys. An aesthetic style that enhanced real-life heroism, as with Roosevelt's attention to Rough Rider uniforms, did not strike men as showy or effeminate because it followed the tradition of decorating the cowboy established in literature and melodrama. In keeping with a military tradition that emphasized the ornamental aspects of officers' uniforms—the brass buttons, campaign

Figure 39. Frederic Remington, *The Bronco Buster*, 1895, remodeled 1909 (courtesy Frederic Remington Art Museum, Ogdensburg, New York)

medals, honorific stripes, and saber—George Custer, the "boy General," had designed his own uniform, complete with double-striped trousers, a red necktie, and a jacket with gold braids. William Cody, too, decked himself out; for his extravaganzas he wore black velvet with scarlet trim, silver buttons, and lace.[141] As Mahan assured readers of his naval reminiscences, "pride in personal appearance, dandyism, is quite consonant with military feeling."[142]

So to nobody's surprise, the Rough Riders, "in their slouch-hats, blue flannel shirts, brown trousers, leggings, and boots, with handkerchiefs knotted loosely around their necks," Roosevelt said, "looked exactly as a body of cowboy cavalry should look."[143] Just as he had once decorated himself as a cowboy, with spurs, neck scarf, belt buckle, pearl-handled revolver from Tiffany's, and tailor-made fringed shirt, of which he owned one hundred, he now appointed his Rough Rider image with an ornamental saber, a personal revolver, and an army uniform tailored by Brooks Brothers, topped with a neck scarf tucked in the collar.

For consumers of the cowboy cult in its Rough Rider variation, Roosevelt's self-fashioning evoked Wister's fictional emphasis on the cowpuncher's "barbaric pleasure in finery." He "sews tough leather fringe" on shirt and pants, stamps leather pockets with "a heavy rose," and sports a leather cartridge belt "sagging in a slant upon his hips . . . buckled with jaunty arrogance." Knotted at his throat, his handkerchief is "chosen for its color and soft texture . . . to draw the eye of a woman." His pistol, used "with murderous skill," appears "pretty, with ivory or mother-of-pearl for a handle." He sits on a "heavy, splendid saddle," likewise adorned with a "luxury of straps and leather thongs."[144]

Crafted cowboy action followed crafted appearance. In language familiar to American readers of tales of male outdoor exploits, Roosevelt drew an aura of militant savagery around the Rough Riders. Each of the "sinewy, saturnine, fearless" soldiers stood out as a "killer of game, a tamer of horses, or a queller of disorder among his people," he wrote. Even more ominously, each one "stood out with a more evil prominence as himself a dangerous man" who was "given to the taking of life on small provocation, or who . . . [lived] outside the law if the occasion demanded it."[145] To Roosevelt, the Rough Riders' usefulness to the nation lay in this very unruliness, a natural outcome of their life on the range. They were "accustomed to handling wild and savage horses," he wrote in his account of the war, "used, for all their lawless freedom, to the rough discipline of the round-up and the mining company." They were "children of the dragon's blood" on whom "danger acted like wine," he told Bradley Tyler Johnson, emphasizing what seemed to him their murderous charm. "They are great big, goodhearted, homicidal children."[146] Jacob Riis reported that it was predicted that Rough Riders could not be disciplined, and Roosevelt agreed. On the frontier, "his men" had fought Indians, Mexicans, and wild beasts. They had served in sheriffs' posses, and they had also taken the law into their own hands as "those bodies of armed men with which the growing civilization of the border finally puts down its savagery." Although "one or two of them needed rough discipline and they got it," Roosevelt savored his men's existence on the savage edge and thrilled at their easy capacity to appropriate its anarchic violence. Some of the Rough Riders, he wrote, were tainted by "those fierce kinds of crime into which the lawless spirits who dwell on the border-land between civilization and savagery so readily drift."[147]

After the war, Roosevelt understood that many of the Rough Riders found it difficult to resume "a life of peaceful regularity" and was sympathetic when they wrote to him for assistance when they were in various kinds of trouble, including bigamy, horse thievery, and in one case the accidental shooting of a "lady." The Rough Rider pled that it was a mistake: "But, Colonel, . . . I was not shooting at the lady. I was shooting at my wife." According to Roosevelt, the former Rough Rider thought that upon hearing the tale the president would consider it a "sufficient excuse" between "men of the world" to distinguish between his accidental and his intended victim. Evidently so. Roosevelt's friend John Burroughs told of Roosevelt's reaction to news of the shooting: "the presidential laughter rang out over the tree-tops."[148] According to William Roscoe Thayer, "Roosevelt had large charity for sinners of this type."[149] Roosevelt, however, omitted his jolly reaction to the story from his official autobiography.

At war's end in the fall of 1898, when Roosevelt campaigned for governor of New York, he and Republican party officials discovered the popular appeal of the veteran cavalrymen despite—or, seemingly, on account of—their wild habits. In this first bid for major public office, Roosevelt invited uniformed Rough Riders to officially accompany his whistle-stop tour through New York towns, and before each speech he had the Rough Rider bugler, Emilio Casse, sound "Charge."[150] "You have heard the trumpet that sounded to bring you here," Roosevelt told eager audiences; "I have heard it tear the tropic dawn when it summoned us to fight at Santiago." He welcomed the Rough Riders' colorful presence and told war stories that commended their "iron endurance."[151]

On one occasion in 1900, when Roosevelt was running for vice president, a former member of his regiment shot a populist newspaper editor who had criticized the candidate. "We had to leave [the Rough Rider] to be tried," Roosevelt said, "and, as he had no money I left him $150 to hire counsel." At a regimental reunion after Roosevelt became president, he greeted a former Rough Rider who had recently been released from jail for killing a man. "How did you do it?" Roosevelt asked the man about his release. "With a .38 on a .45 frame, Colonel," the man replied. "I chuckled over the answer," Roosevelt said, as he mentally shifted an account of an actual death into yet another amusing anecdote.[152] In these and other stories of former Rough Riders that Roosevelt related while he was president, he seems to have been unapologetic and not a little proud of their lawlessness.

While making his 1904 presidential bid, Roosevelt kept a keen eye on the versions of his Rough Rider cowboy-soldier image that appeared in the national media. He complained to James Ford Rhodes that it would have "looked ridiculous" for his campaign supporters to have pictured him like those hostile newspaper illustrators did, who "invariably represented me in the rough rider uniform, or else riding a bucking broncho and roping a steer, or carrying a big stick and threatening foreign nations."[153] Nevertheless, such cowboy-soldier renditions and the media attention flattered Roosevelt. Just ten days before he wrote to Rhodes, he had negotiated the details of his image with the sculptor Frederick Mac-Monnies, who was busy designing a bronze statue of Roosevelt as Rough Rider for the White House. MacMonnies had asked for a photo of Roosevelt jumping a fence in his "soldier suit," to which Roosevelt replied that he jumped fences in a riding habit on a horse with a short tail and never "with a sword and revolver in my belt." Roosevelt tried to persuade the sculptor against representing him in this Eastern hunting attire, which smacked of the effete pastimes of decadent English noblemen. Instead, when Roosevelt imagined his wartime Rough Rider self immortalized in bronze, he saw himself armed and riding a "war horse with a long tail" that would presumably appear less frivolous and more soldierly than a bobtailed hunter-jumper. "Now which way do you want to make the statuette?" Roosevelt wrote MacMonnies. "It seems to me it would be better in uniform."[154]

Better indeed, because the cowboy soldier had become part of how most people sensed themselves to be American and because Roosevelt had cultivated this sense, promoting himself as one of the cult's central action figures. As he endlessly told his readers, he "lived and worked like any other frontiersman"; he could ranch, hunt, and "put down evil-doers, white and red . . . exactly as did the pioneers."[155]

If the imagined cowboy had emerged from "fictions of the real" into reality in 1898, he later retreated back into fantasy, nowhere more vividly than in Roosevelt's Inauguration Day parade in 1905. By then, most Americans had begun to see the Indian wars as a nostalgic and colorful episode in the nation's past, and it seemed perfectly appropriate for the army to take the famed Chiricahua Apache chief Geronimo out of an army stockade and bring him to Washington to ride in the parade. Equally appropriate to the parade's fantasy, the actor Tom Mix dressed in a Rough Rider uniform and joined Roosevelt's regiment as it rode up Pennsylvania Avenue; he was a pure imposter posing as a veteran.[156] Although in 1902 Roosevelt privately castigated General of the Army Nelson Miles for his role in the Wounded Knee massacre and in Sitting Bull's death, the prevailing public image of heroic Indians and even more heroic Indian- and Spaniard-fighting cavalry pivoted around the nation's manly president.[157]

HUNTING

For Roosevelt, wild-game hunting was as dangerous as cowboying and frontier warfare, and every bit as serious a producer of men. War, for him, was simply "bigger hunting."[158] In 1880, when he was hunting in Illinois, Roosevelt wrote to his sister Anna, "We have had three good days shooting, and I feel twice the man for it already."[159] Roosevelt had been raised amid the relatively tame Eastern hunting culture, and from an early age he had learned to shoot, jump fences, and ride to hounds. As a youth, he read Mayne Reid's *The Boy Hunters; or, Adventures in Search of a White Buffalo,* which portrayed white men's forays against Indians and wild animals in the exotic wilderness. In this story, boys engage in primitive struggles with nature, yet remain white. They hunt buffalo, stalking and killing a white—and thus superior—beast and finding their manhood in the process.[160] Restoring the white hunter's lost virility became a lifelong theme in Roosevelt's writings, and he encouraged other writers to help create a national literature of masculine hunting prowess. "I am immensely impressed with your hunting trip with those two dogs and the knife," President Roosevelt wrote in 1904 to Stewart Edward White, who had just returned from a two-week foray during which he had killed 105 boars with a knife and dogs, an average of over seven a day. You must "write a straight-out hunting book in perfectly serious style with scientific accuracy," for the nation is "lacking enough really first-class hunting books." Roosevelt, who rarely missed a chance to assure his friends that the nation's president did not lack for hunting ardor, added in his letter to White: "I have a bully knife with a fourteen-inch blade, and I firmly believe that one thrust would do the business . . . even against a boar."[161]

For devotees of the cowboy-soldier cult, killing and trophy taking had long been a necessary part of developing manliness on the American frontier. Buffalo Bill Cody's reputation rested on his having killed over 4,280 buffalo in an eight-month period in 1867 when he was a five-hundred-dollar-a-month commercial meat hunter for the Kansas Pacific Railroad.[162] It was this feat of marksmanship that gave rise to the name Buffalo Bill and ensconced in the public mind not just his bravery as a buffalo hunter, but also his role as a cavalry scout in ending the militant struggle of the nomadic plains Indians. In the 1860s, approximately 225,000 Indians and fifteen million buffalo lived on the Great Plains, and the hunting and killing of both merged in the minds of Easterners. Indeed, by the early

1880s, a new form of hunting tourism arose in the West, in which wealthy Eastern sportsmen joined the stream of land speculators and surveyors, railroad men, fur traders, and ranchers who incorporated the mountains and plains into the nation's economy. The sports tourists lived in elite resorts and shot buffalo from Pullman cars, and the more daring among them lived in camps and traveled on horseback and relied on guides to find the big game that provided adventure, danger, and most of all, a grand background against which they could portray to friends and family back home their manly experience.[163]

By 1885, when the buffalo's near extermination effectively ended the Indians' resistance, Cody deftly transported whites' hunting and killing of wild buffalo and recalcitrant Indians into his Wild West Show, leading the consuming public to expect ordinary entertainment in macabre form. As Alexander Nemerov has pointed out, middle-class American men did not have to experience danger and death by killing Indians or Spaniards or by hunting game; they had only to imagine it. They were helped along in their imagination by the glorification of hunting and warfare in popular entertainments and outdoor monumental sculpture, and the walls of their parlors, bars, and men's clubs were adorned with countless decorative heads and hides of killed animals.[164]

In midlife, Roosevelt remained his generation's most widely publicized and avid hunter. Certain that he had inherited the racial and civilizing mission of those two frontiersmen of buckskin authenticity Daniel Boone and Davy Crockett, he sought to reinvigorate Eastern men with their vitality, a task he believed would best be accomplished when Easterners found blood brotherhood in the wilderness. In 1887, he cofounded the Boone and Crockett Club with George B. Grinnell, the Yale naturalist and editor of *Forest and Stream*. In the name of those two characters symbolic of the advance of civilization—Boone, closer to the noble savage, and Crockett, the bloodthirsty scalper—this gentlemen's social and conservation club encouraged patrician hunter-naturalists to recapture the wilderness, reclaim their primitive selves, and perpetuate the outdoors for their descendants. Unlike the transcendentalists, whose passive and bloodless affinity with nature Roosevelt thought "slightly anaemic," Boone and Crockett Club members envisioned a Darwinian struggle with nature that would test and strengthen men.[165] Their deeply sought and highly charged hunting and killing experiences flowed directly into the nation's and even the race's virility, in Roosevelt's estimation, because they fostered the development of "vigorous and masterful people" with "energy, resolution, manliness, self-reliance, . . . without which no race can do its life work well."[166] Francis Parkman belonged the club, as did Madison Grant, Henry Fairfield

Osborne, Gifford Pinchot, Henry Stimson, Carl Schurz, Aldo Leopold, Henry Cabot Lodge, Owen Wister, and Frederic Remington. The club was instrumental in the establishment of the American Museum of Natural History.

As Roosevelt pursued wilderness hunting on three continents, he not only identified with and bonded with the white hunting partners and guides who accompanied him, but also appropriated the "primitivism" of men he met on his hunting forays. In South America, he noted, the traveling sportsman "will take pleasure" in the "daring and reckless horsemen" of the plains and the "dark-skinned paddlers" of dugout canoes in the equatorial jungle. Likewise, in America the hunter reveled in the "white and red and half-breed hunters of the Rockies," and in Africa, in the "faithful black gunbearers who have stood steadily at his elbow when the lion came." Roosevelt "became really attached," he admitted, to such men "still in their hunting stage" because he believed he could glimpse civilized men's remote past in their "courage and loyalty and devotion to duty" and their legends and myths of "supernatural beasts." In Africa, Roosevelt felt as if he had "traveled and hunted in the Pleistocene" with hunters of "later Paleolithic times." To historian George Baxter Ward, Roosevelt was "very consciously groping his way back to that more primitive stage for the character-building . . . value of the experience."[167]

Through these attempts to craft a manly primitivism, Roosevelt elevated the bloody killing of animals and men to the most self-realizing act, partly because it supplied an authenticity little available in contemporary urban life. Besides infusing hunters with a sense of power, killing also brought them a pleasure that came from the anticipation of the chase and the suspension of ordinary thoughts and feelings in favor of emotions raised at the moment of death. While Roosevelt's youthful bird collecting and taxidermy was motivated at least in part by a desire for scientific preservation, as an adult, he came to love killing, and he advertised it for its "strong, eager pleasure." Roosevelt's Winchester rifle provided "great satisfaction," he wrote to his sister Bamie in 1896. "Certainly it was as wicked-shooting a weapon as I ever handled, and knocked the bucks over with a sledge-hammer."[168]

No wonder that in a 1904 article, "Deer Stalking," *Sandow's Magazine of Physical Culture* held hunting to be "the most fascinating sport we have left us." Fascinating at least to the "we" of the assumed fraternity of white hunters, because of the high drama surrounding the actual death. "The rifle rings out, the bullet finds its billet in his heart," and in the "act of leaping [the stag] drops with a dull thud among the heather," where he writhes in the "throes of death." Around the felled deer, *Sandow's* observed, "the excited stalkers gather to relieve their pent-up feelings in a wild hurrah, and witness that last desperate struggle. Slowly the convulsions grow feebler, the eyes that some minutes before had sparkled full of life . . . grow cold; a hunting knife releases the fleet, tireless spirit and he stretches out on the blood-stained heather, beautiful in death."[169] Similar emotions were of such prime importance for Roosevelt that many hunting guides remarked on his wild exuberance. "I never saw anyone so enthused in my life," guide Joe Ferris commented, remembering when Roosevelt killed a great bull bison in Montana in 1883. As he watched Roosevelt dancing and whooping around the carcass, he recalled, "By golly, I was enthused myself."[170]

As Klaus Theweleit explains in *Male Fantasies*, during the act of killing, "the unaccustomed release of emotion indicates that psychic defenses have been lowered or dropped altogether." These defenses ordinarily function to prevent the individual's consciousness "from having access to repressed desires and clusters of fear-charged drive" and to protect it "against the force of forbidden excitation, against emotional intensities which he is incapable of 'working over' and which might lead to feelings of 'inundation.' "[171] If indeed those ordinary protections explain Roosevelt's desperate fashioning of white unity and wholeness, then purposeful acts of stabbing, wounding, flaying, and beheading all constituted personal, intimate, exciting forms of physical violence that were sublimated and transferred to the dead or dying animal. During and immediately after these acts, the deepest, most fundamental emotions were projected onto the carcass in order to purge them, to save oneself from them. For Roosevelt, who insisted that he was not a "game butcher," killing wild beasts represented the overcoming of the primitive emotionalism that a man feared in himself—the savagery he must differentiate himself from, the eroticism he must not lust for, and the effeminacy he must not be contaminated by. Through cruel treatment of animals, Jane Tompkins observes, "the spontaneous, exuberant, fleshly, and passionate part of human beings is a continual object of punishment, manipulation, and control."[172]

Dropping those defenses, releasing emotion unexpectedly and giving over to it, explains the satisfactions, if not the pleasures, of killing. Repressed emotions are unleashed in radically excessive ways and directed alternately toward objects of desire, in the case of an eight-point buck, and of aversion, in the case of a Spaniard in Cuba. The moment of a hunted animal's death brings the killer as horrifyingly close to the edge of death as a living being comes, producing alternately a lurid fascination with the violence at hand and the exquisite pleasure of sadistic emotional release.

Roosevelt, of course, would not have put it this way. For him, war and hunting released the "hot life of feeling," returning men to an earlier evolutionary stage at which, he imagined, they were forced to struggle for survival on its most raw and elemental terms. For him, the bearers of modern civilization inherited the responsibility to preserve and pass on to their sons those fiercest and most virile values men could tap only during the "intensity of terror" and the "hideous horror which was the regular and frequent portion of his ages-vanished forefathers."[173] Recall Roosevelt's account in *The Winning of the West* of General Rutherford's killing of Indians. He "wasted and destroyed to his heart's content," producing "deep satisfactions only hinted at."[174] Roosevelt lived out the same satisfactions in hunting venues throughout his entire adult life. As late as 1909, three weeks into his African safari, he wrote Henry Cabot Lodge with great satisfaction that he had "killed most of the things that I specially desired to kill—the lions and rhino. Indeed I simply had to kill them!"[175]

For a man like Roosevelt to unleash his own "primitivism" required an adversary equal in strength and danger to the power of his repressed desires; for a man to dominate his repressed emotions required an emotional experience that was equally fearsome. Hence Roosevelt's accounts of the wilderness were replete with daunting horses to be broken, beasts to be killed, and Indians to be fought. An African lion's life, Roosevelt wrote in *African Game Trails* after his return from safari in 1910, "had been one unbroken career of rapine and violence." Now stalked by equally primitive men in the form of Nandi warriors in eastern Kenya, "the maned master of the wilderness, the terror that stalked by night, the grim lord of slaughter, was to meet his doom at the hands of the only foes who dared molest him."[176] In the primal battle between savage men and savage beasts on the African plain, big-game hunting was, as Roosevelt portrayed it, a morality play of civilized manhood against a bestial savagery that most men thought lay in the animal, not the man. Roosevelt's unique service to civilized manliness was to elevate and purify such savagery when produced by the hands of cultured men. Thus, early in his 1908 safari, he wrote to Edward North Buxton that he hoped to bag elephant, giraffe, eland, gnu, lion, and buffalo. His next sentence came quickly as an assurance that his acts would remain civilized: beyond what the expedition needed for food, he would only shoot one of each species: "I know I need not tell you that I shall do nothing in the nature of butchery."[177]

When the killing was over, the man raised himself above the "forbidden excitation" of his repressed desires and restored his psychological armor by picturing himself as rational, pure, and masterful. The innumerable poses of triumphant hunters perched atop or alongside the huge, inert bodies of conquered game attests to the importance they ascribed to this

Figure 40. Roosevelt and rhino, c. 1909 (Library of Congress Prints and Photographs Division, Washington, D.C. LC-62-10308)

moment of satisfaction (figure 40). The act of ritually ending the killing with photographic identity-making pushes the horrible freshness of the killing into a corner of consciousness, making the act more psychologically tolerable.[178] Frederic Remington recognized the importance of normalizing this satisfyingly bloody moment in his painting *His Second Shot* (figure 41). Here, the painter enlists an unseen, presumably male audience to join two gentlemanly hunters memorializing the death of a large moose. The guide cradles the animal's jaw so that camera captures the faces of the moose and his killers as a third hunter bends over a camera and shoots with the same finality as the death-shot.

Hunters devised institutions that would recognize the validity of their kills and advertise them throughout the nation's burgeoning communities of hunting enthusiasts. One of the earliest, Roosevelt's Boone and Crockett Club, established a system for recording and publishing the names of the killer of the largest, fastest, and most formidable specimen of each species. Along with photography and formal record keeping, taxidermy

Figure 41. Frederic Remington, *His Second Shot*, 1902 (courtesy Frederic Remington Art Museum, Ogdensburg, New York)

further ensured the official capture and public display of the killed beast for the hunter's reputation. Heads were cut off the bodies of recently killed animals, cleaned out, stuffed, and mounted on walls in fashionable downtown men's clubs, in barrooms and hunting lodges, in museums in the nation's capital, and in the parlors of upper-class homes, where they signified the ostensible prowess of men over the animal kingdom. The trophy wing that Roosevelt built onto his home at Sagamore Hill held stuffed American buffalo, water buffalo, cougar, elk, antelope, and bear. On the floor lay cougar and wolf pelts, and under a table lurked a stuffed badger. Though guns, knives, and sabers abounded in Roosevelt's home, the taxidermy eliminated all signs of blood and violence, attesting to the re-repression of the hunter's primal emotions and rendering the tamed, staring residue of the once-living beast fit for the setting of social and family life.[179] With the evidence hanging on the wall, the hunting story became embedded in men's identity. As *Sandow's* observes, "incidents of the chase will be gone over again when pipes are lighted and chairs drawn close" to the fire, becoming "history in the lives of those who took part in the chase."[180]

Animals were not the only living things in danger of being captured and displayed on walls, as one could discover upon entering any men's club or bar. The Hoffman House, an upscale New York hotel, was a popular watering hole for male celebrities. In the drawing *Interior View of Hoffman House Bar*, men enjoy themselves drinking and smoking cigars in a sump-

Figure 42. *Interior View of Hoffman House Bar,* c. 1890 (lithograph, published by Thomas & Wylie; Library of Congress 15315 262 2081; image provided by David Lubin)

tuous bar redolent with chandeliers, dark wood, Corinthian columns, and the stuffed heads of several beasts with antlers, probably deer (figure 42). The room's most prominent object, however, is Adolphe William Bouguereau's *Nymphs and Satyr,* painted in 1877 and purchased that year by Edward Stokes, part owner of the Hoffman House. A premier icon of pre-Raphaelite French salon art, this large canvas features the "romanticized realism" of the genre, so popular among wealthy American patrons, in which size and subject count over actual artistic worth. Although pictures of naked women had long appeared in working-class bars, *Nymphs* immediately became a national sensation, and Stokes sold reproductions that appeared in respectable middle-class hotel bars and clubs, as well as on playing cards and even on the label of his Hoffman House brand of cigar. The original was so popular in New York that Stokes set aside a special "ladies day" to allow women to see the painting in the otherwise all-male establishment. Anthony Comstock stimulated increased sales when he declared the French salon nudes obscene.[181]

Situated on the same wall as the trophy heads, the naked nymphs, beings who were known to consort with beasts, invited "capture" by the male gaze rather than the hunter's gun. The medieval and classical themes of pre-Raphaelite art were redolent with voluptuous naked women who exposed what Dante Gabriel Rossetti, the genre's foremost painter, called the "marvelous fleshiness of the flesh."[182] Inside the hothouse preserve of the barroom, sporting males "talked with great voices [of] wild and valiant adventure," Jacob Riis said in 1913, transforming women and game into dual decorative objects of desire that inspired fantasies of chase and capture.[183]

To hunters, the ideal killed animal specimen was a large, adult male in the prime of life, one with "an unusually fine head"; unspoiled plumage or pelt; or long horns, fangs, or claws, which could be measured, photographed, entered in record books, carried home, and mounted on a wall. To become a member of the Boone and Crockett Club, an initiate was required shoot one adult male from each of the species of North American large game. Club members considered it a triumph for a virile white hunter only if he killed—in a Darwinian triumph of the species—a virile and singular animal, the largest or fastest, most dangerous, muscular, and resplendent male of his kind.[184] For white hunters, or soldiers for that matter, no equivalent prey was to be found in an animal that appeared female, disfigured, injured, juvenile, or otherwise unworthy, nor glory to be had in killing one. Roosevelt disdained the white-tailed deer as inferior prey, calling it a "skulker" that, refusing to stand and fight, had to be killed "by stealth and stratagem and not by fair, manly hunting."[185] Killing a mature male in the prime of life mirrored the logic with which the hunter conceived himself as the highest, most evolved specimen in the world of living beings. Hunting, as Kathleen Dalton says, required a worthy prey for a worthy predator.[186] "It is to such men as [Roosevelt] that the big game legitimately belongs," John Burroughs said, to the naturalists and sportsmen "who share with the world the delight they experience in the chase."[187]

Roosevelt, understanding the popular appeal of this legitimacy, returned to hunting themes and told his readers how many of each kind of animal he had shot and, with emotional intensity, just how each animal died. From boyhood on, he captured, killed, mounted, classified, and otherwise accounted for numerous animals and birds. His lifetime tally easily numbered in the thousands, prompting one biographer to remark that his diaries amounted to "a monotonous record of things slain." At age fourteen, while on a twelve-hundred-mile trip up the Nile to Aswan, he used a rifle to shoot "between one and two hundred" birds. One warbler was "the first bird I ever shot and I was proportionately delighted."[188] We may presume that as the number of kills increased so did the delight, proportionately. In one forty-seven-day period in the Dakotas in 1884, he killed 170 bears, deer, elk, grouse, rabbits, and game birds. Afterward he wrote descriptions of the "harsh grating" of a dying elk's teeth, the smell of a newly killed bear's blood, and the sight of a wounded deer running away, dragging its entrails. On 17 August, he "broke the backs of 2 blacktail bucks with a single bullet."[189]

Killing game unlocked deep emotions in Roosevelt, and he shared these most intimate moments, as in this 1884 description to his sister Anna of the killing a bear that measured over nine feet long and weighed a thousand pounds.

> I found myself face to face with the great bear . . . not eight steps. He turned his huge head slowly toward us. The blue barrel was as steady as a rock. I could see the top of the bead . . . between his two sinister looking eyes; as I pulled the trigger I jumped aside, . . . the great brute was struggling in the death agony, and, as you will see when I bring home his skin, the bullet hole in his skull was . . . exactly between his eyes. I had great sport with elk too, . . . but after I had begun bear killing other sports seemed tame. . . . unless I was bear hunting all the time I am afraid I should soon get as restless with this life as with the life at home.[190]

The more bears Roosevelt killed, the more he seemed to demand that the brute's size, ferocity, and evil meet increasingly higher thresholds of expectation. Five years later, as he left on another hunting trip, he could write to Henry Cabot Lodge that he remained "especially hot for bear."[191]

Knives figured prominently in Roosevelt's killing, especially the "bully hunting knife" given him by a former Rough Rider. Upon receiving the gift, Roosevelt said he wished to "kill a big grizzly or silver tip, which would be great sport."[192] In January and February of 1901, Roosevelt hunted for five weeks in northwest Colorado, where he killed twelve cougars. Eight were treed by dogs and shot with a rifle, and four the dogs cornered on the ground. After a "savage worry" among the dogs and a cougar, Roosevelt wrote to Ted, "I ran in and stabbed him behind the shoulder, thrusting the knife you loaned me right into the heart. I have always wished to kill a cougar as I did this one, with dogs and the knife." Of these twelve animals, three were full-grown males weighing from 160 to 237 pounds. The dogs, though they would be killed or horribly "cut up . . . were quite competent to kill the cougar by themselves," and Roosevelt's "chief fun" in the "great sport" came upon seeing the dogs fight the cougar. One might suppose great fun might also be had in the writing of numerous letters written to friends and relatives in Europe and America detailing the hunt, along with the parceling out of trophy skins, teeth, horns, and claws to the "hundreds" who asked for them.[193]

But by April of that same year, the amount of bloodshed had given Roosevelt pause. "As I grow older," he confided to Hamlin Garland, "I find myself uncomfortable in killing things without a complete justification" and reported that he had killed only "varmint" lately and enjoyed just looking at the deer.[194] In September of 1901, he became president, and his hunting trips were greatly reduced in number for the next few years. In the spring of 1904, having overcome his temporary ambivalence, he returned to Texas for a wolf hunt, where "it was . . . first class fun . . . galloping over prairie dog towns, flats, creek bottoms, everything," and where he was "personally" present at the death of eleven wolves. "One run was nine miles long, and I was the only man at the finish except the professional wolf hunter, [who caught] the wolves alive by thrusting his gloved hands down between their jaws."[195] That hunt extended into Colorado for bear. There, in an incident in which six one-year-old bears were treed, it became impossible to call the dogs off, so the guide shot the bears with his revolver. Roosevelt wrote excitedly to Elihu Root that he had "congratulated [the guide on] having gotten six animals whose skins would make such excellent doilies."[196] In 1905, Roosevelt was again riding at "breakneck speed after the greyhounds," hunting coyote, wolves, rattlesnakes, and bear in Oklahoma and Texas. He wrote to Lodge, "I killed a big bear. It is great sport and I am enjoying it to the full."[197]

Roosevelt's letters and articles on hunting and outdoor exploits poured eastward, garnering admiration and linking his hunting prowess and bloodthirstiness to his presidential stature in the public mind. His close friends joined or were enlisted in the cultivation of his national image. In November of 1904, Roosevelt was elected president by the largest popular

majority ever to date. Two days after the election, he was planning a bear
hunt in Yellowstone for the spring of 1905, a hunt that he said must end
successfully since it promised to augment his fame. "If I come out [to
hunt] as President," he wrote his guide with an eye to his newly elected
status, "we must be dead sure that there is no slip-up and that I get the
game."[198] He seemed to put this hunt's failure or success in the context of
having considered his presidency a "political accident," since he became
president in 1901 as the result of McKinley's assassination. A successful
hunt would, he thought, help fix his legitimacy in the public mind. Lodge
seemed to think that Roosevelt's second term as president was more secure
than his first. "Your place in history was already safe," he wrote to Roosevelt the day after the latter's overwhelming victory in the 1904 presidential
election, "but it has now been signed and sealed by the . . . men of your
own time—and you have four years in which to add to the fame."[199] To
Lodge, hunting prowess infused the presidency with importance: he
wrote the next June after reading Roosevelt's description of the presidential hunt in Yellowstone: "I should like to have seen you slaying bears and
running coyotes."[200]

When in 1909 Roosevelt left the presidency in popular triumph, he
headed for an eleven-month safari in East Africa. Large crowds attended
his departure from New York harbor, but "it was not merely the crowd but
the feeling . . . which was so striking," Lodge remembered. Roosevelt
waved from the ship as it moved slowly down the Hudson. "The picture
will always be vivid in my mind," Lodge said, and presumably it would be
in the country's too. "I knew you would be missed, but I was not prepared
for the intensity of the popular interest . . . after you had left office."
Newspapers were "filled daily with minute accounts of your progress; of
how you looked, what you wore and what you said . . . from moment to moment." Roosevelt's African exploits became a serial story, and the nation
followed them "with the absorbed interest of a boy who reads *Robinson
Crusoe.*"[201]

In his popular account of the safari, *African Game Trails: An Account of
the African Wanderings of an American Hunter-Naturalist* (1910), Roosevelt
took careful pains to paint his image as that of the disinterested naturalist
on a scientific mission for the Smithsonian Museum of Natural History.
Yet he also fit his hunting tropes into his larger worldview of American
manhood's racial and civilizing destiny. He pictured his safari as a white
foray into "dark savagery," a trip backward in time to the Pleistocene, and
likened his hunting exploits to those of his own primitive but white European ancestors, projecting, as Gail Bederman points out, his primitivism
onto Africa and Africans.[202] For readers of *African Game Trails,* he reen-

acted the age-old battle of man proving his manhood against beast in that land where "hot, laughing, tropical beauty" existed side by side with "grisly horror." He compared his motives and behavior to those of his African porters and gun bearers, laying claim to his racial and masculine superiority against that of "real savages who filed their teeth and delighted in raw flesh." East Africa is a "white man's country," he said, "ripe for settlement," and he approvingly described the "true white settlers, white homemakers" who rescued the land from "the black oblivion of a lower barbarism," turning it into "productive" farms and instructing its "grown-up children" in the arts of civilization.[203]

More than simply an outpost of white settlement, Africa also supplied "an ideal playground . . . for sportsmen." On his safari, Roosevelt killed nearly three hundred animals, including lions, hippos, elephants, giraffes, and antelope, and he boasted that "we did not kill a tenth, nor a hundredth part of what we might have killed had we been willing." True to his civilizing mission to unleash and channel masculine primitivism, he claimed to have acted both with civilized restraint, in the sense of not being entirely "willing," and to have indulged his "hot feelings." Just as he distinguished between the "mushy" and muscular forms of peacemaking, he distanced himself from charges of being a "game butcher" or an effeminate man who indulges in mere sport for "ease and luxury." His type of hunting, he said, was a "craft" for "exercising and developing hardihood of body and the virile courage . . . which lie at the base of every strong and manly character." He raised the issue of why one should kill the animals at all and showed that their deaths were necessary by recounting crop devastations, the killing of native villagers and white hunters, and the Darwinian struggle of savage beast against savage beast. "I object to anything like needless butchery," he repeatedly told his readers, claiming that beyond the "several dozen trophies" he kept, all the animals were used for feeding the expedition (of over one hundred persons) or as scientific specimens.[204] Such protestations aside, Roosevelt's accounts make clear that he killed many animals entirely for sport, and the most important part of the sport were the "perilous adventures" and "strange experiences with birds and beasts" that renewed white manhood.

Many animals ran off wounded or sank beneath the water. Roosevelt shot a rhino in the buttocks, and Kermit shot another in the face, hoping, Roosevelt said, to "avoid inflicting a serious injury" and to drive them off. He admitted that he would "always" shoot a crocodile "when I get a chance."[205] Indiscriminate killing led to the inadvertent death of two lion cubs—"each was badly wounded, and we finished them off"—and the perfunctory slaughter of at least eight elephants, numerous crocodiles, and seven hippos, even though the latter were "usually no sport."[206] Many other animals were killed and discarded since they were not the "hoped-for" trophy males, like this unfortunate lion:

> Right in front of me, thirty yards off, there appeared . . . [a] tawny, galloping . . . lion. Crack! The Winchester spoke; and as the soft-nosed bullet ploughed forward through his flank the lion swerved so that I missed him with the second shot; but my third bullet went through the spine and forward into his chest. Down he came . . . his hind quarters dragging, his head up, his ears back, his jaws open and lips drawn up in a prodigious snarl, as he endeavored to turn to face us. His back was broken; but of this we could not at the moment be sure, and if it had merely been grazed, he might have recovered, and then, even though dying, his charge might have done mischief. So Kermit, Sir Alfred, and I fired, almost together, into his chest. His head sank, and he died.[207]

In Roosevelt's fantastic primordial world, a snake became an "evil genius," a lion the "grim lord of slaughter," and an "uncouth" rhino "a monster surviving from the world's past" when "prime" beasts "ran riot in their strength." Describing animals in this manner, he was figuring them as forbidden and repressed desires. He filled the pages of his book with carefully rendered, nearly gleeful accounts, complete with photographs and action drawings, of wounded animals staggering, falling, rising, taking more bullets, and falling again. He anthropomorphized them, writing of their "fortitude under pain." He "could not sufficiently admire" the "splendid" elands, with "their sleek, handsome, striped coats, their shapely heads, fine horns, and massive bodies." Yet the animal had little use for him until its "formidable," "massive," "tremendous muscular power" was sacrificed to his own need for mastery and his simultaneously feared and hoped-for "primitivism." It was when he broke a large bull's back with a "full-jacketed, sharp-pointed bullet" that "made a terrific rendering" and brought the animal "plunging and struggling to the ground" that he felt "elation," perhaps because the barriers dropped away and he could finally touch his most forbidden "excitations." He witnessed the killing of a lion by Nandi hunters and described it as "a scene of as fierce interest and excitement as I ever hope to see." "A fine sight he was," Roosevelt said of one large elephant, "a sight to gladden any hunter's heart, as he lay in the twilight, a giant in death." Of the day on which he killed his largest elephant, he wrote, "We had triumphed; and we were thoroughly happy."[208]

Concluding his safari happily, Roosevelt made a whirlwind tour through Europe in 1910, and was entirely unprepared for the "extraordinary reception" he received. Between April and mid-June, Italy's king and queen, the Austrian emperor, and the German kaiser extended him invitations. He became the first private citizen to review the German army, he lectured on the subject of civilization at the University of Berlin, he represented President Taft at King Edward VII's funeral in London, he spoke on success at Cambridge, and he delivered the prestigious Romanes Lecture at Oxford. As Europe's sovereigns "vied with one another" to entertain him, he claimed, the popular reception included "dense throngs of people cheering and calling." Puzzled at this attention, he attributed it to the average European's image of the American republic, which he called "a queer attractive dream, . . . a kind of mixture of Bacon's utopia and Raleigh's Spanish Main, . . . a field for wild adventure . . . [of a not] necessarily moral type." But he knew, he confided to Lodge, that if on one hand his popularity came from his representing "democracy, liberty, honesty and justice," it also flowed from his heroics in a field of adventure that stretched from the American West through Cuba to the African savanna.[209]

Even as they satirized Roosevelt's heroics, writers and cartoonists in every country he visited advertised his notoriety as a hunter. Cartoonists drew Europe's stone statues of lions—from those on bridges approaching Budapest to those guarding the British museum—fleeing for their lives. The Berlin *Ulk* pictured Roosevelt shooting birds indoors in the Royal German Palace. And the Berlin *Kladderadatsch* sited him surrounded by African animals, with the German eagle perched on his shoulder, having presumably captured that bird not with his guns but with his popularity (figure 43).

A *Collier's Weekly* cartoonist depicted his return from Europe and Africa as the Napoleonic "Return from Elba" of a popular and presumably still politically dangerous ex-president (figure 44). From the Boston *Traveler* came an image of "the faunal naturalist at work" gleefully bounding after a small bird with a ludicrously outsized cleaver and machete, both dripping with blood (figure 45). In decorating Roosevelt's body with killed beasts after his safari, or in showing him killing political opponents during his presidency, cartoonists transported bloodletting into political agency. In a cartoon entitled "Drive the Knife in up to the Hilt!" Roosevelt the president, bloody knife in hand, slays the wolves of post office graft, corporate corruption, evil trusts, and Panama Canal obstructionists (figure 46). Roosevelt himself used the language of killing and wounding political

Figure 43. "Back to Europe with His African Spoil," *Kladderadatsch* (Berlin)

opponents. He said of a fellow politician, "I put the knife into him up to the hilt"; he remarked of a speech of Lodge's, "it has drawn blood"; and in his own "straightout party speech" he declared, "I'll cut for blood."[210]

Cartoonists also sensed the emotional edge and the excesses of physical strenuousness that Roosevelt's cowboy persona introduced into the nation's political culture. "The Unmuzzled Teddy Runs Amuck!" reads the title of a cartoon that appeared in the *Verdict* in 1900 (figure 47). This cartoon repeats the outlandish denunciations of the Democrats that New York governor Roosevelt made while running for vice president in the campaign of 1900. "The democrats stand for lawlessness, for dishonesty and dishonor, for license and disaster at home and COWARDLY SHRINKING

Figure 44. F. G. Cooper, "The Return from Elba," *Collier's Weekly*

Figure 45. Phil Porter, "The Faunal Naturalist at Work," *Traveler* (Boston)

from duty abroad," states a wild-eyed Roosevelt, slinging muck at opponents from the back of an equally pie-eyed, barely controlled, and un-
bridled horse. In another, more ominous characterization of Roosevelt's
capacity for violence, the Atlanta *Constitution* used weaponry to construct
an armed and armored presidential Rough Rider who disdainfully wears
the Constitution as a neck scarf (figure 48).

As these exploits of the president entered the nation's consciousness
through countless representations, killing bounded the trophy heads' otherwise bestial presence with purposeful, rational acts, making the beast
within subject to human will. Images of its president as a hunter went
along with those of him as a cowboy and soldier, and gave Americans
metaphors by which to normalize what were otherwise brutal acts. Hunting, war, and cowboying furnished the only socially acceptable venues

Figure 46. Gillam, "Drive the Knife in up to the Hilt!" *Judge*, 12 December 1903

Figure 47. "The Unmuzzled Teddy Runs Amuck!" *Verdict* (New York), 6 August 1900

where one could kill animals freely and men if one must, to get one's Spaniard, as Roosevelt did, and return to civilization with bloody hands. Serious stuff to the fraternal brotherhood, the trophy heads of adversaries reinscribed in the nation's museums, magazines, newspapers, and political discourse the hunter's control over the primitive powers of recently tamed yet still potentially violent beasts—the very qualities the country lacked.

Men of Roosevelt's era did not invent the martial ideal, as Jackson Lears points out, but they perfected it and handed it to the twentieth century as a means to providing the modern self a more authentic life despite the concerns of modernity. Cartoonists and satirists, of course, made fun of Roosevelt's excesses and, in doing so, pointed up the limitations and contradictions in the unifying capacity of the white hunter. Yet the skills and muscularity of the cowboy-warrior together with his capacity to wreak havoc on lesser beings begged an explicit psychological insularity and aggressiveness that men strove to achieve by imagining themselves upright, rigid, armed, and unfeeling. By endlessly calling for Americans to "nerve" themselves for "labor and peril" and to prepare for a national "cleansing and hardening," Roosevelt posed a new American hero who used spontaneous primitivism to fight the "forces of evil."[211] He evoked a barbarism based on blood, will, and instinct as a means to heroic experience and as an antidote to retrogression and certain death. He transformed a horror of

Figure 48. L. C. Gregg, "For President!" *Constitution* (Atlanta)

killing into an apologia for violence. Through the ecstasy of extreme, outlandish acts, the sacrificial bloodletting of animals and men performed in
the all-male arenas of the West and war, his political vision suggested that
Americans would transcend soft selves, lewd living, and a national failure
of nerve.

War

No triumph of peace is quite so great as the supreme triumphs of war. The courage of the soldier . . . stands higher than any quality called out merely in time of peace. The men who command our ships must have in them the dogged ability to bear punishment, the power and desire to inflict it.
—Roosevelt to the Naval War College, 1897

He who has not seen war only half comprehends the possibilities of his race.
—Frederic Remington, "With the Fifth Corps"

No leading American foregrounded war in a theory of history more than Theodore Roosevelt. Still, although he earned the reputation of a warmonger among contemporaries, Kathleen Dalton points out, he did not seek war as president.[1] As international affairs go, his was a rather restrained and peaceful presidency, punctuated on one hand by the Philippine campaign and the aggression against Colombia, but on the other by his handling of the Venezuela crisis of 1902 and by his peacemaking role in the Russo-Japanese War. Roosevelt did live through two wars and stood in each as the nation's premier advocate for fighting, first against Spain and then against Germany. As both wars approached, he challenged a reluctant administration by calling for military readiness, and indeed, he was known throughout his public career for his efforts to aid the nation in realizing its military potential. In both wars, he advocated quick and determined intervention in place of negotiation.

More importantly, at the very point where politics touched men's emotional lives, Roosevelt articulated their fear and loathing of enemies and called them to unify around military ideals of brotherhood and self-sacrifice. Mastering these political arts, he repeated the litany of punishing weak selves in order to produce hardened men who would then derive psychological satisfaction from war's thrills. From the cowboy cult, Roosevelt appropriated hyperbolic war talk laden with agonistic suffering and reckless disregard for life. Not a small part of his appeal lay in inviting men to displace their everyday lives with one that embodied the grand themes of life and death, will and fate, and men's duty and legacy to civilization. "The preoccupation with large scale politics, with the destinies of the race and humanity," Klaus Theweleit writes, "implies a negation of the small, the close-at-hand, of microhistory . . . the private, the intimate."[2]

For Roosevelt and for almost all Americans, the nation was an abstraction represented in its essential maleness by the military and its nominal raison d'être, war. In that figuring, as a male body of warriors competing to prove its evolutionary fitness, the nation was potentially at its strongest and yet most vulnerable. For Roosevelt, if a nation failed to compete with other nations, if it appeared weak or vacillating, if it endorsed pacifism, or worst of all if it were invaded, it would be taking the female role. Alfred Mahan allegorized the navy as a body that became impotent when forced to submit to emasculating evils like civilian control of military budgets. The nation must act like a man in its relations with other nations, and the military, more than politics or any other aspect of national life, carried the potential to unify men around that belligerent manliness most admired by the end of the century. War created duty, provided risk, and confirmed bravery. By its organizational nature, the military created brotherhood where men resisted danger and protected one another in common, finding along the way unimagined heights and depths of emotion and commitment.

War gave access to the martial virtues, Roosevelt said, especially for the "timid man, the lazy man . . . who has lost the great fighting masterful virtues . . . the man of dull mind whose soul is incapable of feeling the mighty lift that thrills 'stern men with empires in their brains.' "[3] More aggressively minded men like Roosevelt believed that war's skills—stalking, targeting, shooting, and a willingness to suffer and cause suffering—could be activated among the less aggressive by military training or, short of that, by hunting. Military training would hone men into prime specimens like the king of beasts, ripe for sacrifice and worthy of redemption. Not every man or nation deserved the "supreme good fortune" of honorable death in battle, Roosevelt said.[4] The strongest and bravest would meet the test, and weaklings would fail. But how would we ever know, he asked, if they did not fight?

War, alongside working and breeding, served for Roosevelt as one of the three male activities that drove the nation's civilizing mission and established America's place in the historical trajectory of the world's civilized race-nations. Like his favorite poets Tennyson and Kipling, Roosevelt glorified the aristocratic military traditions of the British and the Germans as America's racial precursors. Along with his friends Owen Wister and Frederic Remington, as we have seen, he envisioned ancient and medieval heroes evolving through Western Europe and emerging in the Americas with Daniel Boone, Davy Crockett, Civil War generals, and Great Plains cavalry officers. He included Washington, Jackson, and Lincoln in this lineage and ended with himself. These heroes' careers provided the martial energy that steered the nation's evolutionary development from fledgling frontier colony to world military power.[5] For those white expansionist peoples, warring, working, and breeding secured a territorial, cultural, and racial legacy, thus positioning the nation to survive history's annihilating forces. Formerly successful militarily powers that were now in decline nevertheless had redeemed themselves through the racial and cultural antecedents that survived the loss of their colonial empires. Though Spain "expanded and fell," Roosevelt wrote, she left a "whole continent" of Spanish-speaking peoples. "England expanded and England will fall," but she will leave a legacy of continents dominated by English language and culture. Most nations, however, were cursed doubly by military and racial stagnation. The Dutch "tried to expand," but stronger powers forced them to "assume a stationary position" from which they sank into "nothing," leaving no lasting racial or military presence.[6]

Roosevelt's war eagerness and his moments of self-destructive behavior arose as much from the need for saving his and other men's bodies from the pleasures of modern life as it did from military-strategic considerations. Modern men had transgressed, Roosevelt said, by giving in to the dirty, corrupt, and weak parts of themselves, so he couched his theory of war in a quasi-religious logic of sin, punishment, redemption, and martyrdom. "I am very glad the Spanish war came when it did," Roosevelt later wrote to a British adventurer-sportsman in 1899, "for a little more of the sedentary life would render it hopeless for me to ever . . . stand labor and hardship."[7] To atone for weakness and "lewd" living, Roosevelt said, the nation's men needed and deserved the "grim necessities" of military training and war. Sacrifice forces men out of boredom, Roosevelt wrote to Cecil Arthur Spring Rice, into deep interaction with nature or battle, teaching them "the necessary brutal heroism in attack and defense."[8] If the "mighty deeds" of the Civil War had been "left undone," Roosevelt told Civil War veterans in 1901, then all the nation's accomplishments "would have turned into apples of Sodom under our teeth."[9] Terrible though the destruction of the Civil War was, he said at the 1908 unveiling of General Sheridan's monument in Washington, "the blood and the grim suffering marked the death-throes of what was worn out, and the birth pangs of a new and more glorious national life."[10] By 1916, despite two memorable wars, American white men had not suffered enough, a never-satisfied Roosevelt told Owen Wister. "The country is now ripe for a stronger lesson. Our people need to be roused from their lethargy. Some are silly and sentimental; some are steeped in the base materialism of mere money-getting or the even baser materialism of soft and vapid or vicious pleasure; some are influenced by sheer downright cowardice."[11]

In Roosevelt's military ethos, men must suffer privation and pay with their lives. They must be chastised for easy and corrupt living in order to redeem themselves as men. War must necessarily hurt, deprive, and best of all, kill, and in doing so, it would cleanse. War's pain, work, and death brought the "moral lift" that would "purge this Republic" of racial and ethnic pollutions, of weaklings and pacifists, and of commercial greed. Only through war's purifying fire, Roosevelt said, would the fraternal nation reclaim republican virtue and make itself worthy to lead other democratic nations and to be the vanguard of civilization.

What constituted the "debt" that soldiers must "pay" to the nation? Why was the nation ripe for a yet stronger lesson? Who required such lessons? It was "God," Roosevelt said, quoting the Reverend Sydney Smith, who "calls all the passions out in their keenness and vigor for the present safety of mankind." For those uncertain as to exactly what God's passions were, Roosevelt enumerated the Old Testament emotions: "anger and revenge and the heroic mind, and a readiness to suffer—all the secret strength, all the invisible array of the feelings—all that nature has reserved for the great scenes of the world."[12] Roosevelt, who almost never invoked any divinity, imagined a nation-God-father who beckoned the passions of his deserving male clients and imposed suffering and punishments upon them. To gain the nation-God-father's approval, bestowed as honor, wounded or killed men laid their bodies on the altar of national sacrifice.

Concerns with death and sacrifice are religious in nature, and indeed, Christian notions of sacrifice understand Christ's willingness to suffer as the cleansing of the sinful body and a devout submission to the Father. European art is rife with images of saints, such as Sebastian, Stephen, and Anthony, writhing in exquisite pain, their bodies tormented by demons, bruised by stones, or pierced with arrows as they attempt to prove loyalty to God. In the absence of religious interpretations, modern forms of sacrifice substitute loyalty to the state for loyalty to the divine, and in place of Christ's willingness to die, an astonishing eagerness to kill and be killed. In this figuration, modern sacrifice provides a thick layer of meaning that removes outright killing from its immediate horrors, transforming it into a giving of one's life for a higher cause. As leaders like Roosevelt invested in this eagerness, they enlisted the modern, secular state as a vehicle for making meaning out of death. Sacrifice linked a man's death, if not to God, to the nation's past and future, but also to his own psychological desires.

Such a linking opens a way toward understanding why punishments and self-sacrifice figured so largely in Roosevelt's theory of war. His fear of his own effeminacy drove his desire for punishment and elicited the same concerns in other men. For Roosevelt, as for any man who would rather have his own sons "die than have them grow up weaklings," war tested a man's willingness to suffer. By Roosevelt's rationale, a man tolerated pain in order to prove that he was not the coward or weakling who shirks or flinches. A man must suffer because he feared he might be that coward. Wounds and death effectively punished the little boy within who feared or who preferred to flinch or shirk, a punishment more exquisitely sacrificial for having been borne stoically by the exteriorized armor-self of the unfeeling warrior. What else would rescue the body, which for many Victorian men was a source of sexual dirtiness from an early age? What else would silence the child within even as it killed him?

The most important point to understand in this dangerously simple logic is how men knew what they had to defend against. This understanding might begin to explain the extremity of the sacrifices. Military training, especially if compounded by previous harsh treatment in childhood, hardened a man against his own emotions and impulses; it taught him to act automatically in order to defeat self-doubt and to punish effeminacy, and hence it instilled an astounding willingness to inflict pain.[13] Men turned these sufferings inward to address conditions in their emotional makeup—the homosocial and homoerotic in all-male endeavors, the relentless flight from the erotic, and the unmet need for emotional sustenance since childhood.

SACRIFICE

In Roosevelt's theory of war, the mandate for men to pay bodily debts was embedded in sacrificial languages that gave moral sanction to killing and provided an ethos of self-punishment. His dark penchant for forcing himself into danger and hardship, his quest for the toughest, harshest, and most dangerous adversaries, landscapes, and situations is well known among present-day historians and biographers.[14] However his relentless adoration of pain and suffering across venues and experiences in war and hunting has not been sufficiently noted. More than any other public figure, Roosevelt perfected the psychology of pain, suffering, and sacrifice—and their enjoyment. For would-be hunters, cowboys, and soldiers, war and the Western experience, like no other arena of national life, elevated sacrificial violence to a central defining moment in male self-actualization and made male agency the driving force of history. For Roosevelt, acts of sacrifice spurred men to reach deep into their psyches for new definitions of an authentic self, what he described to Minnesota state fairgoers in 1901 as the "daring, endurance, [and] desire for victory [that] make up the essential manliness of the American character."[15]

Roosevelt's letters and popular writings on Western life, hunting, and

war overflowed with repetitive, detailed accounts of expectations of pain to
come, experiences of giving and receiving pain, and recollections of remembered pain. He could never endure enough pain himself, and he never
tired of exacting it from those around him. He tallied his own manhood
through broken bones, "drubbings" in sports, and the numbers of
wounded and dead Rough Riders in the Cuban campaign. "Men," he told
the Rough Rider recruits in training before the Cuban campaign began, "I
shall not hesitate to spend your lives as I spend my own."[16]

Once the pain was found and the proof of sacrifice was secured, the tradition of the stiff upper lip required its denial. "It did not hurt me at all,"
he said of his arm after he broke it in a fall from his horse. He remounted
his horse and continued the foxhunt. Although subsequent jumps over
fences "made the bones slip past one another . . . I got in at the death."[17] "I
don't grudge the broken arm a bit," he wrote Henry Cabot Lodge once it
had been set. "Every now and then I like to drink the wine of life with
brandy in it."[18] Roosevelt, who broke bones four times in falls from horses,
invited such pain because, he said, it hardened him. Against what, the
question begs—against his own perceived weakness. And just like him, he
argued in "Brotherhood and the Heroic Virtues," American men would
benefit from "a little actual experience with the rough side of things."[19]

As the forty-year anniversary of the Civil War drew him to give com-
memorative speeches at battlefields and memorials, Roosevelt invoked sacrificial language through which he helped the nation come to terms with its
own dead. As these ceremonies increased in fervor and frequency toward
the end of the decade, politicians like Roosevelt taught patriotic Americans
to enjoy them as high moments in their own emotional lives. The ceremonies, many of which featured President Roosevelt as the nation's most
recent near-sacrificial solider, brought together religion, destiny, and patriotic images to explain ultimate loss for warriors and their families. In
Roosevelt's high-minded and rousing speeches, Lincoln figured as a high
priest who stood on an altar and "poured out his own lifeblood for the nation whose life he had saved."[20] With the suffering and deaths of the soldiers at Gettysburg and Valley Forge, Roosevelt said, Americans had
earned the right to "rejoice with exultant pride in the . . . supreme height
of self-sacrifice."[21] His eulogy for Americans who had died in the Cuban
war emphasized the self-fulfillment rather than the pathos of early death.
One must not take pity on them, Roosevelt said, but have "respect and admiration for those to whom the supreme good fortune comes of dying well
on the field of battle."[22]

Significant amounts of blood flowed ritually into national memory in
these battlefield commemorations. Roosevelt said in 1909 that "both

Washington and Lincoln were willing to pour out the blood of the bravest and best in the land for a high and worthy cause." In November of 1918, in an article in the Kansas City *Star*, he assured relatives of the Civil War dead that it was untrue, as some had charged, that their kin's "precious blood" had been "sacrifice[d] on cold altars." Nobody gave his life in vain. Everyone who died laid his life on the warm altar of national appreciation, in "service and sacrifice and honor and glory."[23] War's function as a unifying sacrament of historical memory was not lost on William James either. "Those ancestors, those efforts, those memories and legends, are the most ideal part of what we now own together, a sacred spiritual possession worth more than all the blood poured out."[24]

Many observers understood the languages of ritual sacrifice that endorsed Roosevelt's appeal. Jacob Riis reported that Roosevelt had led the Rough Riders with "a mixture of affection and respect that makes troopers go to death as to a dance."[25] After the war, as they followed Roosevelt on the campaign trail, former Rough Riders themselves used the language of sacrifice: "Vote for my Colonel," said Buck Taylor while on Roosevelt's whistle-stop campaign in 1900, "*He will lead you, as he led us, like sheep to the slaughter!*" The crowd enthusiastically "took to [Taylor's] speech," Roosevelt wrote, also enthusiastically, suggesting that the thousands of men in each town who crowded around the back of the train identified with Taylor's call to national sacrifice.[26]

Roosevelt interpreted his closest brush with death in such a spirit of sacrificial duty. When shot and wounded by a would-be assassin while campaigning as the Progressive Party presidential candidate in Milwaukee in 1912, he was saved by the folded speech and metal glasses case in his breast pocket. Seizing the political moment, he removed the speech from his pocket, unfolded it and held it out to the crowd, showing that the bullet had pierced every page. The former president and candidate went on to deliver the hour-and-a-half speech before seeking medical help, an act of bravery that, he said, "puzzled" the crowd's "city types." Former Rough Riders and Western friends, he was certain, instinctively knew that his actions were "the right thing for a man to do under the circumstance." Just as the Rough Riders would not expect someone "wounded in such fashion" to desert a battlefield, Roosevelt wrote, "they saw no reason why he should abandon a . . . less risky duty."[27] For the quintessential Rough Rider, the sacrificial expectations of military brotherhood, even in a peacetime setting, exceeded the more pragmatic requirement that the candidate survive the campaign.

Did Roosevelt's eagerness to be tested arise not only from childhood frailty, but also, as many have suggested, from a son's shame over what he took to be his father's weakness in the Civil War?[28] Both his daughter Alice and his sister Corrine thought so.[29] The elder Theodore had received his draft notice in 1863, and, with his wife insisting that he not fight against men of her family, he had hired a replacement, a young immigrant who was dead within the year. The father served out the war as civilian allotment commissioner, helping soldiers send money home. Seemingly robust and healthy, he died unexpectedly at age forty-six of stomach cancer. Roosevelt was nineteen then and may have repressed rather than confronted his feelings of humiliation and loss. In moments of reflection about his own life, he often stressed the importance of his children's view of his own achievements, a way, perhaps, of indicating the importance of his view of those of his father. Roosevelt sought military and political life, he wrote in 1901, so that "if foreign or domestic strife arose I would be entitled to the respect that comes to the man who actually counts in the conflict."[30] And in his *Outlook* serialization of his autobiography, he said, "I wished to be in a position to explain to my children why I did take part in it, and not why I did not take part in it."[31]

Throughout Roosevelt's life, the words *shrink* and *flinch* appeared everywhere in his emotional universe, enjoining his sons and all young men to sacrificial extremes. This is why Roosevelt considered his father's otherwise exemplary life flawed without the risk of battle. True to his own extreme sense of duty, he felt incomplete just being a husband, father, provider, civil servant, and honest man of character. He had to punish, suffer, sacrifice, and hopefully die in order to find himself worthy. Only the emotional intensity with which Roosevelt urged the declaration of war in 1898, the glee with which he injected himself into it, the energy with which he drew brave men around him, the recklessness with which he sought wounds or death, and the desperate attempt to secure a medal when it was over, displaced his father's legacy. "I could now leave something to my children" he wrote to Douglas Robinson in 1899, "which will serve as an apology for my having existed."[32]

Roosevelt interpreted lives other than his father's by the same standards. John Hay's death in the summer of 1905 was a deep personal loss for Roosevelt, who as a boy of eleven had met the older family friend who would become his own lifelong friend and later his secretary of state. Roosevelt evinced a son's pride in the masculine Hay, who might have represented a father figure on whom he could look with pride. In a letter to Spring Rice, Roosevelt eulogized the secretary of state: "It must be pleasant to feel that you have done your part as a man and not yet been thrown aside as useless, and that your children and children's children . . . have just cause for pride in your actions."[33] "When it comes our turn to go into the blackness," Roosevelt mused to Lodge that summer after Hay's death, "I only hope the circumstances will be as favorable."[34]

His own experience in the Cuban campaign brought Roosevelt face-to-face with the "blackness" and provided the honor that he hoped would make his children proud. "I think I could face death with dignity," he said before he embarked for Cuba, though "it will not be pleasant to die of fever in some squalid hospital without ever having seen an armed foe."[35] Being injured in a fight was preferable to disease or death, of course, and desirable for its image of smug martyrdom. "Don't ever pretend," Roosevelt wrote Winthrop Chanler, "that you are not as proud as a peacock at having been wounded in action in the late war! I should be, if I were in your place. We have both cause to feel profoundly satisfied that . . . we did actually do our part, and had the luck to get into the fighting."[36] Despite his luck, however, Roosevelt's sacrifice proved insufficient. "I have always been unhappy, most unhappy," he wrote, "that I was not severely wounded in Cuba . . . in some striking and disfiguring way."[37]

For men to be grievously wounded or to die terrible and grand and satisfying deaths, like the one Henry James longed for Wister's *Virginian* to enjoy, suspended men's ordinary cultural restraints and unleashed what Elaine Scarry calls theirs and the nation's "sadistic potential." Political discourses of pain and sacrifice allowed the nation to inflict punishment on its foes and attest to men's endurance. Withstanding extreme physical pain, Scarry observes, creates an immediacy of time, place, and sensation that clears the mind of bourgeois concerns; enhances one's awareness of the body's reality; and proves that men have control over their feelings. Sacrifice, shared between like men for noble causes, produces the intense satisfaction of mutually reinforced heroism and earned glory.[38] Once men had endured and survived battlefield pain, military-minded men surmised, they emerged purified and stronger, and men's collective pain purified the nation and made it stronger. This is the argument of masochists and sadists, though military-minded men considered it uplifting and entirely normal.

Why seek pain other than to punish weak selves? Violence, pain, and the idea of imminent death could seem erotic to those men disposed to their invigorating effects, the titillation of combined proximity and proscription.[39] Exceeding the body's proscriptive boundaries, coming face-to-face with blood and death enabled some men to embrace, incorporate, or otherwise ritually give themselves over to the horror. The eruption of hidden desire, the longing for raw emotional contact, the thrill of breaking civilized barriers, the risk of transgression, and the helplessness of surrender amount to what Scarry refers to as learning to love pain and its corollary, death. In David Savran's account, the entire litany of radical excess suggests that the eroticized wild beast is "none other than the profoundly masochistic thrill of losing control, of submission, of surrendering one's self completely, of forcing one's self to endure the unendurable."[40] In the extreme moments of war, some men give free play to long-avoided emotions—they shout and they kill.

Desire for and surrender to the sexualized self, however, provokes the ascetic self to punish its erotic counterpart. Savran, after Freud, calls this reflexive sadomasochism, a sadism turned inward away from the usual external targets of sadistic violence and toward the perpetrator's own self, wherein the heterosexualized and racialized divided masculine self works violence on its own feminized, maternal-longing other. Men prove their toughness by subjugating the female within. Men's own pain and suffering, indulged in order to master frail bodies, to make them submit "absolutely and repeatedly to the cruelty of his will," turn pain into pleasure, allowing the man to play the part of victim, dominating the feminine while leaving intact the masculine "wild beast within."[41] In this view, the masculine self is split between a masculine, sadistic part and a feminine, masochistic part, creating a reflexive sadomasochism wherein the man can play both the role of aggressor and that of victim, turning the impulse to inflict pain back upon himself. A repressive sexuality that codes male bodies as potentially erotic actually defeats eroticism by brutalizing the body and allows the sadomasochistic man to appear as more of a man for having done physical violence to his own body.[42]

In this way, the cowboy soldier spoke to those yearnings in men's hearts that made Henry James "thirst for . . . blood" and spurred Roosevelt's affinity with frontiersmen who "wasted and destroyed to their heart's content." Suffering seemed necessary, a matter of continual maintenance since a man directed it against the parts of the self that marked him as weak, that made him prey to his own desires for emotion and joy, empathy and mercy, or the love of women. But men also, as we have seen, found it needful to punish and disavow the alternately horrific and enticing parts that Roosevelt termed the "beast within." This is the emotionally satisfying part of the masochism; this is what made men love their own pain and seek death.[43]

EVIL WITHIN AND WITHOUT

As war approached in 1898, Roosevelt's friends remarked on his desperate need to prove himself. To William Roscoe Thayer, "the vital fact [for Roosevelt] was that war was at hand," that "great object for which he had striven during two years and eight months" while he was assistant secretary of the navy. As the U.S. yellow press provoked a public outcry over the excesses of the Spanish occupying regime in Cuba, Roosevelt grew increasingly frustrated by what he considered his superiors' reluctance to declare war, and he tried desperately to convince them. "We will have this war," he exploded at one point. Once McKinley declared war, Roosevelt tirelessly provisioned ships and crews, planned fortifications, and coordinated with the war department. "I doubt whether Roosevelt ever worked with greater relish than during the weeks following the blowing up of the *Maine*," Thayer said. "War, the test—delighted him. At last he had his opportunity."[44]

Once Roosevelt had resigned his secretary's position and was helping to organize the Rough Riders, he told General William Shafter how avidly he anticipated the rigorous military training that "would make us all fit as fighting cocks, as able as we are eager to take a leading part in the great campaign against Havana in the fall."[45] Many contemporaries had remarked on Roosevelt's war eagerness even before 1898. During the Chile incident in 1891, John Hay told Henry Adams that "For two nickels, Teddy Roosevelt would declare war himself and wage it solo." His daughter Alice remembered, "we had always quite simply taken it for granted that if there should be a war, Father would be in it."[46] In 1898, President William McKinley called Roosevelt and Leonard Wood "the war party."[47]

Roosevelt's war desires were only whetted in his Cuban experiences, and when the European war loomed in 1914, he eagerly anticipated his next warrior service in spite of his age of fifty-six. "A great exultation came over him," Thayer observed, "as he believed that at last he himself having put on his sword, would be allowed to join the American Army bound overseas, share its dangers and glories in the field, and, if Fate so willed it, pay with his body the debt of patriotism which nothing else could pay."[48] Reminiscing in 1913 over his earlier public pledge to free Cuba, Roosevelt used the same words. "When a man takes such a position," he wrote, "he ought to make his words good by his deeds. . . . He should pay with his body."[49] Roosevelt desired to make such a payment himself and so, presumably, did the thousands of men who immediately volunteered after he wrote to Secretary of War Newton D. Baker in February 1917 asking permission to raise a volunteer division.

The language of sacrifice loomed ever larger in the nation's culture when the United States declared war on Germany on 6 April. Sacrifice captured the imagination of illustrators like William Allen Rogers, who drew a fatally wounded soldier collapsing into the mud as Liberty rescues his courageous spirit to carry it onward (figure 49). Despite news reports of the trench stalemates of the previous three years, American cartoons

Figure 49. William Allen Rogers, "Let Us Pay with Our Bodies—Theodore Roosevelt," *New York Herald*, 17 April 1917 (Library of Congress Prints and Photographs Division, Washington, D.C., CAI 1996002967/PP)

depicted the heroic and uplifting aspects of early death. Rogers's drawing appeared in the *New York Herald* on 17 April 1917, captioned with Roosevelt's call for sacrifice: "Let us pay with our bodies for our soul's desire." Roosevelt's *The Foes of Our Own Household* had appeared that year with an appendix that reprinted the correspondence and recounted the conversations between Roosevelt, Woodrow Wilson, and Newton Baker.[50] Men must have read the president's and secretary's polite rebuff of Roosevelt's eager plans with a mixture of pathos upon seeing a former officer and com-mander-in-chief of the army pleading his war readiness to the present ad-ministration, and admiration for his desire to back up his words.

The "great advantage to the nation" of suffering in war, Roosevelt said, came from the "moral lift" that protected men against pacifism and fac-tionalism and redeemed the nation's honor.[51] War and expansion, Roose-velt thought, made Americans more courageous. It would cleanse the nation and would "make Americans alone dominant in America and so purge this Republic of the taints of pro-Germanism, of commercial greed, and of ignoble worship of material safety, that it could take its part again at the head of the democracies of the world."[52]

Within the cultural swing toward exaggerated masculinity, the Cuban war and the Philippine insurrection further popularized a trendy, amoral love of war, much of which writers attributed to Roosevelt. In "War as a Moral Medicine," which appeared in the *Atlantic Monthly* in 1900, Gold-win Smith argued that Americans had begun to approve of war as a tough antidote to the "softening of manners" and the "satiety of civilization." In his opinion, the "prevalence of the physical over the moral view of man" had become a "general cast of thought," producing a "moral hygienics" that overshadowed traditional morality. "The present ideal is the 'strenu-ous life,' " he wrote, signifying the general cachet for Roosevelt's term. For Americans, "the life of combativeness and aggression" produces a curious morality of its own, one probably necessary, Smith conceded, in the soldier who "faces the shot, submits to the discipline, endures the hardship." But he worried about the hardening effect that it had "on people who gloat over the [battlefield] picture at home." Ordinary citizens should be ashamed, he thought, when they considered the effects of such amoral, militaristic urges on their politics. Government that was "supposed to be the quintes-sence of practical wisdom," had instead become motivated by mystical "fancies" about "destiny," the "white man's burden," and the "mission of the Anglo-Saxon race."[53]

In 1901, anti-imperialists condemned the supramoral ethos adopted by the nation's modern military, not just in the 1898 war, but in the resulting Philippine War. In "The Military Idea of Manliness," published in *The In-dependent,* the Reverend Ernest Howard Crosby reviewed the assassina-tions, random killings of civilians, and tortures used by U.S. troops in the Philippine campaign against Aguinaldo's guerrillas. It was clear, he told his readers, that the soldier's code of honor was "less stringent than that which applies to ordinary people." For Americans, Crosby felt, this had not always been the case. Until very recently the martial "spirit of West

Point and Annapolis" had not "penetrated into our blood," and traditional military codes of honor had enjoined men and nations to pick on someone their own size. But modern martial virtues encouraged "searching the ends of the earth for little peoples to massacre and rob," and the modern public reflected this desire for domination by deliriously celebrating Admiral Dewey, who merely, in Crosby's view, "sank a few water-logged Spanish ships." Furthermore, the new martial ideal countered antebellum ideals that called for moral thinking on the part of a civilian militia. The modern ideal made men abandon "conscience and reason" in favor of an "absolute obedience [and] readiness to obey orders, [or] to do anything." For Crosby, the motto "My Country, right or wrong" was increasingly being used by the army to get men to obey orders blindly and the American public to approve.[54] Crosby identified President Theodore Roosevelt as the leading proponent of this new and seemingly amoral code.

What Crosby denounced as the U.S. Army's "deception" and "wanton slaughter" in the Philippines, other, more military-minded journalists lauded as the manly attributes of soldiers.[55] Indeed, the new moral code enjoyed wide popularity, and the nation's press had begun to defend the U.S. Army's actions. As early as 1891, in an *Atlantic Monthly* essay, "The Praises of War," Agnes Repplier reveled in the "earlier, easier days" of medieval lore when poets were "untroubled" by moralists and could "sing of slaughter with bellicose cheerfulness." Modern "political economists and chilly historians" had overanalyzed motives for fighting. It was better for soldiers and civilians at home to be "disencumbered of mental luggage" and to forswear moral introspection. "It is best to leave ethics alone," she said, "and ride as lightly as we can." She admired Walter Scott, who alone of all the modern poets had ridden lightly, presumably free of Christian ethics, when he had "sung Homerically of strife" and made his readers feel they were in the thick of battle, where action arose from "good old-fashioned simplicity."[56]

Roosevelt would have found Crosby overly concerned with militarism's negative effects and placed him among the hated anti-imperialists. He would have agreed with Repplier that the martial ideal took precedence over civilian moral considerations for the nation's well-being, and he would have seconded her sense that a muscular morality flowed directly from action. His moral vision understood tenderness and empathy toward adversaries as weakness, as that "morbid self-consciousness which made Hawthorne's 'faun' go out of his head because he had killed a man." If someone gave up such morality in favor of a higher moral test, a call to duty that involved painful sacrifice, then he would find, instead, a readiness to kill that marked him more of a man.[57]

Roosevelt's war vision found plenty of company in the views of other military-minded writers and politicians of his generation. Indeed, with the important exception of Mark Twain, few social critics took on the utter mercilessness and senselessness of the Spanish War, the Philippine campaign, or the Great War. Frederic Remington, in his graphic rendering of the American assault on Santiago, depicted war as both a service to civilization and the ultimate test of manliness. In 1897, William James, who later came to oppose the war with Spain, touted war's salutary effects in language that appropriated Roosevelt's bellicosity. The only way nations could engage in contests of virile strength with equally strong nations, James said, was through war. He advised Americans who might otherwise be tempted to forgo having a national army to keep their "military characters as preservers of our ideals of hardihood . . . if not for use, [then] as ends in themselves." Functioning as "pure pieces of perfection" in the midst of a civilization gone soft, soldier males, by their very presence, protected against a type of man James called "Roosevelt's weaklings and mollycoddles."[58]

Like James and Roosevelt, G. Stanley Hall linked his prescriptions for militarized strenuousness to national and racial ends. In the 1870s, he said, Germany had raised gymnastics to a "special art," and in one generation had become the greatest military power since Rome. Through physical exercise, Germany had fashioned "a better race of man and a united fatherland." "Military ideals" enlisted in individual men's "warfare against evil within and without" ensured that the nation remained intact, strong, and ready to meet its enemies. The "best nations of the future," Hall predicted, would be those giving the most "intelligent care to the body."[59] Hardy, self-denying, sexually pure soldiers, representing the vanguard of white civilization, deflected softness, maintained virility, protected moral and racial purity, supplied clean entertainment, and brought world peace.

COLD ALTARS

To many American men living in a rising industrial nation that was just beginning to play the international game of power politics, international relations were essentially military, and therefore an empire based on sea power seemed the best way to protect the nation. Roosevelt argued in his first published book, *The Naval War of 1812* (1882), that the nation must achieve a high state of preparedness through the building and the strategic positioning of seagoing battleships. The world's authority on sea power, Alfred Mahan, argued in *The Influence of Sea Power upon History, 1660-1783* (1890) that the uncertainty of international rivalry required great nations to control adverse circumstances through armed physical power.[60] A nation *qua* nation could not exist without its armored exterior. "This is not advocacy of war," Mahan added, but simply a rational response to diminishing imperial opportunities in an increasingly crowded world. "I am frankly an imperialist."[61] In the 1880s and 1890s, magazine articles written by naval advocates, including Roosevelt and Mahan, began to use such arguments to sell the idea of a heroic modern navy's international role, laying the groundwork for the transformation to an all-steel navy and thence to global importance. Both men expressed gratitude to the German empire for having transmitted to America its "military impulse."[62] Mahan's and Roosevelt's advocacy won out against that of the anti-imperialists, and in the 1880s, Congress committed to the nation's first peacetime naval buildup. Modern steam-powered steel battleships replaced the wooden naval fleet, and coastal defenses gave way to strategic controls by armored fleets in open ocean lanes and sectors. When despite his misgivings about Roosevelt's bellicosity President William McKinley appointed him assistant secretary of the navy in 1897, Roosevelt began a public relations campaign for an even stronger navy.

Imagining the navy as the manliest of the nation's military incarnations, Roosevelt described its protective powers in the context of a Darwinistic world of armored predators and effeminate prey. "The army and the navy are the sword and the shield which this nation must carry," he said in his Hamilton Club speech of 1889, "if she is to do her duty among the nations of the earth."[63] Despite initial U.S. neutrality in the dispute between Spain and her Cuban subjects, in the year he became assistant secretary of state Roosevelt gave a speech at the Naval War College arguing for a strong navy to defend America. He told his audience that the United States lived in the "uncertain and rapacious world" of naval rivalry on the high seas and that the navy was its only defense.[64] There was little risk of actual attack by another naval power, although soon the United States would interpret German actions as hostile and would make a navy necessary by choosing to enter a European war. Thus, Roosevelt's rationale for naval buildup devolved to problems of image defined in terms of rivalry. If the United States did not build a strong military, it would be "left behind" in the power game nations played among themselves. Even worse, stronger nations would see the present army and navy, America's most visible icons of national strength, "as small." A small and weak navy placed the United States in a sexually subordinate position, subject to penetration in a rapacious world. Having watching the North Atlantic squadron's "dismal" target practice, Roosevelt expressed his fear to Admiral William Sims that the navy was "crushingly inferior," that at the hands of an enemy of equal size it would "inevitably suffer humiliating defeat."[65] Despite the international attention, Admiral Dewey's daring exploits at Manila had "ceased to strike wonder among foreign peoples," Roosevelt warned, "after they heard how small and almost contemptible, judging by the new standards, the Squadron was."[66] The United States had to play catch-up by enabling the fleet to develop enough striking power to project an aura of strength to other nations with fleets of their own.

However receptive to bellicosity the nation had grown following the Spanish-American War, Roosevelt and preparedness advocates still knew that the navy's size was not nearly sufficient for it to join the world's naval club, dominated by the British and the Germans. They worried that Congress and the public had become indifferent to navalism and reluctant to spend for armaments as the war receded in memory. When he became president, Roosevelt pushed Congress to build four new battleships a year.

The appeal of Roosevelt's call for naval expenditures, to military-minded men at least, lay in his expressing the nation's offensive capacity in terms of plated steel and firepower. On the basis of chivalric notions of fortified courage and the ability to withstand assault, repel formations, and deflect penetration, armor and artillery also served as a tangible surround for the emotions of the vulnerable living beings who manned it. However unconsciously, arming fulfilled men's desire to protect the vulnerable self behind an impenetrable defense that projected mastery and courage to other armored and similarly needy men. Some men sensed that the largest warships, the heaviest artillery—and later the deadliest tanks and planes—somehow represented the most virile aspects of themselves and the ultimate expression of the nation's being, not the least for those weapons' assumed capacity to target and destroy anything weaker.

To Roosevelt and Mahan, virility—albeit strongly self-disciplined and ascetic virility—formed the central element of naval and other war professions. Mastery was everything. Mahan grounded military virility in men's ability to separate themselves from female influence, to collectively discipline their own sexuality, and to emerge cleansed and capable of violence. For Mahan, soldiers were at once paragons of "self control, and of resistance to evil." In his book *From Sail to Steam: Recollections of Naval Life* (1907), Mahan insisted that military life remain a sanitized sanctuary, uncluttered by "extraneous matter—love-making and the like . . . intimate knowledge and idle trash."[67] True sailors and soldiers, "those of unrelenting heart who tear and break down every obstacle," remain immune to their own emotions and never exhibit "womanly qualities" or "trudge through life with kindness." Emotions should be "managed, economized, guided, and disciplined," he wrote, in a form of "self-repression."[68]

The collective fraternity of military life provided the means of this self-repression and seems to explain why, in recounting war experiences, Roosevelt and Mahan emphasized military life's cleansing and purifying effects against effeminacy, indeterminacy, and pacifism. Just as the Western hero avoided sexual encounters of any kind, military men too emphasized their cleanliness with abstractions of precision and order, duty and sacrifice. Military life's bonds often emerged in metaphors of mechanical coldness or surgical precision, what the newly professionalized officer corps began to call military science, or the art of bringing warfare under rational control. "I love military science . . . where human beings . . . do these things which science dictates," Remington said while in Cuba. "Our ten regiments of cavalry are the most perfect things of all Uncle Sam's public institutions."[69] In a similar vein of military precision, Jacob Riis observed that Roosevelt's and the Rough Riders' reciprocal loyalty bound them together "with hoops of steel."[70] Roosevelt's description of soldiers as "perfect specimens" with bodies of "steel" echoed William James's terming of them as "pure pieces of perfection" and Remington's characterization of the German army as "perfection . . . about as near right as things get in this world."[71]

With an ethos invoking precision, hierarchy, and the "necessity" of military discipline, soldier groups bound themselves together into unified, homogeneous, mechanized bodies that discouraged any interaction with would-be seducers or sources of decay, decline, or degeneration. Military formations heightened the intensity of synchronized and ritualized acts and mirrored for each member a fraternal brotherhood of ideal and sanitized manliness. "I do wish you could meet some of the nice fellows in my regiment," Roosevelt wrote to Spring Rice in 1900; "they are such good men, manly, clean, straightforward,—just the type you would like."[72] It was the hardy discipline of a soldier group that drew the Rough Riders together, Thayer observed, not in an equal brotherhood but in an authoritarian hierarchy that "bound [them] together by one common bond, devotion to Theodore Roosevelt."[73] Such discipline united bodies of martial men with the "unquestioning obedience essential to unity of action under a single will," Mahan wrote, reminding his readers that to enforce this obedience hazing still existed in the navy and flogging had been used as recently as 1849.[74]

Military life is coolly professional, Mahan said, and entirely dependent on surrounding men with a chilly and defensive but emotionally comfortable group exterior. Like the fictional cowboy who could make uneasy fraternity with others but preferred to be a loner, the navy man was bonded into a corps that established a common outside armor against what would ostensibly harm it. Navy discipline, with its tough, regimented loyalties and necessary secrets, provided common group exteriors for soldiers leaving behind hearth, home, and women. At the moment of boarding warships, men symbolically shed the corruption, degeneration, and effeminacy that might have plagued them in their onshore lives. War's simplicity and extremity liberated men from ordinary lives and allowed the state to appropriate individual bodies into its collective. Military training and warfare provided the ultimate solidarity among men, with seamless exteriors required by the common ego boundaries of soldier males. Only honorable battlefield death could break this union, hence the heavy penalties imposed on informers and deserters and the more subtle ones on individualists and loners.

Mahan considered the individual ego in the form of a pseudoprofessional "pride" or "conceit" to be an "alien temperament" that must be subsumed under the all-encompassing "body" of the corps. In this sense, group exteriors, especially when constructed and performed en masse, protected men from evil diversions on shore and encouraged them to direct their emotions toward other members of the corps. Mahan's projection of emotions away from the feminine and toward homoerotic satisfactions that arose among men living in military settings, Ronald Takaki argues, suggests that he hid his personal relations with other men. Mahan did say his father's friendship with Jefferson Davis at West Point was "approaching intimacy."[75] And Mahan, who was married and outwardly heterosexual, developed an intimate relationship with Samuel Ashe, a fellow student at Annapolis, that lasted forty years. In letters to Ashe, Mahan admitted that he preferred men to women: "When you come to a simple question of sex, on the whole commend me to men."[76]

However well he hid his preferences, Mahan reminisced fondly about the ways in which the intensely disciplined all-male shipboard society relieved homoerotic tension. The "game of detective," for instance, allowed men to circumvent shipboard rules against fraternization and engage in "after-hours' fun." One lieutenant's "favorite stratagems" consisted of "night surprises, inroads on the enemy's country, at the hours when we were mistakenly supposed to be safe in bed." If Mahan suspected sexual involvement in these nighttime excursions, he skirted the question with sly humor. Midshipmen, he said, who were caught visiting other men's rooms, must have been "lured thither, let us hope, by the charms of intellectual conversation."[77]

Mahan's strategies of managing sexuality open a window to understanding how artfully military authorities had to script the erotic content of shipboard and barracks life. Heavily disciplined group military formations and drills superimposed by authoritative officers created a common protective shell that bound the corps narcissistically and libidinally through mutual admiration and feeling. It was the "military methods of psycho-physical education" that created this fraternal aesthetic, G. Stanley Hall explained in the language of nineteenth-century medicine. Marching in step gave soldiers a "corporate feeling of membership" that drew from the "erectile value" of physical activity, which, especially when directed to-ward martial ends, provided "a subtle but potent intersexual influence" that could "exalt the spirit almost to the point of ecstasy." Feeling one's "full store of energy" imparts a "sense of joy," Hall found, "a reflex of pleasure that is sometimes a passion and may fairly intoxicate."[78] At times, the intoxicating joy of adventure for its own sake, in this case bordering on rape fantasy, trumps the justification of war on moral grounds. Roosevelt recognized this love of battle in himself and also ascribed it to members of the Rough Rider regiment in the veiled eroticism of conquest. The "eager longing" and the "sheer love of adventure" that energized the Rough Rid-ers, he wrote, were the same emotions that impelled America's "dauntless [and] restless" frontiersmen "to each penetrate deeper than his neighbors into the remote forest hunting grounds where the perilous pleasures of the chase and of war could be best enjoyed."[79]

In the battlefield's emotionally heightened state of perpetual readiness for death, strong enjoyments often provoked this same aesthetic of mutual caress. The Rough Riders Roosevelt described in his book about the regi-ment, especially the Western cowboys among them, "were a splendid set of men . . . tall and sinewy, with resolute, weather-beaten faces, and eyes that looked a man straight, without flinching." In a similar vein, Roosevelt de-scribed a scene in Cuba with homoerotic longing if not sadistic envy. En-camped in Cuba the first night of the campaign, standing with fellow soldiers around a fire, "I caught myself admiring the splendid bodily vigor of [Captain Allyn] Capron and [Sergeant Hamilton] Fish," who stood there as "perfect specimens. Their frames seemed of steel, to withstand all fatigue; they were flushed with health; in their eyes shone high resolve and fiery desire. They were both filled with eager longing to show their mettle. Within twelve hours they both were dead."[80]

Roosevelt's descriptions of the beauty and strength of these healthy men in their thirties was not out of keeping with custom in an age that ap-proved of physically intimate, though not necessarily sexual, and inti-mately expressed same-sex friendships.[81] For Roosevelt, the soldiers' beauty, together with their forthright acts and martial spirit, made them "men to whom I am bound by the closest of all ties."[82] These bonds were, if not physically sexual, at least sexualized and sexualizing.[83] His descriptions rendered the men physically attractive and transformed the training camp and the battlefield into an erotic ground where a purified sexuality could be elicited and indulged in by the participants. That Capron and Fish knew "eager longing" might end in death lends a fatally heroic tone to Roosevelt's description that is reminiscent of Henry James's longing for Owen Wister's Virginian to "perish in his flower and in some splendid and somber way."[84] Such fantasies of harmonious belonging tied men together in deep bonds that Roosevelt judged to be the "fundamental virtues of hardihood and manliness."

As Ronald Takaki explains, imperialists like Roosevelt and Mahan promoted naval life as a "sanctuary of American asceticism," which, with its self-imposed self-denial, was a way for men "to control their own rebellion against repressions of the self that modernism required." In this rebellion against externally imposed repression, imperialists developed an ironically even more repressive sanctuary, one ostensibly of self-control, yet one that tied them more surely to the most repressive institutions, the army and navy. Imperialist violence regenerated a psychologically protective "raw power" in the face of women and corruption, Takaki holds, but in doing so it "yielded to irrational impulses which emphasized power, aggression and death."[85] In the sanctuary of military life, these irrational emotions could be indulged in only in tightly controlled situations such as the scripts for discipline or homoerotic admiration.

But however much the military life encouraged homo-aesthetic fantasy, this deep interpenetration took place not just between men and feminized landscapes, and not just between mutually admiring men standing around campfires or dying splendid deaths. In truth, men's own conflicted identities constituted a war within, whether abstracted as emotional versus rational, female versus male, child versus man, or man versus himself. The surfacing of the male erotic aesthetic in times of intense male bonding made it necessary that men strictly demarcate heterosexual male gatherings from groups of men desiring one another. These strict demarcations are ones each man needs, David Savran explains, to silence or disavow or displace "a dangerous and perverse identity," and they serve to confirm "the homophobic cultural logic that the more closely bonds between men are drawn, the more crucial becomes the injunction" against homosexuality.[86] In many ways, modern masculinity forms around this homosocial-homosexual boundary. A masculine heterosexual man can cleave to groups of exaggeratedly heterosexual men in an effort to reject and dominate his own bodily and emotional frailties. In short, it is G. Stanley Hall's "warfare against evil within and without."

ALIEN MATTERS

In the logic of such warfare, martially bonded sailors could not tolerate weaklings, spies, or detractors. Esprit de corps, Mahan said of the traditional navy, "is the breath of the body, the breath of life. [The corps] could not survive the big introduction of alien matter." Mahan used the term *alien matter* to distinguish a myriad of men with sexual, racial, and ethnic anomalies from "real" seamen. Those not yet battle hardened, the "vast numbers" of new and untrained men who "swamped" the ship, posed threats to the "real" seamen who had served on "men-of-war" from time immemorial when there were "seas to cross and to rule," seamen who had "evolutionized into something entirely different." Modern sailors, fraught with "defects" and "loss" were poor specimens compared to their more robust and highly evolved forebears, and their inexperience could endanger the ship in wartime. The "less worthy men of the present—less professional, less courageous, less manly" needed "strengthening" that only danger and the nearness of death could provide.[87] To achieve strength, soldiers and sailors directed the steely bonds of military life against their own repressed emotions and weaknesses, to wit, against pacifists and cowards in their midst. Seasoned men singled out new inductees for harassment, Mahan said, in order to make them more fit for military life. Once that was achieved, Mahan explained, the "unquestioning obedience essential to unity of action under a single will [became] at once the virtue and the menace of a standing army."[88]

The military's efforts to fashion a homogenized esprit de corps, however authoritarian, helps to explain how pleased Roosevelt was with the national unity that war provided. Painfully remembering the brutal Civil War and haunted by the specter of racial, immigrant, and class warfare, Roosevelt and his generation of middle-class Anglo-Saxon men were ready to preserve unity at whatever cost. "If the Union had been dissolved," Roosevelt wrote of Antietam, "our country . . . would have been split into little jangling rival nationalities, each with a history both bloody and contemptible."[89] Roosevelt's call for unity transformed the Civil War's sectional split into fears of ethnic dissolution of the fraternal white brotherhood. Divisive as it was, Roosevelt told a veterans reunion in Burlington, Vermont, in 1901, the Civil War had unified the nation. It "drew into the field a very large proportion of the adult male population, [who] together, faced toil and risk and hardship side by side, died with the same fortitude, and felt the same disinterested thrill of triumph when the victory came." The Civil War provided a "very good thing," Roosevelt said: "a great mass of our people learn[ed] what it was to face death and endure toil together, . . . all with a community of interest which they could have gained in no other way."[90] The Spanish-American War, Roosevelt wrote in a *Century* article in 1900, was the nineteenth century's "most absolutely, righteous foreign war," for it brought unity between the North and South.[91] Roosevelt's popular account of the Rough Riders' campaign dwelled not on actual killing (he shot only one Spaniard—in the back as he fled) but on the bonds that developed between men in Cuba.[92] In Roosevelt's thinking, only common bloodletting could the hold nation's body together in fraternal unity and singularity of will.

In the muscular morality and search for unified national manhood, the nation's pacifist and anti-imperialist movements committed the unpardonable sin in that they fractured the unity of purpose so painfully won in war. Pacifism, inasmuch as it indicated a failure of manly risk taking and suffering, could never be a neutral, and surely not a positive, political or moral preference; Roosevelt felt it bred certain decline. Pacifists, for him, were "active agents of the devil," who acted out of "sheer, downright physical and moral timidity."[93] Roosevelt shared William James's sentiment that pacifism arose from the debilitating consequences of modernism, that it sapped manly energy, debilitated character, and spread dissension, infusing men with a paralyzing inability to act and a tendency to argue in times of national emergency. Men who take the "sentimental-pacifist view of international relations [are not] good material out of which to build true national greatness," he wrote in an article on Admiral Mahan.[94] More than just advocating an absence of conflict, pacifism implied an unwillingness to fight, a suspiciously eager surrender by weak men or nations to domination by stronger ones. In 1899, on the occasion of the first reunion of the Rough Riders, Roosevelt said to Chicago's Hamilton Club, "we must send out only good and able men, chosen for their fitness, remembering that . . . weakness is the greatest of crimes."[95]

The pacifism of the Russian novelist Leo Tolstoy provided Roosevelt's favorite example of how individual weakness led to national decline. In some of his strongest language ever, Roosevelt deplored an author who produced simultaneously a wildly lascivious national literature and a pathological political pacifism. "The same quality that makes the debauchee and the devotee alternate in certain decadent families," Roosevelt wrote, "the hysterical development which leads to violent emotional reaction in a morbid nature from vice to virtue, also leads to the creation of Tolstoi's 'Kreutzer Sonata' on one hand, and of his unhealthy peace-mysticism on the other."[96] "A sane and healthy mind would be as incapable of the moral degradation of the novel as of the decadent morality of the

philosophy." Were Russians to have followed Tolstoy's philosophy of pacifism and sexual folly in national life, "they would now be extinct, and savages would have taken their place."[97]

Beginning with the anti-imperialist resistance to the coming war with
Spain and spurred by his own impatience for a declaration of war, Roosevelt's abhorrence of a particular kind of pacifism grew throughout the
1890s. In March of 1898, he wrote Douglas Robinson that President
William McKinley and his speaker of the house both appeared "almost
crazy in their eagerness for peace."[98] The "hysterical and morbid" peace
advocates who were against war because of its "attendant evils," Roosevelt
said, were fussing about "incidental damage" that was "inherent in war."
While war is a great evil, it "may be a less evil than cringing to iniquity."
Peace "may lead men to compromise with unrighteousness," he wrote,
quoting Mahan, and soothe their consciences in the belief that there is no
greater wrong than war. Roosevelt's criticisms centered on pacifists'
"compromise with unrighteousness," which he felt was a greater evil than
war because in this capitulation men assumed a position of helplessness
and weakness, a position that, in Roosevelt's concept of manliness, was to
be avoided at all costs.[99] In Roosevelt's opinion, pacifism enjoined men to
avoid calls to heroic action, and it thereby generated a legacy of shame.
Only by undertaking the most rigorous antidote—active, aggressive,
forthright action against enemies—could manly men cleanse themselves
from the shame of being dominated. This is why Roosevelt thought that
from the colonial period onward the military "pacification" of Indians had
provided its own purifications for the nation. So too had the campaigns of
the Revolutionary War and the Civil War. Now, in 1898, he said, the country was ripe for another purification.

After war with Spain ended, the Philippine insurgency against U.S. occupation continued for another four years. The U.S. Army's bloody campaign against the insurgents provoked an outcry at home, leading some
critics to see the United States as another colonial power and to applaud
the resistance. In a 1902 *Independent* essay, "Expansion and Peace," Roosevelt blasted the pacifist feelings that provoked sympathy for the enemy in
any war because such sympathy ultimately placed American men in a position of weakness not just in relation to other American men, but even
worse, in relation to inferior peoples. The "pacifists" who "deliberately in-
cited in the name of peace the Civil War's bloody draft riots" helped the
enemy for the whole four years, just as the "weakling or coward who
babbles for peace" encouraged Aguinaldo and his guerrillas to shoot
American soldiers. "With such peoples—half-caste Christians, warlike
Moslems, and wild pagans—weakness is the greatest of crimes."[100]

Despite Roosevelt's bellicose talk, he emerged as one of the new century's most applauded peacekeepers when he arranged the 1905 peace conference at Portsmouth, New Hampshire, and the resulting treaty that ended hostilities between Japan and Russia. Roosevelt, who believed in balance of power, worried about Japan's designs on the Pacific even as he encouraged them in Korea and Manchuria. He also feared that Russian humiliation would lead to revolution in Russia. Peace would prevent either Japan or Russia from emerging triumphant from their war. Exhausted and ready for an end to the war, both sides accepted his offer for mediation, and, as his secretary of state John Hay lay dying, Roosevelt became the statesman of peace.

For his peacemaking efforts Roosevelt received worldwide congratulations, including praise from the rulers of Britain, France, and Germany, and thanks from Russia and Japan. Yet he took pains in a letter to his new secretary of state, Elihu Root, to substitute for conventional pacifism one more befitting his notions of muscular national manhood. "I particularly do *not* want to appear as a professional peace advocate—a kind of sublimated being of the [E. L.] Godkin or [Carl] Schurz variety," he confided.[101] He distinguished between the "muscular" and the "mushy" peace advocates: the "doer of deeds who actually counts in the battle for life, and . . . the man who looks on . . . without sharing in the stress and the danger."[102] His sense of his own "muscular" peacemaking would have made him recoil at a 1908 *Baltimore Sun* reproduction of a Japanese cartoon of a supplicating "Roosevelt as angel of peace," holding an olive branch and swooping over fighting soldiers (figure 50). The winged and robed angel did not match Roosevelt's description of himself as "the strong man with sword girt on thigh who preaches peace . . . not from fear or distrust of his own powers, but from a deep sense of moral obligation."[103]

Roosevelt sought the image of fighter for peace that was admiringly if a bit nervously supplied by the nation's cartoonists. In the eyes of a New York *World* cartoonist, he preferred to wield a lasso rather than to be the angel of peace (figure 51). Befitting his role as the "muscular" peace advocate who convinced Russia and Japan to stop fighting, Roosevelt forces the angel of peace to the table. "Come and be peaceful," the Rough Rider orders, brandishing his big stick as he fires his pistol. He lassos the fleeing angel, who screams "Help! Help!" In October 1900, before Roosevelt's election as vice president, a New York *Verdict* cartoonist had pictured another helpless female victim, America herself, assaulted by Roosevelt's muscular politics. Forced to dance to a guitar tune punctuated by pistol shots from a gleeful Roosevelt, she fearfully lifts her skirts (figure 52). The

Figure 50. "Roosevelt as Angel of Peace; A Japanese Interpretation," *Baltimore Sun*, 22 November 1908

editors of *Verdict* promised that once elected vice president Roosevelt would "enliven that proverbially sedate and obscure office with his characteristic strenuousness."[104] With images of Roosevelt projecting his own—and by extension the nation's—"mushy" interior onto helpless females, cartoonists helped clarify and popularize the muscular peace advocacy that Roosevelt-as-cowboy brought to politics. The New York *World*'s more imaginative readers were left to conjecture what Roosevelt might have done with the women once they had been shot or lassoed.

INVITATION
TO 2ˢ PEACE CONFERENCE.
"COME AND BE PEACEFUL."
                              T. R.

THE BIG STICK

Figure 51. "The Angel of Peace: 'Help! Help!' " *World* (New York)

When, in 1905, Roosevelt received the Nobel Peace Prize for mediating the peace negotiations between Russia and Japan, he explained to the anti-imperialist Carl Schurz the moral obligation of "strong, civilized nations" to "police the world." England used the might of its great fleet and colonial armies against the likes of Turks, Armenians, and Egyptians in order to prevent "a horrible and bloody calamity to mankind." Roosevelt wanted Schurz to interpret his own peace efforts with Japan and Russia in the same light as England's Pax Britannica. If in the 1905 negotiations he had used what he derided as Schurz's "conventional peace advocacy," a weak position that capitulated to "peace at any price," it would have marked him in the eyes of the world as a man who "hesitated," and from that moment on, he would have been rendered "powerless." In Roosevelt's figuration, peace was not peace in and of itself. It had to be energetically proactive. It was a means to action and a partner of war. It came "only as a sequel to the

Figure 52. "The Teddy Idea of a Vice-President Who Would 'Do Things,' " *Verdict* (New York), 29 October 1900

armed interference of a civilized power."[105] If America refused such moral obligations, he had said in 1899, "some stronger, manlier power would have to step in and do the work, and we would have shown ourselves weaklings."[106]

As the Great War erupted in Europe and Americans, especially those in the heartland, resisted the calls of interventionists, Roosevelt feared that pacifism was on the rise in his own country. The public acceptance of President Woodrow Wilson's and William Jennings Bryan's strategy of neutrality meant that the "iniquitous peace propaganda of the last fifteen years has finally had its effect." It was the "college sissies," the educated men of his class, he charged, who prevented the country from preparing for war and from responding manfully to a series of German provocations. When a German submarine sank the *Lusitania* in May of 1915, Wilson's two notes of rebuke only further enervated Americans who, Roosevelt thought, should be clamoring for war. "They are cold" he fumed to Lodge. "They have been educated by this infernal peace propaganda in the last ten years into an attitude of sluggishness and timidity."[107]

Roosevelt's strong reaction to pacifism connected several themes that he used frequently to assess the nation's problems. He felt that the pacifists' "hysterical" and "unhealthy peace-mysticism" and the effeminate reactions of "weaklings" brought moral degradation to the nation. Like Mahan's sense of the "alien matter" introduced into the navy by the "defects" of modern sailors, Roosevelt ascribed pacifism to degenerate inbreeding since, in his view, it alternated with militancy in "decadent families." "Failure to act when occasion demands," Mahan wrote of the nation's inability to declare war, "indicates a . . . dangerous condition, in that moral inadequacy means ultimately material decline. When the spirit leaves the body, the body decays."[108] And Roosevelt warned that biologically retrograde pacifism might ultimately allow "savages" to destroy the nation. The only alternative for Roosevelt was war, the steely unifier that bound and bonded the white body of national manhood.

ALONE WITH THEIR JOY

For the purveyors of muscular nationalism, battleships expressed fantasies of danger and strength. For Mahan, the beauty of ships made them objects of desire. "Quick as a docile and intelligent animal to respond to the master's call," he wrote, ships inspired "affection and intensified professional enthusiasm. The exercises of sails and spars . . . to the appreciative possessed fascination, and were their own sufficient reward for the care lavished upon them." Mahan remembered one vessel in particular in the Mediterranean twelve years before: the ship "lying quiet, waiting her opportunity, would glide forward with a dozen slow turns of the screws. . . . The bay at the moment was quiet as a millpond, and it needed little imagination to [identify the ship] with a swan making its leisurely way by means equally unseen; no turbulent display of energy, yet suggestive of mysterious power." Modern ships possessed "elements of the sublime," Mahan said, since they represented the culmination of a long evolution of naval expertise with guns, armor, weight, size, and especially great speed, which was admittedly "often pushed beyond the strictly necessary." Dreadnoughts inspired Mahan's awe not the least because they had inherited this evolutionary naval tradition, which he expressed in bodily and racial metaphors. Modern ships retained "survivals," or characteristics, from earlier types of ship similar to primitive traits discovered by "physiologists [who] seek to reconstruct the past of a race from scanty traces still extant."[109]

Remington, too, expressed a love of battleships in an erotic and mechanical sublime, although he seemed to know the difference. Assigned as a journalist to the battleship *Iowa* during the Cuban campaign, he observed the effects of military technology on the officers and men. For "men who have succumbed to modern science, . . . trees and the play of sunlight mean nothing," Remington wrote in *Men with the Bark On.* "I believe they fairly worship this throbbing mass of mysterious iron; I believe they love this bewildering power which they control . . . so leave them alone with their joy."[110] Roosevelt said that Remington's "old love" was Western horses and men but he suspected that Remington had found "another" love in the steely attractions of battleships. Assistant Secretary of the Navy Roosevelt invited Remington to tour the naval fleet in 1897, and after the tour he wrote to Remington: "You will never care for the ship as you do for the horse, but you must like the ship, too, and the man aboard" who "works hard, and if need be is willing to die hard."[111]

Other observers were captured by the erotic sublimity of the battleships that made war against Spain. Reporting in May 1898 from the deck of the fleet's flagship, the battleship *New York*, Richard Harding Davis described the long line of thirty-two troop ships carrying twelve thousand men steaming toward Cuba. Guarded by fourteen warships, he wrote, the gunboats looked "workmanlike and clean." During the assault on Santiago, Davis observed two bombardments of the Cuban coast by the battleships' eight-inch guns, the first upon the Spanish batteries at the port of Matanzas, and the second upon group of Spanish cavalrymen who had fired on the *New York* from the shore. In their "fierce search" for the port's fortified batteries, the American ships' guns, Davis reported, "came crashing from every point; the thick deck jumped with the concussions. . . . The reports seemed to crack the air as if it were a dense body." As troop ships later unloaded the American army at Baiquiri, battleships pounded the shore and the earth erupted in geysers "as though someone had stabbed it with a knife and the blood had spurted from the wound."[112]

Later, moving eastward along the coast toward Cardenas, the *New York* received rifle fire from shore. "Futile and inadequate," the shots were nonetheless "impertinent," Davis wrote, because they were accompanied by laughter from the Spaniards. Provoked by admittedly "harmless" and feminized riflemen on horses, the battleship commenced shelling the shoreline with four-inch guns. As the guns "spoke, . . . the deck of the flagship heaved . . . as an elevator . . . when it rises with a jerk." Against a blazing sunset, a "gridiron of red and gold," Davis reported, the battleship continued to "hurl flashes of flame and clouds of hot smoke" designed to teach impudent Spaniard soldiers "not to interfere with their betters." As the sailors and marines gathered on the deck to watch the bombardment, the officer's mess string band played Scheur's *Dream of Spring,* the strains of which mingled with the pounding of the ship's guns. "This is not a touch of fiction," Davis said, "but the reporting of cold coincidence, for war as it is conducted at this end of the century is civilized."[113]

With the deliberate ferocity of this bizarre and apocalyptic scene, Davis presented his impression of the overwhelming power of the battleship's huge guns. Historian David Nye has identified such responses on the part of Mahan, Remington, and Davis as the technological sublime, an emotional "enthusiasm for technology" that inscribes great bridges, monuments, and skyscrapers with a transcendent, almost religious significance.[114] This enthusiasm is reflected in the phantasmal quality of Davis's description of the battle scene, a quality that provoked his need to explain that it was "not a touch of fiction." Indeed, military men in the act of describing weapons and fights often substitute the sublime for the erotic they deny themselves in ordinary life. The "cold coincidence" of hot feeling and cold steel, the shells shot from the "throbbing mass of mysterious iron" bursting in the "dense body" of the very air, expressed an abstracted and displaced sexual fulfillment for men who considered women and effeminacy threats to military life. Roosevelt's observation that Remington loved battleships and Remington's that sailors "fairly worship" them were expressions of an acceptable variation of male love. Love objects like weapons or units of military men signify a life undertaken to avoid women and from which all taints of femininity have been removed. Expressions of love, so restrained in Victorian sensibilities, were displaced into longings for steely "bursts" and technological perfection. As Remington advised regarding the men who withdrew into military life, one should "leave them alone with their joy."

Ships were the central fact of naval life, Robert O'Connell maintains. They "symbolized everything that was acceptable and orderly about naval life, . . . its rituals, its social structure, its conceptions of power, courage, and fighting etiquette."[115] Naval training required unquestioned obedience and rigid, hierarchical management of tightly synchronized duties, making the men part of the ship's machine power and inviting them to appropriate the thick armor, big guns, and menacing invincibility along with the internalized discipline. Men assigned to naval duty and those who watched from shore projected their own unfeeling and armored selves onto the battleships, which, like men, carried steel plate on the exterior but contained beating hearts inside. The power of such symbols and rituals reassured and stabilized manhood, locating it outside the realm of the mutable and in the massive, permanent objects that demanded and absorbed attention.

In 1907, in a feat of technological sublimity, President Roosevelt had sixteen of the new battleships painted white and sent to carry an impressive show of muscular nationhood around the globe. In the world's naval culture, ambitious powers like Germany and Japan copied the British Royal Navy's ships, uniforms, and the aristocratic outlook. Not the least of these imitators was Roosevelt. With twelve thousand men aboard and led by the S.S. *New Jersey,* the Great White Fleet cruised the world's oceans until he left the presidency in February of 1909. "Isn't it magnificent?" said the president, toasting the fleet's admirals and captains upon its return. One must admit, Thayer asserted, that the Great White Fleet impressed upon the world that the United States had "manpower as well as money-power" and was "prepared to repel all enemies." That Thayer deemed the fleet's aggressive display a "great moral achievement" indicated the changed definition of morality embedded in the new martial national spirit. Ignoring the aggressive nature of the great-power naval race that occurred in the years preceding the Great War, Roosevelt called the fleet "the most important service that I rendered to peace."[116] In the tradition of the cavalry and naval cultures before him, which had since the European military aristocracies of the ancien régime fetishized weapons, horses, and ships, Roosevelt now invested modern battleships with civilization's moral imprimatur.

Davis's adoration must have elicited emotional patriotism in some readers who imagined the scene and the accompanying music. Other readers, from a generation closer to the Civil War or from the ranks of those opposed to the war with Spain, might have been less impressed. Anti-imperialist opposition to the Cuban war and the guerrilla rebellion in the Philippines highlighted a difference of opinion between Civil War veterans and men of Roosevelt's generation, who considered Civil War action the height of manliness. William McKinley and his contemporaries had seen the horror of betrayed youth, self-serving leaders, and senseless slaughter and therefore showed less eagerness for war in 1898. "I have been through one war," he said as he called for a naval board of inquiry into the *Maine* explosion. "I have seen the dead piled up, and I do not want to see another."[117] McKinley then pursued the war effectively, but Roosevelt's generation revealed a fascination with death and dying.

Romanticizing war and weapons with near-childish glee protected Roosevelt psychologically from facing the horror of raw experience revealed in the eyewitness literature of the Great War. Works like Ernest Hemingway's *A Farewell to Arms* (1929) portray a horror that led many men exposed to mass carnage to reject glorified death and dying.[118] As Robert Wohl explains in *The Generation of 1914,* T. E. Lawrence was devastated when he "discovered in himself the capacity for bloodlust and reprisal that he had formerly associated with primitive and non-European peoples."[119] But for many of the warriors and would-be warriors who partook of Roosevelt's cult of strenuousness at the end of the century, romanticizing killing and cultivating the allegorical primitive served as part of the warrior's ego armor and provided a rationale that masked killing fields with courage and glory.

By 1898, the experience of war with Spain had heightened interest in war's effects on the nation's masculine self. While some Americans thought that the war delivered rational benefits in protecting the nation's economic and strategic interests, many more felt its emotional thrill as yellow newspapers assaulted the boredom of Eastern middle-class life. As Americans evaluated the war and its aftermath, references to this thrill began to surface in political culture. Even before 1898, in his histories of the trans–Appalachian frontier, Roosevelt had emphasized war's ability to elicit states of ecstatic emotional stimulation. The "American advance" in the Indian Wars of 1784–1787, he was sure, had produced a "fiery rush" among the frontiersmen. Of his own war experience, Roosevelt remembered that "we had a bully fight at Santiago."[120] War had finally provided the ultimate sport, in Roosevelt's case the opportunity to "get his Spaniard."[121] "We were all there in the spirit of the thing," he said of the Rough Riders, "and greatly excited by the charge."[122] Like Leonard Wood, officers and men of the American naval squadron in Cuba were, in Roosevelt's observation, "in heart, mind, and body, of the very type which makes the best kind of fighting man"; they were "men who got into scrapes in times of peace" and who were "aroused and excited by the chance of battle."[123]

Roosevelt seemed invigorated by showing other men how in war's "teeth of difficulty," he eagerly sought, calculated, and embraced the risk of injury or death for himself and for the Rough Riders. One-third of the officers and one-fifth of the enlisted men were killed in the Cuban campaign. "Frankly," Roosevelt wrote to Douglas Robinson in the weeks following the battle at San Juan, "it did not enter my head that I could get through without being hit; . . . if hit the chances would be about three to one against my being killed, that has been the proportion of dead to wounded here."[124] He and his officers drank a toast before going ashore: "May we be killed, wounded, or promoted."[125] Almost twenty years later, as another war approached, Roosevelt had not lost what must have appeared to some as a death wish. Rebuffed by Woodrow Wilson when he offered to form another volunteer division and take it to the European war, he wrote to John Burroughs: "I shall never cease bitterly regretting that I was not allowed to go to the other side. I would not have expected to come home alive."[126]

Acting out in war feelings that most men rarely let out and perhaps were reluctant to confront in peacetime offered soldiers a chance to look over a radical psychic edge into an emotional universe they rarely ever saw. Some,

like T. E. Lawrence, were horrified at their blood-thirst. Others, like
Roosevelt, gloried in it, as when he described a warrior as "that child of
thunder and lover of the battle's hottest heat, . . . that lightning-blasted
Son of the Morning."[127] Battle-hardened men readily recognized the
community of those who thrilled to battle's heat. "All men," Roosevelt
said, "who feel any joy of battle know what it is like when the wolf rises in
the heart." William James, too, recognized that hunting and war evoked
men's primitive "instincts," what he called the fascination of atrocity, that
"utterly blind excitement of giving the rein to our fury when our blood is
up."[128] Mahan, reminiscing on the lessons of the Spanish-American War,
wrote of the deep need for men to express uninhibited forms of emotional
energy. He called it "raw power," that "mighty hand that crushes everything that stands in its way and the will that makes men giants."[129]

Yet if killing created joy, Roosevelt felt, there was still a point of no return. One still had to watch for the dangers embedded in war's joy. In a sec-
tion of his autobiography called "The Vigor of Life," he described "buck
fever" as "a state of intense nervous excitement . . . that affects [a man] the
first time he sees a buck or goes into battle." A man must, by repeated exercise of self-mastery, get his nerves thoroughly under control when the
wolf rises. "If the man has the right stuff . . . his will grows stronger and
stronger with each exercise of it—and if . . . not . . . he had better keep
clear of danger."[130]

Indeed, the need to civilize savage behavior reconciled the conflict in
men's consciences between traditional morality and the extramoral demands of empire. The logic of violence—on one hand rationally mastered,
yet on the other experienced as something as close to mayhem as possible—prevented civilized men from understanding or confronting their
deep complicity in uncivilized acts. Just as the cult of the cowboy soldier naturalized Western violence, it was necessary to naturalize imperial
violence lest it became a moral burden on the imperial nation itself.
Americans could do horrible deeds and remain pure, the logic of violence
held. Americans are not savages, they merely use savagery to advance civilization against savagery. But this logic did not always hold, since using
savagery for civilized ends imposed emotional hardships. Modern men
had to develop "iron qualities," Roosevelt explained, in order to revive the
hardness that made their forebears "fit to do the deeds they did."[131] This
justification recalled Darwinist and pre-Darwinist racial ideas that had
long informed frontier warfare, ideas that prescribed not an amoral, but a
supramoral assessment of killing. The duties of advancing civilization
bound men to "destroy and uplift . . . people living in barbarism," Roosevelt said, "to see that they are freed from their chains, and we can free them

only by destroying barbarism itself."[132] When white men act to preserve white civilization, they can presumably kill beasts or savages with impunity because they deem them beasts or savages. We are peacekeepers, Roosevelt wrote Ohio Congressman Theodore Elijah Burton, we who "put an end to bloody misrule and bloody civil strife in Cuba . . . because, and only because we possess a navy which makes it evident that we will not tamely submit to injustice."[133] An unruly and armed but peaceful people, Roosevelt inferred, ended the rule of savages.

Freeing people from barbarism might well kill them—the mission was "to destroy and uplift"—but when barbarism appeared in the form of primitive people, it elicited Roosevelt's urge to tame the "wolf that rises in [his own] heart," which some have figured as his recognition of his own capacity for barbarism. Thus Roosevelt wrote to Leonard Wood in April 1899: "In the Philippines we still seem to be having ugly work; but if only our people stand firm and take a little punishment . . . we will have the islands absolutely pacified once and for all."[134] On the level of rhetoric, the imperatives of this "ugly work" justified the U.S. use of force. On the psychological level, one summoned one's capacity for barbaric behavior to punish the perpetrators.

Men's excesses could erupt in savagery, as everyone knew, but the wolf could be mastered and the joy that arose when "our blood is up" contained. Certain forms of ritual bloodletting could constructively be channeled into society and politics in carefully directed ways—through regimented military behavior in wartime and through rule-and-law-bound hunting and rough sports in peacetime. This kind of channeling allowed men to collectively and rationally contain and at times cautiously unleash long-avoided connections with what they could only describe as the savage beast within. Containing excessive emotions within rational explanations and regimented behavior embedded what would otherwise have been senseless bloodletting in the identity of a virile and advanced civilization.

The nation's literature and art pictured moments of this identity making, horrible acts that the nation had begun to admit into its range of officially acceptable imperial behavior. Human beheading, for example, was an act that few Americans before the Civil War would have considered civilized. Remington's drawings completed after his African trips in 1892 and 1894 showed Spanish conquistadors or Arabs as perpetrators of beheading. In the drawing "In the Rear of a Slave Caravan" (1893), he shows a Semitic, turbaned slave driver standing over a collared man who looks black and whom he has just beheaded with his saber (figure 53). The executioner's casual act of wiping the blood from his saber while gazing down at his victim implies that such acts took place in the normal process of trans-

Figure 53. Frederic Remington, "In the Rear of a Slave Caravan," *Harper's Monthly*, March 1893 (courtesy Frederic Remington Art Museum, Ogdensburg, New York)

porting captives. That the executioner was an Arab mirrored the outcry in Europe against the Arab-controlled slave trade in East Africa and allowed Remington to suggest that beheading was a primitive act that occurred in "oriental" slave cultures.

Yet Remington placed beheading squarely in his own country's politics, picturing it as part of the accepted business of conducting warfare on the American frontier, as safely within notions of military morality. In *Satisfy-*

Figure 54. Frederic Remington, *Satisfying the Demands of Justice: The Head,* 1897 (courtesy Frederic Remington Art Museum, Ogdensburg, New York)

ing the Demands of Justice: The Head (1897), an Indian has brought an enemy's head to a U.S. cavalry encampment and placed it on the ground before a seated officer (figure 54). That one Indian beheaded another might initially have shocked viewers, especially if they did not see the head on first glance. But the soldiers had set the event in motion by offering a bounty on the Indian's head, which may explain the seeming ordinariness of the event. While one of the soldiers holds up his hand as if to shield his eyes or guard his mouth, none of them seems particularly alarmed or offended. They gather curiously. Such near-nonchalance indicates that the soldiers expect barbarism from the Indian, as they would from the Arab slave-trader, and that they may indeed be identifying with him as a slayer. In any case, barbarism in the service of justice seems to strike them as perfectly natural—and certainly it was invited since the head belonged not to an enemy of the Indian but to an enemy of the state. Through such representations, Remington encouraged his American viewers to feel the otherwise barbaric act of beheading as an instrument of white men's frontier justice. With their Army-issue weapons, military discipline, and orders to punish Indian resistance to white advances, the soldiers officially represented the mighty industrialized nation at their backs.

Beheading of nonwhite people also appeared in two accounts of the 1898 punitive expeditions against local African rebels undertaken by Leon Rom, the station chief at Stanley Falls, several hundred miles up the

Congo river in the colony of Belgian king Leopold II. In articles appearing in *Century Magazine* and *The Saturday Review,* a British explorer and journalist recounted the aftermath of one fight: "Many women and children were taken, and twenty-one heads were brought to the falls, and have been used by Captain Rom as a decoration round a flower-bed in front of his house!" Insofar as such representations of colonialist savagery had become everyday fare in widely read magazines, it was fitting that Rom served as a prototype for Joseph Conrad's character Mr. Kurtz. Indeed, *Heart of Darkness* was written in the same decade that the young Conrad made his own trip to Leopold's imperialist outpost of white civilization.[135]

The United States produced no contemporary account of racial imperialism equal to Conrad's. Was it because bloodthirstiness, however fictionalized, catered to or stimulated popular tastes sufficiently to enter political culture seamlessly, something not just Remington but political satirists and cartoonists demonstrated? In a Philadelphia *Record* cartoon, "The Calebra Cut," an armed and uniformed Roosevelt wields the sharp sword of national interest to behead political enemies, in this case opponents of the Panama Canal, whose dismembered and stiffened corpses are lined up for military inspection (figure 55). The title refers simultaneously to the canal's geographic severing of the hemisphere and Roosevelt's beheading of his opponents; *calebra* is a corruption of *culebra,* a Spanish term signifying both a zigzag cut and the way dying bodies stumble around when their necks are severed. In a similar and equally macabre vein, the Berlin *Lustige Blätter* published "Teddy's War Cry: 'Hurrah!'" with Roosevelt holding aloft the heads of political opponents, possibly including Bryan and Hanna, which he has just cut from their bodies (figure 56).

Neither Remington's Apache head nor beheadings in political satire were farfetched, given the atrocities reported from the Philippine campaign. In 1901, General Frederick Funston, who captured the Philippine leader Aguinaldo, put a price of six hundred dollars on the head of David Fagen, one of the black U.S. Army deserters who defected to join the insurgents. Funston let it be known that Fagen was "entitled to the same treatment as a mad dog" and was reportedly greatly satisfied when Fagen's head was delivered in a basket to U.S. Army regulars at Bongabong.[136] As in Remington's painting, white man's justice presented demands to be satisfied, namely a legal resolution of whatever offenses the Indian or black soldier may have committed. The presentation of Fagen's head completes a blood rite in which, whether in fiction or in actual warfare, the alien enemy is reduced to pure body by the severance of its seat of governance, the head, which is presented to civilization's duly elected or appointed representatives. White leaders distanced themselves from savagery by ordering

Figure 55. J. L. De Mar, "The Calebra Cut," *Record* (Philadelphia)

it conducted by its scouts and soldiers. Civilization was reaffirmed when the head was presented to those guarding its furthest outposts. The viewer's identification with beheading was wrapped in the imprimatur of civilization's rationalizing, modulating effect.

During the Philippine campaign, war reporters noted that soldiers had to adopt some sort of psychic mechanism to shield themselves from the human consequences of such atrocities. "I am probably growing hard hearted," said A. A. Barnes, who served with the Third Artillery, "for I am in my glory when I can sight my gun on some dark skin and pull the trigger." To reporter Henry Nelson a U.S. Army officer wrote "we must bury all qualms and scruples about Weylerian cruelty, the consent of the governed, etc. . . . We exterminated the American Indian, and I guess most of us are proud of it, or, at least, believe the end justified the means; and we

Figure 56. Feininger, "Teddy's War Cry: 'Hurrah!'" *Lustige Blätter* (Berlin)

must have no scruples about exterminating this other race standing in the way of progress and enlightenment, if it is necessary." In writing of Weylerian cruelty, the officer was referring to General Valeriano Weyler y Nicolau, the Spanish commander in Cuba who issued an order in 1896 for Cubans to "reconcentrate" themselves into towns guarded by the Spanish army. His army then burned their villages and killed many of those who refused to be herded into the towns, a policy subsequently used by the American army in the Philippines.[137] However painfully and ambivalently, the officer buried his qualms about his own use of "Weylerian cruelty" in carrying out civilization's "necessary" extermination of "this other race," echoing Roosevelt's dictum that the United States would have to "take a little punishment" in order to "destroy and uplift."

When allegations of the army's torture of Filipinos surfaced and the administration came under heavy criticism in the press, Roosevelt instructed William Howard Taft, as governor of the Philippines, to investigate "whether or not any brutalities or indignities [had been] inflicted by the army on the natives." The investigation was conducted by Henry Cabot Lodge's Senate Committee on the Philippines from February through June of 1902. Lodge controlled public knowledge of the proceedings and suppressed incriminating evidence, allowing no victims of army atrocities or even the insurrection leader Aguinaldo to testify. When the whitewashed report was released, Roosevelt wrote to Secretary of War Elihu Root that amid "merciful" behavior on the part of most of the army, there had been individual instances of wrongdoing, "blots on the record" that he attributed to the climate and to provocation by the insurgents.[138] He admitted to Hermann Speck von Sternberg that "certain officers . . . and not a few enlisted men" used the water cure as torture and that Brigadier General Jacob Hurd Smith, who had given the order "to kill and burn and make a howling wilderness of Samar," had been dismissed from the army. "I do not like torture [or] needless brutality," Roosevelt wrote, or officers urging "less intelligent or more brutal" soldiers to "commit occasional outrages." But he found these events insufficient to bring about official changes in the policy of occupation and pacification. He explained to von Sternberg, "I . . . am not in the least sensitive about killing any number of men if there is adequate reason."[139]

In 1906, Leonard Wood led another military expedition, this time against the insurgent Muslim Moros of Mindanao and the Sulu Archipelago in the Philippines. The Moros had fortified themselves inside a volcano crater, and there Wood's troops killed six hundred men, women, and children. Mark Twain wrote a scathing report of the incident in his *Autobiography* (1924). "General Wood was present and looking on," Twain related. "His order had been 'Kill or capture those savages.' Apparently our little army considered that the 'or' left them authorized to kill *or* capture according to taste, and that their taste had remained what it has been for eight years, in our army out there—the taste of Christian butchers." The official story of the massacre, however, was more palatable to the American public than Twain's bitter account. At the conclusion of the Moro campaign, Roosevelt, who never wavered in his belief in the military's civilizing mission, congratulated Wood on his "brilliant feat of arms."[140]

Despite the bloody insurrections, Roosevelt thought that the United States should not shirk the obligations inherent in taking possession of and governing the Philippines. It was our duty as civilized men to "put down savagery and barbarism," he told Minnesota state fairgoers in 1901, even though "at times there will be injustice. . . . But shame, thrice shame to us, if we are so foolish as to make such occasional wrong-doing an excuse for failing to perform a great and righteous task."[141] Were the country "too weak, too selfish, or too foolish" to solve the Cuban and Philippine problems, "some bolder and abler people," some "stronger and manlier power . . . would have to step in and do the work."[142]

Roosevelt's argument approaches a political version of a domination or rape fantasy that projects the onlooker's or perpetrator's repressed but now resurgent emotions onto objects of desire. A manly nation carrying out a "righteous task" engages in random "wrong-doing" but largely accomplishes "brilliant feats of arms" to preempt an even "stronger and manlier" power from having to take the prize, a "barbaric" people. Such fantasies in political culture mirrored those in literature and art that appeared in the eighteenth century and gained currency throughout the nineteenth: they pictured, from the viewpoint of a male onlooker-participant, a helpless, often disheveled and partly undressed female, passive yet ecstatic, who invites a man's primitive urge to overpower her. Attracted by the powerful feeling her helplessness and sexual need bring out in him, he gives in to her allure.

The male fantasy that wanton or helpless women invited erotic violence was grounded in the scientific and medical teachings of the latter part of the century. In *Psychopathis Sexualis* (1886), Richard von Krafft-Ebing coined the term *masochism* and identified it as the "wish to suffer pain and be subjected to force," a desire that occurred naturally in women but only unnaturally in men. By nature, he wrote, women are passive and enjoy men's "masterful behavior with secret satisfaction."[143] The fact that women entertained fantasies of male domination, Krafft-Ebing argued, proved that they derived secret pleasure from suffering. This scientific sanction for men's violence against women piqued the interest of men who, having been raised in the nineteenth-century authoritarian manner, had been taught to deny childhood emotions, to fear weakness, and to sublimate their own youthful sexual fantasies. As adults, these men were bombarded with scientific certainties that women were somehow both threats and inert receptacles for men's actions and that male sexual pleasure necessitated female suffering. As adults, some men could psychologically absorb the sadistic satisfaction of hurting savages and women even as they punished themselves.

The social sanctions for individual men's acts of sexual violence thus readily translated into justifications for imperial violence. Imperial discourse coded "oriental" weakness and "primitivism" as the erotic female who, through her inability to govern herself, asked for male dominance and her own suffering. "Such conquests . . . are sure to come," Roosevelt wrote in *The Winning of the West*, "when a masterful people, still in its raw barbarian prime, finds itself face to face with the weaker and wholly alien race which holds a coveted prize in its feeble grasp."[144] In 1904, Roosevelt considered it absurd to abandon the Philippines to "scores of different tribes—in every stage of semicivilization and Asiatic barbarism." "It is not true that the United States has any land hunger," he wrote to Elihu Root. But "brutal wrongdoing, or an impotence which results in a general loosening of the ties of a civilized society, may finally require intervention by some civilized nation."[145] Leonard Wood's duty as governor of Cuba included "preserving order" among islanders "not at the moment fit to govern themselves." Cubans must be governed by men who "know what their needs really are," Roosevelt said, "and who have the power given them to meet those needs."[146]

With such statements, Roosevelt revealed the dark aspect of his personality wherein he seemed to relish punishment and violence, a trait well known to some of his friends. In 1896, Mrs. Bellamy Storer, Roosevelt's wealthy political patron who was instrumental in securing his appointment as assistant secretary of the navy, visited Roosevelt's home in Sagamore Hill. During her stay, Roosevelt got "on the warpath," she said, over Henryk Sienkiewicz's novels about knightly heroics in medieval Poland, *With Fire and Sword* (1890) and *The Deluge* (1898). "When he was quite sated with slaughter his face would be radiant and he would shout aloud with delight."[147] In 1904, Jacob Riis contrasted this violent aspect of the president's character with his softer side. "Appeal to the animal, and watch the claws come out," Riis said. "Appeal to the divine in him, and he will show you the heart of your brother." Riis described a pen sketch of Roosevelt on horseback leading a group of riders. "There he had on his battle face, the dark look I have seen come in the middle of some pleasant chat." In describing this "battle face," Riis told the story of one of the president's Colorado hunting companions, who expressed surprise at Roosevelt's "growing tenderness toward men and animals." The hunter thought that the tenderness was a welcome change, "since Roosevelt's chief weakness has always seemed to me his almost cruel strength." Roosevelt seemed not to have shown Riis his dark side, since the latter retorted to the hunter, "to me he has always seemed as tender as a woman."[148]

Afterword

One of Roosevelt's final acts as the national embodiment of strenuous heroism was his attempt to raise a volunteer cavalry division at the outset of the Great War. Upon hearing Roosevelt's plans, over one hundred thousand men volunteered from all over the country. Three days after the United States declared war on Germany in April of 1917, Roosevelt visited President Woodrow Wilson to offer in person the services of this longed-for division. The "demand for [the division] was weighty and widespread," his daughter Alice remembered. French Prime Minster Clemenceau aired an open letter asking Wilson to send Roosevelt to France: "He is an idealist, imbued with simple, vital idealism. Hence his influence over the crowd. I claim for Roosevelt only what he claims for himself—the right to appear on the battlefield surrounded by his comrades."[1] But Wilson, backed by Secretary of War Newton D. Baker and the army general staff, declined Roosevelt's offer. Conscription, not volunteerism, would be the way the country raised troops for its first war in Europe, especially after the experience of Britain, which saw its best and brightest flock to the front to be sacrificed in notorious numbers. Alice said the refusal "was the bitterest sort of blow for Father."[2]

Roosevelt's heroism, however popular, also carried a note of pathos, even among his own family. Despite "his eagerness and determination to go," Alice remembered, "there were moments when we could not help teasing him a little." Enraged by Wilson's refusal, Roosevelt said that he would volunteer for war from Canada and "put a bull moose or a bison on the British [flag]," to which one family member responded that a dodo would be more appropriate.[3] Perhaps in the minds of Americans, too, the image of cavalrymen among the trenches of France suggested why Roosevelt's swashbuckling heroism provided an inappropriate model for the technological warfare of the twentieth century. In any case, the former president resigned himself to working for efficiency and preparedness on the political front at home and, he said, felt "fairly sick with impotent rage" over his inability to get the Wilson administration to move quickly.[4]

The Roosevelt name, if not the ex-president himself, went to war in the persons of Theodore's four sons, Ted, Kermit, Archie, and Quentin, the latter nineteen and a half when he enlisted in the flying corps, having memorized the eye chart to conceal his poor eyesight. Delighted and worried about Quentin's enlistment, Roosevelt wrote to Grace Lockwood, "Now he too is where he may pay with his body for his heart's desire."[5] As Ted, Archie, and Quentin made final preparations in the week before they sailed for France and Kermit readied himself for Mesopotamia, Roosevelt and the entire family gathered at Oyster Bay for a farewell. Father talked "with a grim elation at the thought that they would soon all be in the war," Alice remembered, and he was certain that "several, perhaps all, would be wounded, possibly killed." It was "bitterly hard" for Roosevelt not to be going to war with his sons, Alice wrote. "The old Lion perisheth for lack of prey."[6] Prey, for Alice, meant the enemy soldiers on which Roosevelt's indomitable and lionized masculinity fed.

By war's end, Ted and Archie had been wounded, and Quentin had been killed. Archie was terribly injured in the knee and arm and was awarded the Croix de Guerre. He emerged from the war with recurring lifetime depression, and he received 100 percent disability. Ted was gassed and wounded, and he also received 100 percent disability. While Ted remained in France, his wife Eleanor could tell his father that he "has always worried for fear he would not be worthy of you." Quentin, well-known for overconfidence and bravado, was killed in aerial combat over Germany on 13 July, fifteen months after Roosevelt's call for sacrifice.[7] Roosevelt acknowledged that it was "pretty serious" that he had "inspired a boy to conduct that has resulted in his death."[8] Though in the final months of his own life Roosevelt did not speak publicly of Quentin, he spoke often of death and sacrifice. It was then that he changed his familiar call "Let Us Pay with Our Bodies" to the theme of his final essay on the subject, "The Men Who Pay with Their Bodies for Their Soul's Desire."[9] Quentin's famous father outlived him by only six months, dying not heroically in service to his country, but of a coronary occlusion. Archie sent a wire to Ted and Kermit: "The Old Lion is dead."[10]

That eventually three of his four sons would die in uniform signifies the long-term viability of Roosevelt's sacrificial ethos for himself and his family. Kermit, Archie, and Ted would survive the First World War only to become casualties of the second. Kermit died at age fifty-four from a alcoholism-induced self-inflicted gunshot wound while on military duty in Alaska in June of 1943. Archie, disabled and forty-eight years old, sought from his cousin President Franklin Roosevelt and secured a lieutenant colonel's commission and command of a battalion in New Guinea, where he again distinguished himself by receiving for his wounds 100 percent disability, the only man in the history of the U.S. armed services to have done so twice. Ted, too, desperately sought more risk in the Second World War. In 1941, he petitioned the army for active duty, whereupon he took command of his old unit and was promoted to brigadier general. He distinguished himself in Sicily and in North Africa, where his son Quentin, who had already earned a Silver Star, was wounded. Sent to join the Normandy invasion, Ted could have declined on several grounds: his age, a heart condition that he had concealed from the army, or the fact that his son Quentin was also taking part in the invasion, but he went anyway. A photograph taken after the invasion shows a uniformed Ted in a U.S. Army jeep on which "Rough Rider" is painted in large letters (figure 57). He earned the Congressional Medal of Honor for his feats on Utah Beach, actions that General Omar Bradley later cited as the bravest that he had seen in forty years in the military. Ted fought on through Cherbourg and beyond, then succumbed to a heart attack on 12 July 1944. He was fifty-seven, the oldest man in the Allied invasion, and the most decorated American soldier in all of World War II.[11]

For many Americans at the turn of the century, Roosevelt's rousing masculinity merged pleasingly and appropriately into the discourse on national identity. As never before in their history, Americans had identified the nation with the body of its president and believed in his struggles to preserve civilization against degeneracy and danger. The cult of the cowboy-warrior posed an Anglo-Saxon male with military bearing and full of athletic vigor who rescued, purified, and saved the nation and its men. By politically sanctioning violence and bloodletting, the cult invited a generation of Americans to think of their nation as the rightful and proper agent for the unleashing of male energy.

Men saw themselves mirrored in Roosevelt's aggressive athleticism and took heart that these qualities insulated the nation against enemies seen and unseen. Roosevelt's action persona all but subsumed virtue under a new set of bodily preoccupations that made virile action equal to character. His appeal lay in his compulsive proving of manhood, his constant reinvention of the insurgent male. Few American men understood the anxieties beneath the aggressive masculinity, because they were too busy using its scapegoats to make themselves men. After all, it was the *act* of resisting, confronting, and rising above unrestrained flesh, aggressive sexuality, and

Figure 57. Ted Jr. in jeep in France, 1944 (Library of Congress Prints and Photographs Division, Washington, D.C., Digital ID: CPH 3b45544. LC-USZ62-99501, black-and-white film copy negative)

domestic entrapment that established manliness, especially in competition with other men.

As the cowboy ethos entered male culture at the millennium, the attractions of sadistic violence became a rationale for the domination of groups deemed dangerous to the nation. Policy makers like Roosevelt, attracted to this violence, created political discourses that couched manhood in hardness, destruction, aggressive confrontation, and obsessive self-control. In Roosevelt's political ethos, the nation and the race served as levers for the militarization of the male self, which, thus armored, could engage in the liberation of dangerous personal desires. Politics devolved into a ritualized contest in which manhood was proven through exclusionary language that pictured rivals as genitally inferior and counseled that the weak invited domination by their very weakness.

In Roosevelt's day of unapologetic imperialism, an exaggeratedly masculine nationalism came to be openly professed. As Kristin Hoganson finds, American policy makers confronted the Philippine insurrection with a martial mentality that was focused on the preservation of American manhood against the effects of civilized life. In the imperialist minds of men like Roosevelt, Henry Cabot Lodge, and Albert Beveridge, military and administrative colonialism served to build character and restore resolve; it served, as Beveridge put it, to "manufacture manhood."[12] The particularly assertive manhood nourished by these colonial endeavors brought a dangerous antimodern form of radical excess to imperialism and militarism.

Although these ideas might be taken as proto-fascist, they served Roosevelt more as a foil against which to articulate his theory of the civilizing nation than as a prescription for social hatred. Indeed, his presidential campaign of 1912 formulated social policies more akin to those of modern social democracy than to those of modern fascism. Nevertheless, in the first two decades of the twentieth century, when anti-German and anti-union hysteria, anti-immigrant legislation, and anticommunist mania were infused with languages of racialized hate and fear of alien socialist politics, Roosevelt's exclusionary language had helped to create an intolerant social milieu and a punitive psychological one. In Roosevelt's hands, the civilizing nation, and particularly its military, became the direct agent of these intolerances, the sole standard bearer against the endless series of degenerate images that promised annihilation.

For the remainder of the twentieth century, modernism continued to deprive men of viable lives and to force them into compromises that many consider feminizing and emasculating. As the middle class searched for meaning in a world of bureaucracy and consumerism, and as purchasing power and real wages began their long decline after 1972, men still needed a muscular proving ground on which to inscribe their antimodern revolt, and the appeal of violence on an official level never diminished. Although, as Emily Rosenberg says, Americans deny to this day that they are imperialist, they conducted a robust and aggressive economic, cultural, and political expansion throughout what became the "American Century," and in the global marketplace and in international politics the rhetoric of racial and muscular nationality continues to inspire men to project anxieties onto scapegoats and to justify aggression.[13] True to its roots in Roosevelt-era political culture, the masculine ethos remains that of the self-made man, whose proving ground continues to be sports, the military, and foreign affairs. If we are to understand what Barbara Ehrenreich calls "our own warrior caste"[14] and how it seems to continually renew and perfect itself, we must look back to Roosevelt and the collective psychic gratifications of exclusionary violence.

Notes

CHAPTER ONE

1. John Morton Blum, *The Republican Roosevelt*, xi.

2. Woodrow Wilson, remarking on Roosevelt's war eagerness in 1916, and Mark Twain both quoted in Peggy Samuels and Harold Samuels, *Teddy Roosevelt at San Juan: The Making of a President*, 30; William James, observing Roosevelt in 1899 upon Roosevelt's return from Cuba, quoted in Kim Townsend, *Manhood at Harvard: William James and Others*, 244; Edmund Morris, *The Rise of Theodore Roosevelt*, 12; William Henry Harbaugh, *The Life and Times of Theodore Roosevelt*, 19.

3. Blum, *Republican Roosevelt*, 6, 123, 157–58, 160.

4. Harbaugh, for example, lists the "stock psychological explanations" for Roosevelt's behavior as his "unfailing compulsion to act, his perpetual gravitation toward the center of the stage, his conviction that glory was the supreme end of life," but concludes that "higher motives" reigned, those of rational self-interest. *Life and Times of Theodore Roosevelt*, 270.

5. Mark Seltzer, *Bodies and Machines*, 74; Eric Santner, *Stranded Objects: Mourning, Memory, and Film in Postwar Germany*, 49; Carroll Smith-Rosenberg found that as the institutions of marriage and the family, which are the loci of gender identity, are transformed by modern social disruptions, bodily and familial images "assume ascendancy." *Disorderly Conduct: Visions of Gender in Victorian America*, 90.

6. T. J. Jackson Lears, *No Place of Grace: Antimodernism and the Transformation of American Culture, 1880–1920*, 98.

7. Michael Kimmel, *Manhood in America: A Cultural History*, 181.

8. Roosevelt quoting Sydney Smith in "Brotherhood and the Heroic Virtues," in *The Works of Theodore Roosevelt*, 13:467 (hereafter cited as *Works*).

9. Brander Matthews, "Theodore Roosevelt as a Man of Letters," *Works*, 12:ix; Henry Cabot Lodge to Roosevelt, 29 September 1903, in *Selections from the Correspondence of Theodore Roosevelt and Henry Cabot Lodge, 1884–1918*, 2:60–61 (hereafter cited as *Selections*); William Allen White and Owen Wister quoted in Morris, *Rise of Theodore Roosevelt*, 21.

10. Nathan Miller, *Theodore Roosevelt: A Life*, 47.

11. Roosevelt, "The Strenuous Life," *Works*, 13:323, 331, 343; Roosevelt to Cecil Arthur Spring Rice, in Elting E. Morison, ed., *The Letters of Theodore Roosevelt*, 2:1049–53 (hereafter cited as *Letters*).

243

12. Roosevelt, "Strenuous Life," *Works,* 13:322–24, 331.

13. Roosevelt, "Christian Citizenship," *Works,* 13:494; "Biological Analogies in History," *Works,* 12:42.

14. Roosevelt to Cecil Arthur Spring Rice, 13 August 1897, *Letters,* 1:646. Periods of national crisis inevitably summon sacrificially heroic men, Roosevelt maintained, chosen for their "ability to bear punishment" and rendered more useful to the state by "their power and desire to inflict it." By this logic, Roosevelt linked individual psychology with the needs of the modern nation state. Roosevelt, "Washington's Maxims," *Works,* 13:193; "Admiral Dewey," *Works,* 13:428.

15. Roosevelt to Cecil Arthur Spring Rice, 12 March 1900, *Letters,* 2:1217.

16. Kimmel, *Manhood in America,* 120.

17. Michael Kimmel, "The Contemporary 'Crisis' of Masculinity in Historical Perspective."

18. Mary Bronson Hartt, "The Play Side of the Fair," 1096. The modern entertainment industry capitalized on this boredom. "The illusion of danger and close brushes with death are a reliable part of theme parks and the experiences will become more and more intense." "Booming Amusement Parks: The Theme Is Extreme," *Newsweek* (March 1998), 12.

19. Agnes Repplier, "Ennui," 775, 777, 779, 783–84.

20. Roosevelt, "Biological Analogies in History," *Works,* 12:52, 55.

21. Roosevelt to Henry Cabot Lodge, 22 May 1903, *Selections,* 2:17.

22. Roosevelt, "Tolstoy," *Works,* 12:321.

23. Quoted in Townsend, *Manhood at Harvard,* 243.

24. Roosevelt, "Military Preparedness and Unpreparedness," *Works,* 13:415.

25. Roosevelt, "The Foes of Our Own Household," *Works,* 19:xxv.

26. Roosevelt, "Manhood and Statehood," *Works,* 13:458. As Sander Gilman has remarked, "no factor in nineteenth-century self-definition was more powerful than the sense of the sexually pathological." J. Edward Chamberlin and Sander Gilman, eds., *Degeneration: The Dark Side of Progress,* 89; this volume summarizes the origins of European preoccupation with degenerate sexuality.

27. Klaus Theweleit, *Male Fantasies,* 1:24.

28. Quoted in Blum, *Republican Roosevelt,* 161.

29. Roosevelt, "Grant," *Works,* 13:438; William Roscoe Thayer, *Theodore Roosevelt: An Intimate Biography,* 261–62.

30. Thayer, *Theodore Roosevelt,* 452.

31. Peter Stallybrass and Allon White, *The Politics and Poetics of Transgression,* 2.

32. Roosevelt, "Biological Analogies in History," *Works,* 12:41.

33. Gilles Deleuze and Felix Guattari, *Anti-Oedipus: Capitalism and Schizophrenia,* 6–29. "We maintain that the social field is immediately invested by desire, that is the historically determined product of desire, and that libido has no need of any mediation or sublimation, any psychic operation, any transformation, in order to invade and invest productive forces and the relations of production. *There is only desire and the social, nothing else*" (29, emphasis in original).

34. Frank Ninkovich, personal communication, March 1999.

35. Richard Slotkin, *Gunfighter Nation: The Myth of the Frontier in Twentieth-Century America,* 193.

36. Ronald Takaki, *Iron Cages: Race and Culture in Nineteenth-Century America;* Frank Ninkovich, *Modernity and Power: A History of the Domino Theory in the Twenti-*

eth Century and *United States Information Policy and Cultural Diplomacy*; Frank Costigliola, "The Nuclear Family: Tropes of Gender and Pathology in the Western Alliance"; Arnaldo Testi, "The Gender of Reform Politics: Theodore Roosevelt and the Culture of Masculinity"; Gary Gerstle, "Theodore Roosevelt and American Nationalism"; Lawrence J. Oliver, "Theodore Roosevelt, Brander Matthews, and the Campaign for Literary Americanism."

37. Dana D. Nelson, *National Manhood: Capitalist Citizenship and the Imagined Fraternity of White Men.*

38. E. Anthony Rotundo, *American Manhood: Transformations in Masculinity from the Revolution to the Modern Era*; Kimmel, *Manhood in America*; Gail Bederman, *Manliness and Civilization: A Cultural History of Gender and Race in the United States, 1880–1917*, 170–215; Kristin L. Hoganson, *Fighting for American Manhood: How Gender Politics Provoked the Spanish-American and Philippine-American Wars*; Townsend, *Manhood at Harvard*; and Kathleen Dalton, "Why America Loved Teddy Roosevelt: Or, Charisma Is in the Eyes of the Beholders." Dalton examines how popular fantasies about Roosevelt addressed men's personal insecurities, themselves windows into the nation's sense of crisis in the Gilded Age. See especially Dalton's biography *Theodore Roosevelt: A Strenuous Life.* The definitive study that employs a psychoanalytic model of regression to show how forbidden childhood emotions, sexuality, and violence reemerge in the adult is still Michael Rogin's *Fathers and Children: Andrew Jackson and the Subjugation of the American Indian.*

39. See Frank Ninkovich, "Cuba, the Philippines, and the Hundred Years' War."

40. Fredric Jameson, *The Political Unconscious: Narrative as Socially Symbolic Act.*

41. Julia Hell, *Post-Fascist Fantasies: Psychoanalysis, History, and the Literature of East Germany*, 35; Klaus Theweleit, *Male Fantasies*, vol. 1.

42. George Mosse, "Nationalism and Respectability: Normal and Abnormal Sexuality in the Nineteenth Century"; Roosevelt, "Grant," *Works*, 13:438; Thayer, *Theodore Roosevelt*, 261–62. In modern industrialized states at the turn of the century, the discourse surrounding imperialism, especially when the national interest seems threatened, serves as the primary venue in which national concerns and issues are aired. Donald E. Pease explains that because the nation, the norm referent, was "vulnerable to internal decomposition" through, for example, immigration and miscegenation, middle-class Victorian men continually employed rhetorical and ideological discourses to reestablish the boundaries between themselves as ideal Americans and others. Amy Kaplan and Donald E. Pease, eds., *Cultures of United States Imperialism*, 11–14, 24–25, 28, 29. The intersection of racial and gendered categories of difference combined in an "organizing grammar" of social control and empire "in which modernity, the civilizing mission and the 'measure of man' were framed." Ann Stoler, *Race and the Education of Desire: Foucault's History of Sexuality and the Colonial Order of Things*, 27, 32, 124–25; Daniel Pick, *Faces of Degeneration: A European Disorder, 1848–1918*, 39.

43. Townsend, *Manhood at Harvard*, 28, see also 196, 200.

44. David Gilmore, *Manhood in the Making: Cultural Concepts of Masculinity*, 28–29.

45. Liam Hudson and Bernadine Jacot, *The Way Men Think: Intellect, Intimacy and the Erotic Imagination*, ix–x.

46. Gilmore, *Manhood in the Making*, 77, 94.

47. Ibid., 50, 76, 113, 117.

48. Quoted in James Livingston, "Modern Subjectivity and Consumer Culture," 421.

49. Dolf Zillman, "The Psychology of the Appeal of Portrayals of Violence," 179, 186.

50. Zillman, "Psychology," 197; Jeffrey Goldstein, "Why We Watch," 214, 216, 217.

51. Young women, Zillman found, preferred watching horror with young men who "radiated a potential for protection" more than with those who were clearly distressed. Young women were "romantically drawn to callous, aggressively more potent male companions than to apparently fearful ones. And young men were more attracted to squeamish girls than those able to fearlessly watch the violence." "Psychology," 198–99.

52. Ibid., 202, 206.

53. The relationship between bad acts and the punishment of them varies cross-culturally, and in many cases the punishment does not fit the crime. Zillman concludes, "displays of monstrous gratuitous slaughter and the distress they evoke are a necessary prelude to the portrayal of righteous maiming and killing that is to spark euphoric reactions." Ibid., 204, 208.

54. Gilmore, *Manhood in the Making*, 209; Michael Kimmel, *The Gendered Society*, 54–55.

55. Gilmore, *Manhood in the Making*, 25–26.

56. James Eli Adams, *Dandies and Desert Saints: Styles of Victorian Masculinity*, 12–13, 16.

57. Owen Wister, *Roosevelt: The Story of a Friendship, 1880–1919*, 339.

CHAPTER TWO

1. Frank Ninkovich, "Theodore Roosevelt: Civilization as Ideology," 226, 234. In this article, Ninkovich summarizes Roosevelt's worldview. For a further examination of Roosevelt's view of civilization as policy, see Ninkovich, *Modernity and Power: A History of the Domino Theory in the Twentieth Century*. On Victorian discourses about civilization, see George W. Stocking, *Victorian Anthropology*.

2. Roosevelt, "In Cowboy Land," 162, 171.

3. Roosevelt, "The Best and the Good," in *The Works of Theodore Roosevelt* (hereafter cited as *Works*), 13:391.

4. Roosevelt, "The Men of Gettysburg," *Works*, 11:324; Mark Seltzer examined the process by which physical culture linked bodybuilding and nation building, and demonstrated how Americans renegotiated definitions of the sublimation of natural desires through machinelike standards of bodily discipline. *Bodies and Machines*, esp. the chapter titled "The Love Master: The Anthropology of Boys."

5. Roosevelt to Cecil Arthur Spring Rice, 29 May 1897 and 12 March 1900, in Elting E. Morison, ed., *The Letters of Theodore Roosevelt* (hereafter cited as *Letters*), 1:620, 2:1216.

6. Henry Cabot Lodge to Roosevelt, 29 September 1903, in *Selections from the Correspondence of Theodore Roosevelt and Henry Cabot Lodge, 1884–1918* (hereafter cited as *Selections*), 2:60–61.

7. Quoted in William A. Williams, "Brooks Adams and American Expansion," 220.

8. Recent evidence points to an inverse relationship between men's ability to em-

brace their own sensuality and their need for controlling and purifying ideals of maleness. These relationships may extend to a nation's collective mind in its attempts to deal with anxiety-producing aspects of modern life. Harry Brod, "The Case for Men's Studies," 58; see also Joe L. Dubbert, "Progressivism and the Masculinity Crisis."

9. Roosevelt, "Manhood and Statehood," *Works*, 13:455–56.

10. Roosevelt, "Expansion and Peace," *Works*, 13:339.

11. Bryan S. Turner explains the importance of the body as a symbolic site, discussing its "symbolic potential" as an "object of regulation and control." *The Body and Society: Explorations in Social Theory*. Similarly, Caroll Smith-Rosenberg, in analyzing the concern over masturbation in Jacksonian America, finds that the "biological body, transformed by the human mind into a cultural construct, undergoes a second metamorphosis, emerging as the symbolic representation of the social forces that created it." *Disorderly Conduct: Visions of Gender in Victorian America*, 48; see also her article "Sex as Symbol in Victorian Purity."

12. Roosevelt, "Brotherhood and the Heroic Virtues," *Works*, 13:463.

13. Roosevelt to Cecil Arthur Spring Rice, 27 January 1900, *Letters*, 2:1147–48.

14. E. Anthony Rotundo, *American Manhood*, 248–55; Michael Kimmel, *Manhood in America: A Cultural History*, 117–55.

15. Roosevelt to Cecil Arthur Spring Rice, 27 December 1904, *Letters*, 4:1083–84.

16. John Burroughs, *Camping and Tramping with Roosevelt*, xiii.

17. Quoted in Geoffrey G. Field, *Evangelist of Race: The Germanic Vision of Houston Stewart Chamberlain*, 220.

18. Roosevelt to Hugo Munsterberg, 3 June 1901, *Letters*, 3:86; see also Gail Bederman's excellent discussion of Roosevelt's pervading fears of race suicide in *Manliness and Civilization: A Cultural History of Gender and Race in the United States, 1880–1917*, 196–206.

19. Roosevelt to Cecil Arthur Spring Rice, 5 August 1896, *Letters*, 1:554.

20. Roosevelt, "National Duties," *Works*, 13:480; see also his "Sheridan," *Works*, 11:223; and Roosevelt to Cecil Arthur Spring Rice, 12 March 1900, *Letters*, 2:1216.

21. Quoted in Arnaldo Testi, "The Gender of Reform Politics: Theodore Roosevelt and the Culture of Masculinity," 1530.

22. William Roscoe Thayer, *Theodore Roosevelt: An Intimate Biography*, 302, 321, 435; John Burroughs accompanied Roosevelt on a three-month Western trip in 1903 during which the President made three hundred speeches. "The crowd always seemed to be in love with him the moment they see him and hear his voice . . . by reason of his inborn heartiness and sincerity, and his genuine manliness." Burroughs, *Camping and Tramping*, 21.

23. Henry Cabot Lodge to Roosevelt, 14 September 1905, *Selections*, 2:193, emphasis in original.

24. William H. Goetzmann and William N. Goetzmann, *The West of the Imagination*, 313; Stephen Ponder, *Managing the Press: Origins of the Media Presidency, 1897–1933*, 3. During his presidential decade, national magazines published more articles on Roosevelt than on anyone else.

25. Ponder, *Managing the Press*, 17, 25–28.

26. Quoted in Kim Townsend, *Manhood at Harvard: William James and Others*, 269.

27. Nathan Miller, *Theodore Roosevelt: A Life*, 313; Owen Wister, *Roosevelt: The Story of a Friendship, 1880–1919*, 6.

28. In Miller's estimation, Roosevelt matured into a politician who combined "imagination, pragmatism, and shrewdness," yet never lost his pious and blustery style. Miller, *Theodore Roosevelt*, 322. New York governor Grover Cleveland called the young state assemblyman "cocksure" for challenging the state political machine. Republican Party regulars sometimes criticized such reckless political judgment—one said, "It was not that he did not love politics, and know the game well enough, . . . but he loved himself more." Edmund Morris, *The Rise of Theodore Roosevelt*, 191, 193, 197.

29. Jacob Riis, *Theodore Roosevelt the Citizen*, 400, 402, emphasis in original.

30. Edward Alsworth Ross, *Social Control: A Survey of the Foundations of Order*, 228.

31. Gail Bederman, *Manliness and Civilization*, 235. After 1886, wealthy politicos in the New York Democratic Party capitalized on the appeal of the sporting style among Irish and German workmen by sponsoring cross-class political gatherings, offering free whiskey at racetracks, baseball fields, and gambling houses. David C. Hammack, *Power and Society: Greater New York at the Turn of the Century*, 101. Timothy J. Gilfoyle, *City of Eros: New York City, Prostitution, and the Commercialization of Sex, 1790–1920*, 81–84, 116; Kimmel, *Manhood in America*, 172.

32. Peter Stearns, *Battleground of Desire: The Struggle for Self-Control in Modern America*, 78, 85, 97.

33. Gilfoyle, *City of Eros*, 116.

34. Rotundo, *American Manhood*, 318.

35. Ibid., 228.

36. Quoted in Townsend, *Manhood at Harvard*, 101.

37. Gilfoyle, *City of Eros*, 115, 141, 163, 261.

38. Rotundo, *American Manhood*, 3–4, 236–39; Townsend, *Manhood at Harvard*, 17.

39. Rotundo, *American Manhood*, 256.

40. Ernest Thompson Seton, *Two Little Savages: Being the Adventures of Two Boys Who Lived as Indians and What They Learned*, 280.

41. Rotundo, *American Manhood*, 35, 42, 45–46.

42. Ibid., 35, 46.

43. Ibid., 37–38, 98.

44. Ibid., 73.

45. Ed Cohen, *Talk on the Wilde Side: Toward a Genealogy of a Discourse on Male Sexualities*, 90.

46. Rotundo, *American Manhood*, 124–25.

47. Sonya O. Rose, "Cultural Analysis and Moral Discourses," 221.

48. Arthur Brittan, *Masculinity and Power*, 75, emphasis in original.

49. G. Stanley Hall, *Youth: Its Education, Regimen, and Hygiene*, 3, 94.

50. George Lakoff, *Women, Fire, and Dangerous Things: What Categories Reveal about the Mind*; Mary Douglas, *Implicit Meanings: Essays in Anthropology*, 53.

51. William James, *Memories and Studies*, 58.

52. Quoted in Richard Drinnon, *Facing West: The Metaphysics of Indian-Hating and Empire-Building*, 307.

53. Max Nordau, *Degeneration*, 2, 6.

54. Roosevelt, "True Americanism," *Works*, 13:17.

55. Roosevelt to Anna Roosevelt Cowles, 13 November 1896, *Letters*, 1:566.

56. Lakoff, *Women, Fire, and Dangerous Things*, 414.

57. See Norbert Elias, *The Civilizing Process: Sociogenetic and Psychogenetic Investigations*, and Jonas Frykman and Orvar Lofgren, *The Culture Builders: A Historical Anthropology of Middle Class Life*.

58. Quoted in Cynthia Eagle Russett, *Sexual Science: The Victorian Construction of Womanhood*, 194.

59. James, *Memories and Studies*, 276.

60. "The creation of a sublimated public body without smells, without coarse laughter, without organs, separate from the court and church on one hand, and the market square, alehouse, street, and fairground on the other—this was the great labor of bourgeois culture." Peter Stallybrass and Allon White, *The Politics and Poetics of Transgression*, 22–23.

61. Roosevelt, "Expansion and Peace," *Works*, 13:337–38, 340; "National Duties," *Works*, 13:474.

62. It is characteristic of the more aggressive formulations of modern imperial nationhood, Simon During has argued, that leaders emerge who tout the glories of exaggerated heroic masculinity and who prefer action and war to diplomacy and peace. Increasingly removed from the civil and the aesthetic, modern nationalism in some countries takes on hyperbolic form to become the mass politics of the racial nation-state. During, "Literature—Nationalism's Other?" 150–51.

63. W. D. Trent, "Theodore Roosevelt as a Historian," 570, 575.

64. Quoted in John Kasson, *Civilizing the Machine: Technology and Republican Values in America, 1776–1990*, 201.

65. Roosevelt, "Grant," *Works*, 13:437.

66. Roosevelt, "The Best and the Good," *Works*, 13:393.

67. Alice Miller, *For Your Own Good: Hidden Cruelty in Child-Rearing and the Roots of Violence*, 195–96.

68. Ibid.

69. Albert Beveridge, *The Young Man and the World*, 75.

70. Stearns, *Battleground of Desire*, 48; see also David Lubin's discussion of Victorian attitudes toward childhood innocence and depravity, *Picturing a Nation: Art and Social Change in Nineteenth-Century America*, 212–23.

71. Miller, *For Your Own Good*, 195–96.

72. Quoted in Takaki, *Iron Cages: Race and Culture in Nineteenth-Century America*, 275.

73. Roosevelt, "Autobiography," *Works*, 20:10–11.

74. Roosevelt to Edward Sanford Martin, 26 November 1900, *Letters*, 2:1443–44.

75. Morris, *Rise of Theodore Roosevelt*, 42.

76. Longworth, *Crowded Hours*, 20.

77. Riis, *Theodore Roosevelt the Citizen*, 7.

78. Roosevelt, "The Vigor of Life," 674.

79. Thayer, *Theodore Roosevelt*, 66.

80. Quoted in G. Edward White, *The Eastern Establishment and the Western Experience: The West of Frederic Remington, Theodore Roosevelt, and Owen Wister*, 63.

81. Roosevelt, "The Vigor of Life," 661.

82. Roosevelt, "Autobiography," *Works*, 20:10.

83. Ibid., 20:55; Morris, *Rise of Theodore Roosevelt*, 767.

84. Herf, *Reactionary Modernism*, 75.

85. According to the psychoanalytical school of object relations, one can analyze masculinity produced during mothering in which the boy's early identification with his mother is interrupted by transference to his father as the object of identity formation during the teens. The interruption of maternal identification produces a male personality that closes itself off to the boundless relationship he had with mother's body and creates an adult with strongly defended ego boundaries and diminished openness to and expectation from relationships. See Nancy Chodorow, *The Reproduction of Mothering*, 1978.

86. Roosevelt, "Autobiography," *Works*, 20:17, emphasis in original.

87. Nathan Hale, *Freud in America: The Beginnings of Psychoanalysis in the United States, 1876–1917*, 45.

88. Roosevelt, "The American Boy," *Works*, 13:406. He did not use the words *homosexuality* or *masturbation*, preferring to use the words "all that is wicked and depraved" in contrast to what is "clean" in the behavior of boys.

89. Roosevelt, "Christian Citizenship," *Works*, 13:497.

90. Quoted in William Harbaugh, *The Life and Times of Theodore Roosevelt*, 20.

91. Roosevelt, "Christian Citizenship," *Works*, 13:497.

92. Quoted in Paul S. Boyer, *Urban Masses and Moral Order in America, 1820–1920*, 211.

93. Roosevelt to Brander Matthews, 21 October 1890, in Lawrence J. Oliver, ed., *The Letters of Theodore Roosevelt and Brander Matthews*, 19–20.

94. Eliot J. Gorn, *The Manly Art*.

95. Roosevelt to Michael Joseph Donovan, boxing instructor at the New York Athletic Club and Roosevelt's sparring partner while he was in New York, 15 November 1904, *Letters*, 4:1032.

96. Roosevelt, "The Vigor of Life," 670.

97. Quoted in Nathan Hale, *Freud in America*, 44.

98. Roosevelt to Thomas Raynesford Lounsbury, 28 April 1892, *Letters*, 1:275–76.

99. Quoted in Nicholas Roosevelt, *Theodore Roosevelt: The Man as I Knew Him*, 62.

100. Roosevelt, "The American Boy," *Works*, 13:401–2.

101. G. Stanley Hall, *Youth*, 9, 27–28; and *Adolescence: Its Psychology and Its Relations to Physiology, Anthropology, Sociology, Sex, Crime, Religion and Education*. See also Dorothy Ross, *G. Stanley Hall: Psychologist as Prophet*, and Bederman's discussion of Hall in *Manliness and Civilization*, 77–120.

102. Hall, *Youth*, 2, 9, 27–28.

103. Roosevelt to Granville Stanley Hall, 29 November 1899, *Letters*, 2:1100.

104. Longworth, *Crowded Hours*, 5.

105. Roosevelt to William Sheffield Cowles, 29 March 1898, *Letters*, 2:803; Roosevelt to Alexander Lambert, 29 March 1898, *Letters*, 2:804.

106. Roosevelt to Theodore Roosevelt Jr., 7 May 1901, *Letters*, 3:73.

107. Roosevelt to Theodore Roosevelt Jr., 19 October 1901, *Letters*, 3:178.

108. Roosevelt to Theodore Roosevelt Jr., 28 November 1903, *Works*, 19:455.

109. Roosevelt to Endicott Peabody, 4 January 1902, *Letters*, 3:216.

110. Roosevelt to Theodore Roosevelt Jr., 31 October 1902, *Letters*, 3:372.

111. Roosevelt to Theodore Roosevelt Jr., 11 October 1903, *Works*, 19:447.

112. Henry Cabot Lodge addressed this problem with Roosevelt: "You take a dark view of Ted and Kermit because they brought back no big game or no game big

enough. Give them my love and tell them that this painful failure will not alter my regard and affection for them in the least." Lodge to Roosevelt, 27 September 1906, *Selections*, 2:233.

113. Roosevelt to Edward Sanford Martin, 6 November 1900, *Letters*, 2:1444.

114. Roosevelt to William Wingate Sewall, 8 July 1899, *Letters*, 2:1031; and to Finley Peter Dunne, 23 November 1904, *Letters*, 4:1041.

115. Roosevelt to Theodore Roosevelt Jr., 9 February 1903, *Letters*, 3:423; Miller, *Theodore Roosevelt*, 85.

116. Roosevelt to Stewart Edward White, 8 October 1904, *Letters*, 4:977–78.

117. Roosevelt to John Burroughs, 9 October 1901, *Letters*, 3:170–71.

118. Roosevelt to Theodore Roosevelt Jr., 18 November 1905, *Selections*, 1:81–82.

119. Quoted in Townsend, *Manhood at Harvard*, 275.

120. Peter Gay, *The Bourgeois Experience: Victoria to Freud*, 239.

121. Roosevelt to Henry Childs Merwin, 18 December 1894, *Letters*, 1:412.

122. Quoted in Townsend, *Manhood at Harvard*, 103.

123. Roosevelt to G. Stanley Hall, 29 November 1899, *Letters*, 2:1100.

124. Quoted in Townsend, *Manhood at Harvard*, 273.

125. Townsend, *Manhood at Harvard*, 273.

126. Roosevelt, "The American Boy," *Works*, 13:403.

127. Quoted in Townsend, *Manhood at Harvard*, 103.

128. A. C. Post, "Judge Oliver Wendell Holmes," *McClure's* 19 (October 1902), 523, quoted in Theodore P. Greene, *America's Heroes: The Changing Models of Success in American Magazines*, 132.

129. Hale, *Freud in America*, 35.

130. Hall, *Youth*, 3.

131. Ross, *Social Control*, 197.

132. Quoted in Hale, *Freud in America*, 35.

133. Hall, *Youth*, 4–5.

134. Hale, *Freud in America*, 110–12.

135. James, *Memories and Studies*, 262, 276.

136. Roosevelt to Ian Standish Monteith Hamilton, 24 January 1906, *Letters*, 5:139.

137. James, *Memories and Studies*, 276–81.

138. Ibid.; T. J. Jackson Lears, *No Place of Grace: Antimodernism and the Transformation of American Culture, 1880–1920*, 11; for James's anti-imperialist response to Roosevelt's 1899 speech "The Strenuous Life" (*Works*, 13:319–31), see Townsend, *Manhood at Harvard*, 240–45.

139. James, *Memories and Studies*, 281, 283, 291–92; "always latent" quoted in Townsend, *Manhood at Harvard*, 184.

140. Townsend, *Manhood at Harvard*, 72.

141. Quoted in Nicholas Roosevelt, *Theodore Roosevelt: The Man as I Knew Him*, 61.

142. Quoted in Townsend, *Manhood at Harvard*, 258.

143. Roosevelt, "The Winning of the West," *Works*, 8:235; 9:61.

144. In World War II Germany, the Nazis called these internal enemies an "emasculating germ." Dominick LaCapra, *Representing the Holocaust: History, Theory, Trauma*, 104.

145. Quoted in Paul Boyer, *Urban Masses and Moral Order*, 225–27.

146. Edward Alsworth Ross, *Sin and Society*, ix–xi.

147. Thomas G. Dyer, *Theodore Roosevelt and the Idea of Race*, 23–24.

148. George W. Stocking, *Victorian Anthropology*.

149. Dyer, *Theodore Roosevelt and the Idea of Race*, 47–48; Geoffrey G. Field, *Evangelist of Race*, 2:466; Roosevelt, "Review of the Foundations of the Nineteenth Century," 728–31.

150. Wister, *Roosevelt: The Story of a Friendship*, 42.

151. Quoted in Irving Greenberg, *Theodore Roosevelt and Labor: 1900–1918*, 45.

152. Mahan, *From Sail to Steam: Recollections of Naval Life*, 74.

153. Quoted in Morris, *Rise of Theodore Roosevelt*, 799.

154. Quoted in Oliver, *The Letters of Theodore Roosevelt and Brander Matthews*, 13–14.

155. Remington to Poultney Bigelow, 19 August 1893, in Splete and Splete, *Frederic Remington: Selected Letters*, 244.

156. Frederic Remington, "Chicago under the Mob," 680–81.

157. Ibid.

158. Ibid., 681.

159. Roosevelt to James Brander Matthews, 9 December 1894, *Letters*, 1:412.

160. Roosevelt, "True Americanism," *Works*, 13:18.

161. Roosevelt, "Brotherhood and the Heroic Virtues," *Works*, 13:465. M. J. Heale locates the origins of anticommunism in the years after the great strikes of 1877 among middle-class, Anglo-Saxon men whose property was most threatened by the rise of labor. M. J. Heale, *American Anticommunism: Combating the Enemy Within, 1830–1970*, 5–20.

162. Roosevelt to Charles Ferris Gettemy, 1 February 1904, *Letters*, 4:1113.

163. Roosevelt to the Department of Justice, 20 March 1908, *Letters*, 6:977–78.

164. Roosevelt to Grafton Dulany Cushing, 27 February 1908, *Letters*, 6:954.

165. Morris, *Rise of Theodore Roosevelt*, 552–53.

166. Roosevelt to Lodge, 12 February 1917, *Selections*, 2:494.

167. Thayer, *Theodore Roosevelt*, 233.

168. Roosevelt to Cecil Arthur Spring Rice, 27 December 1904, *Letters*, 4:1083.

169. Roosevelt, "Phases of State Legislation," *Works*, 13:67.

170. Roosevelt to Eleonora Kissel Kinnicutt, 28 June 1901, *Letters*, 3:102.

171. Roosevelt, "The Strenuous Life," *Works*, 13:329.

172. Roosevelt, "Civic Helpfulness," *Works*, 13:380–81.

173. Roosevelt to Cecil Arthur Spring Rice, 27 December 1904, *Letters*, 4:1083–85.

174. Ibid., 4:1083.

175. Roosevelt to Francis Markoe Scott, 30 October 1884, *Letters*, 1:84.

176. Quoted in Thayer, *Theodore Roosevelt*, 33; Dewey Grantham, *Theodore Roosevelt*, 41.

177. Quoted in Ben Merchant Vorpahl, *My Dear Wister: The Frederic Remington–Owen Wister Letters*, 277, 295.

178. Roosevelt, "The Two Americas," *Works*, 13:449.

179. Roosevelt, "Fellow-Feeling as a Political Factor," *Works*, 13:355, 359, 361, 363, 368.

180. Quoted in Gerstle, "Theodore Roosevelt and American Nationalism," 1300.

181. Roosevelt, "Fellow-Feeling as a Political Factor," *Works*, 13:355, 359, 361, 363, 368.

182. Ross, *Social Control*, 21, 33, 60, 72, 100–103, 196–97, 376, 403.

183. Roosevelt to Eugene Fitch Ware, 30 March 1900, *Letters*, 2:1243.

184. "Aesop's Fables," "The Short-Haired Poet," and "The Tobacco Stemmers," in Eugene Fitch Ware, *Rhymes of Ironquill.*

185. "Twentieth Kansas Infantry" and "A Corn Poem," in Eugene Fitch Ware, *Rhymes of Ironquill.*

186. "Decoration Day," in Eugene Fitch Ware, *Rhymes of Ironquill.*

187. Quoted in Sander Gilman, "Sexology and Psychoanalysis," 77–79.

188. Gilman, "Sexology and Psychoanalysis," 79; Richard von Krafft-Ebing, *Psychopathia Sexualis: A Medico-Forensic Study,* 24.

189. Roosevelt to Arthur Hamilton Lee, 8 April 1908, *Letters,* 6:995.

190. Roosevelt, *The Winning of the West,* 3:98, 101.

191. Ibid., 2:245–47.

192. Eva Trew, "Sex Sterilization," 814.

193. "Backwaters of Humanity," *The World's Work* 26 (June 1913), 149.

194. Roosevelt, "True Americanism," *Works,* 13:22.

195. Roosevelt, "The World Movement," *Works,* 12:64.

196. Owen Wister, *Lady Baltimore,* 69, 226–27.

197. Roosevelt to Arthur Hamilton Lee, 7 March 1908, *Letters,* 6:965–66.

198. Roosevelt, "True Americanism," *Works,* 13:15, 21–23.

199. "Polyglot" quoted in Morris, *Rise of Theodore Roosevelt,* 565; "True Americanism," *Works,* 13:4, 16.

200. Barbara Ehrenreich, foreword in Theweleit, *Male Fantasies,* 1:xv.

201. Mahan, *From Sail to Steam,* 15.

202. Agnes Repplier, "The Praises of War," 801.

203. Quoted in Michael S. Kimmel, "The Contemporary 'Crisis' of Masculinity in Historical Perspective," 147.

204. James, *Memories and Studies,* 269, 303, emphasis in original.

205. William Ian Miller, *The Anatomy of Disgust,* 113; Stallybrass and White, *Politics and Poetics of Transgression,* 191.

206. Twain quoted in Adam Hochschild, *King Leopold's Ghost,* 146.

207. Quoted in Peggy Samuels and Harold Samuels, *Teddy Roosevelt at San Juan: The Making of a President,* 13.

208. *New York Tribune* quoted in G. Edward White, *Eastern Establishment and the Western Experience,* 311; Roosevelt to Cecil Arthur Spring Rice, 5 August 1896, *Letters,* 1:554.

209. Ross, *Social Control,* 28–30.

210. Quoted in Vorpahl, *My Dear Wister,* 300.

211. Anson Rabinbach and Jessica Benjamin, Foreword in Theweleit, *Male Fantasies,* 2:viii.

212. Ross, *Social Control,* 3.

213. LaCapra, *Representing the Holocaust,* 104.

214. Mahan, *From Sail to Steam,* 220–21.

215. Tim Carrigan, Bob Connell, and John Lee, "Towards a New Sociology of Masculinity."

216. Herman Melville, *Moby-Dick; or The Whale,* 172–73.

CHAPTER THREE

1. E. Anthony Rotundo, *American Manhood: Transformations in Masculinity from the Revolution to the Modern Era,* 103–5.

2. Roosevelt to Theodore Roosevelt Jr., 19 October 1901, in Elting E. Morison, ed., *The Letters of Theodore Roosevelt* (hereafter cited as *Letters*), 3:179.

3. Quoted in Edmund Morris, *The Rise of Theodore Roosevelt*, 125.

4. Roosevelt to Maria Longworth Storer, 28 October 1899, *Letters*, 2:1089.

5. Roosevelt to Martha Macomb Flandrau Selmes, 23 September 1904, *Letters*, 4:952.

6. Roosevelt, "In Cowboy Land," 161.

7. Roosevelt to Hamlin Garland, 19 July 1903, *Letters*, 3:520–21.

8. Ibid., 3:521.

9. Roosevelt, "The Strenuous Life," in *The Works of Theodore Roosevelt* (hereafter cited as *Works*), 13:321.

10. Roosevelt to Hamlin Garland, 19 July 1903, *Letters*, 3:521.

11. Cynthia Eagle Russett, *Sexual Science: The Victorian Construction of Womanhood*, 122–23.

12. Thomas G. Dyer, *Theodore Roosevelt and the Idea of Race*, 15.

13. Roosevelt to Leonard Wood, 9 April 1900, *Letters*, 2:1251.

14. William Allen Rogers's cartoon "Father Knick—will this do?" can be found in the Library of Congress Prints and Photographs Division, Washington, D.C., CAI 1996003062/PP.

15. William James, *Memories and Studies*, 277. Roosevelt used the term *mollycoddle* to mean "people who are soft physically and morally." Roosevelt, "The War of America the Unready," *Works*, 20:211.

16. Roosevelt to Helen Kendrick Johnson, 10 January 1899, *Letters*, 2:905, and *African Game Trails: An Account of the African Wanderings of an American Hunter-Naturalist*, 48.

17. Morris, *Rise of Theodore Roosevelt*, 128.

18. Roosevelt to Susan B. Anthony, 12 December 1898, *Letters*, 2:892–93.

19. Morris, *Rise of Theodore Roosevelt*, 128.

20. Bram Dijkstra, *Idols of Perversity: Fantasies of Feminine Evil in Fin-de-Siècle Culture*, 149–50.

21. Nicholas Francis Cooke, *Satan in Society*, 118, 186.

22. Ibid., 86.

23. Eugene Fitch Ware, "The Leap-Year Party" and "A Romance," in *Rhymes of Ironquill*.

24. Alice Roosevelt Longworth, *Crowded Hours*, 156.

25. Morris, *Rise of Theodore Roosevelt*, 263.

26. Longworth, *Crowded Hours*, 60–61.

27. Quoted in Nathan Miller, *Theodore Roosevelt: A Life*, 432.

28. Longworth, *Crowded Hours*, 213–14.

29. Lois Banner, *American Beauty: A Social History through Two Centuries of the American Idea, Ideal, and Image of the Beautiful Woman*, 146, 155–74.

30. Quoted in Miller, *Theodore Roosevelt*, 360, 432.

31. Roosevelt to Cecil Arthur Spring Rice, 3 July 1901, *Letters*, 3:107–8.

32. Adam Hochschild, *King Leopold's Ghost*, 176. A group of black ministers had Ota Benga removed from the zoo. Ten years later he committed suicide.

33. Miller, *Theodore Roosevelt*, 47.

34. John J. Leary Jr., *Talks With T.R.*, vii–viii.

35. Roosevelt to John Hay, 2 April 1905, *Letters*, 4:1156; Morris, *Rise of Theodore Roosevelt*, 24.

36. Rudyard Kipling, "The Seven Nights of Creation."

37. Quoted in Geoffrey G. Field, *Evangelist of Race: The Germanic Vision of Houston Stewart Chamberlain*, 220.

38. Quoted in G. Edward White, *The Eastern Establishment and the Western Experience: The West of Frederic Remington, Theodore Roosevelt, and Owen Wister*, 105.

39. Roosevelt to Frederic Remington, 28 December 1897, *Letters*, 1:749–50. Letter reprinted in Ben Merchant Vorpahl, *My Dear Wister: The Frederic Remington–Owen Wister Letters*, 272

40. Frederic Remington to Roosevelt, Summer 1906, and Roosevelt to Remington, 6 August 1906, in Allen P. Splete and Marilyn D. Splete, *Frederic Remington: Selected Letters*, 359–60.

41. Alexander Nemerov, *Frederic Remington and Turn-of-the-Century America*, 114–18.

42. Quoted in Nemerov, *Frederic Remington*, 114.

43. Roosevelt to Corinne Roosevelt, 24 August 1881, *Letters*, 1:51. See also *Letters*, 1:100 and 120, for two further examples of Roosevelt's insistence that he does not care for "fleshly nudes."

44. Quoted in William Henry Harbaugh, *The Life and Times of Theodore Roosevelt*, 29.

45. Sam Hunter, *Modern American Painting and Sculpture*, 65–73.

46. Henry Street Settlement and Munson-Williams-Proctor Institute, *The Armory Show: 50th Anniversary Exhibition*, 61.

47. William A. Williams, "Brooks Adams and American Expansion," 221.

48. Roosevelt, "A Layman's View of an Art Exhibition."

49. Morris, *Rise of Theodore Roosevelt*, 707.

50. Roosevelt, "Augustus Saint Gaudens," *Works*, 11:285–87.

51. Roosevelt and Stoker met at a literary event in New York in 1895, and the two were mutually impressed with one another. Morris, *Rise of Theodore Roosevelt*, 514.

52. Rudyard Kipling, "The Vampire," in *The Sahib Edition of Rudyard Kipling*, 10:95–96.

53. Ibid.

54. Roosevelt to Elbert Hubbard, 28 April 1899, *Letters*, 2:999. For a similar denunciation of another writer's "morbid . . . everlasting insistence on the unhealthy sides of the sex relationship," see Roosevelt to Anna Roosevelt Cowles, 31 January 1897, *Letters*, 1:577.

55. Roosevelt to Rudyard Kipling, 1 November 1904, *Letters*, 4:1007.

56. Roosevelt, "Tolstoy," *Works*, 12:321; Roosevelt to Robert Grant, 1 September 1904, *Letters*, 4:914–15.

57. Roosevelt to Corinne Roosevelt Robinson, 12 April 1886, *Letters*, 1:96.

58. Roosevelt to Florence Lockwood La Farge, 13 February 1908, *Letters*, 6:942–43.

59. Roosevelt to Robert Grant, 1 September 1904, *Letters*, 4:915.

60. Leo Tolstoy, "The Kreutzer Sonata," in *The Complete Works of Count Tolstoy*, 8:330, 346–48.

61. Roosevelt to Robert Grant, 1 September 1904, *Letters*, 4:914–15.

62. Roosevelt, "The American Boy," *Works*, 13:406.

63. Roosevelt to Amelia Glover, 10 November 1904, *Letters*, 4:1027.

64. Roosevelt to Robert Grant, 14 March 1905. The *Washington Star* responded to Roosevelt's speech with the remark, "It is a curious idea the President has that quantity makes merit." *Letters*, 4:1139–40.

65. Roosevelt to Robert Grant, 14 August 1900, *Letters*, 2:1382–83.

66. Robert Grant, *Unleavened Bread*, 42, 57, 168, 250.

67. Ibid., 51, 146, 160.

68. Ibid., 146, 149.

69. Ann Stoler, *Race and the Education of Desire: Foucault's History of Sexuality and the Colonial Order of Things*, 143.

70. Roosevelt to Owen Wister, 27 April 1906, *Letters*, 5:221–25.

71. Quoted in Kim Townsend, *Manhood at Harvard: William James and Others*, 273; on Wister and Roosevelt, see chapter 5, "Smile When You Carry a Big Stick," 256–86.

72. Owen Wister, *Lady Baltimore*, 65–66, 69, 85.

73. Ibid., 65, 69, 79, 261, 365, 374, 386.

74. Ibid., 330.

75. Roosevelt to Hugo Munsterberg, 3 June 1901, *Letters*, 3:86.

76. Quoted in Miller, *Theodore Roosevelt*, 90, emphasis in original.

77. Roosevelt to Bessie Van Vorst, 18 October 1902, *Letters*, 3:355–56, and "National Duties," *Works*, 13:470.

78. Roosevelt to Cecil Arthur Spring Rice, 11 August 1899, *Letters*, 2:1053.

79. Roosevelt to Helen D. Johnson, 10 January 1899, *Letters*, 2:905.

80. Roosevelt, "National Duties," *Works*, 13:470.

81. Timothy J. Gilfoyle, *City of Eros: New York City, Prostitution, and the Commercialization of Sex, 1790–1920*.

82. Russett, *Sexual Science*, 108; Anson Rabinbach, *The Human Motor: Energy, Fatigue, and the Origins of Modernity*, 4, 19–21, 44.

83. Bill Brown, "Science Fiction, the World's Fair, and the Prosthetics of Empire," 137.

84. Russett, *Sexual Science*, 197.

85. Théodule-Armand Ribot, *Diseases of the Will*.

86. Ibid., 112–16; for James and Wister, see Townsend, *Manhood at Harvard*, 45, 50, 261–62.

87. Rotundo, *American Manhood*, 187–90.

88. George M. Beard, *American Nervousness: Its Causes and Consequences; a Supplement to Nervous Exhaustion (Neurasthenia)*, 67–73.

89. Beard, *American Nervousness*, 73.

90. Rotundo, *American Manhood*, 185–93; Charlotte Perkins Gilman, *The Yellow Wallpaper*.

91. Quoted in Alan Trachtenberg, *The Incorporation of America: Culture and Society in the Gilded Age*, 43; Michael Kimmel, "The Contemporary 'Crisis' of Masculinity in Historical Perspective," 130.

92. Rotundo, *American Manhood*, 272.

93. Ibid., 279.

94. Mary Warner Blanchard, *Oscar Wilde's America: Counterculture in the Gilded Age*, 13; Rotundo, *American Manhood*, 275–76; Peter Stearns, *Battleground of Desire: The Struggle for Self-Control in Modern America*, 129.

95. George Chauncey, *Gay New York: Gender, Urban Culture, and the Making of the Gay Male World, 1890–1940*, 116–18.

96. Rotundo, *American Manhood*, 267.

97. Ed Cohen, *Talk on the Wilde Side: Toward a Genealogy of a Discourse on Male Sexuality.*

98. Rafford Pyke, "What Men Like in Men," 404–5.

99. Tim Carrigan, Bob Connell, and John Lee argue that hegemonic masculinity subordinates all other kinds of masculinity—that of youth, effeminate men, and gays. Joseph H. Pleck observes that "the homosexual-heterosexual dichotomy acts as a central symbol in *all* rankings of masculinity. Any kind of powerlessness or refusal to compete, among men readily becomes involved in the imagery of homosexuality" (emphasis in original). Pleck, "Men's Power with Women, Other Men, and Society," cited in Carrigan, Connell, and Lee, "Toward a New Sociology of Masculinity," 86.

100. "Political hermaphrodite" quoted in Leonard Dinnerstein and Kenneth Jackson, *American Vistas*, 133; Maurice Low as a "circumcised skunk" in Roosevelt to Arthur Hamilton Lee, 2 February 1908, *Letters*, 6:918; "non-virility" in Roosevelt to Henry Cabot Lodge, 19 January 1896, *Letters*, 1:509; "female brother" in Roosevelt to William Allen White, 6 February 1900, *Letters*, 2:1171–72.

101. Roosevelt, "The Vigor of Life," 673.

102. Roosevelt to Martha Baker Dunn, 6 September 1902, *Letters*, 3:325.

103. Quoted in Kathleen Dalton, "Theodore Roosevelt and the Idea of War," 7; and Rotundo, *American Manhood*, 273.

CHAPTER FOUR

1. Quoted in Theodore P. Greene, *America's Heroes: The Changing Models of Success in American Magazines*, 235.

2. For a discussion of how dominant forms of masculinity are socially enforced in part by the state itself, see Arthur Brittan, *Masculinity and Power*, 128.

3. Greene, *America's Heroes.*

4. Ibid., 222–46.

5. Ibid., 114, 129, 136, 237–41.

6. Martin Green, *The Adventurous Male: Chapters in the History of the White Male Mind*, 19.

7. Nina Silber, *The Romance of Reunion: Northerners and the South, 1865–1900*, 125, 141, 174–75.

8. Quoted in ibid., 161; Silber details the rise of this abstracted and amoral form of patriotism.

9. Quoted in ibid., 172.

10. Herman Melville, *Moby-Dick; or The Whale*, 108.

11. Mark Twain, *Roughing It*, 132.

12. Jacob Riis, *Theodore Roosevelt the Citizen*, 272.

13. Greene, *America's Heroes*, 131.

14. Mary Warner Blanchard, *Oscar Wilde's America: Counterculture in the Gilded Age*, 38.

15. Quoted in Peggy Samuels and Harold Samuels, *Teddy Roosevelt at San Juan: The Making of a President*, 50, 53.

16. Nicholas Roosevelt, *Theodore Roosevelt: The Man as I Knew Him*, 63.

17. Roosevelt to Henry Cabot Lodge, 12 August 1884, in *Selections from the Corre-*

spondence of Theodore Roosevelt and Henry Cabot Lodge, 1884–1918 (hereafter cited as *Selections*), 1:7.

18. Quoted in Edmund Morris, *The Rise of Theodore Roosevelt*, 283.

19. Quoted in G. Edward White, *The Eastern Establishment and the Western Experience: The West of Frederic Remington, Theodore Roosevelt, and Owen Wister*, 84.

20. Nicholas Roosevelt, *Theodore Roosevelt*, 63.

21. William Roscoe Thayer, *Theodore Roosevelt: An Intimate Biography*, 66.

22. Roosevelt to Anna Roosevelt, 17 June 1884, in Elting E. Morison, ed., *The Letters of Theodore Roosevelt* (hereafter cited as *Letters*), 1:73, emphasis in original.

23. Quoted in White, *Eastern Establishment*, 90, 188.

24. Ibid., 188.

25. Roosevelt to Henry Cabot Lodge, 24 August 1884, *Letters*, 1:80.

26. John Burroughs, *Camping and Tramping with Roosevelt*, 29.

27. Quoted in Samuels and Samuels, *Teddy Roosevelt at San Juan*, 51.

28. Roosevelt to Henry Cabot Lodge, 12 August 1884, *Letters*, 1:77.

29. Quoted in Morris, *Rise of Theodore Roosevelt*, 205.

30. Ibid., 14, 20.

31. Nicholas Roosevelt, *Theodore Roosevelt*, 13.

32. Roosevelt to Henry Cabot Lodge, 13 May 1903, *Selections*, 2:14.

33. John J. Leary Jr., *Talks With T.R.*, 19; Peter Stearns, *Battleground of Desire: The Struggle for Self-Control in Modern America*, 100–101; Lois Banner observed in *American Beauty* that such size symbolically demonstrated men's wealth and their entitlement to take up space, as did the hefty bodies of their wives, enhanced by bustles and voluminous skirts. Banner, *American Beauty: A Social History through Two Centuries of the American Idea, Ideal, and Image of the Beautiful Woman*, 42–47, 232.

34. Beard, *American Nervousness: Its Causes and Consequences; a Supplement to Nervous Exhaustion (Neurasthenia)*, 310–11, 334–38.

35. Greene, *America's Heroes*, 127, 258–59; E. Anthony Rotundo, *American Manhood: Transformations in Masculinity from the Revolution to the Modern Era*, 223–38.

36. "10,000 Boys at Play Take All by Storm," *New York Times* (7 June 1913).

37. Klaus Theweleit, *Male Fantasies*, 2:n.p., quoted on the front plate of Mark Seltzer, *Bodies and Machines*.

38. Thayer, *Theodore Roosevelt*, 201.

39. Roosevelt, "Autobiography," in *The Works of Theodore Roosevelt* (hereafter cited as *Works*), 20:10.

40. Roosevelt to Anna Roosevelt Cowles, 9 March and 30 March 1896, *Letters*, 1:521, 523.

41. Burroughs, *Camping and Tramping with Roosevelt*, 4, 60.

42. Quoted in Morris, *Rise of Theodore Roosevelt*, 18.

43. William H. Goetzmann and William N. Goetzmann, *The West of the Imagination*, 291.

44. Alan Trachtenberg, *The Incorporation of America: Culture and Society in the Gilded Age*, chapter 4.

45. Quoted in George Baxter Ward III, "Bloodbrothers in the Wilderness: The Sport Hunter and the Buckskin Hunter in the Preservation of the American Wilderness Experience," 303.

46. Quoted in ibid., 302.

47. On 20 June 1887, the kings of Denmark, Greece, Belgium, and Saxony and the

Prince of Wales rode in Cody's stagecoach. Ward, "Bloodbrothers in the Wilderness," 297; Frederic Remington, "Buffalo Bill's Wild West Show in London."

48. Edward J. Renehan Jr., *The Lion's Pride: Theodore Roosevelt and His Family in Peace and War*, 28.

49. Goetzmann and Goetzmann, *West of the Imagination*, 295.

50. Ward, "Bloodbrothers in the Wilderness," 308-9.

51. Frederic Remington to J. Henry Harper, 2 September 1899, in Allen P. Splete and Marilyn D. Splete, *Frederic Remington: Selected Letters* (hereafter cited as *Remington Letters*), 292-93.

52. Quoted in White, *Eastern Establishment*, 100.

53. Frederic Remington to J. Henry Harper, 19 January 1900, *Remington Letters*, 293; Ben Merchant Vorpahl, *My Dear Wister: The Frederic Remington–Owen Wister Letters*, 22; Goetzmann and Goetzmann, *West of the Imagination*, 237-86.

54. Roosevelt to Frederic Remington, 11 November 1897, *Remington Letters*, 287.

55. Roosevelt, "In Cowboy Land," 166.

56. Quoted in Kim Townsend, *Manhood at Harvard: William James and Others*, 267.

57. Roosevelt to Frederic Remington, 25 December 1897, *Remington Letters*, 288.

58. Roosevelt to Frederic Remington, 20 November 1895, *Remington Letters*, 278.

59. Roosevelt, "In Cowboy Land," 166.

60. Roosevelt to Frederic Remington, 28 December 1897, *Letters*, 1:749-50. Reprinted in Vorpahl, *My Dear Wister*, 272.

61. Quoted in Harold McCracken, *Frederic Remington: Artist of the Old West*, 34.

62. Michael E. Shapiro and Peter H. Hassrick, *Frederic Remington: The Masterworks*, 118; Townsend, *Manhood at Harvard*, 266.

63. Owen Wister, "The Evolution of the Cow-Puncher."

64. Morris, *Rise of Theodore Roosevelt*, 549.

65. Roosevelt, "A Teller of Tales of Strong Men," *Harper's Weekly* 40 (1896), 1216, quoted in Vorpahl, *My Dear Wister*, 97.

66. Remington to Wister, 12 April 1894, *Remington Letters*, 248; Shapiro and Hassrick, *Frederic Remington*, 24.

67. Quoted in White, *Eastern Establishment*, 106, 108.

68. John G. Cawelti, *The Six-Gun Mystique*.

69. White, *Eastern Establishment*, 49-50.

70. "Brave fellow" quoted in ibid., 106; Frederic Remington to Owen Wister, February 1895, *Remington Letters*, 265.

71. Samuels and Samuels, *Remington*, 32; Frederic Remington to Eva Remington, 11 June 1888, *Remington Letters*, 54-55.

72. Cawelti, *Six-Gun Mystique*, 65.

73. Wister, "Evolution of the Cow-Puncher," 610.

74. Ibid., 604, 610.

75. Ibid., 614-17.

76. Quoted in White, *Eastern Establishment*, 107.

77. Wister, "Evolution of the Cow-Puncher," 606, 608, 610.

78. Quoted in Goetzmann and Goetzmann, *West of the Imagination*, 239.

79. See Michael A. Belesiles, ed., *Lethal Imagination: Violence and Brutality in American History*, 5.

80. Cawelti, *Six-Gun Mystique*, 16, 112.

81. Wister, "Evolution of the Cow-Puncher," 615.

82. Quoted in Vorpahl, *My Dear Wister*, 75.

83. Ibid., 272.

84. Wister, "Evolution of the Cow-Puncher," 614.

85. Ibid., 614–15.

86. Quoted in Ward, "Bloodbrothers in the Wilderness," 175.

87. Quoted in Vorpahl, *My Dear Wister*, 75.

88. Wister, "Evolution of the Cow-Puncher," 615, 617.

89. Roosevelt, "In Cowboy Land," 148.

90. Quoted in Vorpahl, *My Dear Wister*, 315.

91. Richard Slotkin, *Gunfighter Nation: The Myth of the Frontier in Twentieth-Century America*, 36; see especially the chapter titled "The Winning of the West: Theodore Roosevelt's Frontier Thesis, 1880–1900," 29–62.

92. Quoted in White, *Eastern Establishment*, 190.

93. W. D. Trent, "Theodore Roosevelt as a Historian," 570, 575.

94. Slotkin, *Gunfighter Nation*, 29–36.

95. Roosevelt, *Winning of the West*, 3:106–9.

96. Roosevelt, "King's Mountain, 1780," *Works*, 8:481.

97. Roosevelt, *Works*, 8:252.

98. Roosevelt, "King's Mountain, 1780," *Works*, 8:481.

99. Roosevelt, *Winning of the West*, 3:14.

100. Quoted in White, *Eastern Establishment*, 91–92.

101. Quoted in ibid., 81–82.

102. Roosevelt, "In Cowboy Land," 148.

103. Jane Tompkins, *West of Everything: The Inner Life of Westerns*, 73; Cawelti, *Six-Gun Mystique*, 62–73.

104. Quoted in Townsend, *Manhood at Harvard*, 263.

105. Tompkins, *West of Everything*, 23–34.

106. Roosevelt, "Manhood and Statehood," *Works*, 13:454–55.

107. Quoted in Thayer, *Theodore Roosevelt*, 452; Ninkovich, *Modernity and Power: A History of the Domino Theory in the Twentieth Century*, 17.

108. William James, *The Principles of Psychology*, 2:1028, 1030, 1058.

109. Alfred Thayer Mahan, *From Sail to Steam: Recollections of Naval Life*, 86. For an account of the Senate investigation, see Richard Drinnon, *Facing West: The Metaphysics of Indian-Hating and Empire-Building*, 313–19.

110. Roosevelt, "In Cowboy Land."

111. Roosevelt, "Grant," *Works*, 13:431, 433–34.

112. Quoted in Samuels and Samuels, *Teddy Roosevelt at San Juan*, 13.

113. Roosevelt to William Sturgis Bigelow, 29 March 1898, *Letters*, 2:802.

114. Roosevelt to Henry Cabot Lodge, 2 October 1918, *Selections*, 2:538.

115. Thayer, *Theodore Roosevelt*, 123.

116. Gary Gerstle, "Theodore Roosevelt and American Nationalism," 1287.

117. Thayer, *Theodore Roosevelt*, 123–24.

118. Corrine Roosevelt Robinson, *My Brother, Theodore Roosevelt*, 150.

119. Roosevelt, "The Rough Riders," *Works*, 11:4–5; "Leonard Wood," *Works*, 11:252.

120. Roosevelt, "Leonard Wood," *Works*, 11:252.

121. Riis, *Theodore Roosevelt the Citizen*, 172.

122. Roosevelt to Kermit Roosevelt, 4 December 1902, *Letters*, 3:389; to Henry Cabot Lodge, 5 October 1897, *Selections*, 1:285.

123. Quoted in White, *Eastern Establishment*, 149–50.

124. Vorpahl, *My Dear Wister*, 214, 233.

125. R. D. Evans to Frederic Remington, 28 October 1898, *Remington Letters*, 232.

126. Roosevelt, "The Rough Riders," *Works*, 11:50.

127. Frederic Remington, "With the Fifth Corps," 971–72.

128. Samuels and Samuels, *Teddy Roosevelt at San Juan*.

129. Quoted in Renehan, *The Lion's Pride*, 4.

130. Riis, *Theodore Roosevelt the Citizen*, 168–70, 183; Roosevelt, Leonard Wood, Remington, the cavalry officers, and many of the soldiers were disappointed that the Rough Riders fought mainly as infantry and not as cavalry as they had been trained. Thus the cowboys, polo players, cavalrymen, and others were no longer "Rough Riders," but "Wood's Weary Walkers."

131. White, *Eastern Establishment*, 152–58; Morris, *Rise of Theodore Roosevelt*, 650–56.

132. Quoted in White, *Eastern Establishment*, 158.

133. Riis, *Theodore Roosevelt the Citizen*, 115.

134. Quoted in Nathan Miller, *Theodore Roosevelt: A Life*, 299.

135. Charles G. Washburn, *Theodore Roosevelt: The Logic of His Career*, 23–24.

136. Quoted in Miller, *Theodore Roosevelt: A Life*, 355.

137. Quoted in Alexander Nemerov, *Frederic Remington and Turn-of-the-Century America*, 166–67.

138. Roosevelt, "The Rough Riders," *Works*, 11:157–58; see also Nemerov, *Frederic Remington*, 90–100.

139. Remington to Roosevelt, September 1898, *Remington Letters*, 230–31.

140. Roosevelt, "In Cowboy Land," 149.

141. Blanchard, *Oscar Wilde's America*, 6–7.

142. Mahan, *From Sail to Steam*, 68.

143. Roosevelt, "The Rough Riders," *Works*, 11:25.

144. Wister, "Evolution of the Cow-Puncher," 610.

145. Roosevelt, "The Rough Riders," *Works*, 11:19.

146. Roosevelt to Bradley Tyler Johnson, 31 July 1899, *Letters*, 2:1042; Roosevelt, "The Rough Riders," *Works*, 11:12–13.

147. Roosevelt, "The Rough Riders," *Works*, 11:15, 17. Riis, *Theodore Roosevelt the Citizen*, 189.

148. Burroughs, *Camping and Tramping with Roosevelt*, 53.

149. Thayer, *Theodore Roosevelt*, 279.

150. Morris, *Rise of Theodore Roosevelt*, 319–20.

151. Quoted in Miller, *Theodore Roosevelt: A Life*, 314.

152. Roosevelt, "In Cowboy Land," 169, 171.

153. Roosevelt to James Ford Rhodes, 29 November 1904, *Letters*, 4:1051. When titling his sculpture, Remington had initially spelled *broncho* with an *h* but changed to *bronco*.

154. Roosevelt to Frederick William MacMonnies, 19 November 1904, *Letters*, 4:1035.

155. Quoted in Gail Bederman, *Manliness and Civilization: A Cultural History of Gender and Race in the United States, 1880–1970*, 178.

156. Goetzmann and Goetzmann, *West of the Imagination*, 303–4.

157. Roosevelt to Elihu Root, 18 February 1902 and 7 March 1902, *Letters*, 3:232–33, 3:240–42. Roosevelt told Root that he deplored Miles's having leaked accounts of atrocities in the Philippines, and he blamed Miles's actions on the general's presidential ambitions for the election of 1904.

158. Roosevelt, "The Rough Riders," *Works*, 11:19; Mahan said "war is not fighting, but business." *From Sail to Steam*, 283.

159. Roosevelt to Anna Roosevelt, 22 August 1880, *Letters*, 1:46.

160. Bederman, *Manliness and Civilization*, 173.

161. Roosevelt to Stewart Edward White, 8 October 1904, *Letters*, 4:978.

162. Goetzmann and Goetzmann, *West of the Imagination*, 289; the railroad's company insignia was a buffalo head.

163. John Dorst, *Looking West*, 58–60. Through film and literature, Dorst examines the cowboy hero as part of the construction of the West as a tourist spectacle.

164. Nemerov, *Frederic Remington*, 123; Goetzmann and Goetzmann, *West of the Imagination*, 289.

165. Quoted in Ward, "Bloodbrothers in the Wilderness," 10.

166. Quoted in Slotkin, *Gunfighter Nation*, 37.

167. Ward, "Bloodbrothers in the Wilderness," 365.

168. Quoted in Morris, *The Rise of Theodore Roosevelt*, 383, 549.

169. "Deer Stalking," *Sandow's Magazine of Physical Culture* 13 (September 1904), 196–98, quote from p. 198.

170. Quoted in Morris, *Rise of Theodore Roosevelt*, 224.

171. Klaus Theweleit, *Male Fantasies*, 1:191.

172. Tompkins, *West of Everything*, 125.

173. Quoted in Bederman, *Manliness and Civilization*, 211.

174. Roosevelt, *Winning of the West*, 2:105.

175. Roosevelt to Henry Cabot Lodge, 15 May 1909, *Selections*, 2:336.

176. Roosevelt, *African Game Trails: An Account of the African Wanderings of an American Hunter-Naturalist*, 408.

177. Roosevelt to Edward North Buxton, 23 May 1908, *Letters*, 6:1033.

178. Theweleit, *Male Fantasies*, 1:263; see Nemerov's discussion of flaying in *Frederic Remington*, 21–24.

179. See Donna Haraway, "Teddy Bear Patriarchy: Taxidermy in the Garden of Eden, New York City, 1908–1936." When Roosevelt once came home to Sagamore Hill dripping blood from hunting, his wife told him not to get it on the carpets.

180. "Deer Stalking," 198.

181. Banner, *American Beauty*, 111; Blanchard, *Oscar Wilde's America*, 201.

182. Banner, *American Beauty*, 111.

183. Quoted in Green, *Adventurous Male*, 15.

184. Michael Kimmel, *Manhood in America: A Cultural History*, 168.

185. Quoted in Ward, "Bloodbrothers in the Wilderness," 159.

186. Kathleen Dalton, personal communication, 19 October 2001.

187. Burroughs, *Camping and Tramping with Roosevelt*, 7.

188. Morris, *Rise of Theodore Roosevelt*, 66, 91–92. By his sophomore year at Harvard, Roosevelt had accumulated hundreds of bird and animal skins. He was already a nationally known ornithologist, listed in a national biology directory, and author of

Summer Birds and *Some of the Birds of Oyster Bay*. His vertebrate physiology professor in his sophomore year was William James; Roosevelt described the course as "extremely interesting."

189. Quoted in Morris, *Rise of Theodore Roosevelt*, 285–86, 299.

190. Roosevelt to Anna Roosevelt, 20 September 1884, *Letters*, 1:82.

191. Roosevelt to Henry Cabot Lodge, 1 August 1889, *Selections*, 1:88.

192. Roosevelt to Philip Bathell Stewart, 10 June 1901, *Letters*, 3:91.

193. Roosevelt to Henry Cabot Lodge, 26 February 1901, *Letters*, 3:3; to Frederick Courteney Selous, 8 March 1901, *Letters*, 3:6; to Theodore Roosevelt Jr., 14 January 1901, *Letters*, 3:1; to Cecil Arthur Spring Rice, 16 March 1901, *Letters*, 3:14; to Hermann Speck von Sternberg, 8 March 1901, *Letters*, 3:5; to Fred Brother, 6 March 1901, *Letters*, 3:4.

194. Roosevelt to Hamlin Garland, 4 April 1901, *Letters*, 3:40.

195. Roosevelt to Kermit Roosevelt, 14 April 1904, *Letters*, 4:1160.

196. Roosevelt to Elihu Root, 13 May 1904, *Letters*, 4:1171–72.

197. Roosevelt to Henry Cabot Lodge, 20 April 1905, *Selections*, 2:117.

198. Roosevelt to John B. Goff, 11 November 1904, *Letters*, 4:1029.

199. Henry Cabot Lodge to Roosevelt, 9 November 1904, *Letters*, 2:107.

200. Henry Cabot Lodge to Roosevelt, 3 June 1905, *Letters*, 2:126.

201. Henry Cabot Lodge to Roosevelt, end of March 1909, *Selections*, 2:330.

202. See Bederman's account of the safari in *Manliness and Civilization*, 207–13.

203. Roosevelt, *African Game Trails*, 118, 173, 405, 431.

204. Ibid., 173, 364, 381–82, 534.

205. Ibid., 481, 486, 500.

206. "Bill and Ted's Excellent Adventures," *New York Times*, 5 April 1998.

207. Roosevelt, *African Game Trails*, 85.

208. Ibid., 105, 131, 186, 190–91, 408, 410, 445, 473, 478–79. See Bederman's fuller account of the Nandi hunters' killing of the lion in *Manliness and Civilization*, 207–13.

209. Roosevelt to Henry Cabot Lodge, 5 May 1910, *Selections*, 2:380–81.

210. Roosevelt to Henry Cabot Lodge, 30 October 1889, 17 October 1889, and 11 October 1892, *Selections*, 1:97, 94, 126.

211. Roosevelt, "Grant," *Works*, 13:431.

CHAPTER FIVE

1. Kathleen Dalton, "Theodore Roosevelt and the Idea of War," 6.

2. Klaus Theweleit, *Male Fantasies*, 1:88.

3. Roosevelt, "The Strenuous Life," in *The Works of Theodore Roosevelt* (hereafter cited as *Works*), 13:323; "stern men," Roosevelt quoting James Russell Lowell. On the sacrificial and redemptive aspects of war, see Jeffrey Herf, *Reactionary Modernism: Technology, Culture, and Politics in Weimar and the Third Reich*, 76.

4. Roosevelt, "The Cuban Dead," *Works*, 11:339.

5. Richard Slotkin, *Gunfighter Nation: The Myth of the Frontier in Twentieth-Century America*, 42.

6. Roosevelt to Frederic Rene Coudert, 3 July 1901, *Letters*, 3:105–6.

7. Roosevelt to Walter Gordon-Cumming, 18 February 1899, in Elting E. Morison, ed., *The Letters of Theodore Roosevelt* (hereafter cited as *Letters*), 2:949.

8. Roosevelt to Cecil Arthur Spring Rice, 27 December 1904, *Letters*, 4:1083–84.

9. Roosevelt, "Brotherhood and the Heroic Virtues," *Works*, 13:461.

10. Roosevelt, "Sheridan," *Works*, 11:223.

11. Roosevelt to Owen Wister, 5 February 1916, in Owen Wister, *Roosevelt: The Story of a Friendship, 1880–1919*, 355. In 1889, musing on the possibility of a future war with Germany, Roosevelt fantasized that the burning of New York and other coastal cities would furnish an "object lesson on the need of an adequate system of coast defences." Roosevelt to Cecil Arthur Spring Rice, 14 April 1889, *Letters*, 1:157.

12. Roosevelt, "Brotherhood and the Heroic Virtues," *Works*, 13:468.

13. Dalton, "Theodore Roosevelt and the Idea of War," 10.

14. Edward J. Renehan Jr., *The Lion's Pride: Theodore Roosevelt and His Family in Peace and War*, 22.

15. Roosevelt, "National Duties," *Works*, 13.469–70.

16. Quoted in Peggy Samuels and Harold Samuels, *Teddy Roosevelt at San Juan: The Making of a President*, 35.

17. Roosevelt, "The Vigor of Life," *Works*, 20:33.

18. Roosevelt to Henry Cabot Lodge, 30 October 1885, in *Selections from the Correspondence of Theodore Roosevelt and Henry Cabot Lodge, 1884–1918* (hereafter cited as *Selections*), 1:36.

19. Roosevelt, "Brotherhood and the Heroic Virtues," *Works*, 13:463.

20. Roosevelt, "Augustus Saint Gaudens," *Works*, 11:287.

21. Roosevelt, "Men of Gettysburg," *Works*, 11:325; "Gettysburg and Valley Forge," *Works*, 11:332.

22. Roosevelt, "The Cuban Dead," *Works*, 11:339.

23. Roosevelt, "Sacrifice on Cold Altars," *Works*, 19:337.

24. William James, *Memories and Studies*, 268, 276.

25. Jacob Riis, *Theodore Roosevelt the Citizen*, 9.

26. Roosevelt, "In Cowboy Land," 169, emphasis in original.

27. Ibid., 171,

28. See, for example, Edmund Morris, *The Rise of Theodore Roosevelt*, 255, and Dalton, "Theodore Roosevelt and the Idea of War," 9.

29. Renehan, *Lion's Pride*, 24.

30. Roosevelt to Eleonora Kissel Kinnicutt, 28 June 1901, *Letters*, 3:103.

31. Roosevelt, "The War of America the Unready," *Works*, 20:224.

32. Roosevelt to Douglas Robinson, 27 July 1899, *Letters*, 2:860.

33. Roosevelt to Cecil Arthur Spring Rice, 24 July 1905, *Letters*, 4:1286.

34. Roosevelt to Henry Cabot Lodge, 18 July 1905, *Letters*, 4:1279.

35. Roosevelt to William Sturgis Bigelow, 29 March 1898, *Letters*, 2:802.

36. Roosevelt to Winthrop Chanler, 23 March 1899, *Letters*, 2:968–69.

37. Irving C. Norwood, "Exit—Roosevelt, The Dominant," *The Outing Magazine* 53 (March 1909): 722, quoted in Dalton, "Theodore Roosevelt and the Idea of War," 10.

38. Elaine Scarry, *The Body in Pain: The Making and Unmaking of the World*, 18, 34.

39. Mark Seltzer, *Bodies and Machines*, 162, 168–69.

40. David Savran, *Taking It Like a Man: White Masculinity, Masochism, and Contemporary American Culture*, 311.

41. Ibid., 189. The dangers inherent in acknowledging this feminized identity, even if to dominate it, explains why men in closely knit male communities such as the

military attach so much violence and anxiety to drawing clear boundaries against the homoerotic (p. 196).

42. Ibid., 203. Real and imaginary acts of violence reproduce an individuating, specifically masculine experience that satisfies what Harry Brod calls a "male predilection for clearly demarcated, agonistic situations," especially those that involve pain, suffering, domination, and sacrifice. Harry Brod, "The Case for Men's Studies," 44.

43. The recipe for heroic selfhood, Jane Tompkins observes, is the "the painful experience the protagonist undergoes, the pattern of self-renunciation [he] is required to live out, the regimen of silence imposed where expression is most needed, and the equation of this repression with the highest integrity and authenticity." Jane Tompkins, *West of Everything: The Inner Life of Westerns*, 126.

44. William Roscoe Thayer, *Theodore Roosevelt: An Intimate Biography*, 118, 432.

45. Roosevelt to William Shafter, 3 August 1898, *Letters*, 2:864.

46. Alice Roosevelt Longworth, *Crowded Hours*, 245.

47. Riis, *Theodore Roosevelt the Citizen*, 158.

48. Thayer, *Theodore Roosevelt*, 432.

49. Roosevelt, "The War of America the Unready," *Works*, 20:224.

50. Roosevelt, "The Foes of Our Own Household," *Works*, 19:29, with appendix, 19:187. A large readership of this book can be assumed because subsequent editions appeared in quick succession in 1918, 1919, and 1925.

51. Roosevelt to William Pierce Frye, 31 March 1898, *Letters*, 2:806.

52. Thayer, *Theodore Roosevelt*, 432.

53. Goldwin Smith, "War as a Moral Medicine."

54. Ernest Howard Crosby, "The Military Idea of Manliness."

55. Ibid., 875.

56. Agnes Repplier, "The Praises of War," 797, 801–4.

57. Roosevelt to John Hay, 1903, quoted in Corrine Roosevelt Robinson, *My Brother, Theodore Roosevelt*, 151.

58. James, *Memories and Studies*, 277.

59. G. Stanley Hall, *Youth: Its Education, Regimen, and Hygiene*, 55, 72.

60. Alfred T. Mahan, *The Influence of Sea Power upon History, 1660–1783*.

61. Alfred T. Mahan, *From Sail to Steam: Recollections of Naval Life*, 324.

62. Mark R. Shulman, *Navalism and the Emergence of American Sea Power*.

63. Roosevelt, "The Strenuous Life," *Works*, 13:329.

64. Thayer, *Theodore Roosevelt*, 289.

65. Quoted in Robert L. O'Connell, *Sacred Vessels: The Cult of the Battleship and the Rise of the U.S. Navy*, 9.

66. Roosevelt, "Preparedness and Unpreparedness," *Works*, 13:415.

67. Mahan, *From Sail to Steam*, 8.

68. Quoted in Ronald Takaki, *Iron Cages: Race and Culture in Nineteenth-Century America*, 272.

69. Remington, "With the Fifth Corps," 962, 968.

70. Riis, *Theodore Roosevelt the Citizen*, 282.

71. Roosevelt, "The Rough Riders," *Works*, 11:52; James, *Memories and Studies*, 277; Frederic Remington to Lieutenant Powhatan Clarke, 19 July 1892, in Allen P. Splete and Marilyn D. Splete, *Frederic Remington, Selected Letters*, 142–43.

72. Roosevelt to Cecil Arthur Spring Rice, 27 January 1900, *Letters*, 2:1147.

73. Thayer, *Theodore Roosevelt*, 123.

74. Mahan, *From Sail to Steam*, 11, 50, 54.

75. Ibid., xv, 8.

76. Quoted in Takaki, *Iron Cages*, 273.

77. Mahan, *From Sail to Steam*, 57.

78. Hall, *Youth*, 55, 78, 92, 101–2.

79. Quoted in G. Edward White, *Eastern Establishment and the Western Experience: The West of Frederic Remington, Theodore Roosevelt, and Owen Wister*, 92–93.

80. Roosevelt, "The Rough Riders," *Works*, 11:52.

81. E. Anthony Rotundo, "Romantic Friendship: Male Intimacy and Middle-Class Youth in the Northern United States, 1800–1900."

82. Roosevelt to John T. McDonough, 28 June 1900, *Letters*, 2:1346.

83. I am indebted to David Lubin for the language "sexualized and sexualizing." David Lubin, *Picturing a Nation: Art and Social Change in Nineteenth-Century America*, 258.

84. Quoted in Ben Merchant Vorpahl, *My Dear Wister: The Frederic Remington–Owen Wister Letters*, 315.

85. Takaki, *Iron Cages*, 265, 274, 275, 277.

86. Savran, *Taking It Like a Man*, 196.

87. Mahan, *From Sail to Steam*, 2, 52.

88. Ibid., 11.

89. Roosevelt, "Antietam," *Works*, 11:335.

90. Roosevelt, "Brotherhood and the Heroic Virtues," *Works*, 13:463–64.

91. Roosevelt, "Fellow-Feeling as a Political Factor," *Works*, 13:356.

92. John Burroughs, *Camping and Tramping with Roosevelt*, 59.

93. Quoted in Dalton, "Theodore Roosevelt and the Idea of War," 7.

94. Roosevelt, "Admiral Mahan," *Works*, 11:279.

95. Roosevelt, "The Strenuous Life," *Works*, 13:331.

96. Roosevelt to Florence Lockwood La Farge, 13 February 1908, *Letters*, 6:943.

97. Roosevelt, "Expansion and Peace," *Works*, 13:334.

98. Roosevelt to Douglas Robinson, 30 March 1898, *Letters*, 2:805–6.

99. Roosevelt, "Expansion and Peace," *Works*, 13:332.

100. Ibid., 13:334–45.

101. Roosevelt to Elihu Root, 14 September 1905, *Letters*, 5:26, emphasis in original.

102. Roosevelt, "The College Graduate and Public Life," *Works*, 13:39.

103. Roosevelt, "Expansion and Peace," *Works*, 13:335.

104. Quoted in Albert Shaw, *A Cartoon History of Roosevelt's Career*, 68.

105. Roosevelt to Carl Schurz, 8 September 1905, *Selections*, 2:197–99.

106. Roosevelt, "The Strenuous Life," *Works*, 13:324.

107. Roosevelt to Henry Cabot Lodge, 15 June 1915, and 29 June 1915, *Selections*, 2:459–60.

108. Mahan, *From Sail to Steam*, 325.

109. Mahan, *From Sail to Steam*, 10–11, 29, 35.

110. Quoted in White, *Eastern Establishment*, 115.

111. Roosevelt to Frederic Remington, 26 October 1897, in Allen P. Splete and Marilyn D. Splete, *Frederic Remington, Selected Letters*, 286–87.

112. Richard Harding Davis, *The Cuban and Porto Rican Campaigns*, 91, 117.

113. Davis, *The Cuban and Porto Rican Campaigns*, 30, 31, 37.

114. David Nye, *American Technological Sublime*, xiii–xiv.

115. O'Connell, *Sacred Vessels*, 3.

116. Thayer, *Theodore Roosevelt*, 286, 289–90.

117. Quoted in Morris, *Rise of Theodore Roosevelt*, 266.

118. Ernest Hemingway, *A Farewell to Arms*.

119. Robert Wohl, *The Generation of 1914*, 118.

120. Roosevelt to Douglas Robinson, 27 July 1989, *Letters*, 2:860.

121. Quoted in Slotkin, *Gunfighter Nation*, 41.

122. Roosevelt, "The Rough Riders," *Works*, 11:84.

123. Roosevelt, "Military Preparedness and Unpreparedness," *Works*, 13:410.

124. Roosevelt to Douglas Robinson, 27 July 1989, *Letters*, 2:860; "teeth of difficulty" in "Gettysburg and Valley Forge," *Works*, 11:333.

125. Approximately one-third of the six hundred Rough Riders who landed in Cuba were killed or wounded or suffered disease, a greater loss than any other American unit in the war. Nathan Miller, *Theodore Roosevelt: A Life*, 278.

126. Quoted in Renehan, *Lion's Pride*, 130.

127. Roosevelt to George Otto Trevelyan, 1 January 1908, *Letters*, 6:881.

128. William James, *The Principles of Psychology*, 2:1030.

129. Quoted in Takaki, *Iron Cages*, 275.

130. Roosevelt, "Autobiography," *Works*, 20:35.

131. Roosevelt, "Manhood and Statehood," *Works*, 13:455.

132. Quoted in Gail Bederman, *Manliness and Civilization: A Cultural History of Gender and Race in the United States, 1880–1917*, 189.

133. Roosevelt to Theodore Elijah Burton, 23 February 1904, *Letters*, 4:737.

134. Roosevelt to Leonard Wood, 24 April 1899, *Letters*, 2:995.

135. Quoted in Adam Hochschild, *King Leopold's Ghost*, 145.

136. Richard Drinnon, *Facing West: The Metaphysics of Indian-Hating and Empire-Building*, 313.

137. Ibid., 307–32; quote from p. 314.

138. Roosevelt to Elihu Root, 9 May 1902, *Letters*, 3:260.

139. Roosevelt to Hermann Speck von Sternberg, 19 July 1902, *Letters*, 3:297–98.

140. Quoted in Drinnon, *Facing West*, 347, emphasis in original.

141. Roosevelt, "National Duties," *Works*, 13:478.

142. Roosevelt, "The Strenuous Life," *Works*, 13:325, 328.

143. Bram Dijkstra, *Idols of Perversity: Fantasies of Feminine Evil in Fin-de-Siècle Culture*, 101.

144. Roosevelt, *The Winning of the West*, 4:199–200.

145. Roosevelt to Elihu Root, 20 May 1904, *Letters*, 4:801.

146. Roosevelt, "Leonard Wood," *Works*, 11:253–55.

147. Quoted in Morris, *Rise of Theodore Roosevelt*, 544.

148. Riis, *Theodore Roosevelt the Citizen*, 405, 261–62; see also Morris, *Rise of Theodore Roosevelt*, 549.

AFTERWORD

1. Quoted in Alice Roosevelt Longworth, *Crowded Hours*, 247.

2. Ibid., 246.

3. Ibid., 245.

4. Quoted in Edward J. Renehan Jr., *The Lion's Pride: Theodore Roosevelt and His Family in Peace and War,* 160.

5. Quoted in ibid., 190.

6. Longworth, *Crowded Hours,* 255, 258.

7. For Archie's depression, see pp. 212–13; for Eleanor's quote, p. 220; and for Quentin's flying bravado, pp. 194–95, all in Renehan, *Lion's Pride.*

8. Quoted in Renehan, *Lion's Pride,* 6.

9. Roosevelt, "The Great Adventure," *Works,* 19:248.

10. Gilbert J. Black, ed., *Theodore Roosevelt, 1858–1919: Chronology, Documents, Bibliographical Aids,* 21, 24–25.

11. Renehan, *Lion's Pride,* 236–39.

12. Kristin L. Hoganson, *Fighting for American Manhood: How Gender Politics Provoked the Spanish-American and Philippine-American Wars.*

13. Michael Kimmel, *Manhood in America: A Cultural History,* 269–70; Susan Jeffords, *The Remasculinization of America: Gender and the Vietnam War,* 28, 44.

14. Barbara Ehrenreich, foreword in Klaus Theweleit, *Male Fantasies,* 1:xiii.

Bibliography

Adams, Brooks. *The Law of Civilization and Decay: An Essay on History.* New York: Macmillan, 1895.

Adams, James Eli. *Dandies and Desert Saints: Styles of Victorian Masculinity.* Ithaca, N.Y.: Cornell University Press, 1995.

Balfour, Arthur James. *Decadence: Henry Sidgwick Memorial Lecture.* Cambridge, England: The University Press, 1908.

Banner, Lois. *American Beauty: A Social History through Two Centuries of the American Idea, Ideal, and Image of the Beautiful Woman.* New York: Alfred A. Knopf, 1983.

Beard, George Miller. *American Nervousness: Its Causes and Consequences; a Supplement to Nervous Exhaustion (Neurasthenia).* 1881. Reprint, New York: Arno Press, 1972.

———. *A Practical Treatise on Nervous Exhaustion (Neurasthenia), Its Symptoms, Nature, Sequences, Treatment.* New York: W. Wood and Company, 1880.

———. *Sexual Neurasthenia (Nervous Exhaustion): Its Hygiene, Causes, Symptoms, and Treatment, with a Chapter on Diet for the Nervous.* New York: E. B. Treat, 1898.

Bederman, Gail. *Manliness and Civilization: A Cultural History of Gender and Race in the United States, 1880–1917.* Chicago: University of Chicago Press, 1995.

Bellamy, Edward. *Looking Backward, 2000–1887.* Boston: Ticknor and Company, 1888.

Bellesiles, Michael A., ed. *Lethal Imagination: Violence and Brutality in American History.* New York: New York University Press, 1999.

Beveridge, Albert. *The Young Man and the World.* New York: D. Appleton and Company, 1906.

Black, Gilbert J., ed. *Theodore Roosevelt, 1858–1919: Chronology, Documents, Bibliographical Aids.* Dobbs Ferry, N.Y.: Oceana Publications, 1969.

Blanchard, Mary Warner. *Oscar Wilde's America: Counterculture in the Gilded Age.* New Haven, Conn.: Yale University Press, 1998.

Blum, John Morton. *The Republican Roosevelt.* Cambridge, Mass.: Harvard University Press, 1965.

Boyer, Paul S. *Urban Masses and Moral Order in America, 1820–1920.* Cambridge, Mass.: Harvard University Press, 1978.

Brewer, E. Cobham. *Character Sketches of Romance, Fiction, and the Drama,* ed. Marion Harland. 4 vols. New York: Selmar Hess, 1902.

Brittan, Arthur. *Masculinity and Power.* New York: Basil Blackwell, 1989.

Brod, Harry. "The Case for Men's Studies." Pp. 39–62 in *The Making of Masculinities: The New Men's Studies,* ed. Harry Brod. Boston: Allen and Unwin, 1987.

Brod, Harry, ed. *The Making of Masculinities: The New Men's Studies.* Boston: Allen and Unwin, 1987.

Brown, Bill. "Science Fiction, the World's Fair, and the Prosthetics of Empire." Pp. 129–63 in *Cultures of United States Imperialism,* ed. Amy Kaplan and Donald E. Pease. Durham, N.C.: Duke University Press, 1993.

Buffalo Bill. *Story of the Wild West.* Philadelphia: Historical Publishing, 1888.

Buntline, Ned. *Buffalo Bill.* New York: American Publishers Corporation, 1886.

Burroughs, John. *Camping and Tramping with Roosevelt.* Boston and New York: Houghton, Mifflin and Company, 1907.

Carrigan, Tim, Bob Connell, and John Lee. "Toward a New Sociology of Masculinity." Pp. 63–100 in *The Making of Masculinities: The New Men's Studies,* ed. Harry Brod. Boston: Allen and Unwin, 1987.

Cawelti, John G. *The Six-Gun Mystique,* 2d ed. Bowling Green, Ohio: Bowling Green State University Popular Press, 1984.

Chamberlin, J. Edward, and Sander Gilman, eds. *Degeneration: The Dark Side of Progress.* New York: Columbia University Press, 1985.

Chauncey, George. *Gay New York: Gender, Urban Culture, and the Making of the Gay Male World, 1890–1940.* New York: Basic Books, 1994.

Chodorow, Nancy. *The Reproduction of Mothering.* Berkeley: University of California Press, 1978.

Cohen, Ed. *Talk on the Wilde Side: Toward a Genealogy of a Discourse on Male Sexualities.* New York: Routledge, 1993.

Cooke, Nicholas Francis. *Satan in Society.* 1870. Reprint, New York: Arno Press, 1974.

Costigliola, Frank. "The Nuclear Family: Tropes of Gender and Pathology in the Western Alliance." *Diplomatic History* 21 (1997): 163–83.

Crosby, Ernest Howard. "The Military Idea of Manliness." *The Independent* 53 (1901): 873–75.

Dalton, Kathleen. "Theodore Roosevelt and the Idea of War." *Theodore Roosevelt Association Journal* 7 (1981): 9–10.

———. *Theodore Roosevelt: A Strenuous Life.* New York: Alfred A. Knopf, 2002.

———. "Why America Loved Teddy Roosevelt: Or, Charisma Is in the Eyes of the Beholders." Pp. 269–91 in *Our Selves / Our Past: Psychological Approaches to American History,* ed. Robert J. Brugger. Baltimore: Johns Hopkins University Press, 1981.

Davis, Richard Harding. *The Cuban and Porto Rican Campaigns.* New York: Charles Scribner's Sons, 1898.

Deleuze, Gilles, and Felix Guattari. *Anti-Oedipus: Capitalism and Schizophrenia.* New York: Viking Press, 1977.

Dijkstra, Bram. *Idols of Perversity: Fantasies of Feminine Evil in Fin-de-Siècle Culture.* New York: Oxford University Press, 1986.

Dinnerstein, Leonard, and Kenneth Jackson. *American Vistas.* New York: Oxford University Press, 1971.

Dorst, John. *Looking West.* Philadelphia: University of Pennsylvania Press, 1999.

Douglas, Mary. *Implicit Meanings: Essays in Anthropology.* Boston: Routledge and Kegan Paul, 1975.

Drinnon, Richard. *Facing West: The Metaphysics of Indian-Hating and Empire-Building.* Minneapolis: University of Minnesota Press, 1990.

Dubbert, Joe L. "Progressivism and the Masculinity Crisis." Pp. 303–20 in *The American Man,* ed. Elizabeth H. Pleck and Joseph H. Pleck. Englewood Cliffs, N.J.: Prentice Hall, 1980.

During, Simon. "Literature—Nationalism's Other?" Pp. 138–53 in *Nation and Narration,* ed. Homi K. Bhabha. New York: Routledge, 1990.

Dyer, Thomas G. *Theodore Roosevelt and the Idea of Race.* Baton Rouge: Louisiana State University Press, 1980.

Ehrenreich, Barbara. Foreword in Klaus Theweleit, *Male Fantasies.* Vol. 1, *Women, Floods, Bodies, History,* trans. Stephen Conway. Minneapolis: University of Minnesota Press, 1987.

Elias, Norbert. *The Civilizing Process: Sociogenetic and Psychogenetic Investigations.* Oxford, U.K.: Blackwell, 2000.

Field, Geoffrey G. *Evangelist of Race: The Germanic Vision of Houston Stewart Chamberlain.* New York: Columbia University Press, 1981.

Frykman, Jonas, and Orvar Lofgren. *The Culture Builders: A Historical Anthropology of Middle-Class Life.* New Brunswick, N.J.: Rutgers University Press, 1987.

Gay, Peter. *The Bourgeois Experience: Victoria to Freud.* Vol. 5, *Pleasure Wars.* New York: W. W. Norton, 1998.

George, Henry. *Progress and Poverty.* New York: D. Appleton and Company, 1880.

———. *Social Problems.* New York: Henry George and Company, 1883.

Gerstle, Gary. "Theodore Roosevelt and American Nationalism." *Journal of American History* 86 (December 1999), 1280–1307.

Gilfoyle, Timothy J. *City of Eros: New York City, Prostitution, and the Commercialization of Sex, 1790–1920.* New York: W. W. Norton, 1992.

Gilman, Charlotte Perkins. *The Yellow Wallpaper.* New York: Feminist Press, 1973.

Gilman, Sander. "Sexology, Psychoanalysis, and Degeneration: From a Theory of Race to a Race Theory." Pp. 72–96 in *Degeneration: The Dark Side of Progress,* ed. J. Edward Chamberlin and Sander Gilman. New York: Columbia University Press, 1985.

Gilmore, David. *Manhood in the Making: Cultural Concepts of Masculinity.* New Haven, Conn.: Yale University Press, 1990.

Gobineu, Arthur de. *The Inequality of Human Races,* trans. Adrian Collins. London: Heinemann, 1915.

Goetzmann, William H., and William N. Goetzmann. *The West of the Imagination.* New York: W. W. Norton, 1986.

Goldstein, Jeffrey. "Why We Watch." Pp. 212–26 in *Why We Watch: The Attraction of Violent Entertainment,* ed., Jeffrey Goldstein. New York: Oxford University Press, 1998.

Gorn, Eliot J. *The Manly Art.* Ithaca, N.Y.: Cornell University Press, 1986.

Grant, Madison. *The Passing of the Great Race; or, The Racial Bias of European History.* New York: Charles Scribner, 1916.

Grant, Robert. *Unleavened Bread.* New York: Charles Scribner's Sons, 1900.

Grantham, Dewey W., ed. *Theodore Roosevelt.* Englewood Cliffs, N.J.: Prentice-Hall, 1971.

Green, Martin. *The Adventurous Male: Chapters in the History of the White Male Mind.* University Park: Pennsylvania State University Press, 1993.

Greenberg, Irving. *Theodore Roosevelt and Labor: 1900–1918*. New York: Garland, 1988.

Greene, Theodore P. *America's Heroes: The Changing Models of Success in American Magazines*. New York: Oxford University Press, 1970.

Hale, Nathan. *Freud in America: The Beginnings of Psychoanalysis in the United States, 1876–1917*. New York: Oxford University Press, 1971.

Hall, G. Stanley. *Adolescence: Its Psychology and Its Relations to Physiology, Anthropology, Sociology, Sex, Crime, Religion and Education*. 2 vols. New York: D. Appleton and Company, 1904.

———. *Youth: Its Education, Regimen, and Hygiene*. New York: D. Appleton and Company, 1904.

Hammack, David C. *Power and Society: Greater New York at the Turn of the Century*. New York: Russell Sage Foundation, 1982.

Haraway, Donna. "Teddy Bear Patriarchy: Taxidermy in the Garden of Eden, New York City, 1908–1936." Pp. 237–91 in *Cultures of United States Imperialism*, ed. Amy Kaplan and Donald E. Pease. Durham, N.C.: Duke University Press, 1993.

Harbaugh, William Henry. *The Life and Times of Theodore Roosevelt*, 2d ed. New York: Collier, 1963.

Hartt, Mary Bronson. "The Play Side of the Fair." *The World's Work* (August 1901), 1096.

Heale, M. J. *American Anticommunism: Combating the Enemy Within, 1830–1970*. Baltimore: Johns Hopkins University Press, 1990.

Hell, Julia. *Post-Fascist Fantasies: Psychoanalysis, History, and the Literature of East Germany*. Durham, N.C.: Duke University Press, 1997.

Hemingway, Ernest. *A Farewell to Arms*. New York: Charles Scribner's Sons, 1929.

Henry Street Settlement and Munson-Williams-Proctor Institute. *The Armory Show: 50th Anniversary Exhibition*. New York: Clarke and Way, 1963.

Herf, Jeffrey. *Reactionary Modernism: Technology, Culture, and Politics in Weimar and the Third Reich*. New York: Cambridge University Press, 1984.

Hochschild, Adam. *King Leopold's Ghost*. New York: Houghton Mifflin, 1998.

Hoganson, Kristin L. *Fighting for American Manhood: How Gender Politics Provoked the Spanish-American and Philippine-American Wars*. New Haven, Conn.: Yale University Press, 1998.

Hudson, Liam, and Bernadine Jacot. *The Way Men Think: Intellect, Intimacy and the Erotic Imagination*. New Haven, Conn.: Yale University Press, 1991.

Hunter, Sam. *Modern American Painting and Sculpture*. New York: Dell, 1959.

James, William. *Memories and Studies*. Cambridge, Mass.: Riverside Press, 1911.

———. *The Principles of Psychology*. 3 vols. Cambridge, Mass.: Harvard University Press, 1981.

Jameson, Fredric. *The Political Unconscious: Narrative as Socially Symbolic Act*. New Haven, Conn.: Yale University Press, 1981.

Jeffords, Susan. *The Remasculinization of America: Gender and the Vietnam War*. Bloomington: Indiana University Press, 1989.

Johnston, William Davison. *Theodore Roosevelt: Champion of the Strenuous Life*. New York: Farrar, Straus and Cudahy, 1958.

Kaplan, Amy, and Donald E. Pease, eds. *Cultures of United States Imperialism*. Durham, N.C.: Duke University Press, 1993.

Kasson, John. *Civilizing the Machine: Technology and Republican Values in America, 1776–1990.* New York: Grossman, 1976.

Kimmel, Michael. "The Contemporary 'Crisis' of Masculinity in Historical Perspective." Pp. 121–53 in *Making of Masculinities: The New Men's Studies,* ed. Harry Brod. Boston: Allen and Unwin, 1987.

———. *The Gendered Society.* New York: Oxford University Press, 2000.

———. *Manhood in America: A Cultural History.* New York: Free Press, 1996.

Kipling, Rudyard. *The Sahib Edition of Rudyard Kipling.* New York: P. F. Collier and Son, 1912.

———. "The Seven Nights of Creation." In volume 17 of *The Writings in Prose and Verse of Rudyard Kipling.* 20 vols. New York: Charles Scribner's Sons, 1900.

Krafft-Ebing, Richard von. *Psychopathia Sexualis: A Medico-Forensic Study,* trans. Harry E. Wedeck. 1886. Reprint, New York: Putnam, 1965.

LaCapra, Dominick. *Representing the Holocaust: History, Theory, Trauma.* Ithaca, N.Y.: Cornell University Press, 1994.

Lakoff, George. *Women, Fire, and Dangerous Things: What Categories Reveal about the Mind.* Chicago: University of Chicago Press, 1987.

Lears, T. J. Jackson. *No Place of Grace: Antimodernism and the Transformation of American Culture, 1880–1920.* New York: Pantheon, 1981.

Leary, John J., Jr. *Talks With T.R.* Boston and New York: Houghton Mifflin, 1919.

Livingston, James. "Modern Subjectivity and Consumer Culture." Pp. 413–29 in *Getting and Spending: European and American Consumer Societies in the Twentieth Century,* ed. Susan Strasser, Charles McGovern, and Matthais Judt. Cambridge: Cambridge University Press, 1998.

Longworth, Alice Roosevelt. *Crowded Hours.* New York: Charles Scribner's Sons, 1933.

Lubin, David. *Picturing a Nation: Art and Social Change in Nineteenth-Century America.* New Haven, Conn.: Yale University Press, 1994.

Mahan, Alfred Thayer. *From Sail to Steam: Recollections of Naval Life.* New York: Harper & Brothers, 1907.

———. *The Influence of Sea Power upon History, 1660–1783.* Boston: Little, Brown, and Company, 1890.

McCracken, Harold. *Frederic Remington: Artist of the Old West.* New York: J. B. Lippincott, 1947.

Melville, Herman. *Moby-Dick; or The Whale.* New York: Oxford University Press, 1947.

Miller, Alice. *For Your Own Good: Hidden Cruelty in Child-Rearing and the Roots of Violence,* trans. Hildegarde Hannum and Hunter Hannum. New York: Farrar, Straus, Giroux, 1984.

Miller, Nathan. *Theodore Roosevelt: A Life.* New York: William Morrow and Company, 1992.

Miller, William Ian. *The Anatomy of Disgust.* Cambridge, Mass.: Harvard University Press, 1997.

Morison, Elting E., ed. *The Letters of Theodore Roosevelt.* 8 vols. Cambridge, Mass.: Harvard University Press, 1951–1954.

Morris, Edmund. *The Rise of Theodore Roosevelt.* New York: Coward, McCann and Geoghegan, 1979.

Mosse, George. "Nationalism and Respectability: Normal and Abnormal Sexuality in the Nineteenth Century." *Journal of Contemporary History* 17 (1982): 221–46.

Nelson, Dana D. *National Manhood: Capitalist Citizenship and the Imagined Fraternity of White Men.* Durham, N.C.: Duke University Press, 1998.

Nemerov, Alexander. *Frederic Remington and Turn-of-the-Century America.* New Haven, Conn.: Yale University Press, 1995.

Ninkovich, Frank. "Cuba, the Philippines, and the Hundred Years' War." *Reviews in American History* 27 (September 1999): 444–51.

———. *Modernity and Power: A History of the Domino Theory in the Twentieth Century.* Chicago: University of Chicago Press, 1994.

———. "Theodore Roosevelt: Civilization as Ideology." *Diplomatic History* 10 (summer 1986): 221–45.

———. *United States Information Policy and Cultural Diplomacy.* New York: Foreign Policy Association, 1996.

Nordau, Max. *Degeneration.* New York: Appleton and Company, 1895.

Nye, David. *American Technological Sublime.* Cambridge, Mass.: MIT Press, 1994.

O'Connell, Robert L. *Sacred Vessels: The Cult of the Battleship and the Rise of the U.S. Navy.* New York: Oxford University Press, 1991.

Oliver, Lawrence J. "Theodore Roosevelt, Brander Matthews, and the Campaign for Literary Americanism." *American Quarterly* 41 (March 1989): 93–111.

Oliver, Lawrence J., ed. *The Letters of Theodore Roosevelt and Brander Matthews.* Knoxville: University of Tennessee Press, 1995.

Pick, Daniel. *Faces of Degeneration: A European Disorder, 1848–1918.* New York: Cambridge University Press, 1989.

Pleck, Joseph H. "Men's Power with Women, Other Men, and Society." Pp. 417–33 in *The American Man,* ed. Elizabeth H. Pleck and Joseph H. Pleck. Englewood Cliffs, N.J.: Prentice Hall, 1980.

Ponder, Stephen. *Managing the Press: Origins of the Media Presidency, 1897–1933.* New York: St. Martin's Press, 1998.

Pringle, Henry F. *Theodore Roosevelt: A Biography.* New York: Harcourt, Brace and Company, 1931.

Pyke, Rafford. "What Men Like in Men." *The Cosmopolitan* 33 (1902): 402–6.

Rabinbach, Anson. *The Human Motor: Energy, Fatigue, and the Origins of Modernity.* New York: Basic Books, 1990.

Rabinbach, Anson, and Jessica Benjamin. Foreword in Klaus Theweleit, *Male Fantasies.* Vol. 2, *Male Bodies: Psychoanalyzing the White Terror,* trans. Erica Carter and Chris Turner. Minneapolis: University of Minnesota Press, 1989.

Remington, Frederic. "Buffalo Bill's Wild West Show in London." *Harper's Weekly,* 3 September 1892.

———. "Chicago under the Mob." *Harper's Weekly,* 21 July 1894, 680–81.

———. "With the Fifth Corps." *Harper's Magazine* 97 (November 1898): 971–72.

Renehan, Edward J., Jr. *The Lion's Pride: Theodore Roosevelt and His Family in Peace and War.* New York: Oxford University Press, 1998.

Repplier, Agnes. "Ennui." *Atlantic Monthly* 71 (June 1893): 775–84.

———. "The Praises of War." *Atlantic Monthly* 68 (December 1891): 796–805.

Ribot, Théodule-Armand. *Diseases of the Will.* Chicago: Open Court Publishing, 1894.

Riis, Jacob. *Theodore Roosevelt the Citizen.* New York: The Outlook Company, 1904.

Robinson, Corrine Roosevelt. *My Brother, Theodore Roosevelt.* New York: Scribner's Sons, 1921.

Rogin, Michael. *Fathers and Children: Andrew Jackson and the Subjugation of the American Indian.* New York: Random House, 1976.

Roosevelt, Nicholas. *Theodore Roosevelt: The Man as I Knew Him.* New York: Dodd, Mead and Company, 1967.

Roosevelt, Theodore. *African Game Trails: An Account of the African Wanderings of an American Hunter-Naturalist.* New York: Syndicate Publishing, 1910.

————. *Gouverneur Morris.* Boston: Houghton Mifflin, 1888.

————. *Hunting Trips of a Ranchman.* New York: G. P. Putnam's Sons, 1885.

————. "In Cowboy Land." *Outlook* 104 (May–August 1913): 148–72.

————. "A Layman's View of an Art Exhibition." Pp. 160–62 in *The Armory Show: 50th Anniversary Exhibition,* Henry Street Settlement and Munson-Williams-Proctor Institute. New York: Clarke and Way, 1963.

————. *The Naval War of 1812, or, The History of the United States Navy during the Last War with Great Britain.* New York: G. P. Putnam's Sons, 1882.

————. *Ranch Life and the Hunting Trail.* 1888. Reprint, New York: Scribner's, 1927.

————. "Review of the Foundations of the Nineteenth Century." *Outlook* 98 (29 July 1911): 728–31.

————. "The Vigor of Life." *Outlook* 103 (January–April 1913): 661–75.

————. *The Wilderness Hunter: An Account of the Big Game of the United States and Its Chase with Horse, Hound, and Rifle.* New York: G. P. Putnam's Sons, 1893.

————. *The Winning of the West.* 4 vols. New York: Putnam's Knickerbocker Press, 1889–1896.

————. *The Works of Theodore Roosevelt,* national edition, ed. Hermann Hagedorn. 20 vols. New York: Charles Scribner and Sons, 1923–1926.

Roosevelt, Theodore, and Henry Cabot Lodge. *Selections from the Correspondence of Theodore Roosevelt and Henry Cabot Lodge, 1884–1918.* 2 vols. New York: Charles Scribner and Sons, 1925.

Rose, Sonya O. "Cultural Analysis and Moral Discourses." Pp. 217–38 in *Beyond the Cultural Turn: New Directions in the Study of Society and Culture,* eds. Victoria E. Bonnell and Lynn Hunt. Berkeley: University of California Press, 1999.

Ross, Dorothy. *G. Stanley Hall: Psychologist as Prophet.* Chicago: University of Chicago Press, 1972.

Ross, Edward Alsworth. *Sin and Society: An Analysis of Latter-Day Iniquity.* Boston and New York: Houghton Mifflin, 1907.

————. *Social Control: A Survey of the Foundations of Order.* New York: Macmillan, 1901.

Rotundo, E. Anthony. *American Manhood: Transformations in Masculinity from the Revolution to the Modern Era.* New York: Basic Books, 1993.

————. "Romantic Friendship: Male Intimacy and Middle-Class Youth in the Northern United States, 1800–1900." *Journal of Social History* 23 (1989): 1–28.

Russett, Cynthia Eagle. *Sexual Science: The Victorian Construction of Womanhood.* Cambridge, Mass.: Harvard University Press, 1989.

Samuels, Peggy, and Harold Samuels. *Teddy Roosevelt at San Juan: The Making of a President.* College Station: Texas A & M University Press, 1997.

Santner, Eric. *Stranded Objects: Mourning, Memory, and Film in Postwar Germany.* Ithaca, N.Y.: Cornell University Press, 1990.

Sargent, Dudley A. *Athletic Sports.* New York: C. Scribner's Sons, 1897.

Savran, David. *Taking It Like a Man: White Masculinity, Masochism, and Contemporary American Culture.* Princeton, N.J.: Princeton University Press, 1998.

Scarry, Elaine. *The Body in Pain: The Making and Unmaking of the World.* New York: Oxford University Press, 1985.

Seltzer, Mark. *Bodies and Machines.* New York: Routledge, 1992.

Seton, Ernest Thompson. *Two Little Savages: Being the Adventures of Two Boys Who Lived as Indians and What They Learned.* New York: Grosset & Dunlap, 1903.

Shapiro, Michael E., and Peter H. Hassrick. *Frederic Remington: The Masterworks.* New York: Harry N. Abrams, 1988.

Shaw, Albert. *A Cartoon History of Roosevelt's Career.* New York· The Review of Reviews Company, 1910.

Shulman, Mark R. *Navalism and the Emergence of American Sea Power.* Annapolis: Naval Institute Press, 1995.

Silber, Nina. *The Romance of Reunion: Northerners and the South, 1865–1900.* Chapel Hill: University of North Carolina Press, 1993.

Slotkin, Richard. *Gunfighter Nation: The Myth of the Frontier in Twentieth-Century America.* New York: HarperCollins, 1992.

Smith, Goldwin. "War as a Moral Medicine." *Atlantic Monthly* 86 (December 1900): 735–38.

Smith-Rosenberg, Carroll. *Disorderly Conduct: Visions of Gender in Victorian America.* New York: Oxford University Press, 1986.

———. "Sex as Symbol in Victorian Purity." Pp. 160–70 in *Culture and Society: Contemporary Debates,* ed. Jeffrey C. Alexander and Steven Seidman. Cambridge, Mass.: Harvard University Press, 1990.

Splete, Allen P., and Marilyn D. Splete. *Frederic Remington: Selected Letters.* New York: Abbeville Press, 1988.

Stallybrass, Peter, and Allon White. *The Politics and Poetics of Transgression.* Ithaca, N.Y.: Cornell University Press, 1986.

Stearns, Peter. *Battleground of Desire: The Struggle for Self-Control in Modern America.* New York: New York University Press, 1999.

Stocking, George W. *Victorian Anthropology.* New York: Free Press, 1987.

Stoker, Bram. *Dracula.* New York: Grosset & Dunlap, 1897.

Stoler, Ann. *Race and the Education of Desire: Foucault's History of Sexuality and the Colonial Order of Things.* Durham, N.C.: Duke University Press, 1995.

Sumner, William Graham. *Earth-Hunger and Other Essays,* ed. Albert Galloway Keller. Freeport, N.Y.: Books for Libraries Press, n.d.

Takaki, Ronald. *Iron Cages: Race and Culture in Nineteenth-Century America.* New York: Oxford University Press, 1990.

Testi, Arnaldo. "The Gender of Reform Politics: Theodore Roosevelt and the Culture of Masculinity." *Journal of American History* 81 (March 1995): 1509–33.

Thayer, William Roscoe. *Theodore Roosevelt: An Intimate Biography.* New York: Grosset & Dunlap, 1919.

Theweleit, Klaus. *Male Fantasies.* Vol. 1, *Women, Floods, Bodies, History,* trans. Stephen Conway. Minneapolis: University of Minnesota Press, 1987.

———. *Male Fantasies.* Vol. 2, *Male Bodies: Psychoanalyzing the White Terror,* trans. Erica Carter and Chris Turner. Minneapolis: University of Minnesota Press, 1989.

Tolstoy, Leo. *The Complete Works of Count Tolstoy.* Boston: Colonial Press, 1904.

Tompkins, Jane. *West of Everything: The Inner Life of Westerns.* New York: Oxford University Press, 1992.

Townsend, Kim. *Manhood at Harvard: William James and Others.* New York: W. W. Norton, 1996.

Trachtenberg, Alan. *The Incorporation of America: Culture and Society in the Gilded Age.* New York: Hill and Wang, 1982.

Trent, W. D. "Theodore Roosevelt as a Historian." *The Forum* 21 (March–August 1896): 570–75.

Trew, Eva. "Sex Sterilization." *International Socialist Review* 13 (1913): 814.

Turner, Bryan S. *The Body and Society: Explorations in Social Theory.* New York: Basil Blackwell, 1984.

Twain, Mark. *Roughing It.* New York: Harper & Brothers, 1913.

Vorpahl, Ben Merchant. *My Dear Wister: The Frederic Remington–Owen Wister Letters.* Palo Alto, Calif.: American West, 1973.

Ward, George Baxter, III. "Bloodbrothers in the Wilderness: The Sport Hunter and the Buckskin Hunter in the Preservation of the American Wilderness Experience." Ph.D. diss., University of Texas, Austin, 1980.

Ware, Eugene Fitch. *Rhymes of Ironquill.* Topeka, Kans.: Kellam, 1889.

Washburn, Charles G. *Theodore Roosevelt: The Logic of His Career.* Boston and New York: Houghton Mifflin, 1916.

White, G. Edward. *The Eastern Establishment and the Western Experience: The West of Frederic Remington, Theodore Roosevelt, and Owen Wister.* New Haven, Conn.: Yale University Press, 1968.

Williams, William A. "Brooks Adams and American Expansion." *New England Quarterly* 25 (1952): 217–32.

Wister, Owen. "The Evolution of the Cow-Puncher." *Harper's Monthly* 91 (September 1895), 602–17.

———. *Lady Baltimore.* New York: Macmillan, 1906.

———. *Red Men and White.* New York: Grosset, 1895.

———. *Roosevelt: The Story of a Friendship, 1880–1919.* New York: Macmillan, 1930.

———. *The Virginian: A Horseman of the Plains.* London: Macmillan, 1902.

Wohl, Robert. *The Generation of 1914.* Cambridge, Mass.: Harvard University Press, 1979.

Zillman, Dolf. "The Psychology of the Appeal of Portrayals of Violence." Pp. 179–211 in *Why We Watch: The Attraction of Violent Entertainment,* ed. Jeffrey Goldstein. New York: Oxford University Press, 1998.

Index

112–13. *See also* Victorian society, early
1900s
*Social Control: A Survey of the Foundations of
Order* (Ross), 57
social Darwinism. *See* Darwinism
Social Problems (George), 118
social theory: fear as the antidote to ambivalence, 7, 244n. 18; ideal of social control,
57; investigation into pathological degeneracy in rural communities, 70; logic behind version of barbarism, 75–76; racial
terms used in political discourse, 57; Roosevelt's view of socialism as unpatriotic,
62–63; socialism equated to the surge in
immigrants, 72
society. *See* Victorian society, early 1900s
Spanish-American War, 26, 64. *See also*
Rough Riders
Spencer, Herbert, 6
"sporting" males, 27, 115
sports: male societies' devotion to, 49–50;
popularity of competitive games, 138;
popularity of hunting (*see* hunting); pressure put on boys to participate, 47–49,
250–51n. 112; as a ritualized display of violence, 28; view of aggressiveness bal-
anced by fair play, 75–76
Spring Rice, Cecil Arthur, 6, 63
Stallybrass, Peter, 249n. 60
Stearns, Peter, 28
Steffens, Lincoln, 26
Stimson, Henry, 174
Storer, Bellamy, 235
suffrage movement, 86–87. *See also* New
Woman

Takaki, Ronald, 211, 213
Taylor, Frederick, 57
Thayer, William Roscoe: on Roosevelt's dedi-
cation to improving his body, 42, 127;
on Roosevelt's need for action, 139; on
Roosevelt's need to join a war, 202; on
Roosevelt's personality, 25, 170; on Roo-
sevelt's popularity with the Rough Riders,
162; on Roosevelt's self-discipline, 12;
view of war, 224
Theweleit, Klaus, 15, 138–39, 175, 193
Tolstoy, Leo, 107, 113–14, 215
Tompkins, Jane, 159, 175, 265n. 43
Townsend, Kim, 15, 28, 51
Trachtenberg, Alan, 143
Trent, W. D., 34

Twain, Mark, 1, 75, 125–26, 143, 233
Two Little Savages (Seton), 30

Unleavened Bread (Grant), 108, 109–11

Vampire, The (Burne-Jones), 105, 106f
"Vampire, The" (Kipling), 105–7
Victorian society, early 1900s: boundaries
maintained against degenerate aspects of
modernism, 33–34, 249n. 60; bourgeois
code of civilized morality, 51–52, 53;
child-rearing practices (*see* boyhood in
late 1800s); corpulence associated with
upperclass and health, 135–37, 258n. 33;
creation of moral and social taxonomies,
32; crisis of cultural authority, 13; cultural
direction of modernism, 23–24; disdain
for Darwinism, 5; expectations of self-
control in manhood, 31–32; fear of having
evolved from primitives, 91–92; Gibson
girl and the New Woman, 87; growing acceptance of male violence, 6–7, 18, 27,
235, 246n. 53; growing preoccupation
with homosexuality, 119–20; men's expectations for women, 82; men's fascination with danger and savagery, 74; new
Northern sympathetic view of Southern-
ers, 124–25; Roosevelt's reaction to modernism, 2–3; social changes subverting
male status, 7; social relationships,
changes in 1880s, 29; society-induced repression of fears, 56; view of savagery, 11.
See also social class
violence: allure of brutishness, 93; appeal to
men, 246n. 51; attraction of the cowboy
ethos, 239; basis in curiosity, 16–17; "civilized adventurer's" self-view of own savagery, 75–76; Easterners' demands for
violence in Westerns, 151–52; emotions
associated with hunting, 175; growing acceptance of male violence in 1880s, 6–7,
18, 27, 235, 246n. 53; logic of war's violence, 226; men's fascination with artistic
depictions of bondage and rape, 97–98;
morality affected by cowboys' everyday violence, 152–53; reflexive sadomasochism,
202; relationship between acts and punishment, 246n. 53; scientific sanction for
men's violence against women, 234; sports
and injuries viewed as toughening, 49–50;
sports culture, growth of institutionalized, 28